The Automobile Age

The Automobile Age

James J. Flink

The MIT Press
Cambridge, Massachusetts
London, England

First MIT Press paperback edition, 1990

© 1988 Massachusetts Institute of Technology

This book was set in Bembo by Asco Trade Typesetting Ltd., Hong Kong, and printed and bound by Hailiday Lithograph in the United States of America.

Library of Congress Cataloging-in-Publication Data

Flink, James J.
  The automobile age.

  Bibliography: p.
  Includes index.
  1. Automobile industry and trade—United States—History. 2. Automobiles—Social aspects—United States. 3. Automobiles—History. I. Title.
  T123.F5713 1988   303.4′832   87-26095
  ISBN 0-262-06111-2 (hardcover)
        0-262-56055-0 (paperback)

For Iona, for many reasons

Who can find a wife with strength of character? She is far more precious than jewels. The heart of her husband trusts in her, and he will never lack profit. She does him good and not harm all the days of his life. . . . Many daughters have done nobly, but you transcend them all.

Proverbs 31:10–12, 29

Contents

Preface

The rise of the automobile industry and the socioeconomic impact of the road and the car are central to the history of the advanced capitalist countries in the twentieth century, and explain an especially large part of the history of the American people. A definitive exposition, analysis, and synthesis of this most important phenomenon to mankind has yet to be written, and many aspects of the topic are still generally misunderstood or shrouded in myth.

In this book I have drawn upon the automotive history scholarship of the past decade and have utilized the research strategies of comparative history and the new social history to revise significantly my earlier revisionist synthesis, *The Car Culture*, published by The MIT Press in 1975. Here the perspective is very different. Even in passages abstracted from my earlier books a number of factual errors have been corrected, new information has been added, and the evidence often has been reinterpreted substantially. I am far less polemical here, and I rely much more on statistical data, much less on the assessments of participant-observers in the interpretation of historical events and processes. Most important, this is a comparative history, not in the sense that equal attention has been given to the history of the automobile in the rest of the world, but in the more limited senses of providing perspectives on the American automobile culture and of explaining developments elsewhere that have affected it. Like *The Car Culture*, this book focuses on the United States. It could not be otherwise, for to understand the worldwide automobile revolution one must put center stage the world's foremost automobile culture.

Throughout the text I explore and interrelate six general themes. One is the technological evolution of the motor vehicle, particularly the passenger car. Another is the development of mass-production techniques, their progressive refinement, and their impact upon automobile workers and labor-management relations. A third is the dynamics of the development, business organization, and marketing strategies of the automobile industry. A fourth is the diffusion of the road and the car and the development of a mass market for automobiles. A fifth is the roles of economic and social conditions and public-policy decisions in the creation of our contemporary automobile culture, and in the concurrent decline of mass transit. Finally, there is the transformation of American lifeways and institutions by mass personal automobility.

Because I believe that history is the product of human choice, made by the decisions of men rather than the inevitable result of impersonal forces, cultural or otherwise, due attention is given to the contributions of individuals to the shaping of our automobile culture, particularly to automotive entrepreneurs and engineers. In doing this I have operated on the commonsense assumptions, for example, that the mass production of the Model T was a manifestation of Henry Ford's philosophy of industry and that to understand the annual model change and planned obsolescence of product, one must know Alfred P. Sloan, Jr.'s, conception of the mature corporation. So, unlike most of the new social history, this work deals with motives and personalities as well as with behavior and aggregate statistics.

Similarly, and as in *The Car Culture*, the text is discursive within the literature of automotive history, because I think that it is important for the general reader to be made aware of the contributions of my fellow automotive historians to my arguments. Scholarship is a cumulative process, and a comprehensive synthesis such as this necessarily is based in the main on the primary research on specialized topics of many other people. I have tried to credit in the text by name those who have most influenced my arguments, to point out their specific contributions to my understanding, and to quote them directly when what they said seems either especially significant or striking.

I have tried to keep the notes sparse and simple. My arguments and the evidence essential to support them are entirely presented in the text. The notes are used only to reference direct quotes and to point out significant sources, not to extend arguments or provide supplementary evidence. They are at the back of the book where they can safely be ignored unless the reader wishes to pursue a topic further. Because the reader interested in doing so can most conveniently work through the index, the citations in the text, and the notes, I have omitted a bibliography. Statistical data, unless otherwise referenced, are taken either from the various annual editions of the Motor Vehicle Manufacturers Association (MVMA)'s *Facts and Figures* and *World Motor Vehicle Data,* or from the *Statistical Abstract of the United States.*

A major problem in writing contemporary history with themes that continue to develop into the future is determination of the point in time at which to conclude the narrative. Obviously, one must stop short of tracing events up to yesterday's newspaper. In general, the text treats events through 1985, when the draft manuscript was submitted for publication. The most recent relevant statistical data then available were most often for 1982 or 1983, and in some cases for as early as 1977. I have updated the statistics where it has been possible and seemed essential. Otherwise, they remain as of 1985. I am unaware of any instance where more recent figures, or for that matter any new qualitative information, would alter my generalizations or add anything important to my conclusions.

This book is the culmination of twenty-eight years of research and writing on automotive history. Many people have contributed to it in one way or another.

Gerald T. White first awakened my interest in social and economic history in his undergraduate courses in history at San Francisco State. Thomas C. Cochran strengthened that interest in his seminars at the University of Pennsylvania and first suggested to me that the automobile revolution was an unexplored topic worthy of at least one doctoral dissertation. John B. Rae paved the way for further work in automotive history with his pioneering books and articles and was instrumental in getting my first book, *America Adopts the Automobile, 1895–1910,* published by The MIT Press in 1970. I am grateful for the continuing support for my work and the friendship over the years of Professors Cochran, Rae, and White.

I have also on occasion learned from my graduate students, particularly about the Japanese automobile industry from Alexander D. McLeod and about the triumph of the automobile over rail transit from Gregory Lee Thompson.

The present book grew out of a paper that I presented at the October 1, 1982, conference "The Automobile and American Culture," sponsored by the Detroit Historical Society. David L. Lewis organized the conference and invited me to participate. Another stimulus was the discovery, while doing research for the paper, of James M. Laux's definitive account of the early French automobile industry, *In First Gear* (1976), and the suggestive history of the worldwide automobile industry, *The Automobile Revolution* (first published in French in 1977, then brought out in English by the University of North Carolina Press in 1982), that Laux coauthored with Jean-Pierre Bardou, Jean-Jacques Chanaron, and Patrick Fridenson.

I have drawn on both books for data on the European automobile industry to an extent not possible to acknowledge adequately in the notes. My interpretation of these data, however, is more often than not very different.

My research has been supported at critical points by funding from three sources within the University of California, Irvine: the departmental instruction and research budget of the Program in Comparative Culture, Academic Senate research and travel funds administered by the research committee of the School of Social Sciences, and intramural grants from the Institute of Transportation Studies. Individuals who deserve special thanks are Dickran L. Tashjian, Ross M. Quillian, Wilfred W. Recker, and Gordon J. "Pete" Fielding.

Librarians are the silent partners in research, and their critical role too often goes unacknowledged by scholars. Much of the present book is based on research that I did as long ago as the 1960s at the McKean Automobile Reference Collection of the Free Library of Philadelphia, and I remain indebted to Mary M. Cattie and Dolores B. Axam for many favors. Along with most other automotive historians, I also am indebted to the late James J. Bradley of the National Automobile Collection of the Detroit Public Library. My research was aided immensely by the expertise of Margaret A. Renton, Government Publications, John E. Smith Memorial Library, and of Lyn Long, Institute of Transportation Studies, both at the University of California, Irvine.

For the illustrations, I am indebted to American Motors; John Baeder; the California Department of Transportation; the Chrysler Historical Collection, particularly Karla Rosenbush; the Ford Motor Company, particularly Susan Page; the Free Library of Philadelphia, particularly Lou Helversen; General Motors, particularly Thomas F. Macan; the Henry Ford Museum and Greenfield Village, particularly Randy Mason and Cynthia Read-Miller; Holiday Inns, Incorporated; the Huntington Library; the Library of Congress; Mercedes-Benz of North America, particularly A. B. Shuman; the National Archives; the Smithsonian Institution, particularly Donald H. Berkebile and Roger B. White; and Volkswagen of America, Incorporated.

The manuscript was read and commented on by my fellow automotive historian George S. May, by my colleague Raul A. Fernandez, and by my neighbor Joseph L. Vuckovich. Their corrections and criticisms were invaluable. Joseph G. Jorgensen has patiently endured having his ear bent and provided encouragement and moral support on numerous occasions.

Edna L. Mejia not only typed several drafts of the manuscript but helped secure research materials and illustrations. Her dedication and efficiency in the preparation of the manuscript have been typical of her exemplary secretarial service to me over the past seventeen years.

Despite the help of all these good people, faults undoubtedly will be found in the text for which I must assume full responsibility. That is simply the nature of all scholarly endeavor. I know that Iona Rogers Flink, the love of my life for the past thirty-five years, to whom this book is dedicated, will understand that I have tried my best to make it perfect for her and forgive my inadvertent failings.

The Automobile Age

The Automotive Idea

The idea of the self-propelled road vehicle dates from at least as early as the speculations made by Roger Bacon and Leonardo da Vinci in the thirteenth and fifteenth centuries. Its development during the nineteenth century was multinational. Sociocultural differences reflected by national political boundaries were far less significant than the evolution of a modern urban-industrial social order in Western Europe and the United States. This involved a widely disseminated, shared state of scientific and technical knowledge. It was thus inevitable that a number of people on both sides of the Atlantic should perceive the possibility and social utility of the automotive idea—the combination of a light, sprung, wheeled vehicle; a compact, efficient power unit; and hard-surfaced roads.

The earliest experiments with cumbersome steam-powered vehicles did not get very far. We know next to nothing about two steam-powered, self-propelled vehicles reported to have been constructed in China about 1665 by the French Jesuit missionaries Ferdinand Verbeist and Philippe-Marie Grimaldi. A century later, between 1765 and 1770, Nicholas Joseph Cugnot, a Swiss engineer, was subsidized by the French government to experiment with steam tractors for pulling cannon. Cugnot's 1769 vehicle was less efficient than horses, and further development was halted when a change in government policy cut off his funds. Richard Trevithick, a Cornish engineer who pioneered the development of the high-pressure steam engine in England, built steam carriages in 1801 and 1803. Although his vehicle ran reliably at speeds up to 12 mph, Trevithick was unable to obtain financial backing to develop it further. Oliver Evans, an American inventor, obtained a patent from the Maryland legislature in 1787 giving him exclusive rights to operate steam-powered vehicles on the public roads. In 1805 a steam-powered dredge that he built for the city of Philadelphia, the "Orukter Amphibolos" or "Amphibious Digger," moved under its own power through the streets of Philadelphia at about 4 mph. Onlookers thought the vehicle would be too slow for turnpike travel, and Evans was unable to raise the $3,000 he needed to launch an experimental company to build steam-powered wagons.

These experiments were a prelude to many other demonstrations of self-propelled road vehicles during the first half of the nineteenth century. Great Britain and the United States led the civilized world in the development and application of steam power. In both countries attempts were made to establish stage lines utilizing steam-powered road vehicles for the long-distance transportation of freight and passengers. The main reason for the failure of these attempts was that the railroad was a far superior technological alternative, given the bulk and weight of the steam engines and the incredibly poor roads of the day.

Competition from cheaper, more reliable rail and water transportation was a major factor in the United States. Our unexcelled waterways and the rapid development of the railroad network here, heavily subsidized by government, reduced the stage lines to the role of short-haul feeders and discouraged the building of improved roads.

In England, under the influence of horse-drawn transportation interests, the turnpike trusts that administered the highways levied discriminatory tolls against mechanical road vehicles. Then in 1865 Parliament passed on behalf of the railroad monopolists the notorious Locomotive Act. This so-called Red Flag Act limited the speed of "road locomotives" to 2 mph in towns and 4 mph on the open highway and required that an attendant walk sixty yards ahead carrying a red flag by day and a red lantern by night. Until its repeal at the request of wealthy automotive pioneers in 1896, the act militated against development of the automotive idea, for by 1890 light steam vehicles were capable of being driven 15 mph for long distances over British roads.

The automotive idea stood the best chance for early implementation in France. Cugnot's experiments are only one indication of early French interest in the military potential of the motor vehicle. Even before the French Revolution, the government had perceived the need for good roads upon which to move the heavy wheeled traffic of its armies; since the founding of the Ecole des Ponts et Chaussées in 1747 to train competent civil engineers, it had given special attention to building a national highway network. Also, local governments in France were required by an 1836 law to maintain local roads and were authorized to collect taxes for this purpose. The result was that by the advent of the automobile in the 1890s, French roads were unexcelled. Elsewhere in Europe and especially in the United States, implementation of the automotive idea necessitated a massive reawakening of interest in highway transportation.

Precursors: The Trolley and the Bicycle

Land transportation improved very little from the domestication of the horse and invention of the wheel in prehistory until it was revolutionized by several mechanical innovations in the nineteenth century. Of these the first to be perfected were the steam railroad and the electric streetcar. The potential of the former for low-cost long-distance intercity transportation was reaching full realization by the mid-1870s.

In American cities, horsecars running on fixed rails had supplanted horse-drawn omnibuses as the main mode of transit by 1860. The 5¢ fare was beyond the reach of $1-a-day workers, however, so the horsecar did little to change the settlement patterns of the "walking city." People of necessity lived close to their workplaces, and shopping and leisure-time activities were centered in the neighborhood.

The cable car, powered by being linked through a grip to a continuously moving cable, was introduced in 1873 in San Francisco. By the mid-1890s, 626 miles of cable car lines were in operation in American cities.

The first electric streetcar, or trolley, system was installed by Frank Sprague in 1887 in Richmond, Virginia. The electric streetcar rapidly displaced horse-drawn cars and ended the construction of cable car systems. As late as 1890, urban rail transit in the United States was 70-percent horse powered, but by the turn of the century electrified rail transit prevailed. Some 850 electric trolley systems operated over 10,000 miles of track. The first electric interurban track in the United States was laid in 1889. Electric interurban mileage proliferated from 2,107 miles in 1900 to a peak of 15,580 in 1916.

Individualized long-distance transportation in the form first of the safety bicycle (1885) and then of the motor vehicle (1895) followed close behind. Many contemporary observers saw the automobile revolution and the rail revolution as complementary. Improved transportation, whether by auto or by rail, increased personal mobility, brought city amenities to the countryside, decentralized urban space, sanitized the central city, and created an integrated national culture, economy, and society. But the unparalleled flexibility of the motor vehicle made its potential impact far greater.

Early in the nineteenth century, John L. McAdam and Thomas Telford in Great Britain developed new techniques of highway design and construction that made possible much smoother, tougher road surfaces and easier grades. But this "highway renaissance" soon collapsed under competition from the steam locomotive running on fixed rails. Interest in improved roads was heightened in France and revived in Great Britain and the United States by the bicycle craze of the 1880s and 1890s.

The bicycle industry began in Paris in the 1860s with the invention of the velocipede by Pierre Michaux, then spread to the rest of Europe and the United States after Michaux's vehicle was demonstrated at the 1867 Paris Exposition. British output of high-front-wheeled velocipedes soon surpassed French output, and the British in particular continued to develop the vehicle. Use of the bicycle became widespread with the introduction of the modern geared, low-wheeled "safety bicycle" in 1885 by James Kemp Starley of Coventry, England, and after quantity production reduced the price of a bicycle to about $30. By 1893 there were some 150,000 bicylces in use in France. And William Plowden relates that in Great Britain, "for the first time since the rise of the railways the roads were crowded with through traffic; and, for perhaps the first time ever, the idea was born of travelling the road for pleasure." [1]

The bicycle required better roads, with much smoother surfaces, than horse-drawn traffic. Even the excellent French gravel roads of the day left something to be desired. So bicycle periodicals and organizations both in Europe and in the United States energetically began to agitate for improved roads. By the 1890s at least a dozen bicycle periodicals throve in France, the most important of which was the daily *Le Vélo*, founded in 1891 by Pierre Giffard. In Great Britain the Cyclists' Touring Club and the National Cyclists' Union, both founded in 1878, in 1886 jointly organized the Roads Improvement Association, which published and distributed widely a booklet entitled *Roads, Their Construction and Maintenance*. Yet cyclists in Europe, who in general were not men of substance, at best had only limited local successes in getting roads improved.

Cyclists were somewhat more successful in the United States, where the crest of the bicycle movement coincided with the climax of several decades of agrarian discontent. The Farmers' Alliances and the Populist movement had made the abuse of monopoly power by the railroads a prime target. Farmers were beginning to perceive highway transportation as an alternative and to complain about the lack of good farm-to-market roads. Good roads thus became a popular political issue in the United States during the 1890s.

The League of American Wheelmen (LAW) was organized in 1880, one of its main goals being "the improvement of public roads and highways." The major figure in the good-roads movement in the United States was Colonel Albert A. Pope, the nation's leading bicycle manufacturer. Pope aided the bicycle periodicals *Bicycle World*, *Wheel*, and

Wheelman (later *Outing*) in their good-roads efforts, and helped found in 1892 the LAW *Good Roads Magazine* (later the *LAW Bulletin of Good Roads*). At the national level, a petition to Congress drafted by the LAW resulted in 1893 in the creation of the Office of Road Inquiry in the Department of Agriculture. This agency became the Office of Public Roads and conducted the first census of American roads in 1904—revealing that only 7 percent of American roads were surfaced, that only one mile of improved road existed for every 492 inhabitants, and that most of this mileage was of poor quality.

The National League for Good Roads, with branches in most states, was founded by General Roy Stone at the 1893 Columbian Exposition, and later that year a Good Roads Convention was held in Washington, D.C. President Theodore Roosevelt and William Jennings Bryan were among the prominent political leaders attending the National Good Roads Convention at St. Louis in 1903, where resolutions were passed endorsing the principle of state aid to counties and municipalities and the support of the federal government for road construction. At the state level, New Jersey led in the passage of legislation in 1888 and 1891 that instituted the modern system of financing road improvements and maintenance through taxation by county and state governments. Between 1892 and 1913 comparable legislation was enacted by twenty-six more states. At the local level, cyclists succeeded in getting streets paved or repaved to accommodate bicycle traffic in a number of cities.

Apart from its impact on road improvement in the United States, no preceding technological innovation—not even the internal-combustion engine—was as important to the development of the automobile as the bicycle. Key elements of automotive technology that were first employed in the bicycle industry included steel-tube framing, ball bearings, chain drive, and differential gearing. An innovation of particular note is the pneumatic bicycle tire, invented by John B. Dunlop in Ireland in 1888. The bicycle industry also developed techniques of quantity production utilizing special machine tools, sheet metal stamping, and electric resistance welding that would become essential elements in the volume production of motor vehicles.

A number of the more important early automobile manufacturers were first bicycle manufacturers—among others, Opel in Germany; Clément, Darracq, and Peugeot in France; Humber, Morris, and Rover in Great Britain; Pope, Peerless, Rambler, Winton, and Willys in the United States. A substantial proportion of engineering talent as well in the early automobile industry was provided by former bicycle mechanics—including William Morris, who initiated volume production of automobiles in Great Britain; Charles E. and J. Frank Duryea, who built the first successful American gasoline car; and William S. Knudsen, production head first at Ford, then at Chevrolet, and later president of General Motors.

The greatest contribution of the bicycle, however, was that it created an enormous demand for individualized, long-distance transportation that could only be satisfied by the mass adoption of motor vehicles.

The Steamer

During the period 1860–1890, lightweight, high-pressure, self-condensing steam engines with automatic controls were developed; and the invention of the flash boiler, an instantaneous steam generator, by Léon Serpollet in 1889 made it possible to operate a steam-powered car without waiting to get up steam. Beginning in 1872 in France, Amédée Bollée of Le Mans built and demonstrated several steam cars and omnibuses, but he gave up his experiments a decade later. Comte Albert de Dion experimented with steam tricycles between 1881 and 1888. The first Peugeot cars, built in 1889, were heavy tricycles powered by Serpollet steam engines. Serpollet, the only French "apostle of steam," drove one of his own steam tricycles 295 miles from Paris to Lyon in January 1890. The journey took two weeks. After building several more tricycles, he switched to building omnibuses in 1892, and by 1897 about eighty of his steam buses were in use in Paris. When the first lines of the underground Paris Métro opened in 1900, Serpollet reverted to making light steam cars with the backing of an American named Frank Gardner. The Gardner-Serpollet cars set some speed records in France and England, and about 100 a year were produced for a few years, which at £600 sold for about three times the price of an American-made Locomobile steamer. The rapid technological development of the gasoline-powered car in France discouraged there the concurrent development of light, inexpensive steamers.

With experimentation in England stultified by the Red Flag Act, leadership in development of the steamer in the late nineteenth century passed to the United States. At least a dozen American inventors built operable steamers in the period 1860–1890. The most important was Sylvester H. Roper of Roxbury, Massachusetts, who began his experiments in 1859 and built ten or more steam-powered road vehicles in the next two decades. Ransom E. Olds completed steam-powered road vehicles in his Lansing, Michigan, machine shop in 1887 and 1891 and sold the latter vehicle for $400 to a London patent medicine firm for use at its branch house in Bombay, India.

Quantity production of steamers in the United States was initiated in the Boston area in 1898 by George Whitney and by Francis E. and Freelan

O. Stanley. The Stanley design was sold the following year to Amzi Barber, an asphalt magnate, and to John Brisbane Walker, the publisher of *Cosmopolitan* magazine. They formed companies that made identical steam cars—the Locomobile Company of America at Bridgeport, Connecticut, and the Mobile Company of America at Tarrytown, New York. The Stanleys then reentered the manufacture of steam cars by buying Whitney's business. The White Sewing Machine Company began producing steamers in 1901 and was the first American maker to use Serpollet's flash boiler. The Locomobile steamer was the best-selling car in the United States in 1900–1901, and the cheapest Locomobile model sold for only $600. About 5,000 were produced before the company, at the height of the steamer's popularity, switched over entirely to making high-priced gasoline-powered automobiles in 1903. White, too, replaced its famous steamer with a gasoline-powered car in 1910. A Stanley Steamer driven by Fred Marriot averaged 127.66 mph to set a new land speed record at Ormond Beach, Florida, in 1906. By then, in sharp contrast to the gasoline automobile, the steamer had reached a technological standstill. Stanley continued in business until 1925, making a few hundred steamers a year for an ever diminishing market.

Initially, the steam engine had some advantages over the internal-combustion engine. It was more flexible with fewer moving parts and was less critical of exact tolerances to perform at minimal efficiency. It could not stall, as could the internal-combustion engine, and it permitted much smoother transmission of power to the wheels, thus simplifying operation by reducing the formidable problem of shifting gears. It was easier to manufacture.

These apparent early advantages were more than canceled out, however, by the steamer's liabilities. Steam engines operated at lower thermal efficiencies than internal-combustion engines of the same capacity, so the steamer had the great disadvantage of loss of energy due to inherent problems of heat transfer and storage. Mechanical problems also resulted from the high pressures (about 600 psi) necessary to develop adequate power in an engine small enough for a motorcar. Furthermore, the steamer was practical only in places where an abundant supply of soft water was available in horse troughs; and in addition to the water it consumed, the steamer burned as much petroleum fuel as did the gasoline automobile. Therefore, once the internal-combustion engine had been made more powerful for its weight and more flexible through better basic design and closer precision in the machining of parts, the steamer could not compete in the ratio of horsepower generated to the combined weight of the engine and fuel supply carried.

The Electric

A few manufacturers, primarily in the United States, for a short time backed the electric-powered car. The storage battery itself was invented and perfected in France: the first one was devised by Gaston Planté in 1859, and subsequent improvement of its storage cells by Camille Faure about 1880 had the result that sufficiently heavy current could be generated to power road vehicles by electricity. The electric car was pioneered in France by Charles Jeantaud, a Paris builder of fashionable coaches. He completed his first electric in 1894 and made several more as a sideline. Alexandre Darracq also briefly experimented with electric power in 1896. The only significant French manufacturer of electrics, however, was the Société Civil des Voitures Electriques, Système Kriéger, formed in 1895 to produce electric taxicabs. It folded in 1907.

If it found little enthusiasm in France, the electric car briefly played a prominent role in the emerging American automobile industry. Perhaps the first and most successful early experiment was a vehicle built by William Morrison of Des Moines, Iowa, in 1891, which was driven on the streets of Chicago a year later. Given the poor storage batteries of the day, it is difficult to believe the claim that Morrison's car was capable of being operated for thirteen consecutive hours at 14 mph.

Another early American electric was the 1894 "Electrobat," built by Henry G. Morris and Pedro G. Salom in Philadelphia. They formed the Electric Carriage and Wagon Company, which began to operate twelve of its electric vehicles as a fleet of public cabs on the streets of New York City in January 1897. The firm was soon absorbed by the Electric Vehicle Company—a New Jersey holding company established in 1897 by Isaac Rice, a manufacturer of storage batteries—and moved to Hartford, Connecticut.

Still another early manufacturer of electrics was Andrew L. Riker, who built an experimental tricycle as early as 1884. He formed the Riker Electric Motor Company to make electric motors in 1888, then organized the Riker Motor Vehicle Company in 1898 at Elizabeth, New Jersey, to make electric cars. In late 1900 Riker's firm was sold to the Electric Vehicle Company. Riker, one of the foremost early automotive engineers, switched over to designing luxurious gasoline-powered automobiles as chief engineer at Locomobile after 1902. He became one of the founders and the first president of the Society of Automotive Engineers (SAE), a small but influential group of American automobile trade journalists and engineers who organized in 1905 to improve the state of automotive technology through the publication of articles.

The most important early manufacturer of not only electric but all motor vehicles in the United States was the Pope Manufacturing Company of Hartford, Connecticut, the nation's leading bicycle manufacturer until surpassed in production by the Western Wheel Works in 1896. Pope's motor vehicle department, with Hiram Percy Maxim as chief engineer, began to produce electric automobiles in 1897. By the end of 1898 Pope had made some 500 electric and 40 gasoline automobiles. The Pope motor vehicle division became the Columbia Automobile Company and was consolidated into the aforementioned Electric Vehicle Comany in 1899. Pope then reentered the automobile business in 1901 by acquiring several small automobile manufacturing firms, one of which was the Waverly Company of Indianapolis, Indiana, a maker of electric cars since 1896. Pope went into receivership in 1907, but Waverly electrics were produced until 1915.

Probably the most notorious example of misplaced optimism and consequent overcapitalization, combined with poor technological judgment, in the early automobile industry was the so-called Lead Cab Trust, which resulted from the acquisition of the Electric Vehicle Company in 1899 by the William C. Whitney and P. A. B. Widener interests. In large part also a stock-jobbing venture, this holding company, formed with an inflated capitalization of $3 million, had as its announced aim the placing of fleets of public cabs on the streets of major American cities. Its manufacturing subsidiary, the Columbia and Electric Vehicle Company of Hartford, Connecticut, for a short time was the leading motor vehicle manufacturer in the United States. It produced some 2,000 electric cabs plus a few electric trucks in 1899, and it formed operating companies for its cabs in New York, Boston, Philadelphia, and Chicago. "Lead cab fever" affected Europe as well as the United States, with electric cabs of English and French make plus a few Pope-Columbias being put into service in London (1897), Paris (1898), and Berlin (1899).

The Lead Cab Trust's ultimate plans for a fleet of 12,000 vehicles and a $200-million capitalization were squelched by the failing performance of its electric cabs when put into service and by a financial scandal involving a fiscal manipulation that entailed a $2-million loan to a clerk. The operating subsidiaries collapsed, and on June 20, 1900, the Electric Vehicle Company became a manufacturing firm rather than a holding company, which through unwise mergers was again overcapitalized at $20 million by late 1900. The company progressively declined and as a result of the 1907 financial recession went into receivership on December 10, 1907, finally to be reorganized as the Columbia Motor Car Company in 1909 with a more realistic capitalization of $2 million. Ironically, the chief asset of this firm turned out to be its ownership of the Selden patent on the gasoline automobile. The Selden patent engendered a bitter organizational conflict in the early American automobile industry and profoundly influenced the industry's subsequent patent policy.

The electric car was the most conservative form of the automobile, in that it bore the closest resemblance to the horse-drawn vehicle in both appearance and performance. Manufacturers of electrics closely copied fashionable carriage forms. The Woods Motor Vehicle Company, a prominent early American maker of electric cars, for example, hoped to supply "hundreds of thousands of gentlemen's private stables with fine carriages in all variety of styles rather than the creation of a machine which will transport a man from town to town or on long country tours." [2] For city use, the electric offered some advantages over gasoline- and steam-powered cars as well as the horse. It was silent, odorless, and easy to control. Therefore, it was especially favored by women drivers, who were concerned foremost about comfort and cleanliness and who had a hard time either controlling a spirited team or starting a gasoline-powered car with a hand crank and learning to shift gears.

These advantages, however, were greatly outweighed by the many serious liabilities of the electric car. It was far more expensive than the gasoline automobile to manufacture and about three times more expensive to operate. As late as 1910, its range was only 50 to 80 miles on a battery charge; charging facilities were virtually nonexistent outside large cities; the storage batteries of the day deteriorated rapidly; and its hill-climbing ability was poor because of the excessive weight of the batteries for the horsepower generated. These relative liabilities of the electric car persist into the present, despite great recent improvements in storage batteries.

Developing the Gasoline Automobile

Although it was by no means obvious at the turn of the twentieth century, the four-cycle internal-combustion engine was vastly superior as an automotive power plant over alternatives. As an article in the June 1900 *American Monthly Review of Reviews* pointed out, the gasoline automobile had "developed more all-round good qualities than any other carriage. In spite of its clumsy and complicated mechanism, it does not get easily out of order. It will climb all ordinary hills; it will run through sand, mud, or snow; it makes good speed over long distances—say, an average of fifteen miles an hour.... It carries gasoline enough for a 70-mile journey, and nearly any country store can replenish the supply." [3] With the bringing in of the gusher "Spindletop" at Beaumont, Texas, on January 10, 1901, in the United States gasoline became a cheap commodity available at any crossroads general store, and farmers in midwestern hamlets early became familiar with the stationary gasoline engine. Electrics and steamers set speed records over short distances on tracks, but gasoline-powered cars excelled them in virtually all early endurance and reliability runs over public roads. The internal-combustion engine also was amenable to far greater short-range improvement than either the steam engine or the storage battery.

The internal-combustion engine was first perfected in Germany and France, and it is unequivocal that Continental automobile manufacturers were at least a decade ahead of their British and American counterparts in the technological development of the gasoline automobile. Like the automobile itself, the internal-combustion engine had no single inventor. Two-cycle versions were patented by Stuart Perry, a New York inventor, in the United States in 1844 and 1846, and by Etienne Lenoir, a Belgian mechanic, in France in 1860. There were others. Credit for being "first" is generally given to Lenoir, because his engine was commercially successful. A major innovation of the Lenoir engine was the use of an electric spark plug powered by a battery and coil to ignite the fuel mixture of air and illuminating gas.

Demand from farmers and small industrial plants for a cheap and simple source of power stimulated the development of more advanced internal-combustion engines. By far the most important was the four-cycle engine introduced in 1876 by Nicolaus Otto, a German manufacturer. His engine was the first to compress the fuel-air mixture inside the working cylinder, as well as the first to embody the four-cycle principle of consecutive intake, compression, power, and exhaust strokes (instead of every stroke being a power stroke, as in a reciprocating steam engine). The Otto engine was exhibited and won several competitions at the 1878 Paris Exposition. Etienne Lenoir then designed a four-cycle engine in 1883–1884 for the Paris machine builder Rouart Frères. A resulting suit over patent infringement was decided against Otto in the German and French courts, because the four-cycle principle had been conceived theoretically in 1862 by the Parisian Alphonse Beau de Rochas. This decision placed the Otto-type four-cycle engine in the public domain.

The original Otto Silent Engine was too cumbersome and slow to be efficient in a self-propelled vehicle. But by 1885 Gottlieb Daimler, who had been one of Otto's engineers, and his assistant, Wilhelm Maybach, had developed a 1.5-horsepower, 110-pound, 600-rpm vertical "high-speed" engine that proved to be the prototype of the modern motorcar's power plant. To demonstrate the capability of their engine, Daimler and Maybach built four experimental motor vehicles between 1885 and 1889. Then in 1893 Maybach invented the modern carburetor, which sprayed a fine jet of gasoline into the air stream being sucked into the engine.

From this point on, the dramatic improvement of the four-cycle, Otto-type engine stood in sharp contrast to developments not only in electric and steam engines but also in the isothermal-combustion/adiabatic expansion engine patented by Rudolf Diesel in 1893 in Germany. The diesel engine sought to obtain higher efficiencies through introducing the fuel into a cylinder in which air had already been compressed to a very high (ca. 250:1) pressure. The engine had the additional theoretical advantage that it could use lower grades of fuel and needed no ignition system because the fuel-air mixture was ignited by pressure. By 1897 Diesel had produced an engine that would run on heavy oil, with a compression ratio of 30:1 and an efficiency of 26 percent. This was about twice the efficiency of an Otto-type, low-pressure engine of the day, but still far less than the 75-percent efficiency that Diesel had anticipated. In producing a practical engine, he further had to justify a change in his patent from a constant-temperature to a constant-pressure engine, because temperatures inevitably went up as more fuel was burned.

Development of the diesel as an automotive power plant proved quite slow. Achieving a proper mixture of fuel and air in the brief time available for combustion was a major problem. "After seventy years of development," Lynwood Bryant pointed out as recently as 1976, "there are still plenty of uncertainties in this area, and in the first decade getting the engine to run smoothly was mostly a matter of accidentally hitting on the right combination of fuel, injection mechanism, and shape of combustion chamber, and sticking to the right formula with fingers crossed ... it was twenty-five years before the development of direct injection made the small diesel practical." [4] Ultimately, diesel engines would permit heavier loads to be transported over highways at greater economies of operation. But because of the diesel's high weight-to-power ratio, its initial impact was on rail transportation, and even diesel-powered heavy trucks and buses did not come into general use until after World War II.

It was Carl Benz, a German manufacturer of stationary gas engines, who brought the automobile to the stage of commercial feasibility. Benz built his first successful motor vehicle in 1885–1886, a tricycle powered by an 0.8-horsepower, two-cycle, one-cylinder engine. His third vehicle was exhibited at the Paris Exposition in 1889. The tricycle had been purchased the preceding summer and shipped to Paris by Emile Roger, a French engineer who became Benz's agent in France. For several months Roger found no buyers, and as late as 1892 he had sold only about a dozen cars.

Under prodding from Roger, in 1893 Benz came out with a greatly improved four-wheel car with a redesigned 3-horsepower engine capable of 700 rpm. Benz also introduced electric ignition, a great advance over the open-flame ignition used by Daimler. Given the limited market expectations of the day, the 1893 Benz sold well and was fairly reliable, as was a smaller model that he brought out in 1894. The Benz design was widely imitated. Benz is estimated to have sold 1,132 cars by 1898, 509 of them in France, 334 in Germany, 120 in England, and a handful in the United States, where they were first imported for sale by three New York City department stores in 1895. With sales of 603 cars in 1900, Benz was one of the emerging industry's leaders. But he retained the same basic design for a decade and was soon surpassed technologically by other manufacturers.

One of the pervasive myths of automotive historiography is that early automotive pioneers worked largely in ignorance of one another's accomplishments. Hiram Percy Maxim, in particular, gave credence to this notion in his 1937 autobiography. Maxim was "amazed that so many of us began work so nearly at the same time, and without the slightest notion that others were working on the same problems." [5] Maxim's own experiments in the early 1890s do illustrate his appalling ignorance of the state of the automotive technological art at the time. His procedures, for example, included igniting drops of gasoline in empty cartridge cases to determine whether or not they would explode! His experience cannot be generalized, however.

The diffusion of key technological innovations from a single source is generally what occurred in the development of the automobile; simultaneous, independent invention/discovery is far less common. We have noted, for example, that Daimler was one of Otto's engineers and that the Otto Silent Engine and the Benz tricycle were exhibited respectively at the 1878 and 1889 Paris Expositions, where they attracted worldwide attention. It is known that Charles E. and J. Frank Duryea were first motivated to design their own car after reading a description of the Benz tricycle in the 1889 *Scientific American*. The Duryeas were Springfield, Massachusetts, bicycle mechanics; they built the first successful American gasoline car in 1893, then initiated the commercial manufacture of gasoline cars in the United States in 1896. Still another prime example of the diffusion of key innovations is that the most important early French and British manufacturers— Panhard et Levassor, Peugeot, and British Daimler—all powered their cars with Daimler engines produced under license. To be sure, Carl Benz and Gottlieb Daimler developed their very first vehicles independently in the mid-1880s, and it is asserted that they never met. But after the Paris Exposition of 1889 virtually no development of importance in automotive technology went unreported in one or another of the engineering journals, bicycle periodicals, automobile trade journals, newspapers, and popular magazines of the day. Consequently, knowledge about such developments was widely disseminated worldwide from the very beginning of the automobile industry.

The Emerging Industry

Paris was the center of the nascent automobile industry. That this was the case had virtually nothing to do with French culture or social conditions—possibly excepting the French roads, the best in the world at that time. Rather, early French hegemony resulted from the historical accident of a unique network of social relationships emanating from the Germans Benz and Daimler through the French and Belgian intermediaries Emile Roger and Edouard Sarazin to the French industry leaders Emile Constant Levassor and Armand Peugeot.

Gottlieb Daimler himself produced only about a dozen cars in the early 1890s. Production began to expand in 1898, but Daimler Motoren Gesellschaft (later Mercedes) did not become prominent in the early automobile industry until after Daimler's death in 1900. The right to manufacture Daimler engines under license was secured in the United States about 1890 by the piano manufacturer William Steinway, who never got into production. In the United Kingdom, rights were obtained in 1893 by the Anglo-German automotive pioneer Frederick Simms, who had been born in Germany and knew Daimler well. Simms formed the short-lived Daimler Motor Syndicate in London before selling his British rights to the Daimler patents in 1895 to Harry J. Lawson, a leading figure in the British bicycle industry. Simms went on to found the British Motor Car Club and the Automobile Club of Great Britain and Ireland (later the Royal Automobile Club) in 1897, then to collaborate with Robert Bosch in the development of the magneto.

Despite the American and British licensing, technological development of the Daimler engine occurred only in France, where in 1890–1891 it powered the early Panhard et Levassor and Peugeot models. As a young engineer in 1860–1861, Gottlieb Daimler had worked briefly for the Paris metalworking firm of Perin et Pauwles, founded in the 1840s. René Panhard became a partner in the firm in 1867. He was the grandson of a coach builder, had been employed earlier by a wheel-making firm, and married in 1869 into a family of coach builders. Panhard was a graduate of the Ecole Centrale des Arts et Manufactures, a prestigious Paris engineering college, as were many French automotive pioneers. He brought into Perin et Panhard, by then one of the largest machine shops in Paris, his classmate, Emile Constant Levassor, who became a partner in 1872. On Perin's death in 1886, the firm became Panhard et Levassor.

After graduating from the Ecole Centrale, Levassor had worked for three years for the John Cockerill engineering works at Seraing, Belgium, where he became acquainted with Edouard Sarazin, a Belgian engineer. In the early 1870s Sarazin became the manufacturer's representative in Paris for Otto and Langden's Gasmotorenfabrik Deutz. He approached his friend Levassor to take the license to manufacture Deutz gas engines, which Panhard et Levassor produced until Deutz established its own branch plant to make the Otto Silent Engine in 1878. Sarazin remained friends with Daimler and obtained the French rights to the new high-speed Daimler engine, which he approached Levassor to manufacture in 1887. After Sarazin's death on Christmas Eve of that year, the French license to manufacture Daimler engines passed to his widow, who became Daimler's business agent in France. Mme. Sarazin married Emile Levassor in May 1890.

The other major figure in this story, Armand Peugeot, had by 1886 become the leading manufacturer of bicycles in France. His family firm, Les Fils de Peugeot Frères, was a major tool maker that employed some 2,000 workers at three factories in the Montbéliard region of France in 1889. As early as 1886, Armand Peugeot had written to Amédée Bollée expressing interest in a Bollée steam-powered vehicle described in the magazine *La Nature*.

Seeking a market for the Daimler engine, and knowing of Peugeot's interest in self-propelled road vehicles, Levassor contacted him. A meeting of historic importance followed in late 1888 between Levassor, Peugeot, and Daimler at Peugeot's Valentigny headquarters, only 150 miles from the Daimler Canstatt plant. Daimler shipped his 1887 car by rail for the meeting, to demonstrate the capabilities of his engine. Also in 1888, Emile Roger had the Benz tricycle that he had bought at the Benz plant in Germany shipped in crates to Panhard et Levassor for assembly and arranged as well for the French firm to produce the Benz two-cycle stationary engine, for which he had obtained French manufacturing rights. In 1890 Levassor delivered several Daimler engines to Peugeot at Valentigny, where a prototype gasoline-powered car was being developed by Louis

Rigolot, the head of Peugeot's bicycle production. In the same year Levassor began work on his own prototype gasoline automobile.

Motor vehicle design was radically altered in the 1891 Panhard et Levassor car, the prototype of the modern gasoline automobile. Its engine was placed vertically in the front of the chassis instead of under the seats or in the back, which put the crankshaft parallel with the longitudinal line of the car instead of parallel with the axles. This mechanical arrangement, called the Système Panhard, marked a radical departure from the carriage silhouette in automotive design. Its great importance was that it made possible the accommodation of larger, more powerful engines in motor vehicles. In 1895 Panhard et Levassor began to use the new two-cylinder, 750-rpm, 4-horsepower Daimler Phoenix engine. Levassor drove one of these cars over the 732-mile course of the 1895 Paris-Bordeaux-Paris race at the then incredible speed of 15 mph, with the longest stop for servicing being only 22 minutes—a feat impossible for a horse-drawn rig.

That race, which began on June 11, 1895, underlined both French superiority in automotive technology and the superiority of the gasoline automobile over not only the horse but steam- and electric-powered cars as well. Panhard et Levassor began producing motor vehicles in quantity for sale and issued the first regular catalog advertising motor vehicles in 1892; by 1895 several French firms were issuing catalogs, and the automobile was a common sight on the streets of Paris. In 1894 *Le Petit Journal*, aware of public enthusiasm, had sponsored a 78-mile reliability run from Paris to Rouen, in which all thirteen entries powered by internal-combustion engines and four of the eight steam-driven entries managed to finish. The Paris-Bordeaux-Paris race was the far more ambitious undertaking of a committee of journalists and French automotive pioneers—including Levassor, Peugeot, and Serpollet—under the leadership of Comte Albert de Dion and with help from the Touring Club of France, the leading French organization of cyclists. Of the twenty-two vehicles that started, nine completed the then formidable distance, and the best driving time was Levassor's impressive 48 hours. Levassor was disqualified on a technicality, however, and first place was given to a Peugeot that finished 11 hours behind him. Eight of the nine successful entries were powered by internal-combustion engines. The last car to finish was driven by the Michelin brothers, André and Edouard. Their family rubber manufacturing firm dated from 1832 and was the leading French producer of pneumatic bicycle tires. The Michelin car was the first automobile to be equipped with pneumatic tires, which quickly became standard on French cars.

Following the race, on November 12, 1895, the organizing committee, again under the comte de Dion's leadership, founded the Automobile Club of France to encourage the development of the motor vehicle and to regulate future sporting events. By early 1896 the club counted 422 well-to-do Frenchmen as members; by 1900 it had 2,261 members and located its clubhouse on the Place de la Concorde. Among its accomplishments, the club developed the automobile show as a marketing device. It sponsored the first automobile show independent of bicycle exhibits in 1898 in Paris. This became an annual event that attracted attention throughout Europe and in the United States.

About 130 automobile manufacturers are estimated to have been in business by 1901 in the Seine Department of France alone, making the Paris metropolitan area the world center of automobile production. The largest market for cars in France was among wealthy Parisians, and the city had the advantage of being a major manufacturing center, with a number of metalworking firms and an abundance of skilled labor. Paris remains the center of automobile manufacturing in France today, an anomaly: in no other country did automobile manufacturing come to be concentrated in its metropolis or, indeed, in close proximity to its major market for cars. Of the early provincial manufacturers, Peugeot was the most important, ranking third in the industry in 1900, after the Paris-based Panhard et Levassor and De Dion–Bouton; and Peugeot established its non-manufacturing operations in Paris.

By the turn of the century Panhard et Levassor, the industry leader, accounted for only about a tenth of French production. The most important of the many other small firms that had entered the French automobile industry was De Dion–Bouton, inaugurated in 1893 when Comte Albert de Dion approached Georges Bouton to develop an engine for a small car to compete with the Daimler motor. Bouton succeeded by 1895 in developing a reliable 2.75-horsepower, 40-pound engine. The tricycle to which this was fitted became the most popular early low-priced car in both France and England. Between 1895 and 1901 about 15,000 were sold, making it the first car to be sold in significant volume. De Dion–Bouton also initiated planned systematic research in the automotive industry by establishing as early as 1897 a laboratory for metallurgical research in conjunction with its factory. In 1899 the firm began to produce a four-wheeled, 550-pound "voiturette," powered by a one-cylinder, 3.5-horsepower engine, that sold for a modest 3,900 francs (about $780). By producing some 1,500 units in sixteen months in 1900–1901, De Dion–Bouton for a short time became the leading automobile manufacturer in the world. Between 1900 and 1910 some 140 other automobile manufacturers also bought about 200,000 De Dion–Bouton engines. At one time or another the firm supplied engines to Clément, Darracq, Delage, Peugeot, and Renault in France; to Argyll and Humber in England; to Adler and Opel in Germany; and to Packard, Peerless, and Pierce-Arrow in the United States. Its engines were also produced under license in Belgium, Germany, Great Britain, and the United States. No firm was more important in the emerging automobile industry.

Other early entrants into the French industry deserving mention are Clément (1898), Darracq (1896), Delahaye (1894), Mors (1895), and Renault (1898). Of these firms only Renault was to have a significant long-range impact. Renault moved quickly from an assembly into an integrated manufacturing operation and concentrated on small cars equipped with a patented direct-drive transmission. By 1908 the firm was the French industry leader. But like all French automobile manufacturers, Louis Renault, the closest French parallel to Henry Ford in background, failed to recognize the need to concentrate on producing a single model at ever decreasing unit costs. James Laux makes the significant observation that "when a [French] firm entered the industry in these years the common pattern was to offer a small and cheap model. If it met with any sort of success the company then began producing additional designs, bigger and more powerful, rather than improving the first one and lowering the cost."[1]

Coincident with the 1898 Paris automobile show, an automobile boom became evident in France, with demand for cars far exceeding the supply. French automobile production consequently jumped from an estimated 320 cars in 1896 to some 4,800 in 1900 and to 16,900 in 1904, the year that United States production first surpassed French. Between 1902 and 1907 France produced more cars than all other European countries combined. France remained the largest automobile producer in Europe until 1924, after which Great Britain vied for leadership.

The French home market was quickly glutted, and the French industry came early to depend on exports for its profits. Whereas in 1901 home demand accounted for some 5,000 sales versus exports of 2,600, by 1903 the situation was reversed and some 7,200 cars were exported, compared with home sales of only 6,900. A market for cars never had developed in Germany, and a 45-percent ad valorum tariff on motor vehicles effectively sealed against European competition the huge developing American market. Consequently, the United Kingdom became the largest importer of French cars and automotive components, accounting for about a third of French automotive exports in the early 1900s.

The British Industry

Most of the early British cars, explains S. B. Saul, were adaptations or superficially modified versions of French models.[2] The British Talbot, for example, was assembled from Clément parts made in France; the Siddeley was a British-designed radiator attached to a Peugeot chassis. De Dion–Bouton engines and Lacoste and Batemann chassis equipped with single-cylinder engines were exported from Paris and widely used by British makers, who attached their own bodies and sold the cars under their own names.

The first successful British gasoline-powered car was a 2-horsepower tricycle built in 1895 by Herbert Austin, a trained engineer employed at Wolseley, a firm that produced sheep-shearing tools and, beginning in 1895, bicycle parts. In 1895 the Wolseley directors invested £2,000 in a plant that was to produce automobiles under Austin's supervision. In 1899–1900 both Wolseley and Humber, another bicycle manufacturing firm, began to turn out small one-cylinder cars; they were soon followed by Alldays and Onions, Star, and Vauxhall. About this same time, the production of larger two- and four-cylinder cars based on French designs was begun by British Daimler and by Napier.

Some 59 British companies had entered automobile manufacturing by 1900, some 221 more between 1901 and 1905, including such later famous names as Argyll, Crossley, Riley, Rolls, Rover, Singer, Standard, and Sunbeam. Beginning about 1898, a number of Englishmen, including Charles S. Rolls, entered the automobile business by becoming British agents for French makes. Still others invested in or bought outright going French concerns. The first instance of the latter was the formation in 1896 of the short-lived Anglo-French Motor Company, with an inflated capitalization of £300,000, by Birmingham capitalists who bought out Emile Roger's Benz concession.

Metalworking firms, which played such a significant role in the formation of the French automobile industry, were conspicuously absent from the list of entrants into automobile manufacturing in Britain. Promoters and mechanics from the bicycle industry predominated among the British automotive pioneers. As in France, however, trained engineers were well represented. "It is striking," observes Saul, "how many [British automotive pioneers] received what might be called the accepted training for someone intended for an executive position in engineering at that time—a good school followed by an apprenticeship of some kind." [3]

The most prominent personality in the early British automobile industry was Harry J. Lawson, who had promoted the Rudge Cycle Company in 1887, then continued in the bicycle business at Humber. Lawson formed the British Motor Syndicate in November 1895, with a capitalization of £150,000, as an attempt to monopolize automobile manufacturing in the United Kingdom through control of key patents. A manufacturing subsidiary, the Daimler Motor Company, was created in

January 1896, with an initial capitalization of £100,000, as the first of an intended series of such subsidiaries; British Daimler placed an initial order for 100 chassis with engines from Panhard et Levassor. A prospectus claimed that the British Motor Syndicate would be "the original parent syndicate of the whole horseless carriage trade now beginning.... None may manufacture or use in this country any of the latest and successful types of Motor Cars ... without first purchasing Licenses or paying a Royalty."

Lawson's action was timely, for at the behest of Britain's pioneer motorists, led by Sir David Salomons, Parliament had passed the Locomotives on Highways Act on November 14, 1896, abolishing the provisions of the Red Flag Act and establishing a 14-mph speed limit on the open highway. To promote the automobile and Lawson's attempt to monopolize its manufacture in Britain, the Motor Car Club, founded by Lawson and Frederick Simms, staged an Emancipation Day run from London to Brighton. The best performance was turned in by an American-made Duryea.

In addition to the Daimler patents, Lawson in 1896 bought the British rights to the motor vehicle patents of both De Dion–Bouton and Bollée for £20,000 each, and formed the New Beeston Cycle and Motor Company and the Great Horseless Carriage Company as additional manufacturing subsidiaries. British Daimler was to produce high-priced cars for a limited market from Daimler and Panhard patents. New Beeston was pegged to build cars based on the De Dion–Bouton patents for a large-volume market. Humber, Lawson's bicycle manufacturing firm, was to turn out still lower priced Bollée motor tandems and a tricycle based on the patents of an American inventor named E. J. Pennington, for which Lawson paid the exorbitant sum of £100,000 cash.

The Midlands became the center of the young British automobile industry, as they were of the bicycle industry. In 1896 Lawson purchased an abandoned cotton mill in Conventry as the manufacturing center for his enterprises. As the bicycle boom of the 1890s evaporated, many bicyle firms in the Midlands turned to automobile manufacturing.

Lawson's attempt to base his monopoly in a conglomeration of early foreign patents was foolish: the state of the art in automotive technology was rapidly changing, outdating those patents. Effective monopolization stood a chance only if the very concept of the gasoline automobile could be patented—which George B. Selden managed to do in the United States—so Lawson's scheme did not get off the ground. By October 1897 the British Motor Syndicate was unraveling. Daimler shares collapsed from £10 to £4, and Lawson resigned his chairmanship of the company. It survived the demise of its parent company to be reorganized in 1904 and emerge as one of the leading manufacturers of luxury cars in England.

The British Motor Syndicate was reorganized as the British Motor Traction Company in 1900 by Selwyn F. Edge, an Australian-born racing cyclist. The validity of a number of Lawson's patent rights was successfully contested in the British courts by the Automobile Mutual Protective Association, and in 1907 Lawson disposed of the remainder of his patent rights to Edge and Montague Napier for a paltry £1,000, ending his automotive career. Former subsidiary companies, such as Daimler and Humber, "had to struggle for years to overcome the burden of watered stock imposed on them by Lawson," writes Saul, "and the public soon became shy of investing in the [British] industry as a result. Even so, it was a valuable purgative period too; the way was now clear, for neither the swindles of financiers nor the claims of patent holders were ever to trouble the [British] industry seriously again."[4]

The American Industry

Great interest in the automobile was stimulated in the United States by the Paris-Bordeaux-Paris race of 1895. Over five hundred patent applications relating to motor vehicles were on file in the United States Patent Office by September of that year, and the first two American automobile periodicals made their debut with the appearance of *Motocycle* in October and *Horseless Age* in November. On the first page of its first issue, *Horseless Age* reported that "all over the country mechanics and inventors are wrestling with the problem of trackless traction. Much of their work is in an unfinished state; many of their theories lack demonstration; but enough has already been achieved to prove absolutely the practicality of the motor vehicle." The periodical estimated that over three hundred companies or individuals in the United States were or had been engaged in building experimental motor vehicles.[5]

Much more than in the United Kingdom, in the United States the automobile industry developed from native roots. The Duryeas completed their first car in 1893. Their feat was duplicated the following year by Elwood P. Haynes, superintendent of the Indiana Gas and Oil Company, who built his vehicle with the help of two Kokomo, Indiana, machinists, Edgar and Elmer Apperson, and their assistant, Jonathan D. Maxwell. A number of others began to build experimental gasoline automobiles about the same time. Significant among those who had succeeded by 1896 were Hiram Percy Maxim, Charles B. King, Ransom E. Olds, Alexander Winton, and Henry Ford. Compared with the best contemporary French designs, these experimental American cars were primitive motorized horse buggies.

The *Chicago Times-Herald* sponsored the first American automobile race, held on Thanksgiving Day, November 28, 1895. Just six of the eighty-three entrants started, and only two vehicles were able to complete the 55-mile distance: the Duryea car that won and a Benz driven by Charles B. King. J. Frank Duryea's winning average speed was less than 8 mph. But as the *Times-Herald* report the following day stressed, the race had been run in thirty-degree temperatures "through deep snow, and along ruts that would have tried horses to their utmost." Eastern newspapers viewed the contest as a convincing demonstration that the Duryea and Benz cars could perform tolerably under the worst possible conditions and prophesied the demise of the horse. Herman H. Kohlsaat, the publisher of the *Times-Herald*, received an open congratulatory letter from P. H. Studebaker, whose family firm was then the world's leading producer of carriages and wagons. And Thomas A. Edison told a reporter from the *New York World* that "the horseless vehicle is the coming wonder.... It is only a question of time when the carriages and trucks in every large city will be run with motors." It was generally believed that the *Times-Herald* race had advanced by a least five years the formation of the American automobile industry.

Capitalizing on their success in the *Times-Herald* contest, the Duryeas made the first sale of an American gasoline automobile in February 1896 and produced twelve more vehicles of the same design that year. Elwood P. Haynes and the Apperson brothers also took advantage of their early start and in 1898 began to build cars at Kokomo. Alexander Winton, a Cleveland bicycle manufacturer, formed the Winton Motor Carriage Company. In the summer of 1897 he gained national recognition by driving one of his cars 800 miles from Cleveland to New York City in less than 79 hours' driving time. Winton sold his first automobile in March 1898 and by December had delivered twenty-two vehicles.

John B. Rae has established that, as in Europe, most of the successful American automotive pioneers "were less likely to be individual inventors starting a completely new business than men who added the production of automobiles to an existing operation. Most frequently, they were bicycle and carriage and wagon manufacturers, or operators of machine shops, but there were a variety of odds and ends." He also points out that although "the number of college-trained engineers in this first generation of automotive entrepreneurs is surprisingly large, considering that engineering degrees were something of a rarity in the United States until the twentieth century," the great majority of the more important figures in the early American automobile industry had received only practical training as machinists or mechanics.[6]

Allowing for changes of name and early failures, thirty American manufacturers produced an estimated 2,500 motor vehicles in 1899, the first year for which separate figures for the automobile industry were compiled in the *United States Census of Manufactures*. Ten New England firms that concentrated on producing electric and/or steam-powered cars were responsible for the most significant part of that output. The remaining firms were equally distributed between the Middle Atlantic states and the Middle West, which even then was the center for the manufacture of gasoline automobiles. *Motor Age*, one of several recently launched automobile trade journals, estimated in 1899 that in addition to the operations of these manufacturers, experimental work was being carried on in as many as a thousand shops in the United States, "and probably one hundred of them have been in operation for two years or longer without yet having advanced to the stage of manufacture, except in a very few instances." [7]

As experience proved the superiority of the gasoline automobile, the geographic center of automobile manufacturing in the United States shifted from New England, the home of the electric and the steamer, to the Middle West. The early, overwhelming choice of the internal-combustion engine by midwestern manufacturers was influenced by the region's poor roads, which were nearly impossible for electrics to negotiate, and by the universal availability of gasoline for fuel in sparsely settled rural areas lacking electricity. As the demand for electrics and steamers quickly subsided and as rural markets replaced urban ones after about 1906–1907, many New England manufacturers saw their sales dwindle to nothing and faced unfamiliar problems of design and production engineering in trying to switch over to the gasoline-powered car.

Michigan, Indiana, and Ohio in particular provided the ideal environment for the manufacture of gasoline automobiles. Their excellent hardwood forests had made these states the center for carriage and wagon manufacturing, and they were also important in the manufacturing of the stationary gasoline engines widely used on midwestern farms. They thus afforded the assembler of gasoline automobiles access to suppliers of bodies, wheels, and internal-combustion engines. Additionally, Detroit was an open-shop town with an abundant supply of unorganized, skilled labor.

Ohio and Indiana were important producers of cars in the industry's early years. But production came to center in southern Michigan, particularly in the Detroit area. By the end of the 1903–1904 fiscal year, Michigan's twenty-two motor vehicle manufacturers employed 2,133 wage earners and with an output that year of 9,125 units accounted for 42.1 percent of American motor vehicle production. In that the value of Michigan-made cars accounted for only 22.9 percent of the total value of American-made cars, it is apparent that Michigan concentrated on the production of low-priced cars for the rapidly developing middle-class market in the United States.

The favorable objective conditions found in Michigan notwithstanding, Gerald R. Bloomfield points out that in its formative stage motor vehicle manufacturing was not tied either to sources of materials or to markets, because transportation costs were relatively low and the industry was not yet capital intensive. Hence, the industry "enjoyed a relatively free choice of location." Rae asserts that as a consequence, "with due allowance for the influence of economic and geographic factors, Detroit became the capital of the automotive kingdom because it happened to possess a unique group of individuals with both business and technical ability who became interested in the possibilities of the motor vehicle." George S. May sees as the most critical factor in Michigan's early rise to hegemony the accidental one of "an idea that Ransom Olds had in 1896 to build a light, inexpensive gasoline-powered motor vehicle [that] led to production of the [1901–1906] curved-dash Oldsmobile.... When it was quickly followed by such other successes as the Cadillac, Ford, and Buick, which were in varying degrees inspired by the Oldsmobile, Detroit's and, to a somewhat lesser degree, Michigan's reputation as an important center of auto production was established." [8]

French leadership was short lived. American production overtook French in volume in 1904 and in value of product in 1905. In 1907 United States production reached 44,000 units, compared with about 25,000 for France, 12,000 for Great Britain, and 5,150 for Germany. France lost technological leadership as well to the United States with the appearance of moderately priced, light American runabouts in 1906–1908—most importantly the Ford Models N and T and the Buick "Nifty" Model 10. After 1907 not only the American but also the British and German automobile industries grew at a faster rate than the French. By the beginning of the First World War, United States production dwarfed European production. In 1913, the last year of peace and full production of cars prior to World War I, the United States accounted for some 485,000 units out of the world production of 606,124 motor vehicles.

Some 485 companies entered automobile manufacturing in the United States between 1900 and 1908; and 253 remained active in 1908, the year that Henry Ford introduced the Model T and William C. Durant founded General Motors. The new firms operated in an unprecedented seller's market for an expensive consumer-goods item. By 1905 the annual New York automobile show was the nation's leading industrial exhibit. By 1910 automobile manufacturing had leaped from 150th to 21st in value of product among American industries and had become more important to the national economy on all measurable criteria than the wagon and carriage industry. Some 458,500 motor vehicles were registered in the United States in 1910, making America the world's foremost automobile culture. Nowhere else did a mass market for cars materialize so early.

A Car for the Great Multitude

3

No industry in history developed in a more favorable climate of public opinion. By the time the Ford Motor Company was organized in 1903, the belief that the automobile would soon supersede the horse was commonplace. In a statement released in late 1900 through a Boston financial information agency, Colonel Albert A. Pope predicted that "inside of ten years there will be more automobiles in use in the large cities of the United States than there are now horses in these cities." He further declared that 15,000 of his bicycle agents throughout the country were "fairly howling" for automobiles to meet "an enormous demand." The principal examiner at the United States Patent Office stated in early 1901 that "to say the future of the automobile is assured is merely to voice an impression which is as common as it is usually vague." John W. Anderson, one of the original investors in the Ford Motor Company, described the scene in Detroit in a letter to his father just prior to the 1903 Ford incorporation: "Now the demand for automobiles is a perfect craze. Every factory here . . . has its entire output sold and cannot begin to fill orders. . . . And it is all spot cash on delivery, and no guarantee or string attached of any kind."[1]

In many respects the diffusion process was identical on both sides of the Atlantic. The Automobile Club of France, the Royal Automobile Club in Great Britain, and the Automobile Club of America were equivalent organizations of the motoring elite and carried on identical functions—sponsoring tours and tests, lobbying for legislation favorable to motorists, and propagandizing the automobilists' cause. Less affluent middle-class motorists were represented and their practical needs for touring information, insurance, and so forth, were met by the Touring Club de France and French regional clubs, the Motor Union in Great Britain, and the constituent state and local clubs of the American Automobile Association in the United States. Even in Germany, with its few motorists, some thirteen local automobile clubs had been organized by the early 1900s.

In all these countries, as Laux points out, "the earliest buyers of cars came from the same social groups: wealthy sportsmen, doctors, businessmen, and engineers." [2] Saturation of the early urban luxury market for cars and the consequent beginnings of significant diffusion into rural areas and among middle-class purchasers date from about 1904–1905 in Europe as well as in the United States, with the most innovative group being physicians. In France, for example, about a third of those who had adopted the automobile for their work by 1905 were doctors, while by 1905 in the United States in large and medium-sized cities the number of automobiles used by physicians in their practices was usually greater than the combined total of all commercial vehicles including public cab fleets. In the provinces of France as in the American Middle West, the country doctor was generally the first person to adopt the automobile.

In a 1973 dissertation in which he replicated, for France during the period 1900–1914, my own 1970 study of the diffusion of the automobile in the United States from 1895 to 1910, Nicolas Spinga reached the conclusion that "the ways of adopting the automobile in France were very much like those found by J. Flink in the United States. . . . In fact we find the same economic, technical, and moral preoccupations." From utilitarian advantages of economy and efficiency over the horse, through the public health benefits of horseless cities and the breaking down of rural isolation, to enhancing individualism and mobility, every motive for adoption of the automobile that I found in the circulating media in the United States can be found as well in the French media. What was important was not that American expectations and attitudes about the automobile differed from those of Europeans—for to the extent that they can be determined, they appear not to have differed significantly. Rather, as Spinga says, the significant fact is that "if the reasons for adoption are the same in the United States and France . . . they did not congeal in the same way in the plan for the quantitative development of the automobile and its distribution." [3]

One must agree with Joseph Interrante and begin "with the premise that our consumption of cars satisfies a real need for transportation—a need as basic as food, clothing, and shelter. . . . When the automobile first appeared as a mass-produced commodity after Henry Ford's introduction of the Model T in 1908, people bought automobiles because they met old transportation needs better than existing alternatives and offered new possibilities for movement." [4] These appeals of the car were universal, not culturally determined. However, because of a set of historically specific circumstances—most importantly, a far higher per capita income and far more equitable income distribution—Americans were able to actualize the possibilities of mass personal automobility a generation ahead of Europeans.

Proving the Automobile's Reliability

A specialized press that covered all aspects of motoring and crusaded for the mass adoption of the automobile existed on both sides of the Atlantic. As we have seen, French periodicals were active in promoting the first automobile races. Not counting regional automobile club bulletins, which took their news largely from the Paris press, some twenty-five specialized automobile periodicals were being published in France by the turn of the century, and French periodicals of general circulation in addition gave motoring generous coverage. The most important automobile periodical was the daily *L'Auto*, published by Henri Desgrange, followed by the weekly *L'Automation, La France Automobile, La Locomotion Automobile*, and *La Vie au Grand Air*.

The first British automobile journal was *Autocar*, inaugurated in November 1895 by William Isaac Iliffe of Coventry, publisher of *The Cyclist*. Its closest rivals were *Motor* (a successor to *Cycling*), Sir David Salomons's *Automobile Journal*, the *Motor Car Journal*, and *Cars Illustrated*. Like the French, the British motoring press, according to Kenneth Richardson, "proved itself one of the most powerful auxiliary forces in forwarding the development of motoring." [5]

The publishers of newspapers and magazines in the United States, knowing that automobile news fascinated readers from all walks of life, gave the motorcar extensive coverage. Important American specialized periodicals to appear in the wake of *Horseless Age* (1895) were *Cycle and Automobile Trade Journal* (1897), *Automobile* (1899), *Motor Age* (1899), *Motor World* (1900), and *Motor* (1903). As early as the turn of the century, *Automobile* felt that "the unprecedented and well nigh incredible rapidity with which the automobile industry has developed . . . is largely due to the fact that every detail of the subject has been popularized by the technical and daily press." *Horseless Age* in 1903 commented that "fanatical opposition to the automobile is on the whole very rare in this country. The metropolitan dailies occasionally print strong editorials denouncing speed excesses and careless driving, but the whole press is practically unanimous in recognizing the automobile as a legitimate pleasure vehicle and as destined to a great future in the commercial world." [6]

Close cooperation between the press and the automobile industry was established early. On May 13, 1897, Colonel Albert A. Pope initiated the custom of the press interview as a part of introducing new automobile models to the public. He invited reporters to a private showing of his first electric cars, allowed them to operate the vehicles, and supplied pictures for publication. The press interview was soon institutionalized and became more elaborate. Manufacturers commonly brought reporters long distances at company expense to be entertained and given a preview of new models in the hope that "free" publicity would follow.

No automobile manufacturer exploited the press more consciously or to better advantage than Alexander Winton, whose high regard for the power of the printed word can be traced to his 1897 drive from Cleveland to New York. The trip resulted in so much favorable publicity that he decided to repeat it in 1899 with Charles B. Shanks, a newspaper reporter. The articles Shanks wrote to publicize the journey attracted much attention and drew crowds all along their route. James R. Doolittle, writing the first comprehensive history of the industry in 1916, called Shanks's articles "the first real effort at intelligent publicity with which the new industry had been favored." He estimated that a million people watched Winton's arrival in New York "and part of the credit for that crowd must be given to Shanks." The fact that Winton's 1899 Cleveland–New York run had taken less than 48 hours' driving time, combined with Shanks's effective publicity, appears to have stimulated popular demand for automobiles. Other manufacturers gave Winton credit for a general increase in sales. Winton's own records showed that before the trip his sales were made "almost exclusively to engineers who desired to buy and experiment with an automobile that would really run, but after the trip, the sales were made to the public at large." [7]

Winton's practical demonstration of the motorcar was emulated many times during the next few years. Automobiles became drawing cards at county fairs around the turn of the century; and the annual automobile show became a popular institution in the United States after its inauguration in five American cities in 1900. It was the long-distance reliability run that most excited the average person's imagination about the romance of motoring. In contrast, track and road races, which placed primary emphasis speed, were more important for their contributions to automotive technology as tests for weaknesses in design than as publicity for the motorcar. Track races were viewed by the public as little more than exciting spectacles, involving as they did specialized monstrosities designed for maximum speed rather than practical road vehicles. The most important came to be the annual Memorial Day 500-miles race at Indianapolis, inaugurated in 1911. Road races were considered to be dangerous exhibitions, unwarranted because their relation to the development of a reliable family car seemed remote. The only important road race in the United States was the Vanderbilt Cup, run annually between 1904 and 1910 on the back roads of Long Island, New York.

In England, too, racing over the public roads was banned. British contests emphasizing speed on the open road were held on the Isle of Man or in Ireland. More important in developing the U.K. market was a 1,000-mile reliability trial from London to Edinburgh run in the spring of 1900 through many of the larger provincial cities. Of the 65 starters, 23 managed to finish. Britons, like Americans, were more impressed by the imminent personal automobility promised by the long-distance reliability run.

On the Continent, in contrast, widespread public enthusiasm for the automobile was engendered by a series of intercity road races beginning with the 1895 Paris-Bordeaux-Paris race. They were bloody spectacles. Emile Constant Levassor died of injuries sustained in the 1896 Paris-Marseilles-Paris race. Louis Renault's brother Maurice was among the victims of the 1903 Paris-Madrid-Paris race, a particularly lethal contest, stopped at Bordeaux after five drivers and several spectators had been killed. Thenceforward, intercity races in Europe were run on closed circuits.

An event of signal importance to the development of the American market occurred when Ransom E. Olds decided in the fall of 1901 to have Roy D. Chapin, then a tester at the Olds factory, drive a new curved-dash Oldsmobile (1901–1906) from Detroit to the New York automobile show. The one-cyclinder, tiller-steered, curved-dash Olds was the zenith of surrey-influenced automotive design. It sold for a moderate $650, making ownership of a fairly reliable car possible for upper-middle-class Americans. The Olds Motor Works had committed itself to the volume production of the curved-dash, and in 1901 it manufactured about 425 units. A New York City–to–Buffalo endurance run sponsored by the newly formed, New York City–based Automobile Club of America in that year had indicated the possibility of long-distance touring by private owners, and Olds hoped to capture the market in the heavily populated eastern cities by proving that his moderately priced light car was as reliable for touring as more expensive heavy vehicles. Chapin left Detroit on October 27. Despite the handicap of extremely muddy roads, he arrived in New York City on November 5, with an average speed of 14 mph for the 820-mile distance. Olds sold a record 750 cars in New York City alone the following year.

With annual production of some 2,500 and 4,000 units respectively, Olds provided an estimated 28 percent of the total United States output in 1902 and an estimated 36 percent in 1903. Olds thus became the first volume producer of American-made gasoline-powered cars. The 1904 Olds production figure of 5,508 units surpassed any annual production of cars previously accomplished.

Chapin's feat was also a prelude to three successful crossings of the American continent by automobile in 1903. The first was made by Dr. H. Nelson Jackson, a physician from Burlington, Vermont, and his chauffeur, Sewall K. Crocker. They traveled from San Francisco to New York in a new Winton in sixty-three days. Transcontinental tours under the auspices of their manufacturers by a Packard and a curved-dash Olds followed. The reliability of the moderately priced light car was now established in the mind of the public. In 1904 several thousand Americans took automobile vacations, marking the inauguration of long-distance touring by the average motorist.

Charles K. Glidden, a millionaire automobile enthusiast who wished to encourage touring by private owners, sponsored the famous Glidden reliability tours, run between 1905 and 1913 for handsome trophies. To keep the events from becoming simply publicity stunts for automobile manufacturers, Glidden stipulated that each car entered must be driven by its owner. But since any executive in the automobile industry could comply with the rule by driving one of his firm's most recent models himself, most contestants were industry representatives. The first Glidden tour was held from July 11 to July 22, 1905, over an 870-mile route from New York City through New England and back. Twenty-seven of the thirty-four entries finished, the first being a heavy Pierce touring car carrying five passengers. A participant summed up the results: "The tour has proved that the automobile is now almost foolproof. It has proved that American cars are durable and efficient. It has shown the few who took part how delightful their short vacation may be, and it has strengthened our belief in the permanence of the motorcar." [8]

That it was indeed "durable and efficient" in long-distance transportation the motorcar again demonstrated during the 1906 San Francisco earthquake. Walter C. White organized a caravan of motortrucks to bring supplies to the disaster area, and some two hundred privately owned automobiles were immediately impressed for emergency service by the authorities. The gasoline automobiles among them used an estimated 15,000 gallons of fuel donated by the Standard Oil Company. After tires exploded from the heat of the pavement, cars were run for days on their wheel rims as fast a speed as possible over obstacle-laden streets. Passenger cars were called upon to tow several moving vans after the horses pulling them had expired from the heat and strain. Mechanical failures under these severe conditions were surprisingly infrequent. Little need remained to demonstrate the reliability of the motor vehicle. By 1907 gasoline economy runs had replaced reliability runs as the focus of public interest.

Motor vehicle sales in the United States increased substantially, despite the 1907 general business recession and an apparent saturation of the initial upper-class market. No one doubted that a broad middle-class market for cars was becoming a reality. The number of starting cars in the annual Glidden tour dwindled from forty-nine in 1907 to only thirteen in 1909. One of the 1909 Glidden officials explained that the decline had occurred because automobile manufacturers "were enjoying too much prosperity. They said, 'Why should we enter this contest when we are unable to supply the demand now? The advertising will do us no good.'" [9]

Recognizing that the upper-class market was nearing saturation and aware of a great demand for outmoded buggy-type cars and secondhand conventional automobiles, after 1905 the more enterprising American manufacturers, in contrast with their European counterparts, turned to the volume production of lower-priced cars for the developing middle-class market. The most successful was Henry Ford, who led the industry worldwide in developing the reliable, moderately priced, four-cylinder runabout with his $600 Model N (1906–1907). Its successor, Ford's legendary Model T (1908–1927), became the low-priced car for the masses anticipated since the turn of the century.

Reconciling Cost with Quality

The 1901 Mercedes, designed by Wilhelm Maybach for Daimler Motoren Gesellschaft, deserves credit for being the first modern motorcar in all essentials. The Mercedes was named for the elder daughter of Daimler's most important agent in France, Emil Jellinek. Its 35-horsepower engine weighed only 14 pounds per horsepower, and it achieved a speed of 53 mph. The car featured a honeycomb radiator, a pressed-steel chassis, mechanically operated intake valves, and an improved gate gearbox. However, Daimler did not begin to produce the car in quantity until 1904, when its plant was moved to Stuttgart. As late as 1909, at the most integrated automobile factory in Europe, Daimler employed some 1,700 production workers to produce annually fewer than 1,000 cars.

Nothing better illustrates the early superiority of European automotive design than the sharp contrast between this first Mercedes model and the 1901 American 3-horsepower, curved-dash Olds, which was in all significant respects merely a motorized horse buggy. The central problem of automotive technology over the next decade would be reconciliation of the advanced design of the 1901 Mercedes with the low initial price and low operating expenses of the volume-produced 1901 curved-dash Olds.

The typical 1908 gasoline automobile bore little resemblance to the horseless carriage of 1900. The French practice of placing the engine under a hood in front of the driver was quickly adopted after the turn of the century. The hood was lengthened, and the wheelbase became longer as cylinders were added and as the engine became larger and more powerful. Power was conveyed from the transmission to the rear axle either by a propeller shaft and universal joints or by sprocket and chain. A differential gear on the rear axle allowed one wheel to turn faster than the other when rounding corners. A lower-slung body resulted from the replacement of high carriage wheels and narrow solid-rubber tires with smaller-diameter wheels and wider pneumatic tires. Goodyear universal rims and the power tire pump made tires, the weakest part of the car, easier to change.

By 1908 the steering wheel had replaced the tiller on most models, and in the United States the steering wheel began to be placed on the left-hand side, the position best suited to driving on the right-hand side of the road. Elliott's steering knuckle, which enabled the front wheels to turn without the entire front axle turning, came into general use after 1902. Controls became more sensitive after 1903 with the adoption of float-feed carburetors that could be throttled and choked, internal expanding foot brakes that operated on the wheel drums, better-designed cone or multiple-disc clutches, and either the standard H-slot gearshift with three-speed forward selective transmission or the simpler two-speed planetary transmission.

Improved engines gave more power for their size and the amount of fuel expended and were capable of generating sufficient power without stalling at a greater range of rpm. Water cooling, forced-feed lubrication by means of an oil pump, mechanically operated valves, and high-tension magneto ignition systems were other major improvements under the hood.

Shock absorbers and independent spring suspension of the wheels increased riding comfort and reduced strain on the mechanism of the car. The seats were moved forward in the body, and running boards and bumpers were added. Acetylene headlamps made night driving possible, and cape and folding tops made the open car of the period into an all-weather vehicle.

These vast improvements meant that the 1908 state-of-the-art gasoline automobile was a fairly reliable family car. The problem faced by the automobile industry was making such cars available at prices the average family could afford, either by cutting manufacturing costs or by reducing unit profits.

Cheaply built, one-cylinder, buggy-type cars that sold for only a few hundred dollars were available in Europe as well as in the United States from the beginning of the automobile industry. A number of American firms—most notably the W. H. McIntyre Company of Auburn, Indiana, and the H. K. Holsman Company of Chicago—continued to build cheap cars essentially similar to the first Duryea and Haynes models, instead of switching over to the modern form of the gasoline automobile innovated by Levassor in 1891 and perfected in the 1901 Mercedes. These high-wheeled, solid-tired horse buggies, equipped with low-horsepower engines under the seat or in the back, could be manufactured to sell for between $250 and $600, and they were very economical to operate. On muddy roads full of ruts and stumps, the high, narrow wheels provided maximum clearance for the chassis. If the car did get stuck, it was light enough to be easily pushed or lifted out. To meet the growing demand for automobiles in the rural Middle West, by 1909 some fifty firms were turning out buggy-type cars. The problem was that inherent mechanical weaknesses in the surrey design caused them to rattle apart in a short time.

Surrey-influenced design was rapidly abandoned by most manufacturers, especially in Europe. Ransom E. Olds and Thomas B. Jeffery, who followed Olds into volume production 1902 at Kenosha, Wisconsin, with his $750 to $825 Ramblers, both attempted to mass-produce cars that were technologically outmoded. Olds was forced to recognize this after his resignation from the Olds Motor Works because of the interference of his partners, Samuel and Frederick L. Smith, in his control of the manufacturing side of the business. When Olds reentered automobile manufacturing with his REO Motor Car Company in August 1904, he had difficulty in getting dealerships established, until it became known that he intended to abandon the surrey style of design and emphasize a 1,500-pound, 16-horsepower touring car that sold for $1,250. Alanson P. Brush also made a notable attempt to produce a car for the masses, with his Brush Runabout (1907–1912), a light car costing only $500, which combined the body style of the conventional automobile with the solid-rubber tires and chain drive of the buggy-type car. However, Brush went too far in reducing construction costs when he substituted wood for metal in his car. Disgruntled owners complained that the Brush Runabout had a "wooden body, wooden axles, wooden wheels, and wooden run."

At the opposite extreme, a number of manufacturers never wavered from producing finely crafted cars for the luxury market. In Europe this resulted in such outstanding marques as the Mercedes and the Rolls-Royce. American counterparts were the Thomas Flyer, the Pierce-Arrow, and the Packard. The 1910 Packard Thirty limousine sold for $5,450, more than sixteen times the estimated average per capita income in the United States.

The most significant strides in reconciling quality of product with volume production and moderate price were made in the United States—initially by Henry M. Leland at the Cadillac Motor Car Company, then by the Ford Motor Company. Leland had been trained first at the United States Armory in Springfield, Massachusetts, where the interchangeability of parts was pioneered, then at the Brown and Sharpe Manufacturing Company of Providence, Rhode Island, the leading precision toolmaker in the United States in the late nineteenth century. Leland and Faulconer, a nationally prominent Detroit manufacturer of high-quality machine tools, by the turn of the century had introduced processes that allowed castings to be machined to closer tolerances than its competition could duplicate. The firm commonly worked to tolerances of 1/10,000 inch.

When Leland and Faulconer undertook the production of transmission gears and motors for the 1901 curved-dash Olds, Brush, then one of its engineers, set out to improve the Olds motor. Through closer machining alone, the one-cylinder Olds engine was raised from 3 to 3.7 horsepower. The introduction of larger valves and a better timing system resulted in further improvement to 10.25 horsepower. After Olds rejected the improved motor as too radical a change in power plant, it was used in the popular Cadillac Model A. Leland entered automobile manufacturing in 1904 by merging his machine tool firm with the Cadillac Automobile Company (initially the Henry Ford Company, which under Ford's direction had not got off the ground).

Leland became general manager of Cadillac and brought out the improved one-cylinder Model B featuring interchangeability of parts—an essential element of mass production. Concentrating on reconciling high standards of workmanship with quantity production, Cadillac won the Dewar Trophy of the Royal Automobile Club of England in 1908 for the achievement of previously unparalleled interchangeability of parts. In a shed at Brooklands racetrack in England, three Cadillac cars were disassembled and their parts mixed by officials of the Royal Automobile Club. Cadillac mechanics then reassembled the cars, which were immediately given a 500-mile test drive. The cars finished with perfect scores. Leland did not, however, move to lower Cadillac prices by cutting manufacturing costs on a car of advanced design. Instead, he introduced the Model Thirty touring car, more powerful and expensive than the Model B. A moderately priced car of exceptional quality, the Cadillac Thirty sold for $1,400 in 1908.

It was the Ford Motor Company that led the world automobile industry in developing what Henry Ford called "a car for the great multitude." A controversy developed in 1905 between Ford and his principal backer, Alexander Y. Malcomson, who wanted to move toward the production of heavier, more expensive touring cars at higher unit profits. The 1906 Ford Model N, on the other hand, illustrated Ford's increasing commitment to the volume production of light, low-priced cars. The controversy was resolved when Ford bought out Malcomson on July 12, 1906.

The four-cylinder, 15-horsepower, $600 Model N was one of the better-designed and better-built cars available at any price in 1906. *Cycle and Automobile Trade Journal* called it "distinctly the most important mechanical traction event of 1906. This Ford Model N position of first importance and highest interest is due to the fact that the Model N supplies the very first instance of a low-cost motorcar driven by a gas engine having cylinders enough to give the shaft a turning impulse in each shaft turn which is well built and offered in large numbers." Deluged with orders, the company installed improved production equipment and after July 15, 1906, was able to make daily deliveries of 100 cars. Henry Ford boasted to reporters, "I believe that I have solved the problem of cheap as well as simple automobile construction . . . the general public is interested only in the knowledge that a serviceable machine can be constructed at a price within the reach of many." Ford rightly believed that the Model N was "destined to revolutionize automobile construction." At the time he considered it "the crowning achievement of my life." [10]

Encouraged by the success of the Model N, Henry Ford was determined to build an even better low-priced car. At $825 for the runabout and $850 for the touring car, the four-cylinder, 20-horsepower, 1,200-pound, 100-inch-wheelbase Model T was first offered to dealers on October 1, 1908. It featured a novel three-point suspension of the motor, improved arc springs, an enclosed power plant and transmission, and a detachable cylinder head. Extensive use of new heat-treated vanadium steels (first used on French racing machines) made the Model T a lighter and tougher car, and new methods of casting parts (especially block casting of the engine) kept the price still within the reach of the middle-class purchaser. Ford's advertising boast was essentially correct: "No car under $2,000 offers more, and no car over $2,000 offers more except the trimmings."

Committed to large-volume production of the Model T as a single, static model at an ever decreasing unit price, the Ford Motor Company innovated modern mass-production techniques at its new Highland Park plant, which opened on January 1, 1910. These production techniques permitted prices to be reduced by August 1, 1916, to only $345 for the runabout and $360 for the touring car. Production of the Model T in 1916 was 738,811 units, giving Ford about half the market for new cars in the United States by American entry into World War I. Antedating the introduction of the moving assembly line, in 1912 the initial price of the Model T—$575 for the runabout—first dropped below the average annual wage in the United States. By the time the Model T was withdrawn from production in 1927, over 15 million units had been sold, and its price had been reduced to a low of $290 for the coupe.

The Model T was the archetype of the American mass-produced gasoline automobile. Compared with the heavy, European-type touring car of the day—exemplified by American as well as European models intended for the luxury market—this car was significantly lower priced, was much lighter, had a higher ratio of horsepower to weight, and was powered by a larger-bore, shorter-stroke engine. In addition to the growing emphasis on producing cars for a mass market, these characteristics of the American car resulted from the lower price of gasoline here and the absence of European horsepower taxes. The sacrifice of engine efficiency and fuel economy for greater engine flexibility meant that the American-type car could better negotiate steep grades and wretched roads. It was also easier to drive, because the more flexible engine required less frequent shifting of gears. Designed for the average driver rather than for the professional chauffeur, the American-type car was abler to withstand abuse and was simpler to repair than the European-type touring car. However, with a body that sat high above the roadbed, the American car appeared ungainly and showed less attention to the details of fit, finish, and appointment. That the chassis of a car clear the inevitable hump in the center of our unpaved, rutted roads was then more important to the American consumer than style.

The Model T sold well not only in United States but all over the world until it was technologically outmoded. It was especially popular in British Commonwealth countries where roads were primitive, where vast areas remained sparsely settled, and where there was effective demand for an all-purpose family car. On the other hand, a combination of lower per capita incomes, higher gasoline prices, and high horsepower taxes had as its result that European cars designed for a far more slowly developing middle-class market were underpowered bantams—exemplified by the 8.5-horsepower (by RAC formula rating) Morris Oxford and the Austin Seven, introduced respectively in 1913 and 1922. In contrast with the 20-horsepower Model T and the 18-horsepower Buick "Nifty" Model 10, cars under 10 horsepower predominated among the European makes produced for the middle-class market until after World War II. In 1928, for example, cars of 10 horsepower or less accounted for some 80 percent of French production. These low-horsepower cars were fuel efficient and space efficient. But they were not all-purpose family cars, and they left much to be desired in performance.

The French pioneered in the development of "baby cars." Probably the first of note was a one-cylinder, 5-horsepower bantam designed by Jules Salomon, which was put on the market by Zèbre in 1909 at the low initial price of 2,500 francs ($483). Another was the four-cylinder, 6-horsepower, 800-pound, 72-inch-wheelbase Peugeot Bébé, designed by Ettore Bugatti and introduced in 1912.

Still another French innovation was the "cycle car"—a light, low-slung, two-seat, four-wheel car built around a motorcycle engine. The first cycle car was the 8-horsepower, 500-pound Bedelia, which came on the market in 1910 at 1,200 francs ($240). Cycle cars were particularly popular in England, where a journal devoted to them, *The Cyclecar*, began publication in 1912. Bedelia went out of business in 1925, but other manufacturers continued to make cycle cars into the mid-1930s.

Among all European automotive engineer-entrepreneurs, Louis Renault was the closest to Henry Ford in social background and character. The difference, therefore, between Renault's business strategy and Ford's is all the more striking. Renault became the leading French producer of motor vehicles for several years after 1907, because of annual sales of 2,000 to 3,000 of his taxicabs, the most widely used motor vehicles in city taxicab fleets throughout the world. Renault's profit margin in 1907 was a phenomenal $2,000 a unit, compared with Ford's $685. In contrast to Ford's concentration after 1908 on mass-producing one model at an ever decreasing price, after 1910 Renault's strategy was to produce a wide range of models at varying prices and high unit profits. Renault believed that the potential European mass market was not large enough for a producer to concentrate on a single low-priced model. The cheapest of Renault's eight models in 1914 sold for 5,000 francs (about $1,000), the most expensive for 22,500 francs ($4,500). Nothing better illustrates the chasm separating European and American entrepreneurial attitudes on the eve of the First World War.

Fordism

4

Up to the introduction of the moving assembly line at the Ford Highland Park plant in 1913–1914, automobiles were made and sold much the same way on both sides of the Atlantic; that is, they were assembled from jobbed-out components by crews of skilled mechanics and unskilled helpers at low rates of labor productivity, and they were sold at high prices and high unit profits through nonexclusive wholesale and retail distributors for cash on delivery.

Nevertheless, differences in national manufacturing traditions manifested themselves from the beginnings of the automobile industry, particularly those differences that added up to great American superiority over the Europeans in production engineering. As early as the turn of the century, it was accepted as axiomatic that, unlike European producers, "American manufacturers have set about to produce machines in quantity, so that the price can be reduced thereby and the public at large can have the benefit of machines which are not extravagant in price, and which can be taken care of by the ordinary individual." [1]

The initial capital as well as the managerial and technical expertise needed to enter automobile manufacturing was most commonly diverted from other closely related business activities, particularly from the manufacture of machine tools, bicycles, and carriages and wagons. The requirements for fixed and working capital were also met by shifting the burden to parts makers, distributors, and dealers. The automobile was a unique combination of components already standardized and being produced for other uses—for example, stationary and marine gasoline engines, carriage bodies, and wheels. Consequently, the manufacture of components was jobbed out to scores of independent suppliers, minimizing the capital requirements for wages, materials, expensive machinery, and a large factory. So once the basic design of his car was established, the early automobile manufacturer became merely an assembler of major components and a supplier of finished cars to his distributors and dealers. The modest assembly plant needed could be rented as easily as purchased, and the process of assembling was shorter than the thirty- to ninety-day credit period the parts makers allowed. Operating on this basis, the Ford Motor Company was able to start in business in 1903 with paid-in capital of only $28,000, a dozen workmen, and an assembly plant just 250 feet by 50 feet. The chassis (engines, transmissions, and axles) of the first Ford car were supplied by the Detroit machine shop of John F. and Horace E. Dodge, which earlier had supplied transmissions for the curved-dash Olds. The Dodge brothers became minority stockholders in the Ford Motor Company.

Demand for automobiles was so high that manufacturers were able to exact exorbitant concessions from distributors and dealers in exchange for exclusive territorial rights. European makers required advance cash deposits ranging from 10 to 33 percent on all orders, with payment in full upon delivery. In the United States advance cash deposits of 20 percent were required on all orders, with full payment demanded immediately upon delivery through a sight draft attached to the bill of lading. Moreover, cars had to be accepted by dealers according to a prearranged schedule, regardless of current retail sales, thereby allowing the manufacturer to gear shipments to production. Roy D. Chapin recalled that as late as 1909, when the Hudson Motor Car Company was beginning in the industry, "dealers' deposits often paid half the sum necessary to bring out a full year's production; and if the assembling were efficiently directed, drafts against the finished cars could be cashed as rapidly as the bills from parts makers came in." [2]

Skilled machinists, each capable of operating efficiently a large number of general-purpose machine tools, predominated in the work force numerically and directed production in the workplace. They were aided by unskilled helpers, who performed menial labor, such as carting and hauling material, at about half the pay of the skilled machinists. Increasingly, semiskilled specialists, who could operate one or more specialized machines, were also employed, especially in the United States. The skilled machinists had wide latitude in determining the pace of work, in setting the standards of production, and in hiring and firing their unskilled and semiskilled helpers. Consequently, there were few purely supervisory personnel, such as foremen, in the shops and small factories where components were made or assembled into completed automobiles.

General-purpose machine tools predominated over more specialized machines; there was little use of specialized jigs or fixtures to position the work; and tool benches equipped with the machinists' personal hand tools were placed in close proximity to machine tools. Machine tools of the same or similar type were grouped together, and material was conveyed by hand from one group of machines to another to be processed. Final fitting and finishing to acceptable tolerances generally involved hand filing and hand grinding. The principal component remained stationary on the shop floor until assembly was completed, while other components were brought to it and affixed. Thus chassis stood in rows as assembly crews moved from one to another affixing bodies and wheels.

So long as and wherever such artisanal production persisted, labor productivity was extremely low. Among even the larger French producers, at De Dion–Bouton in 1901 some 1,300 workers produced an estimated 1,200 cars; at Renault in 1902 some 500 workers produced 509 cars, and as late as 1913, 3,900 workers produced 4,704 cars. British labor productivity was even lower. At Austin in 1907 it took 400 workers to produce only 147 cars, and in 1913 some 2,300 workers produced only 1,500 cars. Morris Motors, entirely an assembly operation, was the only British maker in 1913 with an annual production of more than one car per worker. Labor productivity was equally low among the makers of luxury cars in the United States. As late as 1913, and after Frederick Winslow Taylor's principles of "scientific" management of labor had been adopted to rationalize production, at Packard in Detroit it still took 4,525 workers to produce only 2,984 cars, an annual production rate of about one car for every 1.5 workers.

Such low labor productivity meant correspondingly high prices for cars. The low production runs of only a few thousand cars annually associated with low labor productivity also militated against the establishment of exclusive franchised dealerships; for to sell enough cars to survive, most dealers had to handle several competitive makes.

Artisanal production lingered on as the norm in Europe long after it was abandoned by American automobile manufacturers. Of Daimler's 1,700 production workers in 1909, for example, 69 percent were skilled, 11 percent semiskilled, and 20 percent unskilled. And over a decade later, in 1920, among the Peugeot workers at Souchaux 65 percent had a skilled rating, 25 percent were semiskilled, and 10 percent were unskilled.[3] The continuing commitment of European manufacturers to artisanal production is also evident in their attempts at late dates to institutionalize the training of apprentice skilled machinists. For example, a 1904 law in France limiting the work hours of persons under age eighteen to ten hours a day brought the dismissal of most apprentices from automobile factories, which operated for longer hours. As a consequence, Panhard et Levassor and Darracq set up separate workshops with three-year courses to train teenage boys as machinists. In England such a technical school was established as an adjunct to the Austin factory as late as 1919.

Data for the Ford Motor Company are in sharp contrast. On the eve of the introduction of the moving assembly line in 1913, the Ford labor force of 13,304 was already classified as only 2 percent "mechanics and subforemen," versus 26 percent "skilled operators," 51 percent "operators," and 21 percent "unskilled workers." Even in its first year of operation, 1903–1904, the Ford Motor Company had produced about 12 cars annually for every worker it employed. A comparable production rate was not achieved by Morris Motors, the largest and most efficient British producer, until a generation later, in 1934, when Morris turned out 11.6 cars per worker. Average annual output at that date for the British automobile industry was only about 6 cars per worker. Similarly, Patrick Fridenson notes that in France in 1927 it took 300 man-days to manufacture a car, whereas in the United States it took 70.[4]

"The American System of Manufacturing"

Harking back to Adam Smith's classic exposition of the division of labor in pin manufacture in his capitalist bible *The Wealth of Nations*, Henry Ford in 1903 told John W. Anderson, "The way to make automobiles is to make one automobile just like another automobile, to make them all alike, to make them come through the factory alike—just like one pin is like another pin when it comes from the pin factory, or one match is like another match when it comes from the match factory."[5] The master of mass production described its constituents in the thirteenth edition (1926) of the *Encyclopaedia Britannica* as "the focusing upon a manufacturing project of the principles of power, accuracy, economy, system, continuity, speed, and repetition." These were all well-known aspects of an evolving American manufacturing tradition by the time they were adapted to the Model T and perfected at the Ford Motor Company.

For several reasons, the United States afforded an unparalleled market for motor vehicles, the most costly durable consumer product of the second industrial revolution. With its vast land area, hinterland of scattered and isolated settlements, and relatively low population densities, the United States had a far greater need for individualized automotive transportation than the nations of Western Europe. Even more important, great effective demand was ensured by a higher per capita income and more equitable income distribution than in European countries—an estimated average annual per capita income in 1914 of $334 for the United

States, compared with only $243 for Great Britain, $185 for France, and $146 for Germany.

Historically, the absence of tariff barriers between the states also had encouraged sales over a wide geographic area. By 1910 this comprised a vast free-trade area of some 92.2 million people. European competition in this high-demand American market was effectively nullified by a 45-percent tariff on motor vehicles imported into the United States, reduced in 1913 to 30 percent on cars costing under $2,000 and on chassis and parts. In contrast, tariffs ranged from only 3 percent in Germany to 12 percent in France and Belgium, and the United Kingdom was free of tariffs on cars until the imposition in 1915 of the $33\frac{1}{3}$-percent McKenna duties, which Ford and General Motors avoided paying by forming British subsidiaries.

Such market conditions combined with low raw material costs and with a chronic shortage of labor, especially skilled labor, to encourage the mechanization of industrial processes in the United States. This necessitated the standardization of industrial products and resulted in the early establishment of volume production of standardized commodities. The consequent American superiority in production was acknowledged by Europeans by the mid-nineteenth century. In the hope of learning from the United States, the British Parliament, for example, in 1854–1855 solicited several reports on what came to be called "the American System of Manufacturing." [6]

The automobile was neither the first nor a unique commodity that Americans excelled over Europeans in producing. Saul in particular has dealt in detail with the so-called invasion of European markets by American products form 1895 through 1914. He views this invasion as being "due to a new technology in which the major elements were standardization and mechanization, the use of interchangeable parts and the development of the art of management to plan and coordinate these processes of mass production. Firearms, sewing machines, typewriters, agricultural machinery, and watches were some of the products of this new approach." Particularly pertinent to the later dominance of the American automobile industry was the "unprecedented import of locomotives," invasion in "an industry in which Britain considered herself supreme." Compared with the British locomotive, the American locomotive, "though less perfect technically, was cheaper, more flexible, and rode better on a poor track.... The Americans also had the advantage in that their locomotives were less complex, parts were made interchangeable, and the design standardized so that it was possible to build for stock." [7]

The British and French automobile industries suffered from the inordinate influence of too many formally trained engineers, who sought technical perfection in automotive design at the expense of standardizing design at the point where an automobile was a commercially satisfactory product, then concentrating on cutting production costs to lower its price. Moreover, French and British automotive entrepreneurs consistently underestimated the potential market for cars. "Even if we set aside the story of what happened in the United States automobile market after 1909 as hardly relevant to the European scene," remarks Laux, "the French development of a mass market for cars in the 1920s (passenger car production climbed from 41,000 in 1921 to 212,000 to 1929) strongly suggests that it was waiting to be tapped before 1914." And Richardson points out that in 1926 it was believed by British automobile manufacturers that no one with an annual income less than £450 could afford to own a car, which meant a possible home market for only 835,000 motor vehicles. Yet British registrations exceeded the million mark as early as 1930, demonstrating that effective demand was greater than had been assumed. Most important, the level of demand was taken as a given by French and British automotive entrepreneurs, and in contrast with the drive at Ford to expand the market for the Model T, little was done by the Europeans either to lower the unit costs of cars or to raise the purchasing power of workers as consumers.[8]

Underlying American excellence in production was a machine tool industry vastly superior to that of Europe. Nathan Rosenberg has demonstrated that technological innovation in the nineteenth-century machine tool industry had an exponential impact, because innovations in machine tools revolutionized the manufacture of not just one but many diverse industrial products.[9] Because of the much larger domestic market in the United States compared with European countries, American machine tool makers had come to specialize in single types of tools that could be produced in volume, while European machine tool makers continued to make a variety of tools for much smaller markets. During the nineteenth century the American machine tool industry had become accustomed to providing specialized machine tools for the quantity production of many items, most importantly firearms, sewing machines, and bicycles. Moreover, "technological convergence" occurred, because machine tools used for the manufacture of these diverse items performed roughly the same functions of boring, cutting, grinding, planing, and otherwise shaping materials. Thus, improvements made in the machine tools for manufacturing one item were incorporated by the machine tool industry in tools performing comparable functions designed for manufacturing other items.

As a consequence, the American machine tool industry was well equipped to meet the great demand of the automobile industry for specialized tools. Early French automobile manufacturers were dependent upon American firms for some 70 to 80 percent of their machine tools. Even when European metalworking factories adopted American-made machine tools, observers reported that they failed to achieve as much production from them as American workers did. And in some cases European workers refused to operate semiautomatic, specialized machine tools because their introduction threatened the craft tradition well established in European factories.[10]

A number of innovations in specialized machine tools for the automobile industry were introduced in the United States even before American output of motor vehicles overtook the French. At the Paris Exposition of 1900 new cutting tools made from High Speed Steel, developed by Frederick Winslow Taylor for the Bethlehem Steel Company, were shown to increase by a factor of three the cutting speed of machine tools. Innovations in 1903 included a multiple drill press to work cylinder blocks and heads, a machine to grind cylinders, a lathe to turn camshafts, and a vertical turret lathe specially designed to turn flywheels. A crankshaft grinder developed by Charles Norton in 1905 duplicated in fifteen minutes what had previously required five hours of skilled handwork. It was these great American improvements in cutting and grinding tools that permitted the use of lighter but tougher hardened alloy steels in mass-produced cars such as the Ford Model T.[11]

Though it led the industry in developing the mass-produced, low-priced car, the Ford Motor Company was far from unique in its effort to increase output greatly after 1908. With the appearance of the first reliable, moderately priced runabouts in the Ford Model N and Model T and the Buick Model 10, many of Ford's competitors also began to attempt to cut manufacturing costs and capitalize on the insatiable demand for motorcars by working out similar solutions to their common production problems. For example, innovations to reduce the time and cost of final assembly similar to those worked out at Ford were independently conceived by Walter P. Chrysler after he replaced Charles W. Nash as head of Buick in 1912. Buick production was more than quadrupled from 45 to 200 cars a day by changing outmoded procedures for finishing the body and chassis, which had amounted to "treating metal as if it were wood," and by installing a moving assembly line that consisted of "a pair of tracks made of two by fours" along which a chassis was moved from worker to worker by hand while being assembled. Chrysler recalled that "Henry Ford, after we developed our [assembly] line, went to work and figured out a chain conveyor; his was the first. Thereafter we all used them. Instead of pushing the cars along the line by hand, they rode on an endless-chain conveyor operated by a motor."[12]

Charles E. Sorensen, who was in charge of production at Ford, was well aware that his company's contribution to mass production lay primarily in its refinement of the integration and coordination of the process of final assembly. In his 1956 autobiography he recalled: "Overhead conveyors were used in many industries including our own. So was substitution of machine work for hand labor. Nor was orderly progress of the work anything new; but it was new to us at Ford until Walter Flanders showed us how to arrange our machine tools at the Mack Avenue and Piquette plants." The significant contribution that Sorensen claimed for the Ford Motor Company was "the practice of moving the work from one worker to another until it became a complete unit, then arranging the flow of these units at the right time and the right place to a moving final assembly line from which came a finished product. Regardless of earlier uses of some of these principles, the direct line of succession of mass production and its intensification into automation stems directly from what we worked out at Ford Motor Company between 1908 and 1913."[13]

Before the moving assembly line was introduced at Ford, continuous-flow production had been achieved in a grain mill designed by Oliver Evans in the late eighteenth century, and in Admiral Isaac Coffin's 1810 oven for baking ships' biscuits in England. By the late nineteenth century in the United States it was common in flour milling, oil refining, breweries, canneries, and the disassembly of animal carcasses in the meat packing industry.

Yet in his definitive history of the rise of mass production, David A. Hounshell concludes that despite these earlier origins and uses of the constituent elements of mass production, "it is only with the rise of the Ford Motor Company and its Model T that there clearly appears an approach to manufacture capable of handling an output of multicomponent consumer durables ranging into the millions each year."[14] Indeed, the very term "mass production" dates from Henry Ford's 1926 *Encyclopaedia Britannica* article of that title. Until then, the system of flow production techniques perfected at the Ford Highland Park plant was popularly referred to as "Fordism."

The Revolution at Highland Park

At Ford the moving assembly line was first tried one Sunday morning in July 1908 at the Piquette Avenue plant during the last months of Model N production. The parts needed for assembling a car were laid out in sequence on the floor; a frame was next put on skids and pulled along by a towrope until the axles and wheels were put on, and then rolled along in notches until assembled. This first experiment, however, was not elaborated into the installation of moving assembly lines until 1913, because the extensive changes in plant layout and procedures, in Sorensen's words, "would have indefinitely delayed Model T production and the realization of Mr. Ford's long cherished ambition which he had maintained against all opposition." [15]

There was general agreement in the automobile industry that the 62-acre Highland Park plant that Ford opened on January 1, 1910, possessed an unequaled factory arrangement for the volume production of motorcars. Its well-lighted and well-ventilated buildings were a model of advanced industrial construction. It is clear, however, from the fact that much of the plant was several stories high that it was not designed with moving assembly lines in mind. Its designer was the eminent Detroit architect Albert Kahn, who earlier had designed the reinforced-concrete Packard plant on Grand Boulevard in Detroit—"the prototype for twentieth-century industry." [16] Kahn went on to design the gigantic Ford River Rouge plant, the General Motors Building, and Chrysler's Detroit facilities.

Elementary time-and-motion studies begun at the Piquette Avenue plant were continued at Highland Park and in 1912 led to the installation of continuous conveyor belts to bring materials to the assembly lines. And with the move to Highland Park, manufacturing and assembling operations began to be arranged sequentially, so that components traveled to completion over the shortest route possible with no unnecessary handling. This entailed the abandonment of grouping machine tools together by type in plant layout.

Magnetos, motors, and transmissions were assembled on moving lines by the summer of 1913. After production from these subassembly lines threatened to flood the final assembly line, a moving chassis-assembly line was installed. It reduced the time of chassis assembly from twelve and a half hours in October to two hours and forty minutes by December 30, 1913. Moving lines were quickly established for assembling the dash, the front axle, and the body. The moving lines were at first pulled by rope and windlass, but on January 14, 1914, an endless chain was installed. That was in turn replaced on February 27 by a new line built on rails set at a convenient working height and timed at six feet a minute. By the summer of 1914 productivity in assembling magnetos had more than doubled, and chassis assembly took under two hours, about one sixth the time required with artisanal production methods. "Every piece of work in the shop moves," boasted Henry Ford in 1922. "It may move on hooks or overhead chains going to assembly in the exact order in which the parts are required;

it may travel on a moving platform, or it may go by gravity, but the point is that there is no lifting or trucking of anything other than materials."[17]

In a plant that employed fewer than 13,000 workers, by 1914 about 15,000 specialized machine tools had been installed at a cost of $2.8 million. "The policy of the company," relate Allan Nevins and Frank E. Hill, "was to scrap old machines ruthlessly in favor of better types—even if 'old' meant a month's use."[18] After 1912 the 59 draftsmen and 472 skilled tool makers in the tool department were constantly devising new specialized machine tools that would increase production. By 1915 they had turned out over 140 specialized machine tools and several thousand specialized dies, jigs, and fixtures. Jigs and fixtures to set up and/or position work were called "farmers' tools," because with them green hands could turn out work as good as or better than skilled machinists. Machine tools became larger, more powerful, more specialized, and semiautomatic or automatic. A prime example was a special drilling machine supplied by the Foote-Burt Company. This machine drilled 45 holes simultaneously in four sides of a Model T cyclinder block and was equipped with an automatic stop and reverse. The cylinder block was positioned by a special jig, so all the operator had to do was pull the starting lever and remove the finished block.

At the industrial colossus that Ford began building on the River Rouge in 1916, Fordism was intensified. Nevins and Hill write that by the mid-1920s "in conveyors alone it was a wonderland of devices. Gravity, belt, buckle, spiral, pendulum gravity roller, overhead monorail, 'scenic railway' and 'merry-go-round,' elevating flight—the list was long both in range and in adaptation to special purpose.... At the entrance of the machining department, the various castings were routed mechanically to 32 different groups of machine tools, each unit then passing through a series of machine-tool operations—43 in the case of the Ford [Model T] cylinder block—before the finished shining element emerged, ready to be routed to assembly." By 1924 the River Rouge foundry cast over 10,000 Model T cylinder blocks a day, and by 1926 the 115-acre plant boasted some 43,000 machine tools and employed 8,000 tool and die makers. At the changeover to Model A production in 1927 the Ford Motor Company was estimated to have about 45,000 machine tools worth $45 million. Part of the Model A retooling involved the introduction of the electric welding of parts by self-indexing automatic welders to replace the traditional bolting together of subassemblies. These automatic welding machines were the forerunners of our current Unimate robots.[19]

This intensified Fordism, notes Fridenson, tremendously raised the capital invested in plant in relation to revenue at Ford—from 11 percent of revenue in 1913 to 22 percent in 1921, and to 33 percent in 1926—even as Ford inventories shrank by half and the time to fabricate a Model T from scratch fell from fourteen days to four. "The result was declining profit margins for Ford beginning in 1923," he observes. "The cost of producing a Ford touring car reached 93 percent of the selling price by 1926, and some models were sold to dealers at less than cost." [20]

The Ford Motor Company set the pace and direction of a new social order based on mass production and mass personal automobility in the United States until the mid-1920s, when Hudson surpassed and other American automobile manufacturers began to equal Highland Park's efficiency in production. The mass-production techniques innovated there were widely publicized and described in detail, most notably by Horace L. Arnold and Fay L. Faurote in their 1915 *Ford Methods and the Ford Shops*. Within a few years moving assembly lines had been installed by all major American automobile manufacturers. Production reached peak efficiency at Hudson, where by 1926 assembling an automobile took only ninety minutes, and cars rolled off its four final assembly lines every thirty seconds.

Although the mass-production techniques developed at Highland Park to meet the tremendous demand for the Model T became synonymous in the mind of the public with Henry Ford's name, the evidence is unequivocal that both the Model T and mass production, in Reynold Wik's words, "represented the efforts of a team of engineers, rather than the inspiration of one man, Henry Ford." C. Harold Wills, the chief engineer, and Joseph Galamb head a long list of Ford employees whose collective efforts were more significant than Henry Ford's inspiration in creating the Model T. Charles E. Sorensen, his assistant Clarence W. Avery, William C. Klann, and P. E. Martin deserve the lion's share of credit for the moving assembly line worked out at Highland Park, while the specialized machinery was designed by a staff of dozens of engineers and skilled tool makers headed by Carl Emde. "Henry Ford had no ideas on mass production," claimed Sorensen, the man best qualified to know. "Far from it; he just grew into it like the rest of us. The essential tools and the final assembly line with its integrated feeders resulted from an organization which was continually experimenting and improvising to get better production." Nevins and Hill agree: "It is clear that the impression given in Ford's *My Life and Work* that the key ideas of mass production percolated from the top of the factory downward is erroneous; rather, seminal ideas moved from the bottom upward." [21]

The business success of the Ford Motor Company depended on the talents of many other individuals. For, as John Kenneth Galbraith says, "if there is any uncertainty as to what a businessman is, he is assuredly the things Ford was not." The marketing of the Model T was handled by

Norval A. Hawkins, a sales and advertising whiz. Fred Diehl was in charge of purchasing. The Ford domestic and foreign branch plants were set up by William S. Knudsen. The man who oversaw the entire operation and provided the main business brains for the company until his resignation on October 12, 1915, was James Couzens, a minority stockholder as well as vice-president and treasurer. Sorensen called the period from 1903 to 1913 at Ford the "Couzens period.... Everyone in the company, including Henry Ford, acknowledged [Couzens] as the driving force during this period." After Couzens left, Ford "took full command, and the company was never so successful again," observes Galbraith. "In the years that followed, Ford was a relentless and avid self-advertiser.... Only the multitude remained unaware of the effort which Ford, both deliberately and instinctively, devoted to building the Ford myth.... He was the first and by far the most successful product of public relations in the industry." [22]

The Selden Patent Suit

Henry Ford missed no opportunity to claim personal credit for both the low-priced reliable car and the mass-production techniques that together revolutionized American life. He promoted himself as the champion of the small businessman and of the common man's personal automobility against the forces of monopoly in the bitter and divisive 1899–1911 Selden patent controversy. Ironically, the man who most strongly opposed the preposterous claim that George B. Selden invented the gasoline automobile emerged from the controversy falling just short of making the same claim for himself. Even more ironically, the opponent of monopolization on the basis of the Selden patent came to account for about half of United States production of motor vehicles by the outbreak of World War I.

Probably the most absurd action in the history of patent law was the granting of United States patent number 549,160 on November 5, 1895, to George B. Selden, a Rochester, New York, patent attorney and inventor, for an "improved road engine" powered by "a liquid-hydrocarbon engine of the compression type." The Selden patent thus covered the basic elements necessary for constructing a gasoline-powered automobile. Selden got his idea for the vehicle after seeing the two-cycle engine patented in 1872 by George B. Brayton of Boston, which was exhibited at the 1876 Philadelphia Centennial Exposition. His own patent application was filed in 1879. He then used evasive legal tactics to delay the patent's acceptance until conditions seemed favorable for commercial exploitation. This enabled him to maintain adequate security for his claim while he deferred the start of the seventeen-year period of exclusive rights to his invention provided by law. His hand was forced in 1895—in part because the patent office was tightening its rules on delayed applications but more because events indicated that the time was now ripe for implementing the automotive idea. Selden had not yet built an operational model of his design when the patent was issued; and, as we have seen, the state of the prior technological art in no sense supported his allegation of priority.

To hedge its bet on the electric car, the newly formed Electric Vehicle Company bought the rights to the Selden patent in 1899 and began litigation to enforce the patent against the Winton Motor Carriage Company, then the leading American manufacturer of gasoline-powered cars. Before a decree was entered on March 20, 1903, that the Selden patent was valid and that he had infringed, Alexander Winton capitulated rather than continue what appeared to be a hopeless legal battle.

Other major American manufacturers of gasoline-powered cars, who initially had viewed the Selden patent as a threat, began to realize that it might provide a means of regulating competition. Under the leadership of Henry B. Joy of Packard and Frederick L. Smith of the Olds Motor Works, negotiations were undertaken with the Electric Vehicle Company to form a trade association under the Selden patent; the fruit of these negotiations was the establishment on March 6, 1903, of the Association of Licensed Automobile Manufacturers (ALAM). Licenses to manufacture gasoline automobiles were granted to a select group of thirty-two established companies. They agreed henceforth to pay the association quarterly royalties, amounting to 1.25 percent of the retail price of every gasoline automobile they produced. One fifth of the royalties was to go to Selden, two fifths to the Electric Vehicle Company, and two fifths to the ALAM for a war chest to finance litigations against infringers.

Although the licensed companies did compete against one another, the ALAM threatened to monopolize automobile manufacturing in the United States. The association tried to exercise arbitrary power over entrances into the industry by granting licenses only to manufacturers with prior experience in the automobile business, which theoretically precluded the admission of new firms. It further tried to preserve the status quo in the industry by setting production quotas. The Mechanical Branch of the ALAM was organized in 1905 for the ostensible purposes of facilitating the interchange of technical information and encouraging intercompany standardization of components. But it was in fact conceived primarily as a legal tactic in the Selden patent litigation against nonmember companies; it collapsed when the patent was initially upheld by the courts in 1909. The ALAM threat of litigation proved an ineffective deterrent to new entrances, and the Selden patent was widely disregarded. The vast majority of gasoline automobile makers operated without licenses.

From the consumer's point of view, the influence of the ALAM was regressive, because the main interest of the licensed makers was in maintaining high unit profits. The ALAM companies did not seriously attempt to cater to the needs of a broad middle-class market until they were forced to by the more responsible so-called independent manufacturers, such as Ransom E. Olds at REO; the Thomas B. Jeffery Company, which made the low-priced Rambler car; Benjamin Briscoe at Maxwell-Briscoe; and Henry Ford. The outstanding exception among the ALAM companies was William C. Durant of the Buick Motor Car Company, who paid his Selden patent royalties reluctantly and was considered a maverick within the ALAM fold. "In any given year between 1903 and 1911, the ALAM [companies] never had more than four makes selling for less than $1,000," William Greenleaf points out. "In contrast, it was generally agreed that the majority of independent makers produced low-priced cars. Their ranks could ... cite an average price that was $1,500 below the ALAM average. In 1909 the independents offered twenty-six models costing $1,000 or less." [23]

Henry Ford had gained a national reputation as a racing driver by beating Alexander Winton at the Grosse Pointe, Michigan, track on October 10, 1901; by that time he had also made two unsuccessful attempts to enter automobile manufacturing, with the Detroit Automobile Company in 1899 and the Henry Ford Company in 1901. When with new backers he organized the Ford Motor Company on June 16, 1903, the ALAM made the mistake of rejecting his application for a license on the ground that he had not demonstrated his competence as a manufacturer of gasoline automobiles. (George Selden's application, as it happens, was rejected on the same ground.)

Assured of the support of the department store magnate John Wanamaker, his eastern agent, Ford determined to stay in the automobile business and to contest to the limit of his resources the lawsuit for infringement that was immediately brought against him by the ALAM. Suit was also brought against Panhard et Levassor and the manager of its New York City branch; the Paris firm of Henry and Albert C. Neubauer, which exported Panhard and Renault cars to the United States; John Wanamaker and C. A. Duerr and Company, agents for Ford cars; and the O. J. Gude Company, a New York City advertising firm that had bought a Ford car from Duerr.

The ALAM advertised, "Don't buy a lawsuit with your car." Ford countered this threat with an offer to bond his customers against any suit for damages that the ALAM, might bring against them. Through a clever propaganda campaign that brought favorable publicity, he turned the Selden patent fight into a great benefit to his business. Ford gained public sympathy by contrasting his own humble midwestern origins and status as a pioneer automotive inventor and struggling small businessman with the image of the ALAM as a group of powerful and parasitical eastern monopolists.

At the 1905 Chicago automobile show, twenty independent makers banded together to fight the Selden patent by forming the American Motor Car Manufacturers' Association (AMCMA). Ford, Maxwell-Briscoe, and REO were the most important of the forty-eight manufacturers that ultimately joined the AMCMA. Ford vice-president James Couzens became the AMCMA's first chairman. He explained to reporters, "We manufacturers on an independent basis have simply decided to take the bull by the horns and cooperate for mutual benefit." Henry Ford promised, "I am opposed to the Selden patent first, last, and all the time and I will fight it to the bitter end." But the other members of the AMCMA lacked Ford's determination. *Automobile* reported in late 1906, "No fight is made against the patent by the association, although the members, along with some forty other makers, do not believe in it. The Ford Motor Company, one of the leading members of the AMCMA, is fighting the idea single handed, in an effort to disprove the claims made." [24] The journal overlooked Panhard et Levassor, which considered capitulation for a time but ultimately stuck it out with Ford "to the bitter end."

The ALAM won a fleeting victory when the United States Circuit Court of the Southern District of New York upheld the claim against Ford and Panhard et Levassor in 1909. The AMCMA immediately disintegrated, and most of its members sought and received licenses from the ALAM, swelling the latter's membership to eight-three. The independent makers who joined were allowed to pay a reduced royalty of 0.8 percent on their production since 1903. The ALAM's new liberality resulted from the recent bankruptcy of the Electric Vehicle Company and from the ALAM's mindfulness that its exclusive rights under the Selden patent were due to expire in 1912. Ford, too, was now invited to become a licensed manufacturer, but he declined, because the ALAM refused to reimburse him for his legal expenses. He decided to continue the fight by appealing the decision in the higher courts.

The collapse of the ALAM followed a written decision of the United States Circuit Court of Appeals for the Second Circuit that was handed down on January 11, 1911. That decision sustained the validity of the Selden patent for motor vehicles using the Brayton two-cycle engine. But it declared that Ford and Panhard et Levassor had not infringed, because they powered their cars with Otto-type four-cycle engines. Almost all other manufacturers used the four-cycle engine, too. The decision made the Selden patent worthless. Its lateness, however, meant that it merely formalized and hastened a bit the imminent breakup of the ALAM.

In the aftermath of the Selden patent fight, the secondary functions that the ALAM and AMCMA had filled as trade associations were assumed by the Automobile Board of Trade, which became the National Automobile Chamber of Commerce (NACC) in 1914, the Automobile Manufacturers Association in 1932, and the Motor Vehicle Manufacturers Association in 1972. The technological functions of the ALAM Mechanical Branch were transferred in 1910 to the Society of Automotive Engineers. To prevent another costly patent controversy from ever again arising in the automobile industry, the NACC instituted in 1914 a cross-licensing agreement among its members. Although the Ford Motor Company was not a party to this agreement, Henry Ford conformed to its principles. The use of Ford patents without payment of royalty fees was liberally extended to competitors, and they reciprocated. Up to the outbreak of World War II, the Ford Motor Company permitted 92 of its patents to be used by others and in turn used 515 outside patents, without any cash changing hands.

The patent-sharing arrangement encouraged the widespread diffusion of technological innovations among competing firms and prevented monopolization of automobile manufacturing based on exclusive control of patents. "The patent policy of the Ford Motor Company and the cross-licensing agreement of other automobile producers," concludes Greenleaf, "are tantamount to radical surgery upon the body of the American patent system. Both patterns have preserved free technology along the frontiers of the automotive industry where conflicts over patent rights might well have hampered it." [25]

Nevertheless, for other reasons the American automobile industry did develop into a joint-profit-maximizing oligopoly by the late 1920s, as Detroit's "Big Three" came to dominate worldwide automobile manufacturing.

The Rise of the Giants

5

Closure of entry into automobile manufacturing did not occur in the United States until the market for new cars reached saturation in the late 1920s. But by 1910 it was evident to perceptive entrepreneurs that the era of artisanal production and freewheeling competition among many small producers was about over. Considerably heavier outlays of capital were becoming necessary to ensure success. With a view to reducing unit costs of production, improving the quality of the product, and ensuring the supply of components, the industry leaders early turned toward a policy of reinvesting their high profits in the expansion of plant facilities, both to increase the output of completed cars and to undertake the manufacture of many components formerly jobbed out. The nature of this trend was evident by 1910 to Walter E. Flanders, the Ford production manager from August 1906 until April 1908, when he left to go into business for himself with the EMF car. Flanders knew that "to equal in quality cars now selling at $700 to $900, it is not only necessary to build them in tremendous quantities, but to build and equip factories for the economical manufacture of every part." The formation of General Motors and the opening of the Ford Highland Park plant gave substance to Flanders's assertion that "henceforth the history of this industry will be the story of a conflict among giants." [1]

As the large-volume producers turned to integrated manufacturing operations, the automobile industry, both in the United States and in Europe, became capital intensive. As early as 1903 Renault made its own engines, and by 1905 it had its own foundry and body shop. Laux notes that Renault's "policy of vertical integration, by which he made more and more of his components himself, a policy that between the wars even led him to make his own steel, rubber tires, and electricity, was followed not for economic motives but because it freed him from dependence on others and gave him a greater sway for his authority." As for the Austin Motor Company in England, although it was still buying some cylinder blocks, wheels, and frames from outside suppliers as late as 1914, from the firm's inception in 1905 its Longbridge factory was in essence a conglomeration of small specialist component manufacturing shops, which turned out all parts except electrical ones for Austin cars, plus assembly facilities. Saul describes the Austin operation as "conventional" in the British industry. Morris Motors, on the other hand, was an apparent anomaly. For its first production model, the 1913 Oxford, "Morris went to great lengths to buy out everything including engine and body—not in itself a new idea but unique for the scale on which it was conceived." [2] William Morris increasingly was forced to invest in his suppliers' businesses and to oversee their operations. However, Morris Motors remained basically an assembler of jobbed-out components until Morris acquired control of his British suppliers of bodies, engines, and radiators in 1923. Like Louis Renault in France and Henry Ford in the United States, Herbert Austin and William Morris still remained in personal control of their enterprises as late as the outbreak of World War II, long after such control was outmoded.

Vertical Integration at Ford

The Ford Motor Company began to move toward both vertical integration and one-man rule in mid-1906 with Henry Ford's buying control from Alexander Y. Malcolmson, his principal backer, and with the initiation of Model N production. A system of branch sales houses and agencies in major cities, situated at strategic points where freight rates changed, had started to replace dependence upon wholesale distributors in 1905. These branch houses carried complete inventories of Ford parts and accessories and closely supervised the prices and standards of service among franchised dealerships in their territories. By 1913 Ford had established branch houses in thirty-one cities in the United States, in nine cities in Canada, and in England, France, Germany, and Austria. "By the end of 1912 the company's sales organization [of some 7,000 dealers] covered practically every town in the United States of 2,000 or more," write Nevins and Hill. "Ford franchises for agencies were by this time regarded as highly valuable and were much sought after, and because of the heavy demand for the car, the company could obtain the best dealers in America and in foreign countries.... By the end of 1912, the company had more agents, more dealers, more salesmen employed by the agents ... than any other automobile company or almost any other manufacturing company which might be named; it had probably more agencies than the rest of the automobile industry put together." [3]

Because cars could be shipped cheaper by rail in knocked-down form, Ford branch assembly plants were built, beginning in 1909 at Kansas City, Missouri. By American entry into World War I, branch assembly plants had been set up at freight-rate breaking points in twenty-eight cities under the supervision of William Knudsen. Outside the United States, assembly plants were built in Canada in 1904 and in England in 1911.

In 1911 Ford purchased the John R. Keim Mills of Buffalo, New York, a leading maker of pressed- and drawn-steel components. The plant's modern machinery and technical experts were moved to Highland Park, giving Ford the capacity to make its own crankcases, axles, housings, and bodies. With the inauguration of mass production at Highland Park in 1913 came complete independence from the Dodge Brothers, Ford's early supplier of both engines and complete chassis.

In the spring of 1915 Henry Ford began buying up huge tracts of land along the River Rouge southwest of Detroit and announced plans for developing a great industrial complex there. John and Horace Dodge were still minority Ford stockholders, despite having formed a rival company in 1912 to build their own car. They brought a lawsuit against Ford to stop his diverting Ford Motor Company profits into expansion of the Rouge plant instead of distributing them as dividends, which the Dodge brothers were counting on to finance expansion at Dodge. On January 6, 1917, the lifting of a restraining order by the court permitted Ford to go ahead with developing the Rouge facilities on the condition that he post a $10-million bond to safeguard the interests of his minority stockholders. A decision handed down on February 7, 1919, forced the Ford Motor Company to declare a special dividend of $19.275 million plus interest. Although, as the principal Ford stockholder, Henry Ford himself received the bulk of this special dividend, the experience left him determined to rid himself of his minority stockholders.

Ford "danced a jig all around the room" when he managed to buy up the options of his minority stockholders for the bargain price of $105.8 million on July 11, 1919. Financing the transaction required a $75-million loan from a financial syndicate composed of the Chase Securities Corporation, the Old Colony Trust Company, and Bond and Goodwin. The reorganized Ford Motor Company's shares were distributed 55.2 percent to Henry Ford, 41.7 percent to Edsel Ford, Henry's only progeny and heir apparent to the throne, and 3.1 percent to Clara Ford, Henry's wife. Edsel became titular president of the reorganized company, a position he held until his untimely death from cancer on May 26, 1943. No one, however, least of all Edsel, doubted that the Ford Motor Company after its reorganization was an autocracy subject to the whims of its aging, egocentric founder.

Turning the gigantic Ford Motor Company into a family-owned and family-managed business defied precedent, business trends, rational canons of business administration, and simple common sense. Henry Ford "wielded industrial power such as no man had ever possessed before," write Nevins and Hill; they point out that John D. Rockefeller never held more than two-sevenths of the Standard Oil Company shares, and J. P. Morgan owned a far smaller portion of U.S. Steel.[4] The trends in American industry were toward wider dispersal of ownership among many small stockholders, the separation of ownership from management, the rise of professional managers and salaried experts within the firm, and democratic decision making by committees of executives. At the Ford Motor Company, in sharp contrast, the champion of small business against the forces of monopoly in the Selden patent suit now fastened onto his mammoth corporation the family ownership and one-man rule fit for a mom-and-pop market. In addition to its main Highland Park and River Rouge plants, by the late 1920s the company had branch plants and agencies scattered across the globe, and had acquired rubber plantations in Brazil, iron mines and lumber mills in Michigan, coal mines in Kentucky and West Virginia, glass plants in Pennsylvania and Minnesota, a railroad, and a fleet of ships.

Durant Builds Up Buick

William C. Durant had much in common with Henry Ford. Both men were egocentric individualists, given to one-man rule and motivated by the risk-taking capitalist's cardinal values of power, prestige, and profits. Both were what Alfred P. Sloan, Jr., called "personal types of industrialists; that is they injected their personalities, their 'genius,' so to speak, as a subjective factor into their operations without the discipline of management by method and objective facts. Their organizational methods, however, were at opposite poles, Mr. Ford being an extreme centralizer, Mr. Durant an extreme decentralizer. And they differed as to products and approach to the market."[5] The mechanically minded Ford, as we have seen, approached the market from the perspective of improving production technology so as to sell the Model T at ever lower prices. In contrast, Durant was a flamboyant supersalesman, stock promotor, and stock manipulator, almost totally devoid of acumen in automotive technology.

Durant came out of semiretirement in 1904 to enter the automobile business as the head of Buick, at the behest of a group of Flint, Michigan investors who were his close personal friends. He had made his fortune in the carriage industry, after buying the patent rights to a two-wheeled cart for $50 and going into business to produce it with $2,000 borrowed money and J. Dallas Dort, a Flint hardware merchant, as his partner. At first, production of the cart was farmed out to a local carriage manufacturer, who provided completed carts for $8 that Durant and Dort sold for $12.50. But as sales outstripped production, the partners undertook to manufacture the carts themselves; and, fearful that the growth of horizontal trusts in ancillary industries would make components and raw materials hard to get at reasonable prices, the Durant-Dort Carriage Company purchased hardwood forests and set up specialized subsidiary companies to manufacture bodies, wheels, axles, upholstery, springs, varnish, and whip sockets. By the turn of the century Durant-Dort had fourteen branch plants, hundreds of sales agencies, and annual sales of over 150,000 carriages. In a day when its competitors were mere order-taking assemblers of components, the company's emphasis upon aggressive sales techniques and its integrated manufacturing operations were major innovations in the carriage industry, as were Durant-Dort's bold conception of a mass market for low-priced carriages and its attempt to blanket the market with a complete line of carriages. Durant would carry these ideas with him into automobile manufacturing.

One of the many Michiganders who attempted to enter the automobile business was David Dunbar Buick, a Detroit manufacturer of plumbers' supplies and an eccentric inventor. He was soon deeply in debt to Benjamin and Frank Briscoe, whose sheet metal firm was his major components supplier. The Buick operation passed through the Briscoe brothers to James M. Whiting, a Flint carriage and wagon manufacturer, who had become alarmed about the potential inroads of the motor vehicle on the carriage and wagon industry. Whiting moved the Buick plant to Flint but was unable to get the floundering company off the ground. Only six Buicks were sold in 1903, sixteen in 1904. The company's principal asset was an intangible one—the patent on the valve-in-head engine, developed by Walter Marr and Eugene Richard, which gave better combustion of the fuel-air mixture and more power. Whiting was under pressure from the Flint banking community, which had supported his venture, to find someone who could put Buick in the black. After putting the two-cylinder Buick car through its paces over the worst terrain he could find, Billy Durant, already a millionaire, whose chief occupation at this time was playing the stock market in New York City, agreed to undertake the management of the Buick Motor Company. He assumed his new duties on November 1, 1904. One of Durant's stipulations was that he exercise "absolute control." Bernard Weisberger has observed that seven of the nine Buick directors were Flint men and that "it was almost a family firm, if the elite of the town, with a total 1900 population of about 13,000, was considered as a form of extended clan, comprising thirty or forty families laced together by shared interests, ancestry, trust, and marriage." [6]

Once in control at Buick, Durant moved with boldness and speed into the volume production of a reliable car in the intermediate price range. Buick's capital stock was increased from $75,000 to $300,000 the day he took over, and it increased again to $1.5 million on September 11, 1905. Durant is said to have sold nearly half a million dollars' worth of the new stock to his Flint neighbors in a single day. The Durant-Dort Carriage Company became a major source of capital for Buick, and Buick cars were exhibited in its showrooms. Companies that had supplied Durant's carriage enterprise were shifted to automobile work. A national network of franchised dealers was established. Large assembly plants were built at Flint and at Jackson, Michigan, turning those cities into boom towns reminiscent of western mining camps.

In just a few years, Buick cars were substantially improved in quality for the price asked. The four-cylinder, 18-horsepower "Nifty" Model 10 was introduced in 1907 as, in Weisberger's words, "Buick's entering wedge into that beckoning low-priced field." [7] Like the Ford Model T, the more rakishly styled, $1,000 Model 10 was equipped with a simple two-speed planetary transmission operated by foot pedals, and it too was an easy car to drive and to maintain.

In 1908 the Buick Motor Company built 8,487 cars, had a net worth of $3.5 million, and occupied the largest automobile factory in the world at Flint. Buick ranked second only to Ford worldwide in production from 1907 through 1910. Nevertheless, Durant was worried in early 1908 about the immediate future. So was Benjamin Briscoe, who had become president of the Maxwell-Briscoe Motor Company of Tarrytown, New York, one of Buick's chief competitors.

Consolidation Attempts

Whereas Henry Ford was confident by 1908 that his Model T was the "car for the great multitude" and concentrated henceforth on lowering its price through standardization and improved production, Billy Durant was more uncertain than ever about the best bet in automotive technology. Rather than put all his eggs in the Model 10 basket, he continued at Buick to make several models in different price ranges. He further decided to adopt the marketing strategy of forming an industrial combination of firms making a wide variety of types of cars. Durant later lamented: "They say I shouldn't have bought Cartercar. Well, how was anyone to know that Cartercar wasn't going to be the thing? It had the friction drive and no other car had it. How could I tell what these engineers would say next? Maybe friction drive would be the thing. And then there's Elmore with its two-cycle engine. That's the kind they were using on motorboats; maybe two-cycle was going to be the thing for automobiles. I was for getting every kind of car in sight, playing it safe all along the line." [8]

Benjamin Briscoe also found conditions in the spring of 1908 "somewhat ominous, especially for such concerns as had large fixed investments in plants, machinery, tools, etc." Briscoe was worried about the "menace to the industry" posed by "concerns which did not have a worthy car or any manufacturing ability, but with large stock issues to sell, and [which] by ingenious exploitation would succeed in stirring up the trade and the public, creating the impression that ... they, through some newly discovered combination of geniuses, were enabled to sell gold dollars for fifty cents in automobiles." He blamed the parts makers for threatening "demoralization by encouraging into the business undercapitalized concerns and inexperienced makers" that in the aggregate did a large business. But the main problem was that many companies were outright "manufacturing gamblers," driving the others to risk unduly large amounts of capital, given the existing technological uncertainties. The bolder companies were forcing "even the sanest among the manufacturers ... into business risks which they would not have entered had they not been fearful that some other concern would gain a few points on them." [9]

Briscoe and Durant conceived that the answer to these problems was a horizontal and vertical trust. They decided to team up to try "to form a combination of the principal concerns in the industry ... for the purpose of having one big concern of such dominating influence in the automobile industry, as, for instance, the United States Steel Corporation exercises in the steel industry, so that its very influence would prevent many of the abuses that we believed existed." [10] The easiest way was to merge their own firms, Buick and Maxwell-Briscoe, with several other leading producers of gasoline automobiles. But the merger plan failed when Henry Ford and Ransom E. Olds at REO each demanded $3 million in cash to sell out, instead of accepting the securities offered in exchange for their companies by Briscoe and Durant.

A second plan was to form an "International Motors Company" around the nucleus of Buick, Maxwell-Briscoe, and Oldsmobile. That fell through, too, when J. P. Morgan and Company, Briscoe's backer in earlier automotive ventures, refused to underwrite the stock issue. During the negotiations with the House of Morgan, Durant correctly prophesied that half a million automobiles would soon be sold annually in the United

States. George W. Perkins, who represented the Morgan interests, thought he was dealing with an unbalanced mind and curtly suggested that Durant, when he wanted to borrow money, had better keep such crazy notions to himself.

Ed Cray provides even more substantial reasons for the collapse of the negotiations with the House of Morgan. Upon learning that Buick stock was changing hands during the course of the discussions, Francis Stetson, the Morgan attorney, became suspicious that Durant intended to enlarge his personal Buick holdings at the expense of other stockholders by neglecting to inform them of the terms of the anticipated merger, which would greatly increase the value of Buick stock. When questioned, Durant confirmed that the Buick stockholders did not know the terms of the proposed merger but had deposited their stock with him on the basis of trust. Stetson then insisted that those who had sold stock to Durant in ignorance be permitted to buy back their shares. Durant refused. More important, undoubtedly, the bankers were cooled by Durant's casual offer of $1.8 million for Oldsmobile, without even examining the company's books, on the basis of Frederick Smith's verbal estimate of its worth. The straw that broke the camel's back was Durant's insistence that he, rather than the bankers, would control the combination's finances, while Briscoe would manage its manufacturing operations.[11]

Briscoe and Durant went their separate ways. Briscoe formed the ill-fated United States Motor Company, which in its brief existence came to involve some 130 affiliated companies and an inflated capitalization of $42.5 million. His principal backer in this venture was the traction magnate Anthony N. Brady, who earlier had been associated with the Whitney and Widener interests in the Electric Vehicle Company debacle. Maxwell-Briscoe was the only manufacturing unit in the combination that made money, and its earnings could not support the heavily watered stock and the heavy investment Briscoe and Brady made in too many weak firms producing unpopular automobiles, such as the Brush Runabout. United States Motor went into receivership in September 1912, with liabilities of $12.3 million versus realizable assets of only $9.3 million.

Its reorganization by the banking firm of Eugene Meyer, Jr., and Company brought in Walter E. Flanders, at the price of purchasing his weak Flanders Motor Company for $1 million cash plus $2.75 million in stock of the reorganized combination. After leaving Ford in 1908, Flanders had joined with Barney Everitt, general manager at the Wayne Automobile Company, and William E. Metzger, an organizer of the Northern Automobile Company, to form the Everitt-Metzger-Flanders Company (EMF) from Wayne, Northern, and three Detroit parts and accessories firms. EMF's operations were integrated organizationally and centralized geographically in Detroit, where it produced the EMF car and the smaller Flanders. Wags of the day joked that EMF stood for Every Mechanical Fault.

As a means of expanding its business into gasoline automobiles, the Studebaker Brothers Manufacturing Company of South Bend, Indiana, bought a one-third interest in EMF in 1909. Studebaker was the world's largest manufacturer of carriages and wagons and a maker of electric cars. The new combination, Studebaker-EMF, ranked fourth among American automobile producers in 1909 and 1910, and second only to Ford in 1911. Then, with the help of financing by J. P. Morgan and Company, Studebaker bought complete control of EMF for $5 million, reorganized as the Studebaker Corporation, and dropped the use of the EMF name on its cars. From 1912 through 1914 Studebaker ranked third in the American industry after Ford and Willys-Overland; it dropped to sixth place in 1915 but remained among the top ten American producers through the 1920s and was one of the few independents to weather the Great Depression and survive into the post–World War II period.

Flanders remained with Studebaker as general manager only until 1912, when he rejoined Everitt and Metzger to organize the ephemeral Flanders Motor Company. The policy he had followed at Studebaker-EMF—that of merger to strengthen a single company's competitive position, rather than a strategy of combination—was continued when he took control of the reorganized United States Motor. Here Flanders instituted a severe program of consolidation and liquidation. Only the Maxwell Motor Company (formerly Maxwell-Briscoe) emerged as a going concern. Although Benjamin Briscoe was to found several more automobile companies, his days of prominence in the industry were over. Flanders resigned from Maxwell in 1914. He was associated with the short-lived Rickenbacker Motor Company briefly before his untimely death in 1923 in an automobile accident.

General Motors

Durant fell harder than Briscoe, but his career as an automotive tycoon was far from over. On September 16, 1908, he formed the General Motors Company as a New Jersey holding company with a nominal capitalization of only $2,000. The holding company structure allowed Durant, who was short of both cash and bank credit, to finance his combination mainly through the exchange of stock. Cadillac, bought dear at $4.75 million, was the most notable of the few companies for which cash had to be paid. But Cadillac proved worth its price: it returned a net profit to General Motors of $1,909,382 for its operations in the fiscal year ending August 31, 1909, and in addition the Lelands ended up by accepting $75,000 of the purchase price in GM stock. Without much cash changing hands, General Motors soon acquired control of thirteen motor vehicle and ten parts and accessories manufacturers that varied considerably in strength, prominence, and potential. Within a year its capitalization reached an astonishing $60 million. On July 31, 1911, General Motors became the first automobile company to have its stock listed on the New York Stock Exchange.

General Motors under Durant was in trouble from the start. His strategy of "getting every car in sight, playing it safe all along the line," turned out to be disastrous. He bought too many weak units that drained off the profits from a few strong companies. Of the thirteen automobile manufacturers in the combination he threw together, only Buick and Cadillac were making money. As Durant dispersed his energies, Buick too began to lose money, threatening to leave Cadillac alone among the manufacturing units to support the heavily overcapitalized holding company. Durant's minor mistakes included paying $140,000 for the Cartercar Company in order to obtain its patent on a poorly designed friction drive and buying the Elmore Manufacturing Company for $600,000 on the slim chance that its outdated two-cylinder, two-cycle engine might prove popular in the future. His most spectacular error was purchasing the Heany Lamp Company for $7 million in GM stock to obtain a patent on an incandescent lamp that turned out to be fraudulent. Compounding these blunders, Durant was so optimistic about demand that he failed to build up cash reserves, relied on cash from sales to pay his operating expenses, neglected to inform himself about the combination's financial condition, and made no attempt to achieve economies through coordinating and integrating the constituent units of General Motors.

The crunch came when sales unexpectedly dropped as a result of a slight business recession in 1910. Durant was unable to meet his payroll and pay his bills from suppliers. General Motors was saved by a $12.75-million cash loan fully secured by its tangible assets from a banking syndicate composed of Lee, Higginson and Company of Boston and J. and W. Seligman and the Central Trust Company of New York City. The loan was proffered only after the bankers had been given assurances of GM's fundamental soundness by Wilfred C. Leland of Cadillac at a private meeting. The stiff price the bankers demanded for the rescue was $6 million in GM stock plus $15 million in five-year, 6-percent notes. Durant was forced to retire from active management, and the banking syndicate gained control of the combination through a five-year voting trust. Durant was named one of the trustees, but the other four represented the bankers: James J. Storrow of Lee, Higginson; Albert Strauss of J. and

W. Seligman; James N. Wallace of the Central Trust Company; and the seemingly ever-present Anthony N. Brady. Storrow, a senior partner at Lee, Higginson, first took over as the temporary president of General Motors, then directed operations as chairman of the finance committee. Charles W. Nash, who had worked his way up from a day laborer at Durant-Dort to succeed Durant as head of Buick in 1910, was moved to the presidency of General Motors in 1912.

Banker control of GM was a mixed blessing. On the positive side, the Storrow-Nash regime followed a conservative policy of retrenchment that liquidated all manufacturing units except Buick, Cadillac, General Motors Truck, Oakland (which would become Pontiac), and Oldsmobile. The product was improved, and a program of systematic research and testing was instituted. Great strides were made in attracting top-flight administrative talent and in improving communication and cooperation within the combination. By wringing out the heavily watered assets, in a few years banker control restored GM to solvency.

These pluses were offset, however, by the failure of the banker-dominated management to move ahead aggressively in the low-priced market being developed by Ford. Cray points out that "in their five-year reign ... [the bankers] spent as little as possible modifying the production lines to emulate Ford's moving assembly lines. They had not kept pace with the industry's growth, and were the company not to be overwhelmed, it had to be expanded." [12] Indeed, production costs at Cadillac increased, as Henry M. Leland, obsessed with mechanical precision, refused to adopt faster assembly-line techniques that would make the Cadillac car more competitive in price. Similarly, in a move to raise unit profits, Charles Nash at Buick in 1910 ended production of the Model 10, which was competitive with the Ford Model T and had accounted for about half of Buick's sales since 1907. Buick sales as a result plunged from 30,525 units in 1910 to only 13,389 in 1911. Under Walter P. Chrysler's aggressive leadership they recovered to 32,889 by 1914. Nevertheless, during the five-year period of banker control, GM's share of the automobile market skidded from 21 percent to only 8.5 percent.

The Chevrolet Takeover

As well as being a trustee and a member of the board of directors, Durant was still a substantial stockholder in General Motors. From this strong position he began to make his comeback shortly after the bankers had taken control. In 1911 he formed the Mason Motor Company and the Little Motor Car Company in Flint and the Chevrolet Motor Car Company in Detroit. Then he bought the Republic Motor Car Company of Tarrytown, New York, and converted it into a holding company capitalized at $65 million. The Mason, Little, and Republic cars were soon discontiued to allow Durant to concentrate on the Chevrolet. Designed by the Swiss-born Frenchman Louis Chevrolet, who had gained fame shattering speed records in the Buick "Bug" as a member of the Buick racing team, the Chevrolet Classic Six was a powerful six-cylinder car selling for $2,150. "The car was a market disaster," writes Weisberger. "Louis Chevrolet, oddly for a racing man, had produced something ponderous rather than whippet-like ... the Six had only a scattering of sales after its introduction at the 1912 auto show."[13] Like David Dunbar Buick before him, Louis Chevrolet slipped into personal obscurity while his name became a household word.

In 1913 Chevrolet was reorganized. Its manufacturing operations were moved to the former Little factory at Flint, its business headquarters to New York City. To impress eastern financiers, an assembly plant was located in Manhattan at Twelfth Avenue and Fifty-sixth Street. From there components made in Flint were shipped back to midwestern customers as Chevrolets. The Chevrolet advertising people called this economic illogic "stagecraft."

Two new four-cyclinder models were introduced in 1914, the $875 Bady Grand touring car and the $750 Royal Mail roadster. Over the two years ending on August 14, 1915, Durant sold nearly 16,000 Chevrolets, at a net profit of over $1.3 million. He announced that he would bring out a new $490 model to compete with the Model T, which was selling at that price.

On September 23, 1915, Durant organized the Chevrolet Motor Company of Delaware as a holding company for all Chevrolet activities. Raising its capitalization to $80 million, all in common stock, Durant offered to trade five shares of Chevrolet for one share of General Motors. There were so many takers that the offer was closed on January 26, 1916. It is estimated that by the end of 1915 Durant personally owned about 90,000 of Chevrolet's 200,000 shares of common stock and over 71,000—44 percent—of the 165,000 General Motors common shares outstanding. With his associates, he controlled by then the voting rights of some 100,000 shares of GM common.

A takeover was imminent when the General Motors voting trust expired on October 1, 1915. Earlier that year Durant and the du Pont interests had begun buying up General Motors stock in the open market with the aid of Louis G. Kaufman, president of the Chatham and Phoenix Bank of New York City. Whether and to what extent Durant and the du Ponts acted in collusion remains clouded. Durant claimed Pierre S. du

Pont as an ally, while du Pont maintained that he was acting independently and as a neutral in Durant's battle with the GM bankers. The key figure in alerting the du Ponts to the GM stock opportunity was John J. Raskob, treasurer of E. I. du Pont de Nemours and Company, who saw General Motors as a large potential customer for du Pont products and as an ideal place to reinvest mounting profits from World War I munitions sales. Raskob himself invested liberally in GM. Some $27 million of du Pont money helped push General Motors common stock from a quotation of $82 per share on January 2, 1915, to a high of $558 for the year. Five shares of Chevrolet at this time were worth at least $700, making Durant's offer of a five-for-one trade a profitable proposition for GM stockholders. Additionally, the Storrow-Nash regime had sown the seeds of its own destruction by withholding common stock dividends. This made GM stockholders anxious to sell out to Durant and the du Ponts.

At a meeting of the directors and large stockholders of General Motors on September 16, 1915, Kaufman and Pierre du Pont were elected to the board of directors, with du Pont as its chairman. A belated attempt by the bankers to mobilize stockholder support for a three-year continuation of the voting trust failed. Durant called a meeting of the board of directors in May 1916 to announce that he once again controlled the company. On the first of June he took over again as GM president with the resignation of Charles Nash. Durant reincorporated the General Motors Company, a New Jersey holding company, as the General Motors Corporation of Delaware, an operating company, on October 13, 1916.

Out of General Motors, Nash with Storrow's backing remained in automobile manufacturing. He became president of the Nash Motor Car Company, formed from the bankrupt Thomas B. Jeffery Company of Kenosha, Wisconsin, after its purchase by Storrow for $5 million. Nash was never to be an industry leader, but the firm managed to hang on through the next four decades; in 1954 it merged with Hudson to become the American Motors Corporation.

Walter P. Chrysler had replaced Nash as head of Buick when Nash moved to the GM presidency in 1912. Storrow invited him to join in the Kenosha venture, but Chrysler declined after Durant offered him $500,000 a year, ten times what he had been getting, to stay at GM as president of Buick and GM vice-president in charge of operations.

By 1919 Buick was making about half the money that GM earned. But GM was spending money at a much faster rate than Chrysler could earn it at Buick, and Durant's erratic decision making and arbitrary interference in Buick's operations made Chrysler's job impossible. Chrysler knew that they could never work together when Durant told him, "Walt, I believe in changing the policies just as often as my office door opens and closes." Without consulting Chrysler, Durant sold the lucrative Detroit Buick branch house to one of his cronies. The last straw for Chrysler occurred when a telegram from Durant was read at a booster luncheon of the Flint Chamber of Commerce promising the city a $6-million frame plant that would cost more in five years than GM would pay for frames from other sources in ten. Chrysler told Alfred Sloan, who tried to talk him into staying, "No, I'm washed up. I just can't stand the way the thing is being run. All I'm anxious about now is to sell my stock." [14]

The Rise of Chrysler

Walter P. Chrysler has been called the last great individual constructive force in the American automobile industry. After Chrysler, automotive entrepreneurs were anonymous organization men, team players who were not personally identified in the public mind with the achievements of their companies. Chrysler's particular genius was for incorporating advanced automotive technology in moderately priced production cars.

Chrysler came out of a brief retirement in 1920 to try to rescue Willys-Overland from the brink of bankruptcy as its executive vice-president. The Willys-Overland Company had been formed in 1908 from the small Marion and Overland companies of Indianapolis, Indiana, by John N. Willys, a bicycle and automobile salesman from Elmira, New York. Production was moved to the former Pope-Toledo plant in Toledo, Ohio, and upped from 4,860 cars in 1909 to 15,598 in 1910, making Willys-Overland the third-largest American producer that year, after Ford and Buick. In 1911 Willys-Overland surpassed Buick, and until 1918 it ranked second only to Ford in production. During these years Willys acquired the Deusenberg Motors Company of Elizabeth, New Jersey; two small Ohio producers, the Garford Automobile Company and the Gramm Motor Truck Company; and several parts and accessories firms. Willys-Overland produced several models that used a sleeve-valve engine designed in 1905 by Charles Y. Knight. This engine, quieter but more complicated than those using poppet valves, was much more popular in Europe than in the United States. Willys models varied greatly in power and in price. One of its best-selling cars was the four-cylinder Overland 79, priced at $950 in 1914. The four-cylinder Willys-Knight sold for $1,4000 in 1919, and the classic L-head Overland, introduced that year to compete with the Model T, was priced at a moderate $495.

After trying unsuccessfully to merge Willys-Overland with Hudson and Chalmers, John Willys created the Willys Corporation in 1917 as a holding company owning the stock of his various operating companies.

These companies, which came to include the Curtis Aeroplane and Motor Company during World War I, were never integrated organizationally. Capitalization of the Willys Corporation was raised to $50 million with ill-timed expansion plans that were shattered in the brief but severe recession that followed World War I.

Chrysler bought time for the Willys Corporation but failed to save it. It was liquidated in 1921. Willys-Overland, however, was salvaged and survived until 1933, when it again went into receivership in the midst of the Depression. Resurrected during World War II, the firm became important as a producer of general-purpose military vehicles, nicknamed jeeps. It was absorbed by the Kaiser Motor Company, created from Kaiser-Frazer in 1953, and continued to manufacture four-wheel-drive vehicles for the commercial market after Kaiser withdrew from other motor vehicle production in 1957. The Willys jeep business was sold to American Motors in 1970.

Chrysler moved from Willys to another victim of the 1920 recession, Maxwell, which had merged with Chalmers but soon afterward gone into receivership. He supervised its reorganization as the Maxwell Motor Corporation and became president of the new firm, capitalized at $40 million, in 1923. In 1924 Maxwell introduced the stylish Chrysler Six, the first medium-priced car to use a high-compression engine; the company made profits of over $4 million that year.

Chrysler reorganized Maxwell in 1925 as the Chrysler Corporation and discontinued the Maxwell line. By 1928 Chrysler had made some $46 million in profits and held third place in the industry, after General Motors and Ford. The Dodge brothers had died in the 1920 influenza epidemic, and their business was sold in 1925 to the banking house of Dillon, Read, and Company, which in turn sold it to the Chrysler Corporation in 1928 for $170 million in Chrysler stock. The acquisition of Dodge doubled Chrysler's sales outlets and gave the corporation the plant capacity to bring out the Plymouth and compete in the low-priced field with Ford and Chevrolet.

Oligopoly

The number of active automobile manufacturers in the United States dropped from 253 in 1908 to 108 in 1920 and to 44 in 1929, with about 80 percent of the American industry's total output accounted for by Ford, the constituent units of General Motors, and Chrysler. In that short time the large-scale, integrated manufacturing operations of these giants had created competitive conditions that could not be borne by the small firms and their suppliers of components. While the large producers could count on their own ability to manufacture parts or on concessions in price from independent suppliers, the small automobile makers found it increasingly difficult to obtain components at reasonable prices and lacked the volume of sales to manufacture them for themselves.

The main industrywide effort of the small firms to remain competitive was made through a standards committee of the Society of Automotive Engineers (SAE). The SAE blossomed into an important force in the industry under the leadership of Howard E. Coffin, the vice-president of Hudson, who was elected president of the society in 1910. The standards committee, headed by Henry Souther, a former consulting engineer for the ALAM, was a product of the SAE's takeover of the ALAM Mechanical Branch upon its dissolution in 1909. The committee reflected the interests of the small automobile producers, who made up the bulk of the SAE membership in 1910. These small producers were eager to inaugurate a drive for intercompany standardization of parts, which would enable them to buy readily available standard components at much lower prices than they had been paying for small orders of specially designed parts. The lack of intercompany standardization was, in Coffin's view, "responsible for nine tenths of the production troubles and most of the needless expense entailed in the manufacture of motorcars." [15]

The SAE carried out a vigorous standards program that resulted in the adoption of 224 different sets of standards in the industry by 1921. The program failed miserably, however, in its principal objective of keeping the small producers in a competitive position. Despite intercompany standardization of components and the NACC cross-licensing agreement, mass-production techniques leading to increased standardization of product at lower unit costs could be effectively implemented only by the large, well-financed firm with a car of superior design. Scientific American recognized as early as 1909 that "standardization and interchangeability of parts will have the effect of giving us a higher grade of motorcar at a lower price, but this is dependent in considerable degree upon the production of one model in great numbers and the elimination of extensive annual changes in design that necessitate the making of costly jigs, gauges, and special machinery." [16]

Henry Ford grasped this point long before most of his competitors. By the time they had come to understand it sufficiently, he was so far ahead in design and production engineering that most lacked the capital and talent to catch up. With about half the market for new cars at the outbreak of World War I, the Ford Motor Company might well have moved to monopolize automobile manufacturing in the United States. However, in addition to making some grave errors that allowed General

Motors to surpass him in sales by the late 1920s, Henry Ford early recognized that oligopoly was preferable to monopoly. At the pinnacle of the Model T's success, Ford was urged by Charles Sorensen to build a near monopoly by shooting for 75 percent of the market for new cars. Ford responded that he did not want more than 30 percent. Sorensen reflected in 1956 on the wisdom of Ford's position: "How right he was! If Ford Motor Company had seventy-five percent of the auto business today, it would be prosecuted as a monopoly. He actually welcomed the competition that loomed before us, though in later years he had suspicion amounting to hallucination that bankers and General Motors were out to ruin him." [17]

War and Peace

6

After the Paris fleet of Renault taxicabs proved indispensable in moving troops to the front to stop the German advance at the Marne in 1914, military experts came to believe that "in this war the exploding of gasoline is playing a more important part than the exploding of gunpowder." An entire army was supplied by motor transport over the road to Verdun. Even Lawrence replaced the camels of his Arab troops with Model Ts to fight the Turks in the desert. Lord Curzon, a member of the British war cabinet, declared in 1919 that the Allied cause had been "floated to victory on a wave of oil." [1]

At the 1897 annual maneuvers of the French army, a technical commission headed by artillery officers was charged with conducting experiments with motor vehicles. The British army early introduced motor vehicles into the colonial service and used them in the 1899–1902 Boer War; then in 1903 the British War Office made extensive tests of military tractors entered in a £1,000 prize competition that it sponsored. By 1908 the military budgets of France, Great Britain, and Germany contained special appropriations for subsidies to be paid out to owners or manufacturers of motor vehicles suitable for military use who agreed to turn them over to the government in the event of a national emergency. These subsidies amounted to as much as $2,250 per vehicle over a five-year period in Germany and averaged about $1,400 in France and $584 in Britain. German buyers of heavy trucks were reimbursed by the government not only for part of the purchase price but for part of their annual maintenance expenses as well. In France several thousand trucks of two-ton or heavier load capacity were purchased under a special military subsidy inaugurated in 1910. The Italian army made its first large order of truck chassis from Fiat in 1909. By the outbreak of World War I, officers rode in staff cars and couriers drove motorcycles in European armies; the artillery tractor had been developed in France, the tank in Britain, and the armored car in Britain and in Germany.

The United States War Department, in contrast offered neither prizes nor subsidies to encourage the development of motor vehicles suitable for military use. Major J. B. Mott, representing the United States as an observer at the 1899 French maneuvers, told an Associated Press reporter, "Our needs differ considerably from those of European countries. The latter must always prepare for possible war on their own soil, and their [road] conditions favor the use of autocars, while the possibility of hostilities within the United States [is] remote, and their utility is highly problematical." [2] General Nelson A. Miles was one of the few American officers who early recognized the military potential of the motor vehicle. Upon his retirement in 1903, Miles urged Secretary of War Elihu Root to replace five regiments of cavalry with troops using bicycles and motor vehicles and to establish a road-building corps of at least five thousand men. He believed that the conditions encountered in the 1898 Spanish-American War indicated that the horse was obsolete in warfare and that the large preponderance of cavalry over infantry in the American army compared to European armies was both useless and more expensive to maintain than motorized units would be. In 1904 the Signal Corps purchased a few light trucks, and in 1906 the American army bought its first automobile ambulance, a White steamer with a lengthened chassis. But serious trials of military motor vehicles in the United States did not begin until the 1909 annual war games: that year a mock invasion of Massachusetts was umpired by General Leonard Wood in a White steamer.

Nevertheless, the most prominent motor vehicle on World War I battlefields turned out to be the rugged Model T. Over the typically rutted, shell-pocked, and muddy terrain of the combat zones, the Model T greatly outperformed the far heavier European touring cars and trucks ostensibly more suitable for military use. Consequently, the Model T chassis was adapted to serve a variety of purposes by the Allied armies. It indeed proved itself to be the "universal car" that Henry Ford had envisaged. About 125,000 Model Ts had seen service in the Allied cause by the war's end.

Military Production in Europe

It was inevitable that governments would call upon the automobile industry to play a key role in the world's first mechanized war. In Europe conversion to the war effort was rapid and total. The European industry continued to turn out a few passenger cars, mainly for military use, while truck and tractor production was greatly expanded, and the production of tanks was initiated. In France, for example, 65,592 trucks and cars and some 3,200 tanks were made for the military during the war, versus only about 2,500 motor vehicles for the private sector. Berliet stuck with its peacetime specialty and was the top French producer of trucks. Ford Motor Company of England, the largest prewar British automobile manufacturer, also continued to concentrate on making motor vehicles and alone produced at least 50,000 Model T cars, trucks, and ambulances for the Allied cause between 1914 and 1918. Percival L. D. Perry, the managing director of Ford-England, was knighted for this in 1918. About 40 percent of British military truck production was accounted for by the newly formed Associated Equipment Company, with annual production after 1915 of about 40,000 units. After Italy entered the war on the side of the Allies in May 1915, the production of motor vehicles—most importantly trucks for the military—at Fabbrica Italiana d'Automobile Torino (Fiat) surpassed prewar levels, reaching 16,542 units in 1918 alone. German motor vehicle production rose dramatically during the war but still was insufficient to meet military needs.

The European automobile industry also rapidly diversified into the manufacture of munitions, aircraft engines, airframes, and a wide variety of other items useful to the military. In France the prewar industry leaders Renault and Peugeot diversified most widely, dominating most of the groups into which the French automobile manufacturers organized themselves for the purpose of fabricating specialized items. Fiat was as widely diversified in Italy, manufacturing munitions, aircraft engines, and airframes as well as motor vehicles. The most diversified British firm was Austin. In addition to trucks, ambulances, and over 500 armored cars, the Austin Longbridge plant produced over 8 million shells, 650 guns, 2,000 airplanes, and large quantities of other equipment, including airplane engines, generating sets, and pumping equipment. Herbert Austin was knighted in 1919 for his contribution to the British war effort. Morris Motors turned out only 1,344 motor vehicles while concentrating on making a variety of munitions. Similarly, André Citroën resigned as general manager of Mors to establish his own factory specializing in the volume production of shells. Hispano-Suiza in France, Rolls-Royce in England, and Benz and Daimler-Mercedes in Germany led in diversification into the manufacture of aircraft engines.

As a result of this involvement in the war effort, the European automobile industry underwent phenomenal expansion. Both plant capacity and number of employees quadrupled in the French industry over the four war years. At the Austin Longbridge factory expansion financed by the British Ministry of Munitions resulted in employment skyrocketing from 2,300 in 1914 to 20,000 in 1919, while value of output increased from £600,000 in 1914 to £9 million in 1918. Fiat overnight became the third-largest Italian corporation, after the Ilva and Ansaldo steel firms. Daimler-Mercedes quadrupled its capital.

Wartime exigencies also encouraged a movement toward modernization in French, British, and Italian factories. The shortage of skilled labor was reflected in the utilization of more semiskilled and unskilled operatives, including women. Improved machine tools, and in a few instances conveyors, were adopted. Integrated manufacturing operations became more common. In Germany, in contrast, artisanal production by skilled mechanics continued with little change throughout the war.

Although reconversion to peacetime production was to prove catastrophic for a number of firms on both sides of the Atlantic, there can be no doubt that the war itself was immensely profitable for European automobile manufacturers. Despite the destruction of the Panhard et Levassor factory at Reims and the German pillaging of machinery from the Peugeot plant at Lille, despite the delay in Morris's bringing out his Cowley to compete with the Model T, despite further American inroads into the civilian car market owing to the massive conversion of the European industry to the needs of the war effort, European automobile manufacturing enjoyed a period of prosperity.

In contrast, the war was not profitable for the U.S. industry leaders, particularly Ford. Yet in the long run the war proved an irrelevancy. American technological, marketing, and organizational superiority was evident well before 1914; and for at least a decade after the war the Europeans were uncompetitive in world markets despite a quadrupling of world demand for cars and the erection of formidable tariff and other tax barriers against American imports. The situation on the eve of the war was sized up well by Giovanni Agnelli, the founder of Fiat. "I have just returned from America, where I wanted to see for myself the danger which is threatening, not only Italian industry, but that of France and Germany too. It would be difficult to deny it," confessed Agnelli in 1912. "Competition is becoming more and more difficult every day."[3] By creating a huge military demand far in excess of the effective European peacetime demand for passenger cars at the prices Europe's auto makers could produce them, the war for a short time obviated this competition. However, military experience during the war did demonstrate unequivocally the superiority of the Model T over European models.

American Preparedness

The automobile industry inevitably came to play a key role in American preparedness. Support within the U.S. industry for preparedness and the war effort came almost entirely from the small automobile manufacturers that dominated the SAE. As we have seen, the position of these companies was deteriorating rapidly. Not only had they less to lose from a drastic curtailment of civilian production, but their much smaller fixed investments in highly specialized plants and equipment made conversion to military production easier and far less costly for them than for Ford and General Motors.

The first call upon the industry came on August 10, 1915, with the appointment to the Navy Department Advisory Committee of Howard E. Coffin, vice-president and chief engineer at Hudson, and five other SAE dollar-a-year volunteers. Coffin became chairman of the Council of National Defense, which was formed in 1916 to organize the American industrial system for war. The council's Motor Transport Committee, chaired By Alfred Reeves of the NACC, planned for the mobilization of motor vehicles, and its Highway Transport Committee, under Roy D. Chapin, the president of Hudson, coordinated all highway transportation. With American entry into the war on April 6, 1917, hundreds of automobile industry executives volunteered, and 463 members of the SAE were in government employ by the war's end on November 11, 1918.

Henry Ford at first took a stand against conscription and preparedness, going so far as to sponsor in December 1915 the abortive voyage to Europe of a so-called Peace Ship carrying a delegation of pacifists in a naive attempt to stop the war. But with the severing of American diplomatic ties with Germany on February 3, 1917, Ford abruptly reversed himself, declaring that "we must stand behind the president" and that "in the event of war [I] will place our factory at the disposal of the United States government and will operate without one cent of profit" [4]

Durant, too, had pacifist leanings and at first opposed undertaking war production. The Lelands resigned from Cadillac to form the Lincoln Motor Car Company on June 18, 1917, over Durant's vehement refusal at that late date to endorse their proposal that it was a patriotic duty for Cadillac to switch over to the production of the new Liberty aircraft engine. Within a few months, however, Durant succumbed to the mounting pressure of public opinion and undertook token production of Liberty engines at both Buick and Cadillac.

Designed by Packard engineers to be mass-produced, the Liberty aircraft engine was turned out by Ford and Marmon as well as by the firms already named. Dodge and General Motors led the industry in making munitions. Ford produced the widest variety of items—including aircraft motors, armor plate, caissons, shells, steel helmets, submarine detectors, and torpedo tubes. Sixty Eagle Boats (submarine chasers) were completed by Ford too late to see action, and two tank prototypes developed by the company had just reached the stage where quantity production could begin when peace came.

The automobile industry's principal contribution to the Allied cause, however, was made in its normal role of mass-producing motor vehicles, especially trucks. The chassis of luxury cars could easily be converted to support two- or three-ton truck bodies. American truck production quintupled from 24,900 in 1914 to 128,000 in 1917, largely to meet European demand. Early war orders for trucks went mainly to the makers of luxury cars—Locomobile, Packard, Peerless, and White. But by the end of the war the leading producer of trucks was the newly formed Nash Motor Company. Even before American entry into the war, 40,000 American-made trucks had been delivered to the Allies. Over half of the 238,000 motor vehicles, mainly trucks and ambulances, that the industry contracted to make for our own government had been completed by the Armistice. Following the war, the army sold many of these trucks as surplus at low prices to state governments, which used them in road building in the 1920s.

The railroad arteries to eastern points of embarkation to Europe were clogged by 1917. So Highway Transport Committee Chairman Chapin organized caravans of trucks to be driven from assembly plants in the Middle West to the docks. The trucks were loaded with other freight. Some 30,000 trucks were delivered in this way by the war's end, inaugurating the long-distance trucking of freight as an alternative to rail transportation and calling attention to the great need for a national system of interconnected, improved highways.

The Fordson Tractor

On April 8, 1917, Henry Ford cabled British authorities that he would "comply with every request immediately" to help them mass-produce the Fordson farm tractor. Tractors were desperately needed by the British to help alleviate food shortages caused by German U-boat attacks on ships importing foodstuffs and by the loss of 80,000 farmhands to the military services. Experiments with a number of makes of tractors conducted by the Royal Agricultural Society had convinced the British of the Fordson's superiority.

The first commercially successful gasoline-powered tractors in the United States were built by the Hart-Parr Company of Charles City, Iowa, in 1902–1903. By 1907, when Henry Ford began the experiments that led to the Fordson, about 600 gasoline-powered tractors were in use on American farms. These early machines were too heavy, clumsy, complicated, and expensive to meet the needs of the average farmer. Between 1910 and 1915, when the Fordson was announced, several tractor demonstrations in the Middle West drew an estimated 50,000 farmers and showed that there was a large potential market for smaller machines, such as the 4,650-pound, $650 tractor introduced in 1913 by the Bull Tractor Company of Minneapolis. The 2,500-pound Fordson was introduced by Henry Ford personally in August 1915 at a plowing demonstration at Fremont, Nebraska. With a wheelbase of only 63 inches, the Fordson could turn in a 21-foot circle. It was cheap to operate because its four-cylinder, 20-horsepower engine ran on kerosene. And, like the Model T, the Fordson was designed to be mass-produced at low cost. Henry Ford and Son was organized to manufacture the Fordson as a separate corporation from the Ford Motor Company on July 27, 1917.

The Fordson tractor contributed little toward alleviating food shortages during the war. By March 1, 1918, only 3,600 of the 8,000 Fordsons ordered by the British government had been delivered, and privately owned steam tractors were plowing considerably more acres of British farmland than the government-owned Fordsons. Most Fordsons were bought by American farmers, who, faced for the first time in decades with expanding markets for agricultural commodities, were anxious to comply with the patriotic slogan, "Buy Tractors and Win the War." Although it was not until April 23, 1918, that the first Fordson for domestic use came off the assembly line, by the time of the Armistice 26,817 had been manufactured at Ford's Dearborn tractor plant. Too late to have any significant impact on wartime food production, these Fordsons were distributed to the agricultural states in quotas and sold to farmers through permits granted by the county war boards.

Despite the impression given by Henry Ford that he was selling his tractors at cost as a contribution to the war effort, the $750 price of the Fordson included a tidy profit of $182.86 for Henry Ford and Son. Mass production of the Fordson reached fantastic heights justs as the market for American agricultural commodities began to evaporate in the postwar period. Some 750 Fordsons a day were being produced by 1924. Total production rose to 486,800 units in 1925 and to over 650,000 units in 1927, making Ford responsible for about half the tractors manufactured in the United States up to that time. This proliferation of the Fordson farm tractor was the major factor in creation of the ruinous combination of higher fixed costs and overproduction of staple commodities that plagued American farmers during the 1920s.

Wartime Automobile Production at Ford

Civilian motor vehicle manufacture had continued unabated for some months even after American entry into the war, making 1917 a year of record production. Then the War Industries Board, chaired by Bernard Baruch, cut the steel tonnage allocation to the automobile industry for 1918 civilian production to half the allocation for the last six months of 1917. This led to a 45-percent decline in passenger car production by the end of 1918, as far less lucrative military truck production doubled. New car prices shot up 42 percent with excess consumer demand, and the government in addition imposed a 5-percent luxury tax on new cars. Profits slipped significantly for the American industry leaders.

The cutback in automotive work brought a substantial loss of revenue for Ford, the world industry leader. By July 31, 1918, no motorcars were being made at the Highland Park plant, although almost 3,000 a day still were being assembled from stocks of parts at the twenty-eight Ford branch assembly plants. By Armistice Day, however, assembly at the branch plants had dropped to only about 300 cars a day, practically all for the government. The production of Ford motor vehicles declined from a high of 734,800 units in 1916 to 438,800 units in 1918. Conversion back to full civilian production apparently was no problem, for the Ford factories turned out 820,400 units in 1919. The sharp drop in Ford production to 419,500 units in 1920 demonstrates that the postwar recession had a greater impact than the war effort on production of the Model T.

Participation in the war effort was costly for the Ford Motor Company in terms of profits. Net income fell from $57.1 million for the fiscal year 1915–1916 to $27.2 million for 1916–1917 and $30.9 million for 1917–1918, and the bulk of the company's profits during the war came from its civilian production. After corporate taxes, the Ford Motor Company made only $4.357 million on its war contracts. As the owner of 58.5 percent of the Ford stock in 1918, Henry Ford's share of the company's war profits after paying personal income taxes on them came to a mere $926,780.46—a fraction of what he could have made had civilian production continued uninterrupted.

The Postwar Recession

The abrupt termination of war contracts with the unanticipated coming of peace on November 11, 1918, caused little concern in the automobile industry. To fill the huge accumulation of back orders for new cars, plants were quickly reconverted—a process that at Highland Park took only about three weeks. Automobile manufacturers embarked on ambitious expansion programs, confident that the demand for motorcars was insatiable.

There was especially great optimism in the United Kingdom that development of a domestic mass market for motorcars was imminent. "The home market recovered rapidly with the return to peace, as pent-up demand, rendered more effective by the existence of forced savings and servicemen's gratuities, was generated not only by the need for replacements but also by the growth in new owner demand," Roy Church relates. "Whereas before the war the purchase of a motorcar was associated with conspicuous consumption or the occasional sportive jaunt, greater familiarity with motorized transport resulting from its widespread use during the war, together with the removal of petrol restrictions, produced a climate of expectancy and optimism among would-be consumers and potential suppliers alike, a climate whose temperature can be gauged by the crusading motto coined by the British Motor League, of 'Motoring for the Millions.'" Despite warnings from the financial press, "mass production" became a rallying cry in the trade press, and British automobile manufacturers announced plans for greatly increased output.[5]

The British bubble soon burst. Reconversion was hampered by raw material shortages and strikes, particularly by strikes of the coal miners in the winter of 1918–1919 and of the iron molders in the winter of 1919–1920. Despite the 33⅓-percent McKenna duties imposed in 1915 to stave off further American penetration of the home market, imports increased from 5,000 units in 1919 to 29,000 units in 1920, as the prices of American cars dropped relative to British models. Ford of England , exempt from the McKenna duties, continued up to 1922 to be the leading U.K. producer and in the fifteen months from October 1919 to December 1920 sold some 46,000 cars and trucks to make £852,652, the highest profit thus far in its history. Reconversion presented little difficulty for Ford of England, because its contribution to the war effort had been overwhelmingly the production of motor vehicles.

Conversely, the costs of reconversion for British automobile manufacturers who had diversified into the manufacture of munitions and other nonautomotive items proved far higher than could be justified by their low volumes of sales. And their joint demands for loans created a shortage of capital from the banks for expansion of the British automobile industry. Austin, the most widely diversified British firm during the war, is the prime example. Following the war Austin at first attempted to compete with the Model T and other American cars with a single model—the four-cylinder, 20-horsepower (by RAC formula rating) Austin Twenty. The cheapest Austin Twenty was priced at a relatively high £495 in 1919 and at an absolutely uncompetitive £695 in 1920. In comparison, in 1920 an imported 21.9-horsepower Chevrolet cost £450 and an 18-horsepower Overland £495. The market for the Twenty shrank further when in January 1921 the British horsepower tax was raised £1 per horsepower; and in that same year, at the nadir of the postwar recession, William Morris lowered the price of his Oxford from £590 to £415 and that of his Cowley from £465 to £299. Conversion from munitions production at the Longbridge plant's North and West Works, which were acquired from the government, alone cost £289,624 in 1919–1920, while up to July 1920 only about 3,000 units of the Twenty had been sold. Additionally, only small reserves had been accumulated to meet large tax liabilities incurred under the Excess Profits Duty levied during the war.

Disaster was for a short time forestalled by a 1919 public issue of preferred stock that created the Austin Motor Company, Limited. But by the end of 1920 Austin owed the bankers £187,087 and showed for the two years 1920 and 1921 a combined net loss of £381,922. In April 1921 the company was put into receivership by its creditors. The receivership lasted only a year, and Sir Herbert Austin survived the crisis. But he emerged with a more circumscribed control of the reorganized Austin enterprise.

While the Austin experience was not entirely representative, neither was it unique. The British automobile industry in general was hit hard by the recession. Wolseley, one of the more important producers, with a volume of 12,000 units in 1920, was knocked to its knees and finally collapsed in 1926. Angus Sanderson and Harper Bean, two consortia with great resources that tried to enter automobile manufacturing immediately after the war, failed before getting off the ground. Unlike other manufacturers, who were much more integrated, William Morris was able to spread his financial risk among his various suppliers. Consequently, Morris met his need for capital, except for two £10,000 loans in 1920, out of retained earnings, and in 1921 he made a £128,000 profit. Nevertheless, he sold only 3,000 cars that year, and before he led the U.K. industry in lowering prices, the storage of unsold cars at his Cowley factory had begun to interfere seriously with the production process.

In the United States only the few firms that had resisted mounting ambitious expansion programs in the postwar euphoria managed to escape relatively unscathed from the 1920–1921 recession. Among these firms were Dodge, Hudson, Nash, Packard, and Studebaker. On the other hand, as we have seen, the recession resulted in receivership for Maxwell-Chalmers and for Willys-Overland. Among the firms entering the industry in the postwar expansion, Rickenbacker and Wills Sainte-Claire soon failed, and Lincoln survived only as a peripheral operation of the Ford Motor Company. In 1919 there were over a hundred companies manufacturing motor vehicles in the United States; the 1920–1921 recession reduced that number very considerably.[6] Ford, with about half the market, and General Motors, with about a fifth, together already exercised monopoly power over the industry in 1919. Both firms would narrowly avoid receivership while undergoing internal crises that altered fundamentally the organization of the American automobile industry.

General commodity prices in the United States continued to rise after the war, in May 1920 reaching a peak of 121.7 percent of the November 1918 level, with automobile prices continuing to rise to a peak of 124.9 percent in August. A new Model T touring car that had sold for $360 in August 1916 cost $575 in August 1920. Responding to this upward spiral in the cost of living, some 4.16 million American workers, about 20 percent of the labor force, engaged in 3,630 work stoppages during 1919, making that year a high point of industrial unrest. Except for a major strike at Willys-Overland, the automobile industry experienced minimal direct labor-management strife. But with a million workers out on strike in the steel and coal industries and on the railroads, the automobile manufacturers felt the impact of work stoppages. Most important, new car sales slackened with the general decline in purchasing power. This decline was compounded as rural America's demand for new cars, the automobile industry's mainstay for over a decade, began to evaporate. The American farmer returned to hard times with the collapse of foreign markets after 1919. Gross agricultural income dropped from $15 billion in 1919 to only $9.2 billion in 1921 as agricultural exports declined 50 percent. And finally, the Federal Reserve Board helped burst the automobile manufacturers' balloon when, concerned about a rapid expansion in installment sales of cars, it raised the rediscount rate in November 1919. The effect was to up the down payment required on automobile time sales from a fourth or a third to about half the purchase price of the car.

Prussianization at Ford

The recession caught Henry Ford in the midst of carrying out his plans to develop the huge River Rouge complex and deeply in debt from his successful drive to buy out his minority stockholders. As the full impact of the recession began to be felt in the summer of 1920, Ford still owed $25 million, due in April 1921, on the bank loan that had enabled him to obtain control of his company; he had pledged to distribute a $7-million bonus in January; and he had to pay between $18 million and $30 million in taxes. Over the past three years $60.45 million had been spent on developing the River Rouge plant and between $15 million and $20 million on purchasing mines and timber tracts. Ford estimated that he needed $58 million, and he had only $20 million in cash on hand. The thought of seeking another loan was abandoned once it became apparent to Ford that the bankers would demand in return a voice in the management of his company. So Henry Ford turned to alternatives that preserved his one-man rule at the expense of the long-range well-being of the Ford Motor Company.

The only progressive move that Ford made was to lead the industry in a long-overdue reduction in the price of cars. On September 21, 1920, the Ford Motor Company announced price cuts averaging $148 on the Model T in its various body styles. This reduction theoretically meant a short-term loss of about $20 on every car sold, but the loss was covered by the profit on the $40 worth of parts and accessories sold to dealers with every new Model T. Other automobile manufacturers claimed that the drastic Ford price cuts were ruinous for the industry, and some banded together in an attempt to preserve the old price levels. Within a few weeks, however, twenty-three of Ford's competitors followed his lead and reduced prices on their cars.

As the fall wore on, it became evident that the price cuts were failing to check the decline in sales. By the end of 1920, automobile production had been halted at Buick, Dodge, Ford, Maxwell-Chalmers, Nash, Packard, REO, Studebaker, and Willys-Overland; and the automobile plants that remained open were staffed by skeleton work forces. The number of employed automobile workers in Detroit dropped from 176,000 in September to only 24,000 by the end of the year.

The Ford Motor Company closed its plants "for inventory" on Christmas Eve, 1920, and kept them closed until February 1, 1921, while it disposed of "stocks on hand." Unlike most of his competitors, Henry Ford maintained full production up to the shutdown of his plants, curtailing only the purchase of raw materials. The strategy implemented at Ford was first to turn the huge inventory of raw materials that had been bought at inflated prices into a reservoir of finished cars, then to stop production until those cars were disposed of at a profit and raw material prices had declined. Consignments totaling about 100,000 unordered cars were forced on over 6,300 Ford dealers, who had the choice of borrowing heavily from local banks to pay cash on delivery for them or forfeiting their Ford franchises. Henry Ford thus avoided going to the bankers himself and preserved his own autocracy and profits by arbitrarily unloading his financial problems onto the backs of thousands of hard-pressed small businessmen.

The shutdown at Ford was accompanied by stringent economy measures that went beyond what was necessary for survival and jeopardized the future health of the firm. Plants were stripped of every unessential tool and fixture—including every pencil sharpener, most desks and typewriters, and six hundred extension telephones. The sale of this equipment netted $7 million. The company benefited from replacing some of it with improved machinery and methods that increased output per manhour of labor. These gains were canceled out, however, by a ruthless halving of the office force from 1,074 to 528 persons as most departments, including such critical ones as auditing, were overly simplified, merged, or eliminated. Many capable executives were lost to the company. Even more important, the development of the organized bureaucracy essential to a mature corporation in a technologically sophisticated, consumer-goods industry was stultified.

Henry Ford always considered the financial end of his company to be unessential and therefore expendable. So it was inevitable that he should take the first opportunity to emasculate the administrative staff after buying out Couzens, who had built it up, along with the other minority stockholders. "To my mind there is no bent of mind more dangerous than that which is sometimes described as 'genius for organization.'" Ford explained in 1922. "It is not necessary for any one department to know what any other department is doing." He boasted that "the Ford factories and enterprises have no organization, no specific duties attaching to any position, no line of succession or of authority, very few titles, and no conferences. We have only the clerical help that is absolutely required; we have no elaborate records of any kind, and consequently no red tape." [7]

The lack of "red tape" amounted to what an increasing number of ex–Ford executives called Prussianization, as the entrepreneurial team responsible for the Model T disintegrated in the early 1920s. A complete list of the Ford executives who were arbitrarily fired or who resigned in disgust between 1919 and Henry Ford's retirement in 1945 would add up to a small town's telephone directory. Although this critical loss of executive talent defies adequate summarizing, the most significant departure— after that of James Couzens, who resigned in 1916 over Ford's mixing his personal pacifism with company policy—was William S. Knudsen, who went to General Motors and was responsible for Chevrolet's outselling Ford by 1927. Of more symbolic importance were the 1919 departures to build the Wills Sainte-Claire car of C. Harold Wills, the chief designer of the Model T, and John R. Lee, architect of the Ford prewar progressive labor policies. Charles E. Sorensen, who became Henry Ford's chief hatchet man, seemed to take perverse pleasure in the discharges and resignations of his fellow executives, and he managed to stay in Ford's favor by saying yes longer than any of them. But on March 2, 1944, Sorensen too ended up by resigning—at the request of a senile Henry Ford, who feared that Sorensen had ambitions to take over his company.

The postwar Ford purge extended to operations abroad. Sir Percival Perry was dismissed as managing director of Ford-England in 1919. Perry, who had been the main ingredient in the domination of the British market by Ford, is praised by Church as the "only Englishman" who before 1913 "successfully displayed a sensitivity to the commercial needs of the motoring public."[8] He had to be rehired in 1928 to restore Ford's European operations to a competitive position. In April 1921 George Brubaker, Ford's brother-in-law, and Charles T. Lathers, the Ford Detroit branch manager, made a sweep of Ford's profitable South American operations that has been described as "a tornado." Ellis Hampton, who had set up the lucrative Latin American branches, and all Latin American branch managers were replaced. "The two angry emissaries threw out typewriters, desks, file cabinets and other office equipment at the Buenos Aires, Sao Paulo, and Montevideo branches, discharged 'superfluous' employees, and evicted managers from plush offices," write Mira Wilkins and Frank E. Hill. "So clean a sweep of alleged extravagance and inefficiency did the two visitors make that their work is still vivid today [1964] in the minds of those who watched them." In late 1926 a comparable sweep of Ford's European branches was made by Brubaker, Fred Hoffman, who had charge of American branch assembly plants, and J. J. Harrington, the assistant sales manager at Dearborn. The trio became known as the "yougos," because they dismissed so many men so capriciously in so short a time that the phrase "you go" was constantly on their lips.[9]

Crisis at General Motors

While Henry Ford weathered the postwar crisis by cutting expenses not only to the bone but into the marrow, Billy Durant, an inveterate expansionist who could thrive only in flush times, came to grief. He lacked the technological expertise to discriminate among the many ideas about which he became enthusiastic, and his idea of "playing it safe all along the line" meant backing every impulse in the hope that some would pan out. His performance was brilliant when he concentrated his considerable energies on building up a single company in an expanding market, as at Buick and at Chevrolet. But his bents toward indiscriminate expansion and one-man rule spelled disaster when times got tight and the profits from a few phenomenally successful bets began to dwindle. For every Buick there was a Cartercar, for every Chevrolet a Heany Lamp. Durant believed that the market for automobiles would become saturated "only when they quit making babies," and he expanded GM accordingly. His alleged genius was almost wholly as a stock jobber, and he was deeply involved in speculative market activities in GM and other stocks at the onset of the recession.

When Durant regained the presidency of General Motors on June 1, 1916, he took over a much stronger corporation than the one he had left to the bankers five years before. The decline in GM's market share under banker control was somewhat illusory, for GM was on other grounds in a stronger competitive position. Storrow and Nash had paid off the GM loan in full and restored solvency. Internal administration and product had been improved. The du Pont alliance eased the problem of obtaining working capital and assured the supply at reasonable prices of several commodities needed for the construction of automobiles. Chevrolet was a moneymaking addition to the GM manufacturing units.

Some of Durant's moves turned out to be brilliant. The Fisher Body Company was purchased in 1918. Against everyone's advice he paid $56,000 for a faltering, one-man electric refrigerator company that served only forty-two customers, on the dubious reasoning that refrigerators were related to automobiles because both were essentially cases containing motors. He named the company Frigidaire. Strength was added to GM by the acquisition of the United Motors Corporation, a holding company owning the securities of five leading automobile accessory manufacturers that Durant had put together in the spring of 1916. With United Motors came the Delco laboratories of the engineering genius Charles F. Kettering, and Alfred Sloan's Hyatt Roller Bearing Company. A graduate of MIT, Sloan possessed an organizational talent unmatched in entrepreneurial history. Recognizing early that the automobile industry could not continue on a cash-on-delivery basis, Durant pioneered in time sales for expensive consumer goods with the creation of the General Motors Acceptance Corporation in 1919.

For no apparent reason, however, Durant added two new passenger cars to the General Motors line: the Sheridan and the Scripps-Booth. Both were losers. But even had they proved popular, they would merely have competed in the same general price range with Buick, Chevrolet, Oakland, and Oldsmobile. Durant never bothered to rationalize the various car lines he offered. Sloan objected: "Not only were we not competitive with Ford in the low-price field—where the big volume and substantial future growth lay—but in the middle, where we were concentrated with duplication, we did not know what we were trying to do except to sell cars which, in a sense, took volume from each other." [10] As in 1910, by 1921 only Buick and Cadillac were making money for General Motors.

Durant's enthusiasm for getting into the farm machinery business was more understandable. Impressed by the initial success of the Fordson tractor, he formed the Samson Tractor Division of General Motors from the Samson Sieve-Grip Tractor Company of Stockton, California, the Janesville Machine Company of Janesville, Wisconsin, and the Doylestown Agricultural Company of Doylestown, Pennsylvania. Plans called for the production of tractors, other agricultural machinery, trucks and household appliances. A light, four-cylinder tractor, the Samson Model M, was designed to compete directly with the Fordson, and some 3,000 Model Ms were produced in 1919, together with 56,000 other agricultural implements. Then, at the August 1919 Milwaukee State Fair, Durant introduced the Iron Horse, a tractor guided by reins that was heralded as "a man of all work" around the farm and "the greatest invention up to date for the farmer." Faulty transmission belts sent the Iron Horse into "senseless meanderings." Fewer than 200 were produced, and these had to be recalled from irate farmers. The Fordson continued to outsell the Samson Model M. Plans for a nine-passenger farmer's car that would sell for only $700 never materialized, because it became obvious that there was no way to build it at a profit. The Samson Tractor Division was liquidated in 1920. Estimates of its cost to GM have run as high as $42 million, although Durant's biographer Weisberger believes that $12 million is more realistic because the Janesville plant was converted into a Chevrolet factory.

Executives became frustrated by Durant's chaotic schedule, his inability to recognize priorities, and his increasing involvement in the stock market. As stock trading came to absorb his attention, he relied on cronies and made decisions, in Sloan's words, "right out of his head." Sloan was aghast at the testing of a car model on a cross-country trip by the same man who had designed it, and at Durant's waxing enthusiastic over telegraphed reports the man dispatched "by conniving with hotel porters along his scheduled route while he rested nearer home." Sloan was even more aghast at Durant's casual attitude about the location and price of the new General Motors Building in Detroit, a $20-million project that Durant later opposed as too costly. Sloan recalled: "He started at the corner of Cass Avenue, paced a certain distance west on West Grand Boulevard past the old Hyatt building.... Then he stopped for no apparent reason, at some apartment houses on the other side of the building. He said that this

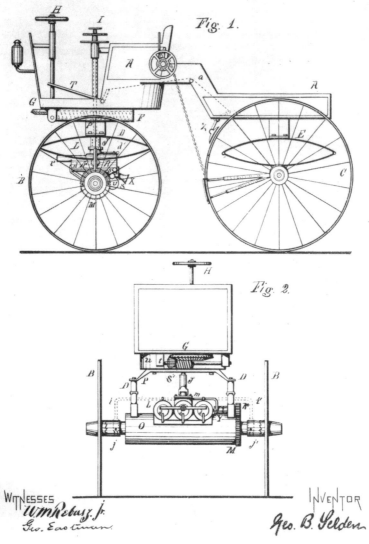

Illustration from the Selden patent papers, showing plan views of the vehicle. In 1895 the U.S. Patent Office awarded a patent on the gasoline automobile to George B. Selden, even though the vehicle in these views was inoperable as illustrated and the state of the technological art did not support Selden's allegations of priority. The gasoline automobile had already been pioneered to the stage of commercial feasibility in Europe. The Selden patent became the basis for an unsuccessful attempt to monopolize automobile manufacturing in the United States. (Courtesy Smithsonian Institution)

Reproduction of the Detroit shop in which Henry Ford built his first car in 1896. By the 1890s, in shops such as this scattered throughout the United States, hundreds of backyard mechanics and amateur inventors were trying to build automobiles that would really run. (Courtesy Henry Ford Museum and Greenfield Village)

Assembling the first American cars made from the same pattern: the Duryea factory in Springfield, Massachusetts, 1896. The scene typifies the artisanal production methods of early automobile manufacturing. Poor plant layout, excessive labor content, and primary reliance on highly skilled labor kept output low and car prices high. Whereas American manufacturers quickly moved toward volume production involving far fewer and less skilled workers, inefficient artisanal production methods remained the norm in European automobile factories until after World War II. (Courtesy Smithsonian Institution)

1901 Mercedes, in all essentials the first modern motorcar. It featured a honeycomb radiator, a pressed-steel chassis, mechanically operated intake valves, and an improved gate gearbox. Its 35-horsepower engine weighed only 14 pounds per horsepower, making the car capable of 53 mph. Lowering the price of such an advanced design through quantity production posed a formidable problem for early auto manufacturers. As late as 1909, in the most integrated automobile factory in Europe, some 1,700 production workers produced fewer than 1,000 Mercedes cars. (Courtesy Mercedes-Benz of North America)

Opposite, top: 1891 Panhard et Levassor, the prototype of the modern gasoline automobile. Placing the engine vertically in the front of the chassis instead of under the seats or in the back marked a radical departure from the carriage silhouette in automotive design and made possible the accommodation of larger, more powerful engines. In 1895 an improved model was driven over the 732-mile course of the Paris-Bordeaux-Paris race at the then incredible speed of 15 mph, with the longest stop for servicing being only 22 minutes. (Courtesy Free Library of Philadelphia)

Sales catalog illustration and specifications of the 1901 curved-dash Oldsmobile, the first gasoline automobile produced in significant volume. This 3-horsepower vehicle was merely a motorized horse buggy. But its $650 price put automobility with the reach of middle-class Americans and made it the best-selling car in the world from its introduction in 1901 to about 1904. (Courtesy Free Library of Philadelphia)

Oldsmobile Regular Runabout

SPECIFICATIONS

CAPACITY -- Two passengers.
WHEEL BASE -- 66 inches.
TREAD -- 55 inches.
FRAME -- Angle steel.
SPRINGS -- Oldsmobile side springs.
WHEELS -- 28-inch wood artillery.
TIRES -- 3-inch detachable.
MOTOR -- 5 x 6-inch 7 H. P. horizontal.
TRANSMISSION -- All-spur gear, two speeds forward and reverse.
FINISH -- Black with red trimming.

EQUIPMENT -- Complete set of tools and pair of large brass side lamps.
RADIATOR -- Copper disk.
CARBURETOR -- Oldsmobile.
IGNITION -- Jump spark.
STEERING GEAR -- Tiller.
DIFFERENTIAL -- Bevel-gear type.
BRAKES -- Differential and rear wheel.
WATER CAPACITY -- Five gallons.
CIRCULATION -- Gear pump.
GASOLINE CAPACITY -- Five gallons.

Dr. H. Nelson Jackson and Sewall K. Crocker, his chauffeur, in their 1903 Winton at a typical stop during the first coast-to-coast trip across the United States by car. Three transcontinental crossings by automobile in 1903 inaugurated informal motor touring by the average motorist. (Courtesy Smithsonian Institution)

Opposite, top: 1906 Ford Model N, the first reliable, low-priced, four-cylinder automobile. Prior to the Model N, cars selling at prices the middle-class family could afford had been one-cylinder motorized horse buggies that soon rattled apart. The Model N was one of the better-designed and better-built cars available at any price in 1906. Its 15-horsepower motor could do 45 miles per hour and got 20 miles per gallon of gas. Ford had hoped to sell the car for $500, but to maintain its high quality, the price soon had to be raised to $600. (Courtesy Ford Motor Company)

Opposite, bottom: 1908 Ford Model T, "the car that put America on wheels." The Model T offered such advanced features as a three-point suspension of the motor, improved arc springs, an enclosed power plant and transmission, and extensive use of new heat-treated vanadium steels. Yet it was initially priced at only $850 for the touring car. Ford advertising boasted that "no car under $2,000 offers more, and no car over $2,000 offers more except the trimmings." Conceived as a static model at an ever decreasing unit price, over 15 million had been sold and the price lowered to $290 for the coupe by the time of the Model T's withdrawal from production on May 27, 1927. (Courtesy Ford Motor Company)

Cadillac Model B (*inset*) and scene at Brooklands racetrack in England, showing interchangeable parts from disassembled Cadillac cars. Cadillac was awarded the Dewar Trophy of the Royal Automobile Club in 1908 for the achievement of previously unparalleled interchangeability of parts, an essential element of mass production. In a shed at Brooklands racetrack, three Cadillac cars were disassembled and their parts mixed. The reassembled Cadillacs then finished a 500-mile test drive with perfect scores. (Courtesy General Motors)

1912 Cadillac, the first car to be equipped with a self-starter and a generator-battery lighting and ignition system. Charles F. Kettering developed the self-starter in 1911 as an adaptation of his electric cash register motor. The self-starter obviated the onerous problem, especially for women, of having to use a hand crank to start an internal-combustion engine. The electric device ironically sealed the doom of the electric car by putting middle-class women behind the wheels of conventional gasoline automobiles. For developing the self-starter, the Royal Automobile Club awarded Cadillac its second Dewar Trophy. (Courtesy General Motors)

Magneto flywheel assembly and chassis assembly at the Ford Highland Park plant, 1913–1914. Magnetos, motors, and transmissions were assembled on moving lines at Highland Park by the summer of 1913. After production from these subassembly lines threatened to flood the final assembly line, a moving chassis-assembly line was installed that reduced the time of chassis assembly from over twelve hours in October to less than three hours by December 30, 1913. (Courtesy Henry Ford Museum and Greenfield Village)

Opposite, top: 1903 Ford Model A sawing wood. Used as a mobile power plant, the automobile lightened farm labor. (Courtesy Henry Ford Museum and Greenfield Village)

Opposite, bottom: Henry Ford (*center*) with Fordson farm tractor plowing a field. Introduced to help alleviate food shortages during World War I, the Fordson tractor mechanized American agriculture and ultimately made the small family farm obsolete. (Courtesy Ford Motor Company)

Stuck in the mud, an all too common experience for the early motorist. The first census of American roads in 1904 revealed that only 7 percent were surfaced and that there was only one mile of improved road for every 492 inhabitants. Roads meandered from town to town without forming an interconnected system and were poorly marked when marked at all. (Courtesy Smithsonian Institution)

World War I Nash Quad Truck. The newly formed Nash Motor Company became the leading American producer of military trucks by the end of World War I, as U.S. truck production quintupled from 24,900 in 1914 to 128,000 in 1917, largely to meet European demand. An entire army was supplied by motor transport over the road to Verdun, and long-distance trucking was inaugurated in the United States as some 30,000 trucks loaded with other freight were driven from assembly plants in the Middle West to eastern ports of embarkation. (Courtesy Henry Ford Museum and Greenfield Village)

Farmer's 1917 Ford Model T with crate carrying goat strapped to side. (Courtesy Ford Motor Company)

Main Street, Henderson, Texas, 1927. The isolation of farm life ended with institutionalization of the Saturday trip to town to market products, shop, and visit with friends. Automobility ended the reliance of farmers on shopping from mail order catalogs, opened up much larger trading areas that killed off the crossroads general store, and brought city amenities, such as better medical care and educational opportunities, to the farm. (Courtesy Henry Ford Museum and Greenfield Village)

was about all the ground we wanted, and turned to me and said, as well as I can remember, 'Alfred, will you go out and buy these properties for us and Mr. Prentice will pay whatever you decide to pay for them.'" [11]

Sloan knew that the day of the colorful entrepreneurial capitalist was about over in automobile manufacturing. Although he had tried to talk Walter Chrysler into staying at GM, by early 1920 he himself was on the verge of resigning. It was clear to Sloan that in order to realize its potential, General Motors "would have to be guided by an organization of intellects. A great industrial organization requires the best of many minds." His ideal executive was the security-oriented technician who, sensitive to evidence and the opinions of others, worked well as a member of an entrepreneurial team. In the GM that he envisioned, there was no place for the autocratic rule of an inveterate gambler like Durant, who made decisions on the basis of "some intuitive flash of brilliance." "Eventually this salesman's optimism, unchecked by facts, became downright disturbing to men who loved him, men whose fortunes he had increased manyfold." Sloan asked himself, "Should they blindly, mutely risk loss of those fortunes?"

Sloan took a vacation abroad to think things over in the summer of 1920. When he returned in August, he "sensed something unusual and decided to ride along awhile and see what happens." What Sloan sensed was that Durant's days at General Motors were numbered. [12]

Durant's postwar expansion program, ill-timed though it turned out to be, had not been entirely his own error. Indeed, there is evidence that he urged caution on several occasions when others wanted to push ahead. The du Pont interests, with a view toward diversification and confident of a tremendous postwar market for automobiles, had invested heavily in General Motors. By 1919 they owned 28.7 percent of the GM common stock and, according to an agreement with Durant of December 21, 1917, had responsibility for the financial management of GM. Pierre S. du Pont, chairman of the corporation's board of directors, had supported the expansion program without objection. John J. Raskob, the du Pont treasurer and chairman of the GM board's finance committee, was at least as responsible as Durant for promoting the expansion program. Durant and Raskob would later each blame the other for the sorry outcome. Both "strong, optimistic expansionists," in Sloan's words, they "seemed to disagree on occasion only on what to put the money into." [13] The problems resulting from expansion were exacerbated, however, by Durant's personal manipulations of GM stock, which would be illegal now and which were even then considered highly unethical.

Raskob initially attempted to raise the money for expansion by an $84-million bond issue and by a ten-for-one split of the GM common stock. But by May 1920 only $12 million of the bonds had been sold, so an issue of $64 million in new common stock was offered for underwriting. An English-Canadian syndicate, composed of Explosive Trades and Canadian Explosives, picked up $36 million of the issue, but that still left $28 million to be disposed of in a declining market.

The price of GM stock was being artificially held up by Durant, who with a syndicate of friends was buying large blocks on 10-percent margin. His intention was to profit personally by cornering GM stock so that the bears in the market could not cover their short lines. After his buying drove the price of pre-split GM common to a high of $420, the New York Stock Exchange intervened to prevent the ruin of dozens of banks and scores of brokers by Durant. A ruling by the exchange that the new GM shares, exchanging at ten-for-one with the old, could be used to cover short sales threatened to flood Durant's corner. So he accepted a compromise in which he placed the nominal value of his average purchase price per share on his GM stock.

As automobile sales slackened, inventories began to pile up and profits shrank. To compound the situation, Durant's slipshod style of management had encouraged the operating divisions to continue to spend large amounts for new equipment and supplies. As a result, the stock issue that had originally been intended for expansion came to be essential to the survival of General Motors.

Large General Motors stockholders, concerned about what was happening, began to unload their holdings. Durant saw that this might collapse the price of GM stock, with the disastrous result that it might be impossible to dispose of the remaining $28 million of the new issue. He also wanted to protect the value of his personal holdings, which on paper were worth $105 million. Despite his attempt now to snap up large blocks as they were offered for sale, GM common slid from its post-split price of $38.50 to under $30 a share before a banking syndicate headed by J. P. Morgan and Company agreed on June 3, 1920, to underwrite the private sale of 1.4 million shares at a still lower $20. The bankers demanded the stiff price of $1.34 million of GM stock as a commission, plus an additional 100,000 shares bonus at an insider's price of $10, and six seats on the GM board of directors. In return Edward R. Stettinius, Sr., a Morgan partner and one of the new directors, agreed to manage a $10-million syndicate that would support the price of GM common over the next six months.

On July 15, 1920, the Morgan interests announced that they had disposed of the 1.4 million shares. But Durant's problems were just beginning. On July 27, 100,000 shares of General Motors stock were dumped on the market, driving the price down to $20.50. It was Stettinius who dumped this huge block of stock that broke the price of GM common.

The bankers had agreed in writing not to sell below $20 a share. They ultimately did sell as low as $9.

The bad faith of the bankers was more than matched by Durant's own double dealing. As president of General Motors and Chevrolet, Durant was bound by the agreement with the Morgan interests that neither of these companies, nor du Pont, nor J. P. Morgan would buy, sell, or borrow GM stock on its own account. This was essential if the price of the stock were to be stabilized. Durant flagrantly violated this agreement by forming other syndicates with his cronies and engaging in personal market operations in GM common without informing either the du Ponts or the House of Morgan. In these operations he unethically discriminated against blocks of GM stockholders. As early as March 1920, for example, he divided a list of GM stockholders into three groups and sent out telegrams urging group A to hang on to its GM stock because something great was about to happen, group B to buy all the additional GM stock it could afford, and group C to give Durant options on its GM holdings.

Perhaps Durant did not think the Morgan interests were acting aggressively enough and rationalized that there was no harm in helping things out on his own. When the bankers found out what he was up to, however, they felt no obligation to uphold their end of the bargain. Their only objective in the first place had been to prevent the price of GM stock from deteriorating faster than the general market dropped, not to protect the paper fortunes of Durant and his cronies. It seemed foolish to the bankers to try to stabilize the price of the stock with several syndicates working independently of one another and with differing goals in mind. From the point of view of the Morgan interests, in fact, the main danger to the value of the stock was Durant's using it as collateral for his personal market operations. Durant, on the other hand, believed that he had been sold out and that his personal market operations were necessary to protect General Motors, his friends, and himself.

As GM common continued to tumble without the support of the bankers, Durant bought frantically. Operating heavily on margin, he supported the stock down to $12 a share before admitting that he was licked. Durant's cash resources were wiped out, and he owed nearly $30 million to twenty-one brokers and three banks.

The du Ponts, Raskob, and the House of Morgan became afraid that if Durant declared bankruptcy he might drag down with him the brokers, the banks, and General Motors. At a series of meetings in November 1920, they worked out an alternative. They would bail Durant out on condition that he hand over to them the control of General Motors.

The full extent of Durant's involvement in the market was not suspected by Pierre du Pont until November 10. At lunch that day Durant dropped hints to the uncomprehending du Pont that the company and he personally were in the hands of the bankers and that he (Durant) would have to "play the game." Durant remained evasive and misled du Pont about the true state of his affairs until the du Ponts and the Morgan interests forced him to review his accounts with them on November 18. In many instances the accounts could only be explained orally by Durant or his son-in-law, Dr. Edwin R. Campbell.

Durant came out of the deal retaining about $3 million of General Motors stock plus a personal loan of $500,000 from Pierre du Pont, which to du Pont and the Morgan interests seemed generous. But Durant later claimed, "There were many things I had forgotten and so when I really cleaned up and protected everybody else, I had nothing left." [14] He resigned as president of General Motors on November 30, 1920.

The du Ponts gained some 2.5 million shares of GM stock, and Pierre du Pont reluctantly succeeded Durant as interim president. The job was to go in 1923 to Alfred Sloan, who for the time being became excutive vice-president. In addition to coughing up $27 million to settle Durant's affairs, the House of Morgan gave General Motors an $80-million loan. To allay fears in Flint about Durant's resignation and the "takeover" of General Motors by eastern bankers, the new management built a $300,000 hotel in Flint and named it the Hotel Durant—the impersonal corporation's final tribute to a founder who had outlived his usefulness to the firm.

Durant Motors

After a brief holiday, Durant set himself up in a modest office and invited sixty-seven friends to back him in a new automobile company. Within forty-eight hours he raised $7 million, $2 million more than he needed.

Durant Motors came into being on January 21, 1921, and grew by leaps and bounds. Facilities were built at Flint and Lansing, Michigan, and at Oakland, California. The first model produced, the Durant Four, was an exceptional value at $850. The Sheridan plant at Muncie, Indiana, was bought to produce the Durant Six. The bankrupt Locomobile Company of Bridgeport, Connecticut, was purchased to add a luxury car with a long-standing, prestigious reputation to the Durant line. With the Willys Corporation in receivership, Chrysler and Studebaker were outbid at $5.25 million to acquire the new Willys plant at Elizabeth, New Jersey, the most modern automobile factory in the world, plus the Willys designs for a medium-priced car that became the Flint. Then, on February 15, 1922, Durant announced that he would bring out the Star, which at $348 would compete with the Model T. Some 60,000 people flocked to see the Star at its first showing in New York City, and by January 1, 1923, Durant had accepted cash deposits on orders for 231,000 Star cars, a full year's production. The Durant Motors Acceptance Corporation was formed to finance time sales and to help dealers store cars over the winter for spring delivery.

Expansion of Durant Motors was financed through the Durant Corporation, which Durant had organized as a sideline while still at GM, to sell on the installment plan to small investors the stock of General Motors, the Fisher Body Company, and other firms. With 146,000 shareholders by January 1, 1923, Durant Motors had more stockholders than any other American company except American Telephone and Telegraph, a much larger enterprise.

Feeling his oats again, Durant tried to achieve another takeover of General Motors. As he had done earlier with Chevrolet stock, he hatched a plan to trade Durant Motors stock for General Motors, which was then priced below Durant. But General Motors had increased its common stock to some 43 million shares, and he soon realized that the task was beyond his powers.

Despite its promising start, Durant Motors never amounted to much. In its best years it was unable to capture more than a fifth of the market for new cars. Henry Ford effectively crushed the threat of competition from the Star car by unexpectedly lowering his prices for the Model T. The Flint and the Durant Six never caught the fancy of the buying public, and the Locomobile could not regain its lost luster. The Durant Four was soon outmoded by competing models. A well-managed firm might have pulled through. Durant, however, failed in recruiting topflight managerial talent; and as his own energies were dispersed into the stock market, Durant Motors came to be treated as a sideline.

Billy Durant and the Bull Market

The liberty loans of World War I had demonstrated for the first time that large blocks of securities could be marketed directly to small investors. And after the war the dominating power that the eastern investment bankers historically had wielded on Wall Street increasingly came to be shared with a new group of self-made millionaires who came mainly from the Middle West. Less cautious and conservative than their predecessors, these high-rolling speculators became the prime movers in the runaway bull market of the late 1920s. By far the most important figure among them was Durant, who after 1924 was widely referred to by the press as "the leading bull."

The "bull consortium" that Durant led was estimated at various times to include between twenty and thirty millionaire investors, who were also known as "Durant's prosperity boys." It was said that Durant himself had $1.2 billion in the market by 1928 and that he directly controlled about $4 billion in investments. The financial press regularly reported the multimillion-dollar killings he made in individual pools. The most impressive involved the Radio Corporation of America (RCA). RCA had never paid a cent in dividends and had been overpriced at $85. Yet the stock was bulled by the Durant group to $420 a share in 1928, and on a split to $570 in 1929. When the insiders began taking profits, RCA dropped some 300 points within a week. Through an investment trust formed in 1924, Durant sold bonds secured by the stock of ten corporations. He also sold the securities of the notorious Goldman Sachs Trading Corporation to the gullible public after Goldman Sachs insiders quit buying their stock themselves in March 1929.

Durant was assailed on the floor of the United States Senate for luring small investors into the speculative orgy by James Couzens, who had become a senator from Michigan, and by Senator Carter Glass of Virginia, author of the legislation establishing the Federal Reserve Board in 1913. Veiled threats made during a secret night visit to the White House by Durant on April 3, 1929, failed to convince President Herbert Hoover to squelch the efforts of the Federal Reserve Board to curb the bull market through a tighter monetary policy. The result was that the "prosperity boys" divested themselves of their huge holdings during May and June.

The *New York Times* reported on June 2 that "rumors of selling by Durant have hung over the market like a pall." The impact on other large investors was tremendous, and by October 1929 the market was being held up by the many small investors. Under Durant's leadership the bulls had done such a good job of killing off the perennial bears in the market during the late 1920s that when prices started to tumble, there were few bears left around to cushion the fall through buy orders to cover their short lines. Thus, the worst financial disaster in American history became inevitable.

The market collapsed on Tuesday, October 29, 1929. Like many other insiders who had managed to unload before the initial disaster struck, Durant assumed that the worst was over. He plunged back into the market to pick up stocks at what he thought were bargain prices, only to find that the market kept deteriorating. His brokers sold him out in 1930.

Durant scraped together his remaining resources and plowed them belatedly into Durant Motors. Conceiving that the American market was ripe for a small car with low initial and maintenance costs, he started to manufacture the French Mathis in New Jersey. Ultimately the Volkswagen was to prove him right, but at the outset of the Depression the corpse that Durant Motors had become could not be revived. It was liquidated in 1933.

Personal bankruptcy followed for Durant in 1936. A stroke suffered in 1942 left him an invalid. He died in relative obscurity on March 18, 1947, in his fashionable Gramercy Park apartment in New York City, attended by his wife, Catharine, and three maids.

Modern Times

7

A few weeks after Durant's death, Henry Ford died too, at his Dearborn estate, Fairlane, during a power failure on the stormy night of April 7, 1947. Ford died at the ripe age of eighty-two, fabulously wealthy, but with greatly eroded mental capacities. He was the most famous man in the world. Power within the gigantic Ford Motor Company had passed some eighteen months earlier to his grandson, Henry Ford II.

More was written about Henry Ford during his lifetime, and he was more often quoted, than any figure in American history. Theodore Roosevelt complained that Ford received more publicity than even the president of the United States. The *New York Times* reported that Ford's reputation had spread to peasants in remote villages in countries where only the elites had heard of Warren G. Harding or Calvin Coolidge. Will Rogers, probably the shrewdest folk psychologist in our history, said a number of times and in many witty ways that Henry Ford had influenced more lives than any living man.

The Russians were fascinated with *Fordizatzia* and viewed Henry Ford not as a capitalist but as a revolutionary economic innovator. A visitor to the U.S.S.R. in 1927 reported that the Russian people "ascribed a magical quality to the name of Ford" and that "more people have heard of him than Stalin.... Next to Lenin, Trotsky, and Kalinin, Ford is probably the most widely known personage in Russia."[1] The 25,000 Fordson tractors shipped to the U.S.S.R. between 1920 and 1927 promised the peasant a new agricultural era free from drudgery and want. Communes and babies born in communes were named Fordson. Ford mass-production methods, widely copied in the U.S.S.R., promised an industrial horn of plenty. Progress in adopting them was chronicled in *Pravda*, and in workers' processions Ford's name was emblazoned on banners emblematic of a new industrial era. Translations of *My Life and Work* were widely read and used as texts in the universities. Russians "used the word 'Fordize' as a synonym for 'Americanize,' " claims Reynold Wik.

Wik's examination of German newspapers similarly "reveals an obsession with Henry Ford." [2] *My Life and Work* became a best seller in Berlin in 1925, and the Germans referred to mass production as *Fordismus*. After the National Socialists seized power in March 1933, Ford had the status of a demigod. "You can tell Herr Ford that I am a great admirer of his," Adolf Hitler told Prince Louis Ferdinand, grandson of Kaiser Wilhelm II and Nazi sympathizer, who was about to depart for an apprenticeship as a production trainee at the Ford River Rouge plant. "I shall do my best to put his theories into practice in Germany. . . . I have come to the conclusion that the motorcar, instead of being a class dividing element, can be the instrument for uniting the different classes, just as it has done in America, thanks to Mr. Ford's genius." [3] Along with rearmament, the rapid development of an automobile culture in 1930s Germany became a major thrust of the Nazi economic recovery program.

Additionally, as the world's most outspoken anti-Semite, Ford was considered a "great man" in the Nazi pantheon of heroes. Ford's magazine, *The Dearborn Independent*, edited by William J. Cameron, began publishing anti-Semitic articles in 1920. Between 1920 and 1922 Ford reprinted them in four brochures and in a more comprehensive book entitled *The International Jew*, which was translated into most European languages and was widely circulated throughout the world. A picture of Ford was displayed in a place of honor at the National Socialist Party headquarters. By late 1933 the Nazis had published some twenty-nine German editions of *The International Jew*, with Ford's name on the title page and a preface praising Ford for the "great service" his anti-Semitism had done the world. At the post–World War II Nuremberg war crimes trials, Balder von Schirach, leader of the Hitler youth movement, testified that he had learned his anti-Semitism at age seventeen from reading Ford's book.

On July 30, 1938, his seventy-fifth birthday, Ford accepted the Grand Cross of the Supreme Order of the German Eagle with Hitler's personal congratulations, "in recognition of [his] pioneering in making motorcars available to the masses." David L. Lewis points out that this was "the highest honor the Reich could then bestow upon a foreigner. Ford was the first American and the fourth person (Mussolini was another) to receive the award." Among other anti-Semitic public statements, in 1940 Ford told a reporter from the Associated Press that "international Jewish bankers" were responsible for the outbreak of World War II. [4]

The people of what Wik calls "grass-roots America" thought Henry Ford a greater emancipator of the common man than Abraham Lincoln. They made Ford our first, and probably our last, millionaire folk hero. He received several thousand letters a day, ranging from simple requests for help and advice to demands that he solve America's remaining social and economic problems. The newspapers of his day called Ford "the Sage of Dearborn" and made him an oracle to the common man. But beyond that, Wik's analysis of letters to Ford "from farmers and middle-class folks ... living in the typical small towns of mid-America" reveals "a widespread and simple faith in Ford and the fixed belief that an understanding existed between the writers and this man of immense wealth." [5]

Henry Ford's Philosophy of Industry

The image of Henry Ford as a progressive industrial leader and champion of the common man that Americans clung to during the 1920s was hardly congruent with the philosophy of industry expounded by Ford himself in *My Life and Work* (1922), *Today and Tomorrow* (1922 and 1926), and *My Philosophy of Industry* (1929).[6]

Far from identifying with the Jeffersonian yeoman farmer glorified in populist rhetoric, Ford looked forward to the demise of the family farm. As a youth he had hated the drudgery of farm labor, and he longed to rid the world of unsanitary and inefficient horses and cows. The Model T was conceived as "a farmer's car" less because Ford empathized with the small farmer than because any car designed in 1908 for a mass market had to meet the needs of a predominantly rural population. "The old kind of farm is dead," he wrote in 1926. "We might as well recognize that fact and take it as a starting point for something better." He looked forward in 1929 to the day when "large corporations ... will supersede the individual farmer, or groups of farmers will combine to perform their work in a wholesale manner. This is the proper way to do it and the only way in which economic freedom can be won."

Ford viewed the common man with a cynical, elitist paternalism, fundamentally at odds with the equalitarian populist philosophy he supposedly represented. "We have to recognize the unevenness in human mental equipment," wrote Ford. "The vast majority of men want to stay put. They want to be led. They want to have everything done for them and have no responsibility." He admitted that the very thought of repetitive labor was "terrifying to me. I could not do the same thing day in and day out, but to other minds, perhaps to the majority of minds, repetitive operations hold no terrors." He believed that the average worker "wants a job in which he does not have to put forth much physical exertion—above all he wants a job in which he does not have to think ... for most purposes and for most people, it is necessary to establish something in the way of a routine and to make most motions purely repetitive—otherwise the individual will not get enough done to live off his exertions." A journalist asked Ford in 1923, "What about industrial democracy?" "The average employee in the average industry is not ready for participation in management," Ford answered. "An industry, at this stage of our development, must be more or less of a friendly autocracy."

Nevins and Hill credit Ford with running his company "as a semi-public entity" through which workers and consumers shared the benefits of increased productivity at a time when profit maximization was the rule in American industry. But beyond the obvious point that the public had no voice in this "semi-public entity," Ford's business philosophy boiled down at best to the simple observation that mass production would yield greater profits only if consumer purchasing power was increased sufficiently to enable people to buy what the machine produced. He called this the "wage motive" and claimed that "we have discovered a new motive for industry and abolished the meaningless terms 'capital,' 'labor,' and 'public.' ... It is this thought of enlarging buying power by paying high wages and selling at low prices which is behind the prosperity of this country."

Ford emphatically denied that higher wages and lower prices ought to follow from the technological progress of a people as a simple matter of social justice. He held, for example, that "it is untrue to say that profits or the benefit of inventions which bring lower costs belong to the worker.... Profits belong primarily to the business, and the workers are only part of the business." Lower prices did not come at the expense of profits but resulted from increased industrial efficiency that permitted profit margins to be enhanced. Ford's policy was "to name a price so low as to force everybody in the place to the highest point of efficiency. The low price makes everybody dig for profits." The continual reinvestment of high profits in improved machinery to increase output to make still more profits for reinvestment was indeed what made the "wage motive" a workable proposition for Ford.

So in Ford's philosophy of industry, the key figure remained the entrepreneurial capitalist, whose supposed superior intelligence enabled him to organize production more and more efficiently through the continual reinvestment of his profits in improved machinery. It followed axiomatically for Ford that this industrial superman had the unquestionable prerogative to determine unilaterally what were fair profits, wages, and prices, free from any interference by the government, workers, or consumers. If the superman erred, he would be punished by the classical economists' bogeymen, the invisible hand of the market and the unenforceable law of supply and demand. Ford's philosophy of industry thus was a pedestrian variation on the conventional business creed that put profits first and foremost, glorified the entrepreneurial capitalist, and accepted as axiomatic the outmoded production ethic of the classical economists' economy of scarcity.

Although the five-dollar, eight-hour day entailed recognition that mass consumption was a necessary corollary of mass production, Ford nevertheless remained committed to most of the beliefs and values of a production-oriented society and economy. He did come to see that mass production made the worker "more a buyer than a seller" and that "the 'thrift' and 'economy' ideas have been overworked." But Ford abhorred waste and held to the central tenet of a production-oriented economy and society—the work ethic. "Thinking men know that work is the salvation of the race, morally, physically, socially," claimed Ford. "Work does more than get us our living; it gets us our life."

Seeing the cure for poverty and want narrowly in terms of more efficient production, Ford held that "hiring two men to do the job of one is a crime against society" and that mass production, despite great increases in worker productivity, would continue always to create more jobs than it destroyed. To Ford, overproduction was a theoretical possibility that would mean "a world in which everybody has all that he wants." He feared that "this condition will be too long postponed," and he believed that in the automobile industry, "we do not have to bother about overproduction for some years to come, provided our prices are right." Meanwhile neither charity nor drones had any place in Ford's conception of the good society. "Fully to carry out the wage motive, society must be relieved of non-producers," he wrote. "Big business, well organized, cannot serve without repetitive work, and that sort of work instead of being a menace to society, permits the coming into production of the aged, the blind, and the halt. . . . And it makes new and better places for those whose mentality lifts them above repetitive work."

The self-styled champion of the small businessman against monopoly power in the Selden patent suit now proclaimed that "business must grow bigger and bigger, else we shall have insufficient supplies and high prices." In a new twist on the Doctrine of Stewardship, which had been the perennial rationalization of American men of great wealth since it was conceived by the Puritans, Ford merely urged the men in charge of these industrial giants to consult their enlightened self-interest and "regard themselves as trustees of power in behalf of all the people. . . . It is clearly up to them now, as trustees, to see what they can do further in the way of making our system fool-proof, malice-proof, and greed-proof. It is a mere matter of social engineering." But in asking for a capitalism stripped of its traditional assumption that selfishness and greed are the natural main-springs of human economic behavior, Ford never went on to call for capitalists free from hypocrisy. Perhaps that would have been too much to expect from a "trustee of power in behalf of all the people" who also declared that "a great business is really too big to be human."

The New Industrial Proletariat

With the transfer of skills at Ford from men to specialized machines, the process that Harry Braverman has identified as the "degradation of work"[7] turned highly skilled jobs into semiskilled and/or unskilled jobs. This revolutionized the workplace.

Fordism meant that neither physical strength nor the long apprentice-ship required for becoming a competent craftsman were any longer pre-requisites for industrial employment. The creativity and experience on the job that had been valued in the craftsman were considered liabilities in the assembly-line worker. "As to machinists, old-time, all-around men, perish the thought!" declared Horace Arnold and Fay Faurote in 1915. "The Ford Motor Company has no use for experience, in the working ranks anyway. It desires and prefers machine tool operators who have nothing to unlearn, who have no theories of correct surface speeds for metal finishing, and will simply do what they are told to do, over and over again from bell-time to bell-time. The Ford help need not even be able bodied."[8]

New opportunities for remunerative employment were opened to the uneducated peasant from southern or eastern Europe, the black migrant to the northern city, the physically handicapped, and the educable mentally retarded. For the machine did not discriminate and did not demand substantial training, physical strength, education, or even intelli-gence from its operator. "Our employment office does not bar a man for anything he has previously done," boasted Ford. "He is equally acceptable whether he has been in Sing Sing or at Harvard and we do not even inquire from which place he has graduated. All that he needs is the desire to work."[9]

The early Ford work force mirrored the ethnic character of Detroit, which at the turn of the century was essentially English and German. About half of Detroit's population in 1900 were native-born whites, the other half overwhelmingly immigrants from northern and western Europe.

The ethnic composition of the Ford work force changed dramatically with the coming of mass production. The first survey of the national origins of those workers, in November 1914, revealed that only 29 percent were American born and that two thirds were immigrants from southern and eastern Europe, with Poles (21 percent) and Russians (16 percent) being the largest ethnic groups. The Ford workers in this survey represented twenty-two national groups. Company announcements were printed in fourteen languages but invariably ended with the injunction, "Learn to Read English." Bilingual foremen were valued, and it became essential for straw bosses to learn how to say "hurry up" in several different languages. Native-born Caucasians were particularly underrepresented in unskilled and semiskilled jobs at Ford. As Nevins and Hill point out, "At the Ford plant the foundry workers, common laborers, drill press men, grinder operators, and other unskilled and semiskilled hands were likely to be Russians, Poles, Croats, Hungarians, or Italians; only the skilled employees were American, British, or German stock." [10]

By 1919 the Ford Motor Company also employed hundreds of ex-convicts and 9,563 "substandard men"—a group that included amputees, the blind, deaf-mutes, epileptics, and about 1,000 tubercular employees. By 1923 Ford employed about 5,000 blacks, more than any other large American company and roughly half the number employed in the entire automobile industry.

Conditions on the assembly line were grudgingly accepted only by workers accustomed to even more repressive systems of labor or whose opportunities for employment elsewhere at a living wage were almost nil. Arnold and Faurote recognized that "the monotony of repetitive production can be alleviated only by a satisfactory wage-rate, and is, perhaps, much more easily endured by immigrants, whose home wage stood somewhere about 60 cents for 10 hours' work, than by native-born Americans." [11] Indeed, one the major reasons why mass-production techniques came to be innovated in the United States is that, in contrast with Europe, automobile manufacturers here could count on the availability of a large labor pool of unskilled, recently arrived, and as yet politically impotent peasants from the most socially and economically backward countries of Europe, and of blacks escaping from the oppressive socioeconomic conditions of the rural American South.

The demands of the assembly line put a premium on youth. Nevins and Hill relate that "the bosses had a natural liking for young, vigorous, quick men not past thirty-five. Experienced hands past that age, if they did not possess some indispensable skill were thus often the first to be dismissed and the last to be re-engaged." In their 1929 study, Robert and Helen Lynd tied mass production to the emergence of a cult of youth in the 1920s. Noting the trend toward employing younger men in Muncie,

Indiana, factories, for example, the Lynds explained that "in modern machine production it is speed and endurance that are at a premium. A boy of nineteen may, after a few weeks of experience on a machine, turn out an amount of work greater than his father of forty-five." [12]

"I have not been able to discover that repetitive labor injures a man in any way," wrote Henry Ford. "Industry need not exact a human toll." Mass production shifted many backbreaking tasks from the worker to the machine, and Highland Park exemplified the clean, safe, well-lighted, and well-ventilated factory essential to efficient mass production. Nevertheless, a human toll was exacted, if only because mass production meant "the reduction of the necessity for thought on the part of the worker and the reduction of his movements to a minimum." [13]

In the 1936 movie *Modern Times* Charlie Chaplin satirized the new breed of semiskilled worker created at Highland Park. Machines were closely spaced for optimal efficiency, and material was delivered to the worker at a waist-high level so that "wasted motion" was not expended in walking, reaching, stooping, or bending. The worker not only had to subordinate himself to the pace of the machine but also had to be able to withstand the boredom inevitable in repeating the same motions hour after hour. A fifteen-minute lunch break, which included time to use the rest room and to wash one's hands, was the only interruption of the fatiguing monotony of repetitive labor, the hypnotic trance that workers were lulled into by the rhythmic din of the machinery.

The precise coordination of the flow of assembly that mass production demanded meant a new ironclad discipline for industrial workers. "The organization is so highly specialized and one part is so dependent upon another that we could not for a moment consider allowing men to have their own way," Ford explained. "Without the most rigid discipline we would have the utmost confusion. I think it should not be otherwise in industry." Consequently, the easy camaraderie on the job that had been normal in American industry for unskilled as well as skilled workers was forbidden at Highland Park. Straw bosses and company "spotters"— another new element in the work force—enforced rules and regulations that forbade leaning against the machine, sitting, squatting, talking, whistling, or smoking on the job. Workers learned to communicate clandestinely without moving their lips in the "Ford whisper" and wore frozen expressions known as "Fordization of the face." "There is not much personal contact," understated Ford. "The men do their work and go home—a factory is not a drawing room." [14]

The impact of Fordism on the worker was debilitating. The individual became an anonymous, interchangeable robot who had little chance on the job to demonstrate his personal qualifications for upward mobility into the echelons of management. Thus, the American myth of unlimited individual social mobility, based on ability and the ideal of the self-made man, became a frustrating impossibility for the assembly-line worker. As the job became a treadmill to escape from rather than a calling in which to find fulfillment, leisure began to assume a new importance. The meaning of work, long sanctified in the Protestant Ethic, was reduced to monetary remuneration. The value of thrift and personal economy became questionable, too, as mass consumption became an inevitable corollary of mass production.

The Five-Dollar Day

The Ford Motor Company had from the beginning been an exemplary employer regarding monetary remuneration. Ford paid top wages, and early Ford labor practices in addition included bonuses, as well as educational, medical, and recreational programs. In 1905 every Ford worker received an incredibly generous Christmas bonus of $1,000. From 1908 through 1911 annual bonuses were paid of 5 percent of wages after one year's service, 7½ percent after two years, and 10 percent after three years. In 1911 the one- and two-year service bonuses were ended, but an "efficiency bonus" was added for salaried and supervisory personnel.

Despite the relatively high wages and bonus incentives paid at Ford, worker dissatisfaction was evident in unacceptable rates of labor productivity and labor turnover at the new Highland Park plant—"a new breed of factory," writes Stephen Meyer III, "with an entirely different pace and intensity of work even for unskilled workers. Like the peasants of the old world, Ford immigrant workers voted and voiced their opinions with their feet and abandoned the Highland Park factory in droves." [15]

John R. Lee came to Ford with the 1911 acquisition of the John R. Keim Mills of Buffalo, New York, where he had been general manager. Lee became director of the Ford Employment Office. In the summer of 1913 he was asked to conduct an investigation to determine the causes of worker discontent and inefficiency at Highland Park. His report concluded that the chief causes were bad housing and home conditions, too long hours, too low wages, and arbitary treatment of workers by foremen and superintendents, who at that time had authority over hiring, firing, and advancement.

As a result of Lee's investigation, in October 1913 the Ford Motor Company instituted a comprehensive new labor program. Wages were increased an average of 15 percent. An Employees' Savings and Loan Association was formed so that workers could have a safe place to save and to borrow money at low rates when family emergencies occurred. Foremen were stripped of much of their authority in the management of the labor force as labor relations were centralized in a new Employment Department.

Probably the most significant of the Lee reforms was the rationalization of job skills and advancement within the Ford factory by a new skill-wage classification system that reorganized jobs into groups with similar levels of skill, and established a graded hierarchy of jobs from the least to the most skilled. This reduced the number of wage rates at Highland Park from sixty-nine to only eight, ranging from a high of 51 cents to a low of 23 cents an hour, for sixteen different levels of skill and competence. A worker received automatic increases as he reached specific standards of efficiency within a grade, and he was advanced to the next grade as his skill increased.

The significance of the Lee reforms was lost in the announcement of the five-dollar, eight-hour day by the Ford Motor Company on January 5, 1914. This plan roughly doubled for Ford's American workers the going rate of pay for industrial workers, and it shortened the work day by two hours as well. It had been foreshadowed on a far smaller scale at Ford-England's Trafford Park plant near Manchester. By paying his English employees the 1s. 3d. an hour, or £3 for a six-day, 48-hour week, in 1911, Ford had paid about twice the prevailing U.K. industrial wage, for a shorter work week.

The five-dollar minimum pay for a day's work was boldly conceived by Ford as a plan for sharing profits with his workers in advance of their being earned. "In accordance with Ford policy," writes Meyer, "wages were the 'earned' result of 'services and labor.' Profits were the conditional gift of the Ford Motor Company." [16] Thus, only workers who met certain criteria established by Ford were entitled to a share of the profits. The normal wage rate of a laborer at Ford was $2.34 per day, for example, while his profit rate under the plan was $2.66. The profit rate was paid to him as an incentive for cooperating in increasing the efficiency of Ford production. Eligible workers were those who had been at Ford for six months or more and were either married men living with and taking good care of their families, single men over twenty-two years of age of proved thrifty habits, or men under twenty-two years of age and women who were the sole support of some next of kin. Almost 60 percent of the Ford workers qualified immediately, and within two years about 75 percent were included in the profit-sharing plan.

The Sociological Department was formed to check on the eligibility of Ford employees to participate in the Five-Dollar Day and to ensure that the profits shared with them were put to uses approved by Henry Ford.

It was first headed by John R. Lee. He was succeeded in late 1915 by the Reverend Dr. Samuel S. Marquis, Ford's Episcopalian pastor, who changed its name to the Educational Department.

An initial staff of over 200 investigators, soon pared down to a permanent staff of 50, visited workers' homes gathering information and giving advice on the intimate details of the family budget, diet, living arrangements, recreation, social outlook, and morality. Americanization of the immigrant was enforced through mandatory classes in English. The worker who refused to learn English, rejected the advice of the investigator, gambled, drank excessively, or was found guilty of "any malicious practice derogatory to good physical manhood or moral character" was disqualified from the profit-sharing plan and put on probation. If he failed to reform within six months, he was discharged, and his profits accumulated under the plan were used for charity. Shockingly presumptuous, repressive, and paternalistic by today's standards, the policies of the Sociological/Educational Department reflected both the long-standing assumption of American businessmen that the employer had a right to interfere in the private lives of his employees and the most advanced theories of the social workers of the Progressive Era.

The Five-Dollar Day defied the conventional wisdom of classical economics, which called for paying wages at a subsistence level. Henry Ford implicitly acknowledged the validity of radical criticisms of income distribution under entrepreneurial capitalism when he told the Reverend Dr. Marquis that five dollars a day was "about the least a man with a family can live on these days." But Marquis knew that the five-dollar, eight-hour day "actually returned more dollars to [Henry Ford] than he gave out. It was unquestionably a shrewd and profitable stroke. To the credit of Mr. Ford be it said that he personally never maintained that his profit and bonus schemes were a means for distributing charity."[17]

Ford's motives for introducing his radical profit-sharing plan undoubtedly were mixed. He recognized ahead of his fellow industrialists that the worker was also a consumer and that increasing workers' purchasing power would stimulate sales. He also wanted to stave off the organizing efforts of the radical International Workers of the World (IWW). His main concerns, however, were increasing labor productivity and stopping an incredibly costly rate of labor turnover at Highland Park. "When the [profit-sharing] plan went into effect, we had 14,000 employees and it had been necessary to hire at the rate of about 53,000 a year in order to keep a constant force of 14,000," recounted Ford in 1922. "In 1915 we had to hire only 6,508 men and the majority of these new men were taken on because of the growth of the business. With the old turnover of labor and the present force we should have to hire at the rate of nearly 200,000 men a year—which would be pretty nearly an impossible proposition." Ford asserted in 1922 that "the payment of high wages fortunately contributes to the low costs [of production] because the men become steadily more efficient on account of being relieved of outside worries. The payment of five dollars a day for an eight-hour day was one of the finest cost-cutting moves we ever made, and the six-dollar day [instituted at Ford in 1919] is cheaper than the five. How far this will go we do not know." [18]

An estimated 15- to 20-percent increase in labor productivity at Highland Park in 1915 was attributed to the Five-Dollar Day. And with inauguration of the eight-hour day, Highland Park switched from running two shifts a day to three. The advertising and public-relations value alone was well more than the $5.8 million that the profit-sharing plan cost the Ford Motor Company during its first year of implementation. Henry Ford was roundly denounced as a "traitor to his class" by his fellow entrepreneurial capitalists, especially by his less efficient competitors in the automobile industry. The public response, on the other hand, was decidedly positive. "Nine-tenths of the newspaper comment was favorable, much of it almost ecstatic," write Nevins and Hill. "Industrialists, labor leaders, sociologists, ministers, politicians, all hailed the innovation in glowing terms." [19]

The Mussolini of Detroit

Although the eight-hour day and forty-eight-hour week quickly became the norm in American automobile factories, Henry Ford's doubling of the daily minimum pay stood for decades as an isolated example of self-interested benevolence. The strategy underlying the Ford profit-sharing plan did not become institutionalized in American industry until after World War II. Nor did the experiment in benevolent paternalism last longer than a few years at the Ford Motor Company. By 1918 the inflation of the World War I years had reduced the $5.00 minimum daily pay to only $2.80 in 1914 purchasing power, wiping out the workers' gains. As we have seen, the war also meant greatly reduced profit margins for Ford, and the company only survived the postwar recession by adopting stringent economy measures. As the 1920s wore on, as the Model T became outmoded and Ford's competitors became more efficient in production, the position of the Ford Motor Company in the automobile industry declined. Working conditions deteriorated with the speedup of the Ford assembly lines to meet the new competition. After the minimum daily pay of Ford workers was raised to $6.00 in January 1919, giving them $3.36 in 1914 purchasing power, there were no further advances in Ford wages until World War II. By the early 1920s $10.00 a day would have been necessary to match the $5.00 minimum pay of 1914. In 1925—Ford's pre–World War II high point in sales both in the United States and worldwide—the weekly earnings of Ford workers were $4.21 below the automobile industry average in the United States, although cutting the Ford work week to five days in 1926 reduced the gap to $1.37 by 1928.

The Educational Department folded and its records were burned after Samuel Marquis resigned as its head early in 1921. He later explained: "The old group of executives, who at times set justice and humanity above profits and production, were gone. With them, so it seemed to me, had gone an era of cooperation and good will in the company. There came to the front men whose theory was that men are more profitable to an industry when driven than led, that fear is a greater incentive to work than loyalty." [20]

Ford benevolent paternalism had actually ended earlier. Over the course of World War I, the company's labor policies had undergone, as Meyer puts it, "a transition from a variant of welfare capitalism, which captured the mood of the Progressive Era, to a version of the American Plan, which typified the more recalcitrant employer attitudes of the twenties." Under the Espionage Act of 1917 and the Sedition Act of 1918, at Ford "more authoritarian and more repressive labor policies moved to the foreground.... Under extremely broad judicial interpretations, both of these laws were used to prosecute German, Austrian, and Hungarian immigrant workers, members of the IWW and the Socialist Party, and finally, any worker who voiced discontent with the war or American society." [21]

The American Protective League (APL) was created as a "semiofficial auxiliary of the Justice Department," composed of some 250,000 volunteer "patriots" who were organized into a nationwide network of spies and informants in American industry. The Ford Educational Department coordinated the activities at Highland Park of about a hundred APL operatives, who were given access to the thousands of individual "records of investigation" maintained on employees under the Ford profit-sharing plan. Should an APL operative report suspicious statements or behavior by a Ford worker, his file would be pulled and a new record started containing an account of the incident. "This new record on the worker often passed into the hands of the Department of Justice, military intelligence officers, and local law enforcement officers," Meyer reports. Ford officials made high worker productivity a patriotic duty and considered any worker activity that retarded production to be, in Meyer's words, "a conscious and treasonable act of sabotage." [22]

APL activities ostensibly ceased at Highland Park with the Armistice. However, under Alex Spark in the Superintendent's Office, the Ford APL organization was converted in 1919 into a network of labor spies and informants whose mission was to thwart the organizing efforts of the Automobile Workers Union (AWU). Although all automobile manufacturers in the 1920s employed labor spies and informants to ferret out union organizers, the Ford Motor Company gained particular notoriety.

Citing the Ford Motor Company as the world's outstanding example of an industrial dictatorship, the *New York Times* on January 8, 1928, called Henry Ford "an industrial fascist—the Mussolini of Detroit." Probusiness *Fortune* magazine commented in December 1933 that it was well known in the automobile industry that "Mr. Ford's organization does show extreme evidence of being ruled primarily by fear of the job." Even Edsel was mercilessly bullied by the elder Ford, who thought his son too soft and held up as a model worthy of emulation Harry Bennett, an ex-pugilist with underworld connections. Bennett enforced discipline in the Ford plants as head of a gang of labor spies and thugs called the Ford Service Department. He came to be Henry Ford's most trusted associate and comrade after the Model A replaced the Model T in 1928 and production was shifted to the River Rouge plant.

From Edsel Ford on down, the Ford executives came to fear and despise Bennett as his influence grew, and by the mid-1930s Ford workers wondered whether Hitler had derived the idea for his Gestapo from Bennett's Ford Service. "As a rule, Ford's managers, having more to lose, came to watch their jobs more nervously than the men at the Rouge who swept the floor," relates Keith Sward. "On the lower tiers of the Ford organization, Ford Service gave rise to any number of unmistakable neuroses. These 'shop complaints' went all the way from mild states of anxiety to advanced nervous symptoms that were fit material for a psychopathic ward. Thus conditioned, the personality of any Ford employee was subjected to a process of subtle and profound degradation." Writing during the depths of the Great Depression, Jonathan Leonard, an early Ford debunker, declared, "Detroit is a city of hate and fear. And the major focus of that hatred and fear is the astonishing plant on the River Rouge." Leonard found almost all automobile factories in Detroit "horrifying and repellent to the last degree. But the Ford factory has the reputation of being by far the worst." The reason was that "over the Ford plant hangs the menace of the 'Service Department,' the spies and stool pigeons who report every action, every remark, every expression.... No one who works for Ford is safe from the spies—from the superintendents down to the poor creature who must clean a certain number of toilets an hour." [23]

Black Workers at Ford

With expansion into the Rouge plant and as labor relations deteriorated in the early 1920s, Ford hired more and more black workers. August Meier and Elliott Rudwick point out that Henry Ford was ambivalent in his attitude toward blacks: he believed that they were racially inferior and that the races should be segregated residentially and socially, but he also believed that blacks had constitutional rights to social justice and rights to decent housing, jobs, and economic security. He thought that the "superior" race was obligated "to give philanthropic service to subordinate races" and that "whenever blacks had received a fair chance their labor made them an asset to the community."[24]

Blacks first began moving en masse into northern cities, including Detroit, to take advantage of the employment opportunities created by the World War I labor shortage. Packard became the first significant employer of blacks in the automobile industry, with 1,000 on its payroll in May 1917. Working in close association with the Detroit Urban League, Dodge also was a substantial early employer of blacks. In contrast, as late as January 1916 the Ford Motor Company had only 50 black employees in a work force of 32,702.

As fears of labor unrest and labor organization mounted in 1919, Ford rapidly expanded his recruitment of blacks and within a year became Detroit's leading employer of them. Ford's black workers were concentrated at the Rouge, where by 1926 they numbered 10,000 and constituted about 10 percent of the work force. Despite cutbacks in employment during the Depression, the number and proportion of black workers at the Rouge remained fairly constant—9,325 in 1937, constituting about 12 percent of the Rouge work force. This contrasts with 2,800 blacks constituting a mere 3 percent of the entire General Motors Michigan work force as late as 1941. By the outbreak of World War II Ford employed about two thirds of the blacks working in Detroit's automobile factories.

Recruitment was carried out through recommendations from Detroit's most prominent black citizens—particularly from the Reverend Robert L. Bradby, pastor of the Second Baptist Church, and Father Everard W. Daniel, pastor of St. Matthew's Protestant Episcopal Church. Authority over black hiring, firing, disputes, and other matters was exercised by Donald J. Marshall, a former policeman and one of Father Daniel's parishioners, and Willis Ward, a black former football star at the University of Michigan. Marshall and Ward belonged to the Ford Service Department and reported directly to Harry Bennett and to Charles Sorensen. In effect, Ford had established a "Negro Department," with special procedures for black employees. And these procedures meant that black workers at Ford were under even more repressive scrutiny than white workers.

Although blacks employed in automobile factories earned relatively high wages in comparison with those employed in other industries, they tended to be concentrated in the most dangerous, dirty, and disagreeable jobs—chiefly in paint spraying and in foundry work. This was true at the Rouge, where fully 38 percent of the black workers were employed in the foundry and an additional 15.6 percent in the foundry machine shop, versus only 5.2 percent in motor manufacturing and assembly, 6 percent in chassis and parts manufacturing and assembly, and a minuscule 1 percent in the tool rooms. A white worker at the Rouge explained to an investigator, "Some jobs white folks will not do, so they have to take niggers in, particularly in duco work, spraying paint on car bodies. This soon kills a white man." Zaragosa Vargas demonstrates that although the relatively small number of Mexicans employed at the Rouge also were concentrated in the most disagreeable jobs, they were significantly less concentrated in them than were the blacks.[25]

Nevertheless, Meier and Rudwick find that "Henry Ford was unique in the wide range of opportunities that he offered Negro blue-collar workers." Blacks could be found in all Ford production jobs working alongside whites. Ford had more black supervisory personnel than the rest of the industry combined. In a few instances black foremen were in charge of all-white crews. Blacks were admitted to apprenticeship schools only at Ford. And in 1924 James C. Price, an outstanding expert in abrasives and industrial diamonds, became the first black salaried employee at Ford. Meier and Rudwick cite the labor economist Herbert Northrup's conclusion that in the pre–World War II period Ford's black workers at the Rouge "came closer to job equality ... than they did at any large enterprise ... recorded in the literature." Significantly, however, this was true only at the Rouge. Outside the Detroit metropolitan area Ford employed blacks in menial jobs only, primarily as custodians.[26]

The racist aspects of Henry Ford's unique treatment of his black workers were overlooked by Detroit's black community at a time when rabid Negrophobia was more characteristic of white employers than self-interested, benevolent paternalism. Black workers at Ford felt themselves superior and wore their company badges to church on Sunday. Black leadership, including the Detroit Urban League, praised Ford as a friend of the race who could do no wrong, "The income of Ford's black workers was the cornerstone for the prosperity of the black community's business and professional people," write Meier and Rudwick. "The latter, acutely aware of how much black Detroit's economic well-being and their own livelihood depended on the company, believed that what was best for Ford was best for the race." [27]

Consequently, Ford's black workers remained amazingly loyal to him despite the repressive activities of the Ford Service Department, the degeneration of working conditions at the Rouge, and the existence of tokenism rather than true equality of opportunity in the Ford plants. They demonstrated this loyalty by remaining in the River Rouge plant as strikebreakers during the 1941 strike that resulted in the unionization of the Ford Motor Company and the inauguration of a new era in Ford labor policy and labor–management relations.

Diffusion

8

Fordist production of the Model T was the most important factor in the development of automobile cultures in the interwar period, most spectacularly in the United States but also in neighboring Canada and in Australia and New Zealand. By 1927 there was one car for every 5.3 inhabitants in the United States; the ratio for New Zealand was 1:10.5, for Canada 1:10.7, and for Australia 1:16. The extent of the gap between these countries and the rest of the world in cars per capita is striking. Argentina ranked fifth with a ratio of 1:43; France and Great Britain tied for sixth place with ratios of 1:44. Germany still had only one car for every 196 inhabitants. Americans at this point owned about 80 percent of the world's motor vehicles. The countries of Western Europe did not achieve the ratio of cars to population of 1920s America until the 1950s and 1960s.

Throughout the 1920s Canada ranked second worldwide in motor vehicle production. For the decade 1919–1929 Canada's total production was 1.649 million motor vehicles, versus 1.452 million for France and 1.344 million for the U.K. The Canadian industry had begun on August 17, 1904, when the Ford Motor Company of Canada was incorporated and began production at Walkerville, near Windsor, Ontario, just across the border from Detroit. Ford assembly plants were added at Montreal, Toronto, Winnipeg, and Vancouver. General Motors operations in Canada began in 1910 with the acquisition of 40 percent of the stock of the McLaughlin Motor Company, which manufactured Buicks under license. In 1918 GM obtained full control of the McLaughlin enterprise. Chrysler, too, had Canadian operations by the late 1920s.

Some 83 percent of the "Canadian" automobile industry was American controlled by 1929. This American-owned Canadian industry exported about 42 percent of its output, with more than two thirds of the exported cars going to other British Commonwealth countries. Canada exported some 101,700 motor vehicles in 1929, versus exports of only 42,200 for the U.K. auto industry. Not only did the American-Canadian industry dominate the market in British Commonwealth countries, but Ford-Canada also took the lead in creating an Australian automobile industry by building a body factory and five assembly plants in Australia in the 1920s. General Motors began assembling cars in Australia in 1923, through a cooperative agreement with Holden Motor Body Builders of Adelaide, a leather firm that had begun to make automobile bodies. GM purchased Holden in 1931.

Australians, New Zealanders, and Canadians vastly preferred American cars over British makes, because American cars were cheaper, more reliable, and better suited to the primitive driving conditions that these countries shared with the United States. As early as 1912, the rugged Ford Model T had captured the Australian and New Zealand markets. By the mid-1920s Ford faced stiff competition down under from GM's Holden operations, and in fact GM came to outsell Ford in Australia. Together GM and Ford dominated the market. For the first six months of 1927, for example, Australian registrations (excluding Western Australia) showed that American cars held 81.4 percent of the market, compared with only 14.1 percent for British makes. Thus, the automobile cultures developing in 1920s Canada, Australia, and New Zealand were tightly integrated with the American car culture, through both manufacturing and marketing.

Contributing to this integration was a shared set of material conditions that permitted Americans, Australians, Canadians, and New Zealanders to actualize the possibilities of mass personal automobility a generation ahead of Europeans. The early automobile cultures developed in countries that had relatively low population densities, great distances to be bridged between small settlements in vast rural hinterlands, high per capita incomes, and equitable income distribution—a combination of conditions that added up to great effective demand for motorcars.

Automobile Ownership and Use: Class and Caste Dimensions

The withdrawal of the Model T from the market coincided with the realization of mature market conditions in the United States. The year 1927 was the first in which NACC statistics showed more new car sales for replacement demand in the United States than sales to first-time owners and multiple car sales combined. By 1927 every American who could afford a car already owned one, and the average life of an American-made passenger car was, according to the NACC, seven years. United States passenger car registrations then dramatically declined some 10 percent during the Great Depression of the 1930s. The record 1929 production of 5.3 million motor vehicles fell to a low of 1.3 million in 1932, and was not to be surpassed until 1949, when 6.3 million units were produced. United States registrations of motor vehicles dipped from 26.5 million in 1929 to 23.8 million in 1934 before bouncing back to 29.4 million in 1938; during World War II, automobile production for the civilian market was halted and severe restrictions were placed upon automobile use.

The patterns of automobile ownership and use in late-1920s America, then, represent a high point not surpassed until after World War II. Not only were the experiences of Americans vis-à-vis the motorcar very diverse, but at least up to the mid-1950s Americans were far less auto-dependent than has generally been recognized. Whereas 44 percent of American families did not own cars in 1927, 41 percent still lacked personal automobility in the form of the family car as late as 1950. This contrasts with only about 13 percent autoless American households at present.

Motor calculated in 1921 that ownership of a $600 automobile necessitated an annual income of at least $2,800 if one lived in a city and at least $1,936 if one lived in the country. The NACC estimated in 1924 that "the entire field of those receiving under $1,500 [in income] yearly is still unsupplied with motor transportation." The NACC thought that "growth in the motor vehicle market depends on the ability of the lower income brackets to purchase used cars, not necessarily new ones," and that industry policy ought to be "pouring in [new cars] at the top, with the used cars being traded in and going to a secondary market." By the mid-1920s the industry was plagued with "the used-car problem." Because each car that was traded in also meant a trade-in when it was sold, several traded-in used cars had to be disposed of—most often at a loss—in order to sell one new model. Still, the income distribution of Coolidge prosperity put the ownership of a $50 junker beyond the reach of most working-class families. The automobile trade journals were agreed in 1923 that "illiterate, immigrant, Negro and other families" were "obviously outside" the market for motorcars.[1]

The pattern of diffusion within the United States, as elsewhere in the world, was determined by the need for personal transportation of an overwhelmingly rural population not adequately served by mass rail transit, and by the distribution of incomes sufficient for the buying and running of cars. By the time the Model T was introduced, the early luxury market for cars among the wealthy in large cities was saturated. Rising farm incomes until the post–World War I recession and declining Model T prices combined to make midwestern farmers yearning to "get out of the mud" the mainstay of the developing automobile market. By the mid-1920s the Model T had become a rural necessity. Few farmers by then remained autoless.

Not only did automobility affect rural families decades earlier and far more deeply than city families, but suburbanites and village residents were affected differently from farm families; and farmers, tenant farmers, sharecroppers, and migrant farm workers were affected differently. "The difference was not necessarily one of car ownership itself," writes Joseph Interrante. "As many tenants as farmers owned cars: for example 89 percent of the tenants and 93 percent of the farmers in Iowa in 1926 had automobiles. More important than automobile ownership per se was their use of the car." Both a family's economic status and the size and character of the nearest village center determined the extent to which the family car could be used for recreation or social activities. And whereas both farmers and tenants used the car primarily to commute to town, "a migrant family's car was not only a means of consumption, but it was also the necessary basis for the migrant household's survival as a unit." [2]

Both automobile ownership and use progressively declined with extent of urbanization. A survey of car ownership among over 4.1 million American families conducted in 1927 by the General Federation of Women's Clubs showed slight differences in the percentage of families owning automobiles in cities of various sizes. The range was from a low of 54 percent of families owning cars in cities of 100,000 population and over, to a high of 60.5 percent for towns under 1,000 population. The survey showed overall that 55.7 percent of the 27.5 million families in the United States in 1927 owned automobiles and that 2.7 million of these families (18 percent of those owning automobiles) owned two or more cars. [3]

Because of the broad categories used, these data underestimated differences. As evidenced, at this time the ownership of automobiles by farmers was nearly universal. In contrast, automobile ownership was rare among the urban working class. Interrante presents data on use, for example, that show that in 1930 motor vehicles accounted for 20 to 30 percent of the daily traffic into the central business districts (CBD) of large cities, as contrasted with 50 to 60 percent in the case of medium-sized cities, while "222 cities with at least 10,000 residents were entirely dependent on motor transportation." He concludes that "the further one lived from the city the more advantageous car travel became." [4]

That two out of three Middletown families owned an automobile by 1924 demonstrates that the automobile had become a necessity to the "business class." Yet in their 1929 study of Muncie, Indiana, Robert and Helen Lynd went beyond their evidence to claim that "a working man earning $35.00 a week frequently plans to use one week's pay each month as payment for his car," and that "the automobile has apparently unsettled the habit of careful saving for some families." They also falsely reported that "the mobility afforded by new modes of transportation combines with ... periodic waves of employment, unemployment, and reemployment to diminish the tendency of workers in a given factory to live together immediately about the plant. This tendency toward decentralization of workers' dwellings means that ... those with whom one works may have their homes and other interests anywhere from one to two-score miles distant."

These generalizations were accurate for Middletown's "business class," but they would not hold true for the working class until the 1950s. This is demonstrated by the Lynds' own data, which they badly misinterpreted.

The Lynds secured data on automobile ownership from 123 Middletown working-class families. They found that among the 60 families that owned cars, 41 also owned homes, and that 26 had mortgages on their homes. In comparison, among the 63 working-class families that did not own cars, 40 owned homes and 29 had mortgages on them. "Obviously other factors are involved in many of Middletown's mortgages," understated the Lynds.

The incomes of 100 working-class families studied by the Lynds ranged from $345 for a family of eight to $3,460 for a family of five, an extremely wide range. Of the 51 families reporting incomes under $1,500 a year, only 16 owned automobiles. The combined expenditure for the year October 1, 1923, through September 30, 1924, reported for "purchase, license, gas, and upkeep" among these families ranged from $25 for a family of seven making $1,287 and $45 for a family of three making $588 to $345 for a family of five making $971. Only 7 of the 16 families owning cars reported a deficit. At the other extreme, 6 of the 9 families reporting an income of over $2,800 owned automobiles. Expenditures on cars among these families ranged from $110 for a family of four earning $2,876 to $777 for a family of four earning $3,356. Interestingly, the only one of these 9 families to run a deficit was a family of seven earning $3,198 that did *not* own an automobile, but spent $1,749 on investment in a home!

Similarly, data collected by the Lynds in 1924 revealed that 27.9 percent of Middletown's workers lived less than one-half mile from work, 27 percent between one-half mile and one mile, and 22.7 percent between one and two miles. Although these distances were measured "as the crow flies" and were consequently lower than actual travel distances, it is clear nonetheless that the overwhelming majority of Middletown's workers lived within walking distance of their work places.[5]

Such systematic data on car ownership and possible use are lacking in the Lynds' 1937 *Middletown in Transition*. We do know, however, that the ratio of cars to persons in Muncie increased slightly from 1:6.1 in 1924 to 1:5.2 in 1935; that new-car sales collapsed to only 29 percent of their 1929 level by 1932, then began to recover; that some Middletown workers lost their cars in the Depression; and that in the trough of the Depression the dollar volume of gasoline sales in Muncie declined by only 4 percent. The Lynds claimed that workers "do not readily segregate themselves from the rest of the city. They want what Middletown wants so long as it gives them their great symbol of advancement—an automobile. Car ownership stands to them for a large share of the 'American dream.'" The Lynds concluded, "Car ownership in Middletown was one of the most depression-proof elements of the city's life in the years following 1929"; "while ... people were riding in progressively older cars as the depression wore on, they manifestly continued to ride."[6] The point missed was that, however much the automobile may have become the "great symbol of advancement" to the working class, the "business class" was doing the bulk of this riding.

In his study of transportation and changing spatial patterns in Pittsburgh from 1850 to 1934, Joel A. Tarr documents both striking differences between middle-class and working-class patterns of automobile ownership and use and the minimal impact of automobilily on the urban working class. In 1934 only 45 percent of the chief wage earners in Pittsburgh owned automobiles, and only 20.3 percent of them drove their cars to work. In the surrounding suburban countryside, 56.7 percent of the chief wage earners owned automobiles and 25.5 percent drove them to work. Yet even these levels of ownership and use were significantly higher than those in predominantly working-class communities. "In the mill-oriented industrial third-class cities," notes Tarr, "even though 38 percent of the wage earners owned cars, only 12.4 percent of them used them to journey to work. Here with homes located close to the mills, 72.6 percent of the workers walked to work." He concludes that up to at least 1934, the automobile "had little impact on the spread of population in those sectors of [Allegheny] county with large mill town populations" and that "it was basically members of the employed middle and upper classes who were able to make the choice between a longer (and costlier) work-trip [by automobile] from the suburbs and lower land costs available on the [city] periphery."[7]

Because the upper and middle classes who could afford to buy and operate automobiles were also overwhelmingly white, urban blacks were especially disadvantaged by auto-induced urban decentralization. In his pathbreaking case study of the impact of the automobile on Atlanta from 1900 to 1935, for example, Howard L. Preston concludes that since whites "could generally better afford the price of an automobile, it gave them a novel advantage over black Atlantans: greater mobility and an opportunity to act out their racist views by moving away to planned suburban neighborhoods on the north side. Many of these communities were outside the city limits, and once there ... residents paid no city taxes and could effectively eschew the responsibility of paying to maintain adequate social services for those Atlantans who were less rich and less white. By 1930, if racism could be measured in miles and minutes, blacks and whites were more segregated in the city of Atlanta then ever before." [8]

Significantly, blacks also were not to share proportionately in the extension of the "American dream" of the automobile commute to a suburban home that was opened to the working class in the post–World War II period through a combination of rising working-class incomes due to the aggressiveness of the industrial unions formed in late 1930s, government guarantees of low-interest home loans to returning veterans, and the innovation of cheaper methods of suburban home construction by Abraham Leavitt in the late 1940s. The pervasive racism of American society continued to confine blacks to rural poverty or to central-city ghettos. "Industries [however] were no longer confined to central urban locations that employees could reach by mass transportation," Dan Lacy observed in 1972. "Suburban locations were especially attractive to electronic and service industries ... the most rapidly growing industries, providing the most attractive job opportunities. ... Consequently, blacks who could not afford to own or maintain cars in the city were hopelessly blocked from employment in precisely those types of plants in which opportunities were largest and most promising." Additionally, as Helen Leavitt documents, because the cheapest land was sought for their routes, ambitious programs for building urban freeways beginning in the mid-1950s resulted in the massive destruction of once viable poor and minority neighborhoods in order to accommodate the automobility of middle-class, white suburbanities. [9]

Automobility as Social Reform

Both the traditional horse culture and the horse and rail culture that superseded it in late-nineteenth-century America had many drawbacks. It is a moot point whether living conditions were worse in the slums of the metropolis or on the isolated farms of the rural hinterland.

In New York City alone at the turn of the century, horses deposited on the streets every day an estimated 2.5 million pounds of manure and 60,000 gallons of urine, accounting for about two thirds of the filth that littered the city's streets. Excreta from horses in the form of dried dust irritated nasal passages and lungs, then became a syrupy mass to wade through and track into the home whenever it rained. New York insurance actuaries had established by the turn of the century that infectious diseases, including typhoid fever, were much more frequently contracted by livery stable keepers and employees than by other occupational groups, and an appeal to the Brooklyn Board of Health to investigate resulted in the institution of new municipal regulations on stables, compelling more frequent removal of excreta and disinfecting of premises. Medical authorities stated that tetanus was introduced into cities in horse fodder and that an important cause of diarrhea, a serious health problem among city children at the time, was "street dust," consisting in the main of germ-laden dried horse dung. The flies that bred on the ever present manure heaps carried more than thirty communicable diseases, and the unsightliness and stench of the stable meant that most urban owners of horses "boarded and baited" them at public facilities an inconvenient distance from their residences. In addition, traffic was often clogged by the carcasses of overworked dray horses that dropped in their tracks during summer heat waves or had to be destroyed after stumbling on slippery pavements and breaking their legs. About 15,000 dead horses were removed from the streets of New York each year. Urban sanitation departments, responsible for daily cleaning up this mess, were not only expensive but typically graft- and corruption-ridden. A 1908 estimate that tried to take all factors into account concluded that the cost of not banning the horse from New York City was approximately $100 million a year. Finally, the city at the turn of the century was hopelessly overcrowded. New York's Lower East Side, for example, was estimated by the urban reformer Jacob Riis to have contained some 290,000 persons per square mile in 1890, making it then the world's most densely settled living area.

Although these conditions were characteristic in varying degree of all of our large and medium-sized cities, they were not experienced in the daily lives of most Americans, because most still lived in small rural hamlets or on farms. The 1920 United States census was the first to report a majority of our population residing in towns with 2,500 or more people. The residents of the rural hinterland, a majority of Americans until well into the twentieth century, were plagued not by overcrowding and unsanitary conditions but by isolation and lack of access to adequate medical care and to other urban amenities. Such profound differences in the environments of the "city slicker" and the "hayseed" underlay a division in turn-of-the-century American society based on residence comparable to those based on race, ethnicity, and class.

Norman T. Moline has examined the impact of transportation change between 1900 and 1930 on Oregon, Illinois, a village in the scenic Rock River Valley some 100 miles west of Chicago, its population ranging from 1,577 to 2,376 over the period of the study. In 1900 the local roads were unpaved and impassable by horse-drawn vehicles for much of the year. Three eastbound and three westbound trains stopped each day on the main Burlington line from Chicago to Minneapolis, and additionally there was twice-daily train service to towns to the northwest. Thirteen proposals to extend electric interurban service to Oregon were made between 1894 and 1913. None materialized.

Oregon's rail service was undoubtedly better than that of most villages and hamlets in the Midwest and the West. Still, it left a great deal to be desired. Travel to places not on the main rail line involved lengthy layovers, because the schedules of different railroads did not coincide. Transfers were in general not available. Routes were circuitous, and mainline trains usually passed through small towns such as Oregon at inconvenient hours, because schedules were arranged to provide convenient departure and arrival times at major cities. Fares averaged 2 or 2½ cents a mile in the early 1900s, which "while not extremely expensive, was sufficiently expensive to be a limiting factor for frequent travel by persons with average economic means." Special rates offered by the railroads for holiday and group travel on special occasions "were exceptions and help to prove the point that regular rail travel was more expensive than the average budget could sustain." It took from one and a half to three hours to get 22 miles from Oregon to neighboring Rockford by rail, four and a half hours to return on the 5:15 P.M. train. The trip took four hours by horse and buggy. To get 16 miles from Oregon to neighboring Dixon took an hour and a half by rail, two and a half to three hours by horse and buggy. The result was that "for many there simply was little or no travel."[10]

Not surprisingly, a major theme of rural reformers was the extension of city amenities to the village, hamlet, and farm, while urban planners and reformers of the so-called Progressive Era stressed the need to decentralize the city. In densely populated Western Europe, where no one lived much farther than ten miles from a railroad, this critical American problem of homogenizing space was not nearly so important.

The electric streetcar was sanitary, not subject to organic malfunctions, and faster than the horse. However, it was not flexible. If a single trolley got stalled on the tracks, the normal flow of traffic was halted. Most important, an urban transportation system based upon electric-powered traction required huge expenditures for its rail infrastructure. As construction costs mounted during the 1890s, it began to become questionable whether even in large cities adequate mass-transit rail systems could be built, especially since freight still had to be moved in the central city by horse-drawn trucks, and passengers had to get from the streetcar stop to their ultimate destinations by horse, bicycle, or foot. In any event, the expense of electric-powered rail systems made them seem practical only in areas with high population densities. It did not seem feasible financially to extend them to the sparsely settled outskirts of the city, much less to villages such as Oregon or to the farm. The potential of electric-powered traction both to decentralize the city and to extend city amenities into rural areas was thus severely limited.

The motor vehicle offered an attractive alternative because it combined the flexibility of the horse with the speed of the locomotive or electric trolley, without the costly liability of a system of fixed rails and overhead wires. General adoption of the automobile promised to relieve taxpayers of the high cost of removing tons of excreta daily from city streets and to eliminate huge expenditures for endless miles of track, overhead wires, and networks of elevated platforms and/or tunnels, and with this the graft and corruption that too often seemed to be associated with building urban mass transit systems. It was facilely assumed that the cost of improving city streets for antiseptic automobile traffic would be negligible. Further, it was anticipated that urban traffic congestion and parking problems would disappear, because automobiles were more flexible than streetcars running on fixed rails and took up only half the space of horse-drawn vehicles. According to an 1896 article in *Scientific American*, for example, "The existence of a double line of cars moving on a fixed track and claiming the right of way over other vehicles is a hindrance to traffic and is itself delayed." If these rails were removed, the street asphalted from curb to curb, and the streetcars replaced by motor vehicles that could pass one another at will, "the whole volume of traffic would move with less interruption than at present, and . . . the cars themselves would make faster time." [11] The idea of asphalt pavement, too slippery for horses, was obviously predicated on a horseless city.

Not only was the motorcar considered cleaner, safer, more reliable, and more economical than the horse, but it promised to be vastly improved and lowered in price in the near future, whereas the expense and liabilities of the horse seemed unalterable. A horse-drawn rig was capable of a top speed of only 6 to 8 mph, and its maximum range was only about 25 miles before the horses had to be rested. The average life of a dray horse was only two or three years. Safety was a major concern. For example, *Harper's Weekly* noted in 1899 that "a good many folks to whom every horse is a wild beast feel much safer on a machine than behind a quadruped, who has a mind of his own, and emotions which may not always be forestalled or controlled." Lacking the physical strength to control a spirited, skittish team, women in particular were impressed with the advantages of the motorcar, especially the noiseless, odorless electric car, which did not require one to learn to shift gears. Even the crude brakes on early motorcars were vastly superior to those on horse-drawn vehicles, and it was widely believed that an automobile going 20 mph could be stopped in less space than a horse-drawn rig being driven at a moderate trot. The motor vehicle was also much more maneuverable than the horse-drawn vehicle, requiring considerably less space for turning around because of its shorter length. In addition, it was impervious to weather conditions and fatigue. Countless tests demonstrated to the public that the motor vehicle was cheaper than the horse. It depreciated less rapidly and did about three times the work for the same amount in operating expenses. Physicians, who drove their horses hard on calls, invariably reported that the automobile was more economical as well as more reliable. There was general agreement at the turn of the century that "the displacement of the horse will cheapen living and travel, certainly not increase them." [12]

Henry Ford once phrased nicely the auto enthusiast's program for urban reform: "We shall solve the city problem by leaving the city." [13] Thus, the facile answer to the slum was that tenement dwellers should buy motorcars and commute to suburbia. Commentators stressed the "autopian" advantages of suburban living. For example, in 1904 William F. Dix wrote in the *Independent*: "Imagine a healthier race of workingmen toiling in cheerful and sanitary factories, with mechanical skill and tradecraft developed to the highest, as the machinery grows more delicate and perfect, who, in the late afternoon, glide away in their own comfortable vehicles to their little farms or houses in the country or by the sea twenty or thirty miles distant! They will be healthier, happier, more intelligent and self-respecting citizens because of the chance to live among the meadows and flowers of the country instead of in crowded city streets." [14]

Similarly, the general adoption of the automobile by farmers promised to break down the isolation of rural life, lighten farm labor, and reduce significantly the cost of transporting farm products to market, thereby raising the farmers' profits while lowering food prices paid by city consumers. A writer in *Outing Magazine* predicted in 1902, for example, that with the general adoption of the automobile "the millions of our rural population will be brought into closer relations with the towns and with neighbors, and the loneliness of farm life, which drives so many to the cities, with detriment to all, will no longer retard our agricultural growth, nor prevent a proper distribution of population for the national welfare." [15]

Mass Motorization in Southern California

California led the nation in 1929 as it had in 1910 in ratio of population to motor vehicle registrations. It remained true as well that the leading regions in motor vehicles per capita were still the Pacific and the West North Central states and that the South continued to lag behind the rest of the country in adopting the automobile. But the gaps among the various regions of the United States already had closed appreciably by 1920. During the decade 1910–1920 automobile registrations increased more rapidly in the Rocky Mountain states and in the South, the early laggards in adopting the automobile, than in the East North Central, Middle Atlantic, and New England states. Although the agricultural states of the trans-Mississippi West continued to be the largest market for new cars, and California remained known as a bottomless pit for automobile sales, regional differences in the diffusion of the motorcar were becoming less significant. With a United States average of 10.1 persons for every motor vehicle registered in 1921, California ranked first with a ratio of 5.2:1 and Mississippi last with 27.5:1. By 1929 the United States average was 4.5:1. California still led the states with 2.3:1, and Alabama ranked last with 9:1. Long-distance trucking and a new mobility of people were beginning to open up the Pacific Coast and the Southwest to commercial development, make specialized regional economies more interdependent, and lessen the distinctiveness of regional lifeways.

A lifestyle based on mass personal automobility first developed in Southern California, and nowhere in the world has mass motorization been more pervasive in its impact. "Mass motorization of the region was largely accomplished during the ... span of the single decade following World War I," Ashleigh Brilliant relates. "Since the earliest days of motoring, Southern California, with its benevolent climate, attractive scenery, and relatively good roads, had been regarded as a 'motorist's paradise.' Until the postwar decade, however, the automobile was considered primarily as a means of recreation. For more practical purposes there was the Pacific Electric Railway, world famous for the efficiency of its service." [16]

Los Angeles has been called "a city built on transport." Its first population boom followed the completion of the Santa Fe Railroad line in 1885. Competition with the Southern Pacific reduced the railroad fare from Kansas City, Missouri, to only one dollar, bringing a flood of tourists and fortune seekers. Invalids and retired couples in particular sought the region's dry air and sunshine. Many came for a winter vacation and stayed on as permanent residents. Midwestern farmers relocated to become citrus growers.

In contrast with the immigrants to eastern and midwestern cities in the late nineteenth century, the immigrants to Southern California were older, overwhelmingly native-born and white, and relatively affluent. The largest proportion came from the rural Middle West, where a highly decentralized residential pattern was the norm. "Americans came to Los Angeles with a conception of the good community which was embodied in single-family houses, located on large lots, surrounded by landscaped lawns, and isolated from business activities," Robert Fogelson points out. "Their vision was epitomized by the residential suburb—spacious, affluent, clean, decent, permanent, predictable, and homogeneous.... Here then was the basis for the extraordinary dispersal of Los Angeles." [17]

A decade prior to this first population boom, the Southern Pacific had built five lines radiating out from Los Angeles to San Fernando, San Bernardino, Anaheim, Wilmington (near the San Pedro port), and Santa Monica. Reyner Banham observes that this rail system "constitutes the bones of the skeleton on which Greater Los Angeles was to be built, the fundamentals of the present city where each of these old lines is now duplicated by a freeway." He goes on to note that "subdivision of adjoining land proceeded as fast as the laying of rails" and that "commuting began almost as soon as the rails were down.... Before 1880 then, the railways had outlined the form of the city and sketched in the pattern of movement that was to characterize its peculiar pattern of life." [18]

Horse-drawn streetcars began to connect the Los Angeles business district with fashionable residential areas in 1876, then suburban development began in 1887 when an electric trolley line began to operate from downtown out Pico Street to serve the Electric Railway Homestead Association Tract. This was the first of a number of trolley lines built by real estate developers out to large tracts of land in outlying areas that they subdivided into homesites. Easy access to downtown by trolley was emphasized in advertising the lots. "Often mechanically unreliable, and even more often on unsound financial footings, the street railways rarely turned profits as transportation businesses, though they often contributed to huge speculative profits in real estate," Martin Wachs writes. Building street railways out to low-density population areas was feasible because of these huge profits and because "Los Angeles ... was just growing to maturity as a city when street railways were introduced and it had never developed a significant commercial and industrial core." [19]

Between 1901 and 1911 some 72 separate street railways were merged, reorganized, consolidated, and extended into the Pacific Electric

Railway by Henry Edmunds Huntington, the heir of Southern Pacific magnate Collis P. Huntington. By 1911 this constituted the largest electric interurban system in the United States. Pacific Electric served 56 communities within a 100-mile radius over 1,164 miles of standard-gauge track with its "Big Red Cars." The associated Los Angeles Railway Company operated streetcars over an additional 316 miles on narrow-gauge track within the city of Los Angeles. Proximity to streetcar lines, observes Mark Foster, "continued to be an important prerequisite for successful development until the 1920s. City maps drawn in 1902 and as late as 1919 show few streets more than five or six blocks from streetcar lines." [20]

Critics of urban sprawl have erroneously blamed the Southern California freeway system for making Los Angeles not a city but a collection of suburbs in search of a city. The unchecked horizontal growth of Greater Los Angeles in fact preceded rather than followed from mass motorization in the 1920s. Wachs notes that by 1910, "largely because of the Pacific Electric System, Los Angeles was functionally integrated with Long Beach, Santa Monica, and San Bernardino. The extent of the metropolitan region has not grown substantially since then, and most of the recent growth has consisted instead of filling in the spaces between outlying areas associated with important stations on the Pacific Electric." The Southern California freeway system closely parallels the 1923 Pacific Electric route map, which, as Banham says, "pretty well defines Greater Los Angeles as it is today." The socioeconomic impact of the Big Red Cars has been most thoroughly examined by Spencer Crump. "Unquestionably," he writes, "it was the electric interurbans which distributed the population over the countryside during the century's first decade and patterned Southern California as a horizontal city rather than one of skyscrapers and slums." [21]

Southern California's second great population boom occurred during the 1920s, when the population of Los Angeles County grew from 1.2 million to 2.2 million. By 1930 only 20 percent of Angelinos had been born in California. At the time, C. Warren Thornwaite characterized this mass movement as "the greatest internal migration in the history of the American people." "Like earlier booms, it was fostered by speculators, bankers, and businessmen," Wachs relates. "In 1921, the 'All Weather Club' was formed to advertise the wonders of Southern California in the East and especially to promote tourism, in the belief that a substantial proportion of those who vacationed in Southern California would be 'sold' on the idea of staying permanently." [22]

Whereas earlier affluent vacationers generally had shipped their open touring cars out from the East by rail, the combined effect in the 1920s of improved roads, better tourist services, and the closed car was that increasingly people came to Southern California in their motorcars. Motorization proliferated much faster than population. Between 1919 and 1929, while the population of Los Angeles roughly doubled, automobile registrations increased 550 percent, from about 141,000 to 777,000. Remarked city planner Gordon Whitnall in 1930, "So prevalent is the use of the motor vehicle that it might be said that Southern Californians have added wheels to their anatomy."[23] Although ridership on the Pacific Electric System increased into the 1930s, it failed to expand proportionately with population growth as more and more riders switched to motorcars. Significantly, the level of mass motorization, as measured by the ratio of motor vehicles to people, has not greatly increased in over half a century. Los Angeles County had one motor vehicle for every 2.85 persons in 1929 and one motor vehicle for every 1.7 persons in 1979, to lead the nation in automobiles per capita at both dates.

Despite Southern California's highly decentralized settlement pattern, a 1931 traffic study showed that over twice as many motor vehicles entered the Los Angeles central business district (CBD) as entered the CBDs of other large American cities. During identical twelve-hour periods, some 277,000 motor vehicles entered the Los Angeles CBD, while among cities with roughly equal-sized CBDs 113,000 entered in Chicago, 66,000 in Boston, and only 49,000 in St. Louis. Moreover, despite the fact that Los Angeles developed as a post-automobile city, its streets were the narrowest and most disconnected and it devoted the least land area to streets in its CBD of any large city in the United States. For example, in 1924 only 21.4 percent of the Los Angeles CBD was devoted to streets, compared with a range of 29 to 44 percent for other large American cities. This gave Los Angeles the most severe automobile traffic congestion in the world in the pre–World War II period. Downtown traffic snarls were already so bad during the 1919 Christmas shopping season that the city put into effect on April 10, 1920, a ban on street parking during business hours. Business dropped off so sharply that the ban was revised on April 26 to apply only during the evening rush hours.

Mass motorization fit hand in glove with a Southern California economy that necessitated the dispersion of business locations. For good reasons, a commercial-industrial core never developed in Los Angeles. To begin with, fear of earthquake damage led after 1906 to a 150-foot limitation on the height of downtown buildings, which remained in effect until the mid-1950s. Citrus growing, the movie industry, and later the aircraft industry required large tracts of land available only in the suburbs. The petroleum industry, central to the local economy, located facilities where oil was found or near the port from which it was shipped. As petroleum exports mounted, by 1930 the port of Los Angeles had come to rank third in total commerce and second in tonnage in the United States. The port facilities and related commercial activity were located along forty miles of waterfront in the Long Beach, San Pedro, and Wilmington areas, whose northern edge was about twenty miles distant from the traditional commercial core of the city. New residential communities sprang up between downtown Los Angeles and the port area. Wachs notes that although manufacturing industries grew, the segment of the work force engaged in manufacturing declined from 28 percent in 1920 to 22 percent in 1930. "Los Angeles was increasingly described as a 'white collar' town; real estate, finance, and tourism expanded most prominently." [24]

Thus, mass motorization neither caused the dispersion of economic activities nor changed the form of residential patterns in Southern California. However, the motor vehicle permitted decentralization that went well beyond what had been possible with electric traction. And this created a new urban lifestyle in Southern California that uniquely combined big-city amenities with low population density, single-family housing, and unparalleled individual mobility and access to outdoor recreation.

In areas close to the central business district that were served well by streetcars—such as Hawthorne, Inglewood, and Gardena in the South Bay area—mass motorization had little impact. There was a substantial increase, however, in the number of new subdivisions opened as mass motorization enabled real estate promoters to develop tracts of land remote from streetcar lines. The development of the San Fernando Valley was the prime example. The number of new subdivision maps recorded soared from 346 in 1920 to peak of 1,434 in 1923. With this new suburban construction, the amount of land converted to urban use in the Los Angeles area increased from 14.2 percent in 1924 to 24.4 percent a decade later. Construction of single-family residential dwellings accounted for 75 percent of this urban land use in the area between 8.6 and 10.3 miles from downtown Los Angeles.

The 1930 United States census revealed that 93.7 percent of the dwelling units in Los Angeles were single-family homes—the highest proportion of any American city—and that population density in the Greater Los Angeles area was only 2,812 persons per square mile. This contrasted with densities of over 23,000 persons per square mile in New York City, nearly 18,000 persons per square mile in Boston, and nearly 17,000 in Chicago. Single-family residences accounted for less than 53 percent of the dwelling units in all three of these cities.

The movement of population outward plus traffic congestion led to the rapid decline of downtown Los Angeles, as businesses and professional offices located outside the central business district. Between 1920 and 1930 the proportion of banks located outside the CBD increased from 45 percent to 89 percent, theaters from 26 percent to 80 percent, dentists' offices from 16 percent to 55 percent, and physicians' offices from 21 percent to 67 percent. The proportion of residents living within a ten-mile radius of the CBD who entered it daily declined from 68 percent in 1924 to 52 percent in 1931.

"The impact of the automobile upon Los Angeles's urbanization process compared to that in other cities is distinguished chiefly by its magnitude," Foster concludes. "Both critics and defenders of Los Angeles's decentralization generally concede that by 1930 the city was in many respects the prototype of the mid-twentieth-century metropolis." [25] This is most forcefully demonstrated by an examination of the parallel impact of the automobile on southern cities during the 1920s.

The Automobile Revolution in the New South

A combination of notoriously poor roads and a per capita income less than half the national average discouraged car makers from developing southern markets until demand began to be met in other regions. Southern interest in the automobile was first sparked by the 1909 National Association of Automobile Manufacturers show in Atlanta—the first national auto show held outside New York or Chicago—then stimulated by Glidden reliability tours from New York City to Texas (1910) and to Jacksonville, Florida (1911). Urban businessmen in the South were particularly enthusiastic promoters of the motor vehicle, perceiving its potential both to bring more customers into downtown commercial districts and to make outlying areas accessible for commercial and residential expansion. "General community sentiment," observes Blaine A. Brownell, "was that the motorcar contributed to 'progress' and to the prospects for material prosperity. An era marked by widespread automobile travel was welcomed as one both modern and affluent." [26]

Brownell sketches the impact of motorization on southern urban areas in the 1920s. Even though the South lagged behind the rest of the country in adopting the automobile, "the motorcar's overall influence on the South was massive. The region's transportation system was probably revolutionized to a greater extent by the motor vehicle than was the case elsewhere, and the traditional provinciality of the rural South was radically altered by new highways." By 1929 the percentage of retail businesses listed in the automobile category by the Bureau of the Census for major southern urban areas ranged from 14.2 in New Orleans to 20.7 in Birmingham. "[The automobile's] total economic significance is virtually impossible to compute with precision, but it would probably be measured in the billions of dollars in major southern cities alone." Sunday blue laws gave way to automobility, and problems caused by the automobile became the most time-consuming item on the agendas of southern city councils.[27]

Howard Preston believes that automobility "has influenced all of southern life and played a leading role in producing the modern South." In his study of Atlanta during the period 1900–1935, he documents "the impact of this new means of horizontal mobility on a relatively young, not yet fully developed, American city, whose spatial and demographic characteristics were in the process of being determined." In 1903 Atlanta was at a similar stage of development to that of Los Angeles. Atlanta had a somewhat smaller population (96,550 versus 116,420), covered a much smaller area (11 square miles versus 42.8 square miles), and consequently had a much higher population density (8,777 persons per square mile versus 2,719). In contrast to Los Angeles, Atlanta was a biracial, bicultural city, with about 43 percent black residents in 1903, the overwhelming majority of whom were poor. Atlanta in 1903 had about a third of the street railway track that Los Angeles had per square mile (0.092 mile versus 0.268), slightly more inhabitants per mile of street railway track (805 versus 795), and an even higher proportion of unpaved streets (68.36 percent versus 50.22 percent). Like Los Angeles, Atlanta was "a progeny of transportation," having been founded in 1837 as a terminus for the Western and Atlantic Railroad. But it was a railroad terminus in the nonindustrial, cotton-dependent, Civil War–devastated South, which had not yet recovered fully from Sherman's march to the sea. Consequently, in sharp contrast with booming Los Angeles, turn-of-the-century Atlanta "was well behind even moderately sized American cities in its development, and with such a slow rate of growth there was little reason to expect the first few decades of the twentieth century to be any different."[28]

Turn-of-the-century Atlanta was a "walking city," where more attention was given to the construction and maintenance of sidewalks than of streets. Its circumferential shape and land area roughly approximated Boston's a half century earlier. Not one of Atlanta's 22 public schools was located more than a mile and three quarters from the central business district, and about half of its 121 churches were located within a mile of the CBD. Some 59 percent of Atlanta's grocery stores were located within one mile of the city's center, with another 37 percent located within two miles. Atlanta's streets radiated in a grid pattern at right angles from the railroad tracks that ran through the city into its central business district. New grid patterns were attached to the original railroad-oriented one by street railways in the late nineteenth century.

The city grew outward in a star-shaped pattern along streetcar lines.

However, the impact of electric traction in dispersing Atlanta's population was minimal. The reason was that, as in all southern cities except Memphis, far fewer people per track mile were served by streetcars in Atlanta than in northern cities.

Because they were conceived as adjuncts to real-estate speculation rather than as profit-making transportation companies, the street railways and electric interurbans in Southern California were able to disperse a population only about a third as dense as Atlanta's over a land area four times as large. Elsewhere, however, expansion depended on making profits from ridership. Compared with Atlanta's 805 persons per mile of street railway track in 1903, New York had 2,809 persons per mile of track, Boston 2,413, and Chicago 2,026.

Yet even with such high densities of potential riders, electric traction could only decentralize the walking city to a very limited degree. For example, the land area of Boston at the turn of the century was about 43 square miles. In his now classic 1962 study of the impact of street railways on Boston's growth, Sam Bass Warner, Jr., credits the electrification of street railways in the 1880s and 1890s with bringing "convenient transportation to at least the range of six miles from City Hall. The rate of building and settlement in this period became so rapid that the whole scale and plan of Greater Boston was entirely made over." He goes on to modify this claim, however: "By 1900 the expansion of crosstown street railway service had carried the band of lower middle class construction to a position 2.5 to 3.5 miles from City Hall. The gross area of this band was about equal to the area of the old walking city." The gain was so minimal that in 1900 even an area this close to City Hall still "had been only partially built upon" and possessed "large suburban lots." Warner further observes that "the costs of new construction were such as to exclude at least half the families of Boston." Awareness of these limitations on the democratic dispersal of population by electric traction leads him to conclude that the automobile "allows a less rigid class arrangement and less dense housing than was possible under streetcar transportation." [29]

As in Los Angeles, the automobile displaced the streetcar as the predominant means of transportation in Atlanta during the 1920s. Of the 20,363 motor vehicles registered in 1920 in Fulton County, 8,525 were registered in Atlanta, a ratio of one car for every 22 people. The population of Atlanta more than doubled from 1903 to 1920, then increased another 34 percent to 252,398 by 1930, while the number of motor vehicles registered in Fulton County tripled to 64,243. Up to the mid-1920s streetcar service in Atlanta was relatively good, and there was a steady increase in streetcar patronage. By the mid-1920s, however, the great expansion of Atlanta's population and the commercialization of its central area had created a severe housing shortage. The combination of low prices for lots in outlying areas, low interest rates, and the automobile consequently led to "an unprecedented wave of suburbanization" in Atlanta. "The inabiltiy of the street railway to serve a growing suburban area then became wholly apparent," Preston writes. "Streetcar tracks did not extend into the new outlying areas under construction, and with the automobile by then in use, the decision on whether or not to construct additional lines into these suburban areas was crucial." [30]

The reason that the lines were not extended is that it did not seem profitable to do so. The Georgia Railroad and Power Company began to show losses on its street railway operations in 1921. By 1923 the company earned an average of only 5 cents a car mile and showed losses on eleven of the twenty-three lines it operated. Even were business to turn profitable, the Georgia Public Service Commission, a state regulatory agency, limited the company's annual profits to 8 percent of capital investment, meaning that the most the company could hope to make each year on a risky $1-million investment was only $80,000.

Suburbs were planned to attract residents able to afford housing within certain price ranges beginning at middle-income levels. And historic patterns of discrimination in education and employment resulted in the close correlation of income with race and ethnicity in the United States. Consequently, whether movement to the suburbs occurred by streetcar or by motorcar, in Los Angeles or in Atlanta, the result was bound to be further segregation of the population into increasingly homogeneous neighborhoods. Mass motorization simply permitted this to happen faster and on a far greater scale than electric traction.

Despite white flight by automobile to the suburbs, the racial composition of Atlanta's population did not change during the 1920s. Thirty-four and one-tenth percent of Atlantans were black in 1920, 33.5 percent in 1930. There was a dramatic change, however, in the racial composition of neighborhoods within the city with the outward movement of population. Ward 1 near the city's center went from 56.8 percent black in 1900 to 66.5 percent in 1910, 78.4 percent in 1920, and 96.1 percent 1930. The newer wards on the outskirts of the city, in contrast, were virtually all white. Blacks comprised only 0.18 percent of the 19,531 Atlantans residing in Ward 12 and Ward 13 in 1930.

In 1917, although only 10,000 motor vehicles were then registered in Fulton County, the *Atlanta Constitution* estimated that automobile-related businesses were annually grossing between $40 and $50 million and that the combined annual salaries of some 5,000 persons employed by them was between $7.5 and $8 million. An annual $50 million of Atlanta's bank clearings was attributed to retail automobile sales. By 1920 there were

80 automobile dealers in Atlanta and 236 other automobile-related businesses, such as gas stations, garages, and accessory dealers. In 1922 there were 153 garages alone. More than 100 new buildings had been constructed to house these new businesses, and an "automobile row" sprang up on formerly fashionable Peachtree Street between Ellis Street and Ponce de Leon Avenue, creating many new jobs.

The economic impact of the suburban construction boom was tremendous. A slump in new housing construction saw only 552 single-family dwellings built in Atlanta in 1920. Between 1921 and 1929, however, 12,768 new single-family homes were built, not even counting those in automobile suburbs outside the city limits. Before motorization, property values had been highest along streetcar lines. With motorization, suburban land values soared.

White flight beyond the city limits occurred in part because of lower property taxes, and had as one result the loss of Atlanta's middle-class tax base, at the very time that the dispersal of population within the city and accommodation to motorization necessitated expanded services. Not only was Fulton County assessment pegged at 70 percent of Atlanta assessment at an 0.5 lower millage rate, but Atlantans were required by law to pay both city and county property taxes. Translated into dollars and cents, this meant that the annual tax on a $10,000 single-family home was $209.10 in Atlanta but only $101.80 outside the city limits. Yet suburban commuters profiting from these lower property taxes daily drove to work over city streets and were dependent on other city services. By 1937 Atlantans living within the city limits were paying five sixths of Fulton County's taxes. "This meant," notes Preston, "that Atlantans within the city limits, one third of whom were black, were subsidizing the necessary municipal services of unincorporated Fulton County residents, who were overwhelmingly white and, as a whole, better able to afford the price of police and fire protection, public health care, sewage, and street repairs than those Atlantans living inside the city." [31]

The decline of Atlanta's downtown and the decentralization of business followed in the 1920s from a combination of the outward flow of population and traffic congestion in the CBD. Gas stations and retail food-related businesses led in following customers out to new neighborhoods. In 1918, 8 of Atlanta's 14 gas stations were one mile or less from the city center; only 64 of its 321 stations were within one mile in 1930. Food-related businesses on Whithall Street, one of the most important downtown retail thoroughfares, declined from 24 in 1902 to 13 in 1916 to only 4 in 1930. Conversely, the proportion of retail grocery stores over two miles from the city center increased from 9.7 percent in 1916 to 25.9 percent in 1930. A typical CBD casualty was Thomas H. Pitts's drug and sundries store, operated at the Five Points intersection of Edgewood Avenue and Decatur Street since the turn of the century. Pitts closed his doors on October 1, 1926. "I think the real thing that did it was automobiles and more automobiles," he explained. "Traffic got so congested that the only hope was to keep going. Hundreds used to stop; now thousands pass. Five Points has become a thoroughfare, instead of a center.... A central location is no longer a good one for my sort of business." [32]

In 1930 the Bureau of the Census ranked Atlanta as a "metropolis," an urbanized area in which "all adjacent and contiguous civil divisions [had] a density of not less than 150 inhabitants per square mile." Population in the area outside Atlanta's city limits grew during the 1920s at about twice the rate of population within the city, with the result that by 1930 some 100,554 of Metropolitan Atlanta's 370,920 people lived outside the city limits. "By 1935 existing governmental boundaries bore little relationship to the pattern of human settlement," Preston concludes. Completion of the Dixie Highway in 1929 "marked the rebirth of Atlanta as a regional metropolis and redefined the city in terms of interstate travel by motor vehicle rather than by rail. Years later, with the automobile as America's primary means of mass transportation, Atlanta became the crossroads of the Southeast—the point at which converged three major southeastern highways: I-20, I-75, and I-85." [33]

Megalopolis

The trends observable in Los Angeles and Atlanta were typical. By the outbreak of World War II, mass motorization had reorganized American urban and rural space into what the President's Research Committee on Social Trends in 1933 called "metropolitanism." "By reducing the scale of local distance," the committee pointed out, "the motor vehicle extended the horizon of community and introduced a territorial division of labor among local institutions and neighboring cities which is unique in the history of settlement. The large [urban] center has been able to extend the radius of its influence.... Moreover, former independent towns and villages and also rural territory have become part of the enlarged city complex." [34]

As early as 1922, some 135,000 suburban homes in 60 cities were already wholly dependent on automobile transportation. During the 1920s, suburbs grew twice as fast as did the cities they encircled, and by 1940 some 13 million Americans lived in communities lacking public transportation. Industry, too, began to move to the suburbs, and every city with a population greater than 100,000 experienced a severe decline in industrial employment in the period from 1920 to 1940. With suburban-ization the nineteenth-century "star" pattern of urban development along "rays" paralleling streetcar tracks was transformed into the development of constellations of interdependent centers within metropolitan regions, and these regions began to fuse into one another.

By 1937 the National Resources Committee could characterize the whole east coast from New York City to Philadelphia as "a single 'con-urbanized' band of metropolitan settlement." In 1961 geographer Jean Gottman described the eastern seaboard from southern New Hampshire to northern Virginia as "Megalopolis," a densely inhabited band of inter-connected and interdependent settlements "more the size of a nation than of a metropolis." He found that in Megalopolis the traditional distinctions between "rural" and "urban" were no longer meaningful.[35]

Associated with this revolutionary transformation of traditional set-tlement patterns by the motor vehicle was the massive restructuring of institutions. "Among the many factors which contributed toward the expansion of local taxes [between 1913 and 1930], probably no single one, price inflation aside, exercised a more potent influence than did the auto-mobile," reported the President's Research Committee on Social Trends. Staggering highway expenditures, the bulk of which came directly out of motorists' pockets in use taxes, accounted for only part of this increased tax burden. The committee found that it "was not merely in its influence on highway costs that the automobile affected the size of the tax bill. Its use in cities created serious problems of traffic congestion and increased crime. Motorized police and traffic control became important items of increased expenditure." The spreading out of the population into new suburban communities "helped to swell the volume of local taxation, since schools and other public facilities had to be provided anew in these outer areas, despite the under-utilization of such facilities in older areas where population declined." Concluded the committee: "Since the changes which came with the motor era are inextricably bound up with other types of change, it is impossible to state in dollars and cents just how much the automobile has cost the taxpayers of the country."[36]

City planners and politicians largely ignored the needs of the autoless for better public transportation, while undertaking a massive restructuring of American cities at public expense to accommodate middle-class motor-ists. As early as 1916, the editors of *Automobile* were expressing concern over "the parking problem," which "every day in big cities ... grows more acute.... We are facing something which was never foreseen in the planning of our towns, a thing which has come upon us so swiftly that there has been no time to grasp the immensity of the problem till we are almost overcome by it." By 1923 the automobile trade journals considered the urban traffic problem caused by automobiles "one of the great problems of the day." Articles in *Motor* warned "Stop! You Are Congesting the Streets," and asked "Will Passenger Cars Be Barred from City Streets?" [37]

Urban officials sought an answer in city planning—"a concept that was advanced as a virtual panacea for a whole range of urban ills, but was always fundamentally tied to the demands posed by motor vehicles," Blaine Brownell observes. "The ultimate failure to significantly ease the impact of the automobile occurred even though the response of city governments and local leaders to the automotive challenge was in the best American pragmatic tradition. As the numbers of automobiles mounted, so did the governmental response: new taxes, improved roads, expanded parking facilities, extensive surveys, and a vast system of regulations enacted to guarantee the auto's operation in the public interest and welfare." Probably the main reason why planners almost totally neglected the needs of the urban working class and the poor for better public transit is that planning commissions were dominated by commercial civic elites. Robert Walker's 1939 study of urban planning in thirty-one of the largest American cities, for example, revealed that more than half of the members of planning commissions were businessmen or realtors, whereas only one percent had any university affiliation. [38]

"In 1925 Middletown youngsters, driven from street play to the sidewalks, were protesting, 'Where can I play?'" the Lynds reported. "But in 1935 they were retreating even from the sidewalks." Jane Jacobs, in *The Death and Life of Great American Cities*, documents the destruction of the urban neighborhood as a community by the decentralization and segregation of activities encouraged by automobility and by the longer blocks, combined with widened streets and narrower sidewalks, that accommodation to the motorcar demanded. [39]

In contrast, automobility conferred substantial benefits while revolutionizing rural life. Not only was the country general practitioner better able to make his rounds to see patients, but the mass adoption of the automobile by farmers made accessible to them city hospitals and medical specialists. Public libraries in cities also were made accessible to farmers. Rural Free Delivery (RFD) mail routes were reorganized in 1915, taking advantage of automobility to improve service. And in the 1920s the daily bus trip to a consolidated school began to replace the long walk of farm children to inferior ungraded schoolhouses. Jacked up and used as a mobile power plant, the farmer's car made many chores easier. The Saturday trip to town in the Model T to market dairy products and garden crops, then shop and socialize, became an institution. By making available a far wider range of recreational possibilities and social contacts, the automobile ended rural isolation. In the "'new' rural America," Michael Berger writes, "everything was more complex. No longer did one choose friends, leisure activities, or the family doctor merely on the basis of proximity. The new associations included people from geographically separate units, and interest rather than location became the primary tie among them.... Time ceased to be the barrier it had once been." [40]

Notwithstanding these great benefits, the cityward migration of farm youth continued. Indeed, the family farm was being killed off by automobility. Although improved roads and the Model T got rural America out of the mud in the 1920s, motorization was also in large part responsible for the depressed condition of agriculture, which involved a ruinous combination of overproduction of staple crops and higher operating expenses for equipment and chemical fertilizers. Along with the farmer's automobile came the widespread displacement of farm horses by the tractor, which necessitated a switch to artificial fertilizers, encouraged the use of other expensive machinery to increase productivity, displaced farm workers, and usually involved a mortgage on the family farm. This combination of circumstances made the small family farm obsolete. As the Hoover Committee on Recent Economic Changes pointed out in 1929, "the most dramatic and probably the most significant single factor which has entered into the productive situation of agriculture within the last few years has come with the increased mechanization of the farm, primarily as a result of the internal combustion engine." The number of tractors in use on American farms had increased from 147,600 in 1919 to over 825,900 by 1929. It was obvious that "the introduction of the tractor implies and necessitates a sweeping revision of the whole character of our agricultural industry and of our ideas with reference to farm organization and management, land values and other phases of rural economy.... We are coming slowly to perceive that it sets a new pace and rather than fitting itself unobtrusively into our agriculture, creates a demand that agriculture be quite drastically readjusted in accordance with its needs and potentialities." The committee concluded that the tractor "permits enormous economies in the production of staple agricultural products, but its effective utilization demands larger operating units and a more specialized type of economic organization; it permits also of a considerable release of manpower." [41]

Just as the "city problem," in the words of Henry Ford, was "solved" for the white middle class by flight from the city, so too the "farm problem" perceived at the turn of the century was in the main "solved" by the mass movement of rural folk off the soil. One conspicuous example of this was the mass migration of blacks from the rural South into northern urban ghettos that began just prior to World War I and accelerated into the post–World War II period. Another was the great "Okie" migration to California of the 1930s. Less dramatically, the movement affected the overwhelming majority of small farmers and agricultural laborers, regardless of race or region, as agribusiness, dominated by multinational corporations headquartered in the metropolis, came to supersede the family farm. The magnitude of the resulting displacement of people is compellingly summarized by John L. Shover: "Between 1926 and 1965 more than 30 million people moved away from American farmlands. . . . Spanning just three and a half decades, this mass outpouring represents one of the great migrations in history, greater in scope and numbers than the great exodus of Europeans and Asians to the United States in the 140 years from 1820 to 1960. An estimated 47 million migrated to the United States during these years, and 22 million returned, leaving a net increment from foreign migration of about 25 million." [42]

Motorization also profoundly changed the character of the small town. Ogle County, Illinois, for example, in 1900 had 79 horse-related service establishments and no automobile-related ones. But by 1930 automobile-related businesses outnumbered horse-related ones 86 to 21; the town of Oregon alone had 10 automobile dealers and 3 filling stations. By 1930 a round trip from Oregon to Rockford in an automobile took only as long as the train ride one way. So shopping trips to nearby Rockford and Dixon increased for Oregon families that owned cars from only once or twice a year to every two or three weeks. More and more out-of-town businesses began to advertise in the Oregon newspapers. And as the automobile greatly expanded trade areas in the 1920s, delivery service from local stores declined. In short, writes Norman Moline, as a result of automobility "persons in rural areas as well as those in towns increasingly had options as to where they could do their shopping. Trading habits which previously had been quite rigid became slightly blurred." [43]

By opening up much larger trading areas, automobility killed off the village general store and lessened deposits in small local banks. The big mail-order houses—Sears, Roebuck and Montgomery Ward—were forced to assume the new business risks involved in opening chains of retail stores. Before the advent of the automobile, the mail-order houses had catered to the isolated rural population. The Sears, Roebuck catalog was placed alongside the Bible in farmhouse parlors and so defined the material universe for farm children that it was used as a primer in one-room schools. Other retailing "had been concentrated into the center of cities and towns into which all avenues of transportation funnelled." Robert E. Wood, the former general merchandise manager at Montgomery Ward who became vice-president of Sears, Roebuck, explained, "When the automobile reached the masses it changed this condition and made shopping mobile. In the great cities Sears located its stores well outside the main shopping districts, on cheap land, usually on arterial highways, with ample parking space."[44] Downtown merchants in medium-sized cities as well as proprietors of small-town general stores consequently saw business move to the periphery of town or to the metropolis and were forced to specialize in a single line of goods.

These developments in retailing completely unsettled wholesale trade. Competition became much sharper among wholesalers, and many firms found that they could no longer operate economically in the expanded trading areas brought about by mass motorization. The Hoover Committee reported as early as 1929 that "relatively few wholesale firms have as yet readjusted their methods for dealing with the new conditions."[45]

The decentralization of business into larger trading areas slowed during the Great Depression and World War II, then accelerated in the post–World War II period with the building of "shopping centers" to accommodate suburban consumers. The electric trolley had decentralized retail businesses outward from the central business district in "taxpayer strips" that developed along streetcar lines. The automobile not only tremendously expanded this decentralization along main routes of travel to suburban residential neighborhoods, but brought about the proliferation of suburban shopping centers with off-street parking for customers. The first regional shopping mall was Country Club Plaza, built on the outskirts of Kansas City, Missouri, in 1922; the first regional shopping center complex, planned as a unified commercial development with its stores turned away from the access street, was the Highland Park Shopping Village, built in Dallas in 1931. A massive shift of retail trade from central business districts to outlying shopping centers occurred after the innovation was brought off on a grand scale with the building of Northgate in Seattle in 1950 and of Shoppers' World in Framingham, Massachusetts, in 1951. Each provided parking for several thousand cars. With the rapid proliferation of such shopping centers in the 1950s and 1960s, the downtowns of medium-sized cities came to be crime-ridden wastelands of vacated stores.

The economies of the smallest villages and hamlets probably underwent the most profound change. Chana, Illinois, a village about 8 miles from Oregon that was not near any major highway, stopped being a general trade center and became more an agricultural supply center as trade shifted to Oregon. But Grand Detour, 10 miles from Oregon on Illinois Route 2, became a popular point for automobile tourists to stop for services. This typified the trend articulated by Joan Halloran in her 1937 study of changes in business services in Iowa agricultural villages over the years 1920–1935: "In many villages the most conspicuous features are no longer those services that cater extensively or chiefly to the resident agricultural population, but the filling station, the garage or repair shop, the restaurant and tavern—types of business that serve an outside world of transients coming and going by automobile." [46]

What happened in the long run to small agricultural communities is documented by John Shover in two case studies—of Ostrander, in Scioto Township, Delaware County, Ohio, and of Bedford County, Pennsylvania. The number of farms in Delaware County declined from 3,073 in 1910 to 2,647 in 1945 and to 1,389 in 1969; only 757 of the latter were full-time operations with gross annual sales over $2,500. "Ostrander's business block about 1920 contained a livery stable, two grocery stores, two restaurants, two barbershops, the bank, a drugstore, the opera house, a pool room, a bakery, a small hotel, a machine shop, the railroad station, and the new grain elevator that towered over the village. At least one physician practiced. Hence, about fifteen economic functions were being performed." Although Scioto Township's population of 1,598 remained at about its 1890 level in 1970, the services provided by Ostrander had been cut drastically. "The residents were serviced [in 1970] by a branch bank, a filling station, a post office, a restaurant, a barbershop, a grocery store, and a general equipment chain store that had taken over the old elevator site. There was no physician in the township. For supermarkets, medical service, hardware supplies, or the movies, the county seat is less than fifteen minutes away by car." An eight-grade elementary school remained in Ostrander, but one of twenty-two school buses in Delaware County bused older students to a consolidated high school 15 miles away. Retired people formed a large percentage of Scioto Township's residents, and its new residences were trailer-type homes. "Only one of Ostrander's businesses in 1973 (the general equipment store) functioned to service farmers, for there was little need. Driving up and down the dusty road, one soon loses count of the weed-grown yards and rotting houses with broken windows that mark the sites of abandoned farm homes." [47]

The number of farms in Bedford County peaked at 3,627 in 1910, then declined to 3,184 in 1930, and continued to decline to only 1,292 in 1970. By that time, although 92 percent of the county remained classified rural, only 7 percent of its work force was engaged in farming, and more than half of these were part-time workers. Agriculture remained the principal economic activity of Bedford County until the opening in 1938 of the Pennsylvania Turnpike, which transects the county and passes 2½ miles north of the city of Bedford. Tourism then became the county's "economic lifeblood." In 1973 Bedford County's 266 tourist-related businesses employed over 2,000 people and pumped over $15.6 million into the local economy.

The bulk of the economic activity occurs within a two-mile-wide belt along the turnpike, particularly at "Turnpike City" around Exit 11 and at the Breezewood Exit ten miles further east. In 1973 Turnpike City had six motels, the two largest owned by national chains, and Pennsylvania Route 220, which runs south into Bedford, was "lined with ramshackle garages with spare tires and assorted truck parts strewn along their fronts and sides." The larger Breezewood Exit complex is located at about the midpoint of the turnpike, where it is intersected by Interstate 70, a main route south to Baltimore and Washington, D.C. The motorist coming off this exit in the early 1970s plunged onto a 300-yard-long "Million Dollar Mile" composed of 17 gasloine stations, 9 restaurants, and 21 motels. "Breezewood on a summer night may accommodate up to 4,000 overnight guests," Shover observes. "Every now and then a bit of authentic Bedford County topsoil breaks the sea of concrete behind the service stations—it's the place you walk your dog. Nearly every billboard advertises some national franchise, but most of the managers and employees would be listed in the rural non-farm category that now makes up the vast majority of the county's population." [48]

With only minor variations, Breezewood is replicated in thousands of tourist traps at limited-access-highway exits across the United States. One can travel by automobile from coast to coast sleeping at a constant temperature in similarly decorated rooms and eating convenience food from the same menus. Home, too, is now much the same for middle-class suburbanites wherever they find it.

The Family Car

9

Beginning in the 1920s for the middle class and in the 1950s for the working class, automobility revolutionized the lifestyle of the typical American family. Despite the development of rudimentary automobile cultures in the advanced capitalist countries of Western Europe and in Japan in the post–World War II period, the family car remains a uniquely American institution; in the words of French sociologist Jean-Jacques Chanaron, "Except for North America, the automobile [still] is not integrated into the banality of daily life." [1]

Family togetherness was a major benefit anticipated by early proponents of automobility. "Next to the church there is no factor in American life that does so much for the morals of the public as does the automobile," E. C. Stokes, a former governor of New Jersey and the president of a Trenton bank, claimed in 1921. "Any device that brings the family together as a unit in their pursuit of pleasure is a promoter of good morals and yields a beneficent influence that makes for the good of American civilization. If every family in the land possessed an automobile, family ties would be closer and many of the problems of social unrest would be happily resolved.... The automobile is one of the country's best ministers and best preachers." [2]

Intergenerational Conflict

Contrary to Stokes's widely shared expectations, by the end of the decade it was evident that any tendency of automobility to bring the family together was ephemeral—although an increasing number of people did find the Sunday drive a preferable alternative to attending church. "No one questions the use of the auto for transporting groceries, getting to one's place of work or the golf course, or in place of the porch for 'cooling off after supper,' " Robert and Helen Lynd found in their 1929 study. "But when auto riding tends to replace the traditional call in the family parlour as a way of approach between the unmarried, 'the home is endangered,' and all-day Sunday motor trips are a 'threat against the church'; it is in the activities concerned with the home and religion that the automobile occasions the greatest emotional conflicts." [3]

Although in theory the family car could bring husbands, wives, and children together in their leisure-time activities, the divorce rate continued to climb in the 1920s, and conflicts between parents and children reached a new height during the decade. A major source of intergenerational conflict in Middletown was the use of the family car. There is no evidence that the motorcar contributed to the divorce rate, but then neither did it, as early proponents of automobility expected, stop the divorce mill from grinding.

That the motorcar undercut parental supervision and authority is unequivocal. "The extensive use of this new tool by the young has enormously extended their mobility and the range of alternatives before them; joining a crowd motoring over to a dance in a town twenty miles away may be a matter of a moment's decision, with no one's permission asked," the Lynds pointed out. "Furthermore, among the high school set, ownership of a car by one's family has become an important criterion of social fitness: a boy almost never takes a girl to a dance except in a car; there are persistent rumors of the buying of a car by local families to help their children's social standing in high school." [4]

In Southern California the automobile had become by the mid-1920s "a social essential" for teenagers: dating now required a car, and "the automobile was seen as a tremendous threat to parental control, enabling children to escape entirely and with great ease from all the restrictions of their home environments." A 1921 report from the captain of the Los Angeles County motorcycle squad to the Board of Supervisors noted, "Numerous complaints have been received of night riders who park their automobiles along country boulevards, douse their lights and indulge in orgies." In a 1925 address the Pasadena police chief complained that "the astounding number of 'coupe lovers' who park on dark streets in the Crown City necessitates the use of nearly all the police machines on patrol duty." High-speed "joy riding" by youths under the influence of alcohol, frequently in stolen cars, became an even more serious problem for Southern California police during the 1920s. [5]

Social workers and teachers put the blame for increasing juvenile delinquency on parents who made cars too easily accessible to their children, yet admitted that if boys were not given use of the family car for dates, they might steal one. An average of about 8,000 cars a year were stolen in Los Angeles during the 1920s, with a peak of 11,541 stolen in 1926. Car theft was described in 1921 as "the least risky and most profitable of all major criminal operations." The chief of the California State Motor Vehicle Division reported in 1929 that stolen cars were associated with at least 70 percent of major crimes in the state. That over 90 percent of the cars stolen were recovered by the police was mainly due to the fact that most were stolen by youths under eighteen years of age, used for a specific purpose, and then abandoned. The superintendent of a state reform school reported in 1929 that 35 percent of his inmates had been committed on a charge of auto theft.[6]

Courtship and Mating

The impact of the automobile on courtship and mating has been most thoroughly studied and wittily portrayed by David L. Lewis. "Cars fulfilled a romantic function from the dawn of the auto age," he writes. "They permitted couples to get much farther away from front porch swings, parlor sofas, hovering mothers, and pesky siblings than ever before.... Courtship itself was extended from the five-mile radius of the horse and buggy to ten, twenty, and fifty miles and more. Sociologists duly noted that increased mobility provided by the motorcar would lead to more cross-breeding and eventually improve the American species." However, autos did more than facilitate romantic love among couples who would marry and settle down to rear children. "They also have influenced American culture by abetting prostitution, creating the 'hot pillow' trade in tourist courts and motels, [and] providing an impetus for drive-in restaurants and movies."[7]

The traditional visit on the veranda or parlor call was replaced by the automobile date to a dance or movie that ended up in the local lovers' lane. No one ever has proved that the 38-inch-long seat of a Model T was more convenient or comfortable than a haystack, and Henry Ford allegedly designed the Model T seat so short to discourage the use of his car as a place in which to engage in sexual intercourse. But determined couples found ways to thwart Ford's intentions, and the auto makers came to facilitate lovemaking in cars with such innovations as heaters, air conditioning, and the tilt steering wheel. The 1925 Jewett introduced the fold-down bed, and the bed conversion option on Nash cars after 1937 became popular as "the young man's model." The height of accommodation to sexual drive in automobile design came in the vans of the 1970s, called by

Lewis "the most sexually oriented vehicles ever built." Van owners tended to be single men under 35 years of age; and vans featured interiors with all the amenities of a bordello and suggestive exterior murals and slogans that, in Lewis's words, "leave no doubt as to their owner's motives.... Vans also are a prostitute's motorized dream." [8]

Thousands of drive-in fast-food stands were built at the edges of towns in the 1920s and 1930s, after the first, Royce Hailey's Pig Stand, was opened in Dallas in 1921, and the Pig Stand Company was formed. The drive-ins served hamburgers and hot dogs washed down with soft drinks or milk shakes, to patrons who remained in their cars. The food was delivered on trays by low-paid teenaged help, called carhops. A&W, which followed the Pig Stand Company into business with its national chain of drive-ins in 1924, introduced "tray girls," who became a major attraction to the main patrons of the drive-ins—youths cruising in cars in search of sexual adventure. In most areas of the country, the drive-in business was seasonal. Many cities passed restrictive legislation to abate the nuisance of drive-in noise and litter. At the height of their popularity in the mid-1960s, there were some 35,000 drive-in eateries in the United States, with California and Texas leading in numbers.

The first drive-in movie theater was opened in Camden, New Jersey, on June 6, 1933, by Richard M. Hollingshead, Jr., who was granted a patent on the idea. With his cousin, Willis Warren Smith, owner of a chain of parking lots, Hollingshead formed Park-In Theaters, opened a second drive-in theater on Pico Boulevard in Los Angeles in 1934, and began selling his idea to other entrepreneurs for a fee of $1,000 plus 5 percent of their gross receipts. The drive-in theater consisted of a giant screen; a building that housed a projection room, a stand dispensing soft drinks and snacks, and rest rooms; and rows of parking spaces on a large lot on the outskirts of town. Relatively low overhead costs compared with those of downtown theaters were passed on in the form of low admission prices, and family patrons had neither to dress up nor to worry about leaving young children at home with a babysitter. The main drawback was that, like the drive-in food stand, the drive-in theater was a seasonal business closed for the winter months in most areas of the country.

Only a handful of drive-in theaters were in operation nationwide as late as 1946. But they proliferated in the 1950s with expanding automobile ownership, and at their peak of popularity in 1958 there were 4,063 of them in the United States. After that the drive-in theaters became a casualty of home television and entered a period of gradual decline.

Drive-in theaters made special attempts to appeal to a predominantly family trade, both in the low admissions charged and in the provision of special facilities to amuse children, such as playgrounds and animal parks.

Nevertheless, they quickly gained reputations as "passion pits" where the show in the cars was usually better than the one on the screen.

Similarly, the cabin camps that came to dot the roadside after 1925 were assailed by FBI chief J. Edgar Hoover in 1940 as "camouflaged brothels." He claimed that many so-called tourist courts refused accommodations to travelers to concentrate on the more lucrative local "couples trade" and that some Texas cabins were rented as many as sixteen times a night, while others provided prostitutes.

Mobile lovemaking has declined appreciably in the United States since the 1970s. Urban sprawl, a result of auto-induced decentralization, has diminished greatly the availability of safe trysting spots. Gas-guzzling vans have become less popular with escalating oil prices following the oil shocks of 1973 and 1979. The downsizing of passenger cars places severe limits on the possible positions for expressing passion. Most important, changing sexual mores and standards of community and parental acceptance have resulted in living arrangements that make mobile lovemaking largely unnecessary. "Who needs cars when beds are so readily available?" Lewis asks rhetorically.[9]

Changing Woman's Role

Motor Trend in 1967 cited a survey showing that out of 1,100 marriages nearly 40 percent had been proposed in an automobile. Motorization profoundly affected the lifestyles of middle-class couples whose "spoon, moon, and June" back-seat romance rhymed with family life in a suburban home.

To begin with, as early as the 1920s automobility was making the role of the middle-class housewife vastly different from her mother's. Despite the traditional association of the automobile as a mechanical object with men and masculinity in American culture, automobility probably has had a greater impact on women's roles than on men's, and women have been enamored of the motorcar from the outset of its diffusion.

Because driving an automobile requires skill rather than physical strength, women could control one far easier than they could a spirited team. They were at first primarily users of electric cars, which were silent, odorless, and free from the problems of hand-cranking to start the engine and shifting gears. Introduction of the self-starter in 1912, called the "ladies' aid," and of the closed car after 1919, which obviated wearing special clothes while motoring, put middle-class women drivers in conventional gasoline automobiles in droves. Most of the comfort and convenience options added to cars since then—including vanity mirrors, plush upholstery, heaters, air conditioning, and automatic transmissions—were innovated with the ladies especially in mind.

Since the 1920s the bulk of automobile advertising has attempted to appeal to women, who generally have the final say in the selection of the family car. One of the major pioneers of this strategy was Edward S. "Ned" Jordan, who eschewed engineering language to focus on the emotional richness of the car for women drivers. His classic 1923 ad for his Playboy car began: "Somewhere west of Laramie there's a bronco-busting, steer-roping girl who knows what I'm talking about. She can tell what a sassy pony, that's a cross between greased lightning and the place where it hits, can do with eleven hundred pounds of steel and action when he's going high, wide and handsome. The truth is—the Playboy was built for her."

Despite a pervasive myth to the contrary, as early as 1925 the American Automobile Association announced that tests had proved conclusively that women drivers were not only as competent as men but even more stable and predictable in their responses to driving situations. Statistics on motor vehicle accidents and traffic violations continue to bear this out and to demonstrate that the most dangerous drivers are young males.

Until the automobile revolution, in upper-middle-class households groceries were either ordered by phone and delivered to the door or picked up by domestic servants or the husband on his way home from work. Iceboxes provided only very limited space for the storage of perishable foods, so shopping at markets within walking distance of the home was a daily chore. The garden provided vegetables and fruits in season, which were home-canned for winter consumption. Bread, cakes, cookies, and pies were home-baked. Wardrobes contained many home-sewn garments. Mother supervised the household help and worked alongside them preparing meals, washing and ironing, and house cleaning. In her spare time she mended clothes, did decorative needlework, puttered in her flower garden, and pampered a brood of children. Generally, she made few family decisions and few forays alone outside the yard. She had little knowledge of family finances and the family budget. The role of the lower-middle-class housewife differed primarily in that far less of the household work was done by hired help, so that she was less a manager of other people's work, more herself a maid-of-all-work around the house.

Automobility freed such women from the narrow confines of the home and changed them from producers of food and clothing into consumers of national-brand canned goods, prepared foods, and ready-made clothes. The automobile permitted shopping at self-serve supermarkets outside the neighborhood and in combination with the electric refrigerator made buying food a weekly rather than a daily activity. The car also permitted attendance at movie matinees followed by downtown shopping sprees or getting together with the girls for lunch or an afternoon of bridge.

Far less household help was needed, as the household stopped being a producer of many items, and as domestic servants were replaced by a bevy of increasingly sophisticated electric vacuum cleaners, ranges and ovens, mixmasters, irons, washing machines, and clothes dryers. Control of the family budget inevitably passed to Mother as she took over the shopping and became the family expert on the technology of household appliances.

She was the primary user of the family car, for shopping, for carting the kids to school and Little League practice, and for a myriad of other activities. Consequently, her views on what kind of car the family needed often became a mandate for the purchase of a nine-passenger station wagon. "By midcentury," writes Ruth Schwartz Cowan, "the automobile had become, to the American housewife of the middle classes, what the cast-iron stove in the kitchen would have been to her counterpart of 1850—the vehicle through which she did much of her most significant work, and the work locale where she could be most often found." [10]

Domestic Economy

Folklore notwithstanding, the impact of the automobile on the bedroom has been far less profound than its impact on the kitchen. And it was the kitchen that was the heart of the turn-of-the-century middle-class home.

In conjunction with electric kitchen appliances, particularly the refrigerator, the automobile transformed shopping and food preparation. The electric refrigerator with freezing compartment, which permitted large amounts of perishable foods to be purchased at one time and stored until needed, was appropriately developed and popularized by GM's Frigidaire Division and by Nash-Kelvinator during the 1920s and 1930s. Now it was possible to load up the car with a week's worth of food—more and more of it partially prepared convenience food—at a one-stop, self-serve market whose prices were lower than those at the specialty stores.

Prior to the widespread diffusion of the automobile-refrigerator complex, shopping for foodstuffs and housewares was virtually an everyday chore, at a series of retail specialty stores operated by the dry goods merchant, the butcher, the fishmonger, the produce dealer, and the baker. Orders read to clerks were boxed from stocked shelves behind a counter in the grocery store. Meats were cut to order and wrapped by the butcher. Fresh vegetables were selected under the peddler's watchful eye. Credit was extended to steady customers, and phoned-in orders were delivered to the door. The large amount of store labor necessitated by this personal service, together with uneconomical wholesale purchasing in small lots, resulted in relatively high retail prices for foodstuffs.

The self-service market was introduced by Clarence Saunders, who opened his first Piggly Wiggly store in Memphis, Tennessee, in 1916 and patented the idea. Instead of reading orders to a clerk behind a counter, the customer entered the Piggly Wiggly through a turnstile, picked up a basket, and followed a one-way "circuitous path" along which groceries were stacked, including perishables in refrigerated cases. The path ended at a "settlement and checking department," where the prices of the goods selected by the customer were totaled on an adding machine and the purchases were bagged by a checker. The innovation won immediate popularity, and the changeover of retail food sales to self-service was evident by the early 1920s. By the end of that decade over 2,600 Piggly Wigglys were in operation.

Simultaneously, there was a movement away from independently owned small specialty stores to chain stores that could purchase in large lots and pass the savings on to customers, and to "combination stores" that sold a full range of foodstuffs under the same roof. The largest corporate chain was the Altantic and Pacific Tea Company (A&P). Founded on the eve of the Civil War, the A&P mushroomed from only 372 stores in 1920 to over 16,000 by 1927, compared to some 4,000 stores for Kroger, A&P's chief corporate-chain rival. The policy of the chain stores was to replace several smaller specialty stores with a larger combination store, resulting in fewer stores serving a given area. By 1932 some 4,500 of A&P's 15,700 stores were combination stores.

The last outpost of the clerk was the meat market, where butchers continued to cut and wrap meat to order through World War II. Pre-packaged meats were introduced by A&P in 1939. Meats packaged in plastic wrap and displayed in self-serve refrigerated cases, along with partially prepared frozen foods, introduced in the 1930s as "frosted foods," became common after World War II with the rise of the discount "super-market," a store several times larger than the typical four- to six-thousand-square-foot combination store of the 1930s.

The marketing concept of the discount supermarket was innovated by Michael Cullen, who opened a chain of fifteen discount supermarkets in the New York metropolitan area during the Depression. The savings from large carload purchases of foodstuffs at bargain Depression prices were passed on to customers at his huge King Kullen markets. The first use of the term "supermarket" in a corporate trademark was probably by Albers Super Markets, Inc., of Cincinnati, in 1933.

The kitchen began to lose its status as the center of household activity as shopping and food preparation came to require far less time, and moreover as automobility encouraged families to eat out far more often. Automobile tourism created a demand for wayside family restaurants, and a meal out became the capstone of the Sunday drive or weekend automobile outing for hungry, tired families. Chester H. Liebs points out that coincident with the rise of mass personal automobility, "the nation … entered a full-fledged eating-out boom, with the estimated number of restaurants jumping 40 percent between 1910 and 1927."[11] The experience of eating out also changed dramatically for the middle-class family—from a leisurely, full-course meal in the formal atmosphere of a hotel dining room, to the quick pickup of a hamburger and french fries in a come-as-you-are roadside diner.

The final blow to the hegemony of the kitchen came with the rise since the 1950s of the limited-menu, self-service restaurant, innovated and exemplified by McDonald's. In 1948 the McDonald brothers, Maurice and Richard, dismissed the carhops from their San Bernardino, California, drive-in restaurant, reduced their menu to a minimum, and began to develop assembly-line techniques for the preparation of food. By 1952 the McDonalds were selling a million fifteen-cent hamburgers and twenty-cent malts and shakes, and 160 tons of ten-cent orders of french fries a year at their food factory, where the combination of a hamburger, french fries, and a beverage could be served to a customer in twenty seconds. Ray Kroc, a former Lily Cup and milk-shake machine salesman, began franchising the McDonald concept and name in 1954 and by 1960 had sold some 200 franchises nationwide. The concept caught on immediately, with Burger King and Kentucky Fried Chicken becoming McDonald's chief competitors. Liebs observes that by the mid-1950s "restaurant trade journals began to thicken with advertisements soliciting franchises for a wide assortment of fast-food ventures.… By 1960 thousands of other limited-menu, self-service roadside franchises serving everything from tacos to doughnuts to pizza had become familiar fixtures along the Miracle Mile."[12]

Hearth and Home

Automobility transformed the architecture of the American middle-class house. Folke T. Kihlstedt describes this process of change, beginning with the pre-automobile era, when "the front porch still functioned as the buffer zone between the privacy of the house and the communality of the neighborhood. . . . The parlor and the front porch supported a formal style of life . . . built around an accepted social hierarchy in which a progression of architectural spaces, from front porch (or veranda) to hall to parlor to library (or sitting room) and to dining room, were related to increasing degrees of intimacy."[13] The unsightliness and stench of the stable kept it located away from the house at the back of a large lot.

By removing leisure-time activities away from the home and the neighborhood, automobility "offset the need for a large house with many rooms into which one could escape and seek privacy." The front porch and the parlor were eliminated as the home became more of a dormitory and rooms lost their former specialized functions. Fear of the danger of gasoline storage, enforced by building codes, zoning laws, and higher insurance rates, generally kept garages detached from houses until after World War II. But under the leadership of Frank Lloyd Wright, architects were designing houses with integrated garages for middle-class clients by the mid-1930s. Wright's 1930s "usonian" houses developed the carport and made it necessary to walk down the driveway and under the carport to find the front door. "In contrast to a turn-of-the century house, the house of 1945 has no hall, no parlor, and a mere vestige of a porch," Kihlstedt observes. "The garage was moved from the back of the lot to the front of the suburban house, and adjacent to the front door. . . . Entry is directly into the living and dining rooms, or into the kitchen through the adjoining garage. The element that projects farthest toward the street to greet the passer-by is no longer a shaded and generous porch. It is the large prominent surface of the garage door."[14]

This prominence of the driveway and direct entry into the kitchen from the garage turned the suburban home into an extension of the street. So much so that sidewalks were eliminated from many post–World War II housing tracts. The blending of the house into the highway has proceeded furthest in auto-dominated Southern California. "A domestic or sociable journey in Los Angeles," notes Reyner Banham, "does not so much end at the door of one's destination as at the off-ramp of the freeway, the mile or two of ground-level streets counts as no more than the front drive of the house." He continues, "Though the famous story . . . about the [Southern California] family who actually lived in a mobile home on the freeways is now known to be a jesting fabrication, the idea was immediately convincing . . . because there was a great psychological truth spoken in the jest. The freeway is where the Angelinos live a large part of their lives."[15]

Community: From Neighbor to Night Dweller

The new mobility of families was destroying the traditional pattern of close relationships among neighbors by the 1920s. Wrote the Lynds, "The housewife with leisure does not sit so much on the front porch afternoons after she 'gets dressed up,' sewing and 'visiting' and comparing her yard with her neighbors', nor do the family and neighbors spend long summer evenings and Sunday afternoons on the porch or in the side yard since the advent of the automobile and the movies." Automobility had made "a decorative yard less urgent." "In the nineties we were all much more together," a Middletown housewife explained. "People brought chairs and cushions out of the house and sat on the lawns evenings. We rolled out a strip of carpet and put cushions on the porch step to take care of the unlimited overflow of neighbors that dropped by.... The younger couples perhaps would wander off for half an hour to get a soda but come back to join in the informal singing or listen while somebody strummed a mandolin or guitar." [16]

Such a scene contrasts sharply with the conception of neighborliness revealed by a 1929 survey of the residents of a twenty-block middle-class section of Los Angeles near the USC campus. The interviewer found that "a new definition of a friendly neighborhood is apparent; it is one in which the neighbors tend to their own business." One householder explained: "We have nothing whatsoever to do with my neighbors. I don't even know their names or know them to speak to. My best friends live in the city but by no means in this neighborhood. We belong to no clubs and we do not attend any local church. We go auto riding, visiting and uptown to the theaters." The interviewer concluded, "This straining against the bonds that hold them in the area makes for many families an uneasy, unsettled, uncertain state." But another observer of 1920s Los Angeles interpreted the phenomenon positively: "The role particularly of the automobile ... has cut down spatial distance and tended to increase social nearness to such an extent that every person may live in wide-flung communalities of his own [making], in place of the old closely circumscribed neighborhoods." [17]

On the Road

10

Before the automobile revolution, extended vacations away from home were the privilege of the rich. The average middle-class family could not afford railroad fares to a remote national park and a long stay at a luxury hotel. With the advent of the Model T and improved roads, the automobile outing and the automobile vacation became middle-class American institutions. As Foster Rhea Dulles points out in his history of American recreation, the automobile "greatly stimulated the whole outdoor movement, making camping possible for many people for whom the woods, mountains, and streams were formerly inaccessible." [1]

Until the late 1920s, however, automobile touring, especially to remote western parks, was severely limited by poor roads. Despite the efforts of bicycle organizations, automobile clubs, and farmers, the good-roads movement had accomplished little up to the outset of the Model T era. Roads meandered from town to town without forming a system of interconnected highways. They were poorly marked when marked at all. Roadside services for tourists were virtually nonexistent. Over 90 percent of the roads were unsurfaced, and impassable much of the year. Only 8.66 percent of the roads in the United States were surfaced at all in 1909, a gain of only 1.5 percent over 1904, when the first census of American roads was taken. These few improved roads most commonly had gravel surfaces, which automobile traffic quickly destroyed by sweeping the gravel into windrows, rather than packing it down as did much slower horse-drawn traffic. Macadam was no solution, for the weight and speed of motor vehicles quickly broke down macadamized surfaces too. Brick roads were satisfactory, but their cost was prohibitive. Until 1909 there was not a single section of paved road in a rural area.

At the Second Annual Good Roads Convention in 1909 at Cleveland,

Ohio, "the two dominating influences ... were the American Automobile Association, representing the autoists and the cities, and the National Grange, representing the farmers. Cooperating with these organizations were the American Road Makers' Association, the National Association of Automobile Manufacturers, and the American Motor Car Manufacturers' Association." Automobile interests predominated in the Lincoln Highway Association, organized on July 1, 1913, to promote the construction of a coast-to-coast highway taking "the shortest, best, and most direct route." The first demonstration "seedling" mile of the Lincoln Highway was opened at Malta, Illinois, in October 1914.[2]

Through the combined lobbying efforts of automobile interests and farmers newly made mobile by the Model T, the primitive road network of 1910 was transformed into an interconnected system of concrete highways by 1930. By the end of 1912 a number of major road-building projects were under way; outstanding county/township road bonds totaled over $155.6 million and authorized state good-roads expenditures totaled nearly $136.9 million. By the end of 1914 the United States had 257,293 miles of surfaced roads, of which 75,400 miles were paved with macadam, 1,591 with brick, and 2,349 with concrete.

Concrete was used to surface the 24-mile stretch of highway built in 1908–1910 out to the Ford Highland Park plant in Wayne County, Michigan. Concrete also was used in the construction, begun in 1908, of the first American limited-access highway exclusively for automobiles—the Long Island Motor Parkway. This privately built toll road ran 45 miles from Great Neck to Lake Ronkonkoma, New York. "Although the northeastern states were still experimenting with the concrete surface," Peter J. Hugill observes in his study of early U.S. road building, "California embraced it enthusiastically, because of the transportation needs of its agriculture and the relative lack of railroads. By 1914, 35 percent of the 2,600 miles of improved roads in California was covered with concrete. In contrast, New York with almost 9,300 miles of improved roads had only 244 miles of concrete surface." California is also credited by Hugill with the innovation of concrete curbs to prevent soil erosion during floods and with banked roadbeds for safety. He reports that concrete roads "were more expensive per mile than other types of roads, but the excellent record of concrete pavement in California and in eastern United States [sic] under wartime conditions and the low maintenance costs contributed to the wholesale adoption of concrete roads throughout the United States in the early 1920s."[3]

The federal government gave its first support to building a national system of roads with passage of the 1916 Federal Aid Road Act, which appropriated $75 million to be spent over a five-year period by the secretary

---

of agriculture for the improvement of post roads. Then, following World War I, the federal goverment made available as military surplus to state highway departments for road building some 25,000 heavy trucks and 1,500 caterpillar tractors. Demonstration of the value of long-distance trucking during the war and growing automobile registrations after the war led to passage of the Federal Highway Act of 1921, which provided federal aid to the states, through fifty-fifty matching grants, for building an interconnected interstate system of highways. Some $75 million was appropriated for 1922 alone, and that year 10,247 miles of federally financed highways were built, 3.5 times more than in the preceding five years under the 1916 legislation. States were required to select and designate not more than 7 percent of their highways as part of an interconnected system eligible for federal aid. In 1924 the amount of federal aid per mile was stabilized at $15,000. In 1925 a uniform plan was adopted for designating and numbering the U.S. highways that were part of the system.

Western states with sparse populations could not pay for roads out of property taxes or general funds. To finance highway construction and maintenance, the gasoline tax was innovated in Oregon, New Mexico, and Colorado in 1919. By 1929 all states and the District of Columbia collected gasoline taxes, which amounted to some $431 million in revenue for highways that year. Rates of three or four cents a gallon were common. In 1921 road construction and maintenance were financed mainly by property taxes and general funds, with only about 25 percent of the money for roads coming from automobile registration fees. But by 1929 gasoline taxes were the main source of revenue for highway expenditures, and twenty-one states no longer used any property taxes or general funds for main roads. The reasoning was that the gasoline tax "was superior as a user tax because the amount of gasoline consumed in a vehicle was a good measure of the use of the road and also of the damage that a vehicle did to a road ... the tax was 'equitable' in itself and also that those who paid it benefited directly." The chief collector of the gasoline tax in Tennessee exclaimed in 1926, "Who ever heard, before, of a popular tax?" John C. Burnham points out that "never before in the history of taxation has a major tax been so generally accepted in so short a period." It is remarkable, he writes, to what extent Americans "were willing to pay for the almost infinite expansion of their automobility." [4]

Automobility and the National Parks

The concept of both democratic access to and preservation of scenic and wilderness areas, exemplified by our national parks, is one of America's most significant contributions to world civilization and has been exported around the globe. On March 1, 1872, by an act of Congress, Yellowstone, our first national park, was "dedicated and set apart as a public park or pleasuring ground for the enjoyment of the people." The 1976 bicentennial years of American independence was celebrated in part by over 267.7 million visits to 293 units of our National Park System, representing "treasured historical aspects of our past, cultural aspects of our people, and natural aspects of our land."[5]

Our national parks were the product of what Alfred Runte calls a "pragmatic alliance" between upper-class preservationists and western railroads seeking to boost their passenger traffic. Jay Cooke and Company, promoters and financiers of the Northern Pacific Railroad extension project, were centrally involved in winning congressional approval for Yellowstone. Southern Pacific Railroad lobbyists campaigned for Yosemite, Sequoia, and General Grant, and the Southern Pacific became the leading booster of West Coast national parks. Grand Canyon was pushed by the Santa Fe Railroad. Louis W. Hill of the Great Northern enthusiastically supported the creation of Glacier National Park as part of his railroad's "See America First" campaign. Western railroads spend vast sums of money advertising the national parks and also were responsible for inaugurating "proper" tourist facilities—the grand hotels at major visitor attractions.[6]

Stays in the parks had to be long, because although the railroad transported one swiftly and in comfort to the park periphery, travel through the park by horse-drawn coach over the few crude roads was slow and arduous. Consequently, the grand hotels and other tourist facilities had to be clustered not only within park boundaries but also in close proximity to major scenic attractions. Because the parks were visited by so few people, Congress was reluctant to provide money for road building. Consequently, roads were built as cheaply as possible, most often following stream beds or connecting major scenic attractions along the easiest natural routes available.

A presidential order of August 25, 1916, established the National Park Service (NPS) to regulate the national parks and the national monuments under a directive "to conserve the scenery and the natural and historic objects and the wild life therein and to provide for the enjoyment of the same in such manner and by such means as will leave them unimpaired for future generations." Stephen T. Mather, the first director of the NPS, recognized that park development was linked intimately to the growth of tourism, so he energetically built a second "pragmatic alliance," this one between the NPS and automobile interests throughout the country. The early impact of automobility on the national parks has been summarized succinctly by Robert Shankland in his biography of Mather: "The auto reached swarming ubiquity fast—faster than people now remember. As the auto prospered so did the national parks." Preservationist Edward Abbey claimed that the slogan "Parks are for people" decoded came to mean that "Parks are for people-in-automobiles." [7]

Automobiles were first admitted into Mount Rainier in 1908, General Grant in 1910, Crater Lake in 1911, Glacier in 1912, Yosemite and Sequoia in 1913, Mesa Verde in 1914, and Yellowstone in 1915. As early as 1916 more visitors entered Yosemite by automobile than by railroad, and the largest source of revenue for the newly formed NPS already was automobile admission fees—levied for paying for park roads and improvements. Along with other prominent preservationists, Mather welcomed the automobile into the parks: he recognized the potential political power of the automobile industry, automobile clubs, and the growing number of automobile tourists. A broad base of popular support was deemed essential to the parks both to obtain adequate congressional funding for development and maintenance and to thwart mounting pressure for the exploitation of park resources from commercial interests and other governmental agencies. The main opposition to opening the parks to the automobile came, significantly, not from the preservationists but from park concessionaires who operated horse-drawn stage lines. Their fears were borne out when Mather ordered Yellowstone's stage lines motorized in 1917, a scant two years after the automobile was admitted into that park. Automobilists also were prominent in many preservationist organizations, a prime example being that the Save the Redwoods League originated at the Pacific Auto Show of 1920.

The Federal Highway Act of 1921 and the universal adoption of the gasoline tax to fund highway improvement by 1929 resulted in an interconnected system of paved highways that made even the more remote western parks accessible from the east coast. Moreover, as the outcome of agitation by the National Parks Highway Association, formed in 1915, a route that interconnected all of the national parks had been laid out and signposted by the early 1920s. This interpark route was not totally paved. Nevertheless, it served as a psychological as well as a physical link among the national parks and encouraged people to travel to them.

Until at least the mid-1930s, however, good roads ended at the boundaries of the national parks. In 1915 Yellowstone was the only park with sufficient road mileage to make driving worthwhile, and all park roads not only were unpaved but were too narrow and had grades too steep for automobile traffic. By 1924 a total of only $3.5 million had been spent on park roads; there were only 12 miles of paved road in the entire National Park System, and Glacier and Mount McKinley still lacked through roads. Although by 1924 Yosemite had 138 miles of rutted wagon road, all except 20 miles were private. With 356 miles of unpaved road for a land area larger than several of our eastern states, Yellowstone still had the best road system of any national park.

The turning point came in 1923, when Congress appropriated $7.5 million for road building in the national parks between 1924 and 1927. Altitude, a short working season, rocky terrain, and preservationist considerations made the cost of building new paved park roads extremely high—$20,000 to $60,000 a mile. Consequently, although some 360 miles of new park roads were planned, paving the bulk of either these or existing park roads was out of the question. So the appropriation was used primarily to reduce grades, straighten sharp curves, and widen existing wagon roads to handle automobile traffic.

The philosophy of park road building early adopted by the NPS was first laid down by Hiram Chittenden, the Army Corps of Engineers officer in charge of building many of Yellowstone's wagon roads: "The park should be preserved in its natural state to the fullest degree possible … and the great body of the park should be kept inaccessible except on foot or horseback. But a road once found necessary should be made as perfect as possible. So far as it may detract from scenery it is far less objectionable as a well-built work than if left in a rough or incomplete state."[8] Translated into policy, this meant a limitation to one well-built, low-speed, scenic through road per park—an NPS policy that remains in effect to this day.

Roads were first made adequate to the demands of automobile traffic in our national parks as a by-product of increased governmental spending to stimulate the economy during the Great Depression of the 1930s. Although the number of park visitors remained about the same as in 1929, park appropriations were nearly doubled in 1931; and between January 31, 1931, and July 21, 1932, Congress appropriated over $13 million specifically for road building and improvement in the national parks and monuments. Where the Hoover administration measured, the Roosevelt administration poured funds, inaugurating what has been called "the golden age of park development." From 1933 to 1940 the National Park Service received $220 million from a variety of New Deal agencies. The major use of these funds was for a massive program of rebuilding and paving park roads, as well as for the addition of several impressive new scenic through roads, including the Zion–Mount Carmel Road and Tunnel, the Wawona Tunnel and Road in Yosemite, the Cape Royal Road in Grand Canyon, the Paradise Valley and Yakima Park Highway in Mount Rainier, the Sylvan Pass Road in Yellowstone, and the Going-to-the-Sun Highway in Glacier.

This represented only a small part of huge New Deal expenditures on road construction from 1933 to 1942. After Roosevelt came to power, federal aid was extended from designated sections of interstate highways to urban segments of primary roads in 1934 and to secondary "feeder" roads in 1936. John Rae points out that this represented "a major change in national highway policy." As a "time-honored method of relieving unemployment," the federal government attempted to offset declines in state and local expenditures for roads and streets. "By 1939 relief and recovery accounted for 80 percent of all federal expenditures for roads and 40 percent of the total outlay on highways from all sources," Rae reports. "Between 1933 and 1942 federal relief agencies spent $4 billion on roads and streets." [9]

With saturation of the market for new cars, informed observers doubted that such expenditures were justified by the volume of automobile traffic. The President's Research Committee on Social Trends, for example, concluded in 1933: "Should there be no further increase in the volume of motor vehicle traffic, the utility of new construction and improvement projects would naturally diminish as present highway programs approached the period of completion. This in turn would lead to a more careful weighing of the relative advantages of additional highway facilities as against a reduction of highway taxes." [10] There was so little enthusiasm for express highways in the 1930s that the Pennsylvania Turnpike Commission was unable to sell its bonds.

During World War II, visits to the national parks declined so drastically that the parks might as well have been closed for the duration of the war. The further development of park roads was abruptly curtailed, as the National Park Service operating budget was cut from $21 million in 1940 to a low of $5 million in 1943. Although the war's end brought a record 22 million visitors to the national parks in 1946, NPS budgets remained stringent through the Korean War. The result was that in 1949 it was estimated that some $321 million was needed to rehabilitate park facilities, whereas the NPS budget was only $14 million. William Everhart points out that by 1954 the parks were receiving 54 million visitors a year, "with a level of staff and the run-down facilities [including park roads] designed for the 17 million visitors in 1940." [11]

In the mid-1950s preservationists viewed these inadequate appropriations and deteriorating facilities as the main problems of the National Park System. Therefore, they enthusiastically supported Mission 66, the 1956 federal program that brought national park facilities up to standards by 1966 at a cost to the taxpayers of over one billion dollars. The increased park use that resulted was further magnified by the reciprocal impact of the Interstate Highway Act of 1956, the most ambitious public-works program undertaken in American history. That act committed the federal government to pay, from a nondivertible Highway Trust Fund, 90 percent of the construction costs for 41,000 miles of toll-free express highways, scheduled to be completed by June 30, 1976.

The Interstate System capped ambitious express highway building programs begun at the state level after World War II. Between 1947 and 1970 the combined highway expenditures of the local, state, and federal governments in the United States totaled $249 billion; and Senator Gaylord Nelson calculated that 75 percent of government expenditures for transportation had been for highways, as opposed to only one percent for urban mass transit. The lion's share of this gigantic, disproportionate expenditure for highways continued to come from the gasoline tax and other special use taxes on cars, automotive parts, tires, and lubricants.

A significant point is that virtually no one was concerned about "overuse" of the national parks prior to the combined impact of express highways and modernized park facilities in exponentially increasing park use by the mid-1960s. Nor was there concern that the impact of the road and the car was deleterious to park environments. Preservationist thinking rapidly changed, however, to the view that Mission 66 had encouraged too many people demanding too many conveniences to spend too much time in our national parks. Because these people came in automobiles, the road and the car came in for particular criticism.

This abrupt change in preservationist attitudes was part of a broader reaction against the road and the car in the late 1960s and early 1970s. Concern about the automobile in the parks coincided with widespread acceptance of what might be called the Yosemite fallacy. On June 24, 1966, the *Wall Street Journal* published a front-page story under the headline, "Ah Wilderness; Severe Overcrowding Brings Ills of the City to Scenic Yosemite." The article claimed that on an average summer day the Yosemite Valley had a population density three times that of Los Angeles County. "The damp night air, heavy with a fall of eyewatering smoke, is cut by the blare of transistor radios, the clatter of pots and pans, the roar of a motorcycle, and the squeals of teenagers. Except for hundreds of shiny aluminum trailers and multicolored tents squeezed into camping areas, this might be any city after dark."

The writer did not mention that the same criticism had been made as early as 1937 by Lewis Gannett, who complained that "the floor of Yosemite is an amusement park, as crowded a city as New York's Central Park, and only twice as large. . . . Nothing in America is less wild than the floor of Yosemite Valley."[12] The grandeur of its scenery notwithstanding, Yosemite had not been a wilderness park for over a generation, and its valley no longer had much of a natural ecosystem to preserve. Yosemite also was one of the few national parks within an easy drive from two major population centers, the San Francisco Bay area and the Los Angeles area. And in no other national park were nearly as many automobile tourists being accommodated—1.7 million annually, in an area only seven miles long by two miles wide that was also particularly pollution prone because it was bounded by sheer granite walls. Nevertheless, facile over-generalization by the media built the case that Yosemite was a harbinger of impending disaster for Yellowstone and Grand Teton—a land area larger than the states of Rhode Island and Delaware combined, remote from population centers, and easily accommodating two million automobile tourists a year.

No firm evidence supported the widely held belief that "the park experience" and park ecosystems faced imminent ruin from too many people in automobiles. These allegations were investigated, for example, by Robert Cahn, who reported his findings in a sixteen-article series for the *Christian Science Monitor*, "Will Success Spoil the National Parks?" that won a Pulitzer Prize for reporting in 1969. After six months of research and 20,000 miles of travel, Cahn found that there was overcrowding in the parks, but "only during the peak periods of use." "On the basis of my observations," he concluded, "the National Park System appears to be in relatively good physical condition. No disaster situation is evident." Similarly, the blue-ribbon National Parks Centennial Commission concluded in 1973 that after two generations of coexistence with mass personal auto-mobility, "the properties entrusted to the [National Park] Service are generally in far better condition today than at the time they were taken into the [National Park] System." [13]

Hysteria in the late 1960s and early 1970s over the alleged destruction of the parks by people in automobiles resulted in large part from the almost complete absence of a historical perspective on park development and problems. To begin with, road building in the national parks had consistently lagged well behind the increase in park automobile traffic and had only moderately exceeded the increase in park area. From 1924 to 1947, for example, $107 million was spent on national park roads, and total park road mileage was increased about five times—from 1,060 to 5,387 miles. During this same period, however, total park area almost tripled—from 13,320 to 33,720 square miles. On the other hand, the number of automobiles entering the parks skyrocketed from 330,000 in 1924 to over 7 million in 1947, an increase of twenty-one fold. Thus the impact of the automobile on road building in the national parks was at most incremental rather than dramatic. John Ise, the foremost historian of the national parks, in 1961 described the minimal impact of the road and the car on wilderness: "In an hour's walk from the most congested area of

Yellowstone, one can lose himself in a wild forest where there is little scent of man. The lover of nature who does not like to drive his car over the glorious Going-to-the-Sun Highway in Glacier can walk or ride horseback across the divide—horseback if he can get a horse. He has about every freedom that he had before the road was built." [14]

The automobile also inherited and minimally changed the ecologically unsound park development patterns established by early dependence on rail and horse-drawn transportation—that is, the clustering of tourist service facilities in close proximity to major scenic attractions and the building of roads along the easiest natural routes to interconnect these scenic attractions. Indeed, dependence on the automobile led to great improvement of the enviroment in the vicinity of the grand hotels at scenic locales. Ise vividly describes conditions in Yellowstone in the preautomobile era: "With hundreds of horses around, stabled near the hotels, it was inevitable that there should be a great deal of unpleasant litter and flies.... The hotels were good but around the stables there were masses of manure, rubbish, waste material, and dump from the hotels, as there were also around the permanent camps. The horse and buggy days lacked a few points in sanitation." [15]

In other respects too the impact of people in automobiles on park ecosystems was not only moderate but even beneficial. Although mass personal automobility tremendously increased the number of visitors to the parks, it also drastically reduced the average length of the park visit—from several weeks in the railroad and horse-and-wagon era to only thirty-one hours in Yellowstone by the early 1970s. The vast majority of automobile tourists have little impact on park ecosystems, because they are content to view wildlife and scenery in close proximity to their cars and spend almost all of their time in the park driving, stopping at a few major visitor centers, or chatting with the people in the next campsite. Paul Schullery, a former Yellowstone ranger, observes that hikers, "who generally regard themselves as the most environmentally holy, dig trail ruts and cause erosion. It can be argued that a single hiker traveling on foot through a park's back country does far more damage to the natural systems than does the average car- and road-bound automobilist." [16]

The speed and flexibility of the automobile permitted the development, in the gateway towns outside park boundaries, of tourist facilities that otherwise, even given a far lower level of park visitors, undoubtedly would have continued to proliferate near major scenic attractions within the parks. Had mass personal automobility not developed in the United States, it also seems doubtful that transportation within the parks would forever have relied on the horse and wagon traveling over primitive roads. Street railways were common in cities, and it seems probable that, lacking the automobile, sooner or later major visitor attractions in the parks would have been interconnected by systems of fixed rails and overhead wires, incurring at least as much damage to park ecosystems as park roads have.

Democratic access by automobile, furthermore, was and remains the main reason for strong public support for the acquisition of park lands and the protection of park resources from exploitation. That the infamous Hetch Hetchy Dam and Reservoir, built in Yosemite in 1913 to provide water for San Francisco, remains the only such structure in the parks is no accident. Schemes to build a series of dams on the Yellowstone River in the 1930s and in the Grand Canyon on the Colorado River in the 1960s failed for one significant reason: congressmen received countless letters from irate constituents who recognized the value of preserving the parks because they had visited one in an automobile.

Even though coach-class fares between Chicago and points west were halved between 1921 and 1926, automobile travel still was cheaper and more convenient for a family than travel by train. "The automobile represented a new democratization of vacation travel," Earl Pomeroy writes. "In the same years [the 1920s] when the average American had more time for trips away from home and more money to spend on them, he could buy gasoline to carry his whole family from his own front door for what he alone would have to pay to ride the train. The growing western highway systems, growing in response to his demands, represented his expanding opportunity and the opportunity of the sections that they fed." Pomeroy continues, "What the motor cars and the motorists did to the outdoors would be long debated, but there is little doubt that the age of the automobile was the age in which the average American vacationer first found the West within his reach." With this democratization of travel, "a mass market became more important to the tourist industry as a whole than the patronage of the elite. The great profits in the western tourist and vacation industry came not from serving squab to the few but from selling gasoline, hamburger sandwiches, and postcards to the many." [17]

The validity of Pomeroy's statements depends on what one considers "democratization" and whom one considers "average." Of the 100 working-class families on whom Robert and Helen Lynd collected data on income and expenditures for their 1929 study, 66 reported spending nothing on vacations, and the amounts spent by the remaining 34 ranged from $1 to $65, with the notable exception that one family of three earning $1,680 a year spent $175 on a vacation and $492 on their automobile. The Lynds concluded, "Use of the automobile has apparently been influential in spreading the 'vacation' habit. The custom of having each summer a respite, usually of two weeks, from getting-a-living activities, with pay unabated, is increasingly common among the business class, but it is as yet very uncommon among the workers."[18]

A 1968 survey showed visitors to our national parks still to be almost exclusively white and middle class. As Everhart says, "No one would seriously contest that visiting parks and historic sites is an activity directly proportional to income. National parks are essentially a middle-class experience.... The culturally disadvantaged are not a significant part of the statistics of national park travel, and black families are seldom encountered in the campgrounds." The extent to which this remains true was revealed in testimony given in the United States Senate on June 8, 1977, before the Subcommittee on Parks and Recreation of the Committee on Energy and Natural Resources. Robert L. Herbst, an assistant secretary in the Department of the Interior, reported that about 75 percent of all national park visitors were "members of the 15 percent upper-income segment of the population (35 million upper-middle-income Americans account for 170 to 180 million park visits). The remaining 180 million Americans, with lower economic status, make up the remaining 85 to 90 million park visits."[19]

Although rail travel to the national parks continued to increase into the 1930s, it had been surpassed in volume by cheaper automobile travel to the parks a decade earlier. The railroads managed to hang on, providing alternative transportation to the parks, until the 1960s, when one by one they discontinued service. The western national parks are still linked, about a day's travel apart, by a system of railroad tracks that fell into disuse with massive indirect government subsidization of competing highway transportation after 1956. Visitation to the western national parks is largely a summer business, whereas the profitable running of an unsubsidized interpark railroad system would require year-round passenger traffic. With the cost of rail transportation estimated at $50 to $75 per person per day in the early 1980s, access to the national parks by motor vehicle remains much cheaper as well as much more convenient for families. Consequently, over 90 percent of the visitors to the national parks continue to arrive in motor vehicles.

Camping in the national parks used to mean tent camping by people in passenger cars or by backpackers who left their wheels at the trail heads. Neither required elaborate facilities. Increasingly in the 1960s, however, visitors tended to arrive in the park in pickup trucks with over-the-cab campers, station wagons pulling house trailers, or enormous "mobile homes" equipped with television sets and noisy generators. Often they came as well with trail bikes hooked fore and aft, and/or a motorboat in tow. These slow-moving, oversize rigs congested narrow park roads and parking areas originally designed for Model Ts. Their operators demanded hookups for water and electricity and waste disposal stations. And in winter snowmobiles came to ply park roads.

Traditional views of camping have been outmoded by these realities. "Many campgrounds, once primitive and small, are now large and intensively developed with water systems, flush toilets, paved roads, increased supervision, and special facilities for trailers that now house nearly half of all campers," Roger N. Clark, John C. Hendee, and Frederick L. Campbell point out in a 1971 study of modern camping culture. "Campers are no longer required to forfeit many comforts of the urban environment to enjoy outdoor recreation. Equally important, the range of available camping behaviors, once limited by primitive conditions, has increased." The pattern has been one of the "invasion and succession" by the masses of naturally attractive locations initially accessible only to wilderness campers. "Consequently, a new camping style emerged with associated behavioral expectations less dependent on direct environmental contact, more compatible with highly developed structures, and increasingly social conditions.... Although recreationists seem to subscribe to the traditional goals associated with camping such as contact with the environment and isolation, they apparently feel that they can pursue such values in highly developed campgrounds." [20]

Preservationists have always considered the appropriate use of the national parks to be for nature appreciation, while recreationists view the parks mainly as arenas for activities such as sport fishing, boating, horseback riding, and snowmobiling. Mass recreation has tended more and more to compete with nature appreciation as the main park use. This is chiefly a result of the overuse and exhaustion of available public recreation land in close proximity to major population centers, a phenomenon attributable in the main to mass personal automobility. In 1969 Secretary of the Interior Walter Hickel estimated that it was in the urban areas that almost 80 percent of current recreation needs were located, and that it would require "in excess of $25 billion above existing expenditure levels to give urban dwellers the same amount of nearby recreation opportunity by 1975 that was available on the average nationwide in 1965." A notable example is that public access to stream fishing of the quality found a generation ago near large cities in several eastern and midwestern states now exists only in remote places such as Yellowstone Park and its environs. In 1978 the NPS issued some 218,000 free fishing permits in Yellowstone, one for every ten visitors. "There are at least twelve states that have fewer licensed anglers than that," Schullery notes. "Fishing is an industry in Yellowstone. Anglers spend about $4 million annually in and near the park, so that a local economy depends in part on their trade." [21]

Despite substantially higher gasoline prices following the 1973 and 1979 oil shocks, demand for the park experience from people-in-automobiles was expanding. Visits to units of the National Park System increased from 276.7 million during the 1976 bicentennial year to 284.2 million in 1979 and to 334.6 million in 1983. However, cutbacks on camping facilities and the imposition of moderate campground fees and two-week time limits have led to a dramatic decline in overnight visits. From a record high of 9.4 million in 1968, overnight stays in NPS-operated campgrounds fell to 7.9 million in 1971. After rising to slighly under 9.3 million during the 1976 bicentennial year, they have stabilized at 7.9 million in 1979 and 7.8 million in 1983. Total overnight stays in the national parks, including hotel and lodge-type facilities as well as campgrounds, have stabilized at about 16 million annually.

More visitors now stay at motels and privately operated campgrounds outside the parks in the gateway towns, and the trend promises to continue. Especially in the large parks, however, maintaining substantial overnight facilities for automobile tourists is essential. "At Yellowstone, for example, a visitor must travel a 140-mile loop to view the park's principal natural features," the Stanford Research Institute reports. "Without overnight facilities inside the parks, each visitor would have to complete the loop between sunup and sundown, substantially diminishing the park experience and congesting the park entrances at sunup and sundown hours." [22]

During the 1970s about one fourth of all travel over 100 miles from home by Americans was for purposes of outdoor recreation or sightseeing. Government statistics make evident the central role that the national parks and other public lands, such as state parks and the national forests, played in encouraging this recreational travel. Even if, as earlier noted, some three fourths of the visitors to our national parks in 1977 were among the richest 15 percent of our population, on the other hand government statistics on participation in outdoor recreation for the bicentennial period July 1, 1976, through June 30, 1977, reveal that fully 62 percent of Americans twelve years old and over participated in sightseeing at historic or scenic national sites, 30 percent camped in developed and an additional 21 percent in undeveloped areas, and 28 percent hiked or backpacked.

Tourism, then—fostered by increased affluence and expanding automobile ownership in the post–World War II period, together with the effects of Mission 66 and the 1956 Interstate Highway Act—is an essential part of American life and the American economy. And that democratic access to wilderness has remained compatible with wilderness preservation in the form of our national parks is both a signal achievement of American civilization and a major benefit of the automobile revolution.

Development of the Tourist Infrastructure

The development of an infrastructure of tourist services from 1910 to 1945 is brilliantly analyzed by Warren J. Belasco. He demonstrates how "autocamping, an inexpensive, individualistic sport with antimodernist implications, gave birth to the motel, a nationally standardized up-to-date roadside business ... how, in an emerging mass-consumption society, hunger for escape was directed into conservative commercial channels." His thesis is that early upper-class automobile tourists were "deliberately seeking to escape crowded, overly institutionalized vacation places. In a consumption-based economy, however, the ability to purchase contrast cannot usually be confined to a small elite.... With numbers comes a specialized tourist infrastructure to control, service, and exploit the increased flow." [23]

Small-town hotels were oriented toward serving the needs of traveling salesmen who journeyed from town to town by train with their wares. Automobile-touring families found hotels expensive and overly formal, yet often lacking in cleanliness. After registering at the desk, tipping the bellhop for carrying up luggage from the curb, and finding a place to garage the car, the family had to bathe to remove road grime and change into suitable attire before going down to dinner. This might not be accomplished before the hotel dining room closed.

An estimated several hundred thousand middle-class families escaped from this expense and inconvenience of "the monopolistic rail-hotel complex" in the 1910–1920 decade by going "gypsying" in their cars, stopping each night along the roadside to cook simple meals over campfires and to sleep in tents. "In five minutes you set up a hotel of canvas that is much more satisfying than any builded of brick and stone," enthused an autocamping advocate. "No more hanging around on a dewy morning waiting for a cafeteria to open, or the sleepy garage owner to appear and release the family Lizzie. They appear with the lark, or a few jumps ahead of him, hustle the breakfast ... dismantle camp, and are on their way once more." [24]

Ingenious autocampers designed their own equipment, including fold-out tents from cars and fold-down beds in them, portable iceboxes and stoves, and equipment racks and trailers. The camping equipment industry grew spectacularly in the 1920s, by marketing equipment that appealed especially to comfort-conscious women—large tents, folding cots with springs, air mattresses, portable gas stoves and lamps, and elaborate yet compact kits of kitchen utensils.

Camping was made still easier by the establishment of free municipal campgrounds on major routes of travel around 1920. This resulted from the pressures of local merchants, who wished to lure the growing automobile tourist trade to their stores, combined with the need for social control of camping as sanitation problems and altercations with property owners proliferated. On 10- to 15-acre sites, the camps accommodated 50 to 60 cars a day with campsites that included running water, electricity, privies, cold showers, laundry rooms, and central kitchens. Groceries and gasoline could be bought at nearby mom-and-pop markets and filling stations, so large amounts of supplies did not need to be carried. Estimates of the number of autocampers in the early and mid-1920s range from 10 million to 20 million annually, and the number of municipal auto-camps from 3,000 to 6,000.

In part to defray rising maintenance expenses in municipal park budgets, but mainly to screen out itinerants and low-budget tourists, in 1923 some towns began to charge small fees at campgrounds, opening the field to competitive private entrepreneurs. A 1921 survey revealed that autocampers included not just middle-class tourists, emigrants, and farmers out to buy supplies, but migrant workers and "plain hoboes," who contributed nothing to local economies while freeloading at municipal parks. Some were year-round tourists who "violated the cardinal rule that motor gypsying be a temporary vacation, not a lasting occupation.... The goal of an auto trip was to reactivate one's loyalty to job, home, and family. Few wanted a permanently wandering population."[25] Consequently, nightly fees of 50 cents, time limits from as short as 24 hours to as long as a week or two, and registration came to be generally imposed after 1924 to screen out the "automobile tramps" from the "better class" of "bonafide tourists."

Between 1925 and 1928 there was a marked shift toward private camps charging fees. The movement began in Southern California, where year-round sunshine not only made tourism a uniquely profitable business but attracted the largest number of undesirable migrants. Municipal camps rapidly reverted to daytime picnic areas, as local entrepreneurs took over the overnight camping trade with the blessings of town officials. By the mid-1930s most of the remaining municipal camps had been shut down by state health inspectors as public nuisances.

Some campgrounds began to provide cabins, which were constantly upgraded in the late 1920s and the 1930s to attract a higher class of patronage. The "cabin camps," as they came to be called, were in the main mom-and-pop operations, cheaply constructed and run with family help. They remained the predominant type of roadside lodging for noncampers until after World War II. They appealed to the "suitcase" tourist, who found autocamping too primitive and difficult and who had continued to patronize hotels. The cabin camps offered easy access from the highway, free parking, no clerks or tipping, informality, and, above all, privacy. As Belasco says, "Privacy spared shy or inexperienced travelers the ordeal of the public lobby 'gauntlet'; it allowed speeding motorists to come and go more freely; and it also attracted middle-class young people and well-dressed unmarried couples desiring to rendezvous in secrecy. Thus the same informality endeared cabin camps to families, mileage fiends, and roadhouse patrons." [26]

Expenditures related to tourism plunged from $872 million in 1929 to $444 million in 1933, while hotel occupancy rates fell from 70 percent to 51 percent. With hard times the patronage of automobile tourists further shifted from hotels to more economical cabin camps. Hotel occupancy recovered to only 56 percent in 1937, and the American Automobile Association (AAA) estimated that the proportion of its touring members staying in hotels had declined from 75 percent in 1929 to 60 percent in 1936.

In the 1930s the first "motor courts" were built in California, Florida, and Texas. These establishments combined the advantages of the cabin camp with sturdier construction and hotel-type conveniences such as indoor plumbing and private bathrooms. The first to use the word "motel" was James Vail's Motel Inn, in San Luis Obispo, California, a hotel with automobile facilities designed by Arthur S. Heineman and opened in 1925. Coast-to-coast chains of such "motor inns," offering full hotel services, professional staffs, and national advertising, were planned by several oil companies. "By 1930 the Holiday Inn style was already outlined: yet such chain schemes proved premature," Belasco explains. "Touring was still too seasonal in most of the country to support a heavily capitalized motor hotel that required year-round patronage to break even ... [and] expensive motor hotels needed very affluent customers, yet wealthier non-campers were only beginning to come to the roadside.... Big capital would have to await the return of prosperity after 1945, by which time the motor hotel concept would be well defined and nationally feasible." [27]

An article in *Harper's* declared in 1933, "The commercial houses, the railroad hotels down by the switching yards, where lonely drummers [traveling salesmen] chew cigars in fetid lobbies, are so infinitely more dreary than even the second-rate tourist cabins that no motorist who has learned the simplicity and cheapness of Camp Joy or U Wanna Kum Back will ever go near such hotels as these again." The AAA reported some 30,000 "tourist cottage and camp establishments" along the nation's highways. This new roadside industry catering to Americans on the move was "one of the few features of the American landscape that the depression is causing to grow by leaps and bounds." [28]

By the late 1930s early domestic cottage and regional themes in tourist cabin architecture were being replaced by modern-style flat-roofed cubes with curvilinear windows and rounded corners. And the motto of tourist courts had changed from "all the comforts of home" to "more than the comforts of home." There was a general tendency to upgrade facilities as, in Chester Liebs's words, "depression-weary manufacturers … discovered that each of the thousands of cabins lining the American roadside was a potential showcase for their wares … [and] wooed court owners with advertising and discounts so their items might be put on display and tried out by thousands of overnight guests. At the same time, the more enterprising court owners, eager to maintain a competitive edge, cooperated by snapping up large quantities of everything from inner spring mattresses and coin-operated radios to deluxe bathrooms with sunken tubs and hot and cold running water." *Business Week* summed up the economic impact of this in 1940: "Their total investment in furniture runs to about $50,000,000 and in plumbing and bath fixtures about $37,000,000. They use 560,000 beds and mattresses (403,200 of them inner spring), 245,000 gas stoves, and over 100,000 fans. So attractive are sales opportunities that such big suppliers as Simmons Co. (mattresses) are creating special divisions to service the auto courts." [29]

Tourism ended in 1942 with the World War II ban on passenger car production for the civilian market and wartime rationing of gasoline and tires, but revived to unprecedented levels with the great expansion of automobile ownership and use after the war. "By the 1950s, the roadside-lodging field was ripe for an invasion by corporate chains," Liebs observes. He cites a *Fortune* analyst who explained in 1959: "You had these thousands and thousands of little courts run by middle-aged, semi-retired couples. They had the world by the tail—a market yelling for improvements—and they couldn't handle it. Then, almost overnight, the big money began to flood in from everywhere—and I mean from everywhere." [30]

Referral chains of motels had their origins in the late 1930s as an outgrowth of the AAA's tourist facilities rating and recommendation service for its members and of the efforts of state and regional associations of tourist court owners, who began setting up minimum standards for members that used common logos and trade names. The best example of a referral chain is Best Western, which was founded in California in 1946 by motel owner M. K. Guertin with 50 member motels and came to have some 2,700 affiliates worldwide by 1980.

The franchised motel chain was pioneered most significantly by Holiday Inn, the brainchild of Kemmons Wilson. "In 1951," he later recalled, "my wife Dorothy and I loaded our five children into our station wagon and started on a vacation to Washington, D.C., from our home in Memphis. It didn't take long to find that motels had cramped, uncomfortable rooms—and they charged extra for children." [31] Wilson joined forces with Wallace E. Johnson, a prefabricated-home builder who had gained a reputation as the "Henry Ford of the home building industry." The first Holiday Inn, three single-story buildings clustered around a swimming pool, was opened on the outskirts of Memphis, Tennessee, in 1952. Wilson and Johnson franchised the right to use their trade name and logo and the benefits of national advertising and a national referral network to local investors, who erected and maintained motels according to Holiday Inn standards of design and service. Hotel corporations that directly owned their properties, such as Sheraton, entered the motel business in the mid-1950s, after which directly owned motels were added to the franchised ones in the Holiday Inn chain.

A year after the first Holiday Inn opened, Howard Johnson began selling franchises for motor inns adjacent to his franchised roadside restaurants. Johnson had, by the mid-1930s, parlayed a Quincy, Massachusetts, soda fountain acquired in 1925 and an ice cream manufacturing business that sold ice cream richer in butterfat at seaside stands into a string of roadside restaurants along the Massachusetts coast. He had begun franchising his restaurants in 1935. By 1940 some 125 Howard Johnson restaurants, a third of them company owned, were in business from Maine to Florida, grossing $14 million a year. Johnson had opened the largest roadside restaurant in the world on Queens Boulevard in New York City to serve visitors to the New York World's Fair. And he had secured an exclusive contract to built restaurants at the rest stops on the recently opened Pennsylvania Turnpike.

"Johnson's success derived from an uncanny ability to recombine current ideas into a new synthesis that unerringly appealed to a middle-class family on the road," writes Liebs. "Ice cream, for instance, was an extremely common treat, but Johnson's restaurants offered an unusual selection of flavors embellished with a touch of showmanship—he served it in a distinctive cone-shaped scoop that formed a rim of extra ice cream at the bottom, suggesting to the customer that he was getting an exceptionally large portion." Another shrewd step was his merging under one roof a full-meal dining room service and a quick-bite lunch counter with a fast-food menu, whereby he "addressed most everyone's needs in a single stop." [32] By the late 1950s some 500 Howard Johnson restaurants across the United States—next to many of which now stood motels belonging to his new standardized chain—were serving up identical menus to middle-class Americans on the road.

Hard Times

11

During the 1920s automobility became the backbone of a new consumer-goods-oriented society and economy that has persisted into the present. By the mid-1920s automobile manufacturing ranked first in value of product and third in value of exports among American industries. In 1926 motor vehicle factory sales had a wholesale value of over $3 billion, and American motorists spent over $10 billion that year in operating expenses to travel some 141 billion miles. The automobile was the lifeblood of the petroleum industry, one of the chief customers of the steel industry, and the biggest consumer of many other industrial products, including plate glass, rubber, and lacquers. The technologies of these ancillary industries, particularly steel and petroleum, were revolutionized by the new demands of motorcar manufacturing. The construction of streets and highways was the second-largest item of governmental expenditure during the 1920s. The motorcar was responsible for a suburban real estate boom and for the rise of many new small businesses, such as service stations and tourist accommodations. In 1929, the last year of the automobile-induced boom, the 26.7 million motor vehicles registered in the United States—one for every 4.5 persons—traveled an estimated 198 billion miles, and in that year alone government spent $2.237 billion on roads and collected $849 million in special motor vehicle taxes. The eminent social and economic historian Thomas C. Cochran, noting this central role of automobility, asserts: "No one has or perhaps can reliably estimate the vast size of capital invested in reshaping society to fit the automobile. Such a figure would have to include expenditures for consolidated schools, suburban and country homes, and changes in business location as well as the more direct investments mentioned above. This total capital investment was probably the major factor in the boom of the 1920s, and hence in the glorification of American business."[1]

The automobile boom was short-lived and illusory, however. It sowed the seeds of its own demise and was shattered with the saturation of the market for new cars after 1925 and the onset of technological stagnation in the automobile industry. It would be simplistic to say that market saturation and technological stagnation "caused" the Great Depression in the sense that they were sufficient conditions for what occurred. There are too many variables that are too complexly interrelated. The argument in this chapter will be rather that mass motorization played a key role in creating the most important necessary conditions underlying the Depression.

This argument is broadly consistent with the Keynesian "spending hypothesis," which attributes the unprecedented economic contraction of the 1930s to a severe decline in aggregate spending. Peter Temin empirically demonstrates the validity of the spending hypothesis over the alternative monetary explanation—that is, the argument that the Depression was primarily a result of a contraction of the money supply. Most important, he demonstrates that, contrary to monetarist claims, the real money supply did not contract during the late 1920s.[2] Despite its being enshrined in popular myth as the fundamental "cause" of hard times, the 1929 stock market crash has long been viewed by economic historians as only another symptom of a fundamentally unsound economy. The steep decline in aggregate spending evident by the late 1920s, then, can be shown to have resulted from the economic dislocations that were an essential ingredient of the automobile boom, and from the inevitable drying up of that boom.

Market Saturation

The automobile boom of the 1920s was in large part the product of an unprecedented extension of consumer installment credit to finance automobile sales. Although a few expensive items, such as pianos and sewing machines, had been sold on time before 1920, it was time sales of automobiles during the twenties that established the purchasing of expensive consumer goods on credit as a middle-class habit and a mainstay of the American economy.

As early as 1910, conservative country bankers were beginning to complain about the growing tendency of farmers to withdraw their savings to purchase motorcars. In New York City a spokesman for the bond house of Spencer Trask and Company declared: "Thousands are running cars who cannot afford to do so without mortgaging property, while thousands of others are now investing in motors who formerly invested in bonds. It is calculated that upward of $300,000,000 will be absorbed by the automobile industry this year [1910], which represents the interest on about two-thirds of our entire prospective crops of the present year." *Horseless Age* estimated that although only about 400,000 automobiles had been produced up to that time, almost a million American families had incomes above $3,000 a year, leaving a large untapped market among purchasers who could well afford to pay cash for a car.[3]

With the coming of the mass-produced car in the next decade, however, this relatively affluent market became saturated. It was then that the industry began to encourage less affluent purchasers to become automobile owners through the extension of consumer installment credit, realizing the worst fears of the conservative bankers.

One person who agreed with them on this point—although he generally had little respect for bankers—was Henry Ford. He advised the Wisconsin Bankers' Association at its 1915 annual convention to adopt the slogan, "Get Cash, Pay Cash," after it was brought out that 90 percent of a $70-million investment in motorcars in Wisconsin represented either money withdrawn from savings, money borrowed, or notes purchased. "It has always seemed to me that this putting off the day of payment for anything but permanent improvements was a fundamental mistake," said Ford. "The Ford Motor Company is not interested in promulgating any plan which extends credits for motorcars or for anything eles." During the Model T era, according to Allan Nevins and Frank Hill, "the sale of Ford cars on credit had never received the company's official blessing. Henry Ford firmly opposed the practice. Edsel, in contrast, recognized its effectiveness, and quickly encouraged its use. Ford dealers often employed it."[4]

The Banque Automobile in 1906 became the first of several French financial institutions to finance time sales of automobiles. In the United States the Morris Plan banks began financing such sales in 1910. The following year the Studebaker Corporation announced that it would accept notes endorsed by its dealers on the purchases of EMF and Flanders cars. Walter Flanders, then the Studebaker general manager, explained, "We have in view the future rather than the immediate present.... We have considered the advent of the credit in this business as inevitable and our move is but the consummation of a plan long since laid."[5] By 1912 commercial vehicles commonly were sold on time, and a few large automobile dealers had inaugurated their own plans for the installment selling of passenger cars.

The manufacturers of moderate-priced cars, under pressure from their dealers, by 1915 had come to see installment selling as an alternative to Henry Ford's strategy of progressively lowering the price of the

Model T. On November 8, 1915, the Guaranty Securities Company was formed in Toledo, Ohio—with John Willys and Alfred Sloan among its directors—to finance times sales of Overland and Willys-Knight cars. Reorganized as the Guarantee Securities Corporation of New York City, the company was financing time sales of twenty-one makes of cars—including all General Motors lines, Dodge, Ford, Hudson, Maxwell, REO, and Studebaker—by April 1, 1916. General Motors became the first automobile manufacturer directly to finance time sales of its products with the creation of the General Motors Acceptance Corporation on March 15, 1919. By the spring of 1921 over 110 automobile finance companies were in existence in the United States. Lagging behind this trend, the Ford Motor Company at last formed its own finance unit, the Universal Credit Corporation of Delaware, in March 1928, with the changeover to Model A production.

By the mid-1920s the market for both new and used cars was being maintained primarily by installment sales. As early as 1922, 73 percent of cars were sold on time. "Take Your Hat Off to the Man Who Buys on Time," *Motor* urged automobile dealers in 1925. "Time-buying has caused more intensive work than any scheme of mere money-saving ever devised—meritorious though such plans may be." [6] By then, however, the automobile finance companies themselves had begun to fear that time sales had been overextended. Dealers facing the onset of market saturation were already trying to extend the customary 12-month maximum for payments to 18 and 24 months, with lower down payments than the usual third. Some were even passing on to the finance companies inflated bills of sale that credited the buyer with a down payment he had never made. Credit losses tended to increase as credit was further extended. In 1926, for example, the credit loss on new-car paper was only 0.16 percent for terms of 12 months with one third down, versus a 4.58-percent credit loss when terms were extended to 19 months or more with 24 percent or less down. So after 1925 the finance companies tightened credit terms. In 1927 the share of new cars sold on time dropped to 58 percent, and there was an estimated sharp decline of $643 million that year in the volume of installment sales of both new and used cars.

Advertising also undoubtedly helped push automobile sales beyond the bounds of sanity in the 1920s. The automobile industry during that decade became "one of the heaviest users of magazine space as well as of newspaper space and of other types of mediums ... the expansion in the advertising of passenger cars and accessories, parts and supplies in 1923 being particularly noteworthy." Expenditures for automobile advertising in magazines alone climbed from $3.5 million in 1921 to $6.2 million in 1923 and to $9.269 million in 1927. [7] But this huge increase in advertising without a concomitant increase in personal disposable income or a more equitable income distribution could not maintain the automobile boom, as the finance companies were forced to recognize.

It would be nice to know precisely when the automobile manufacturers themselves began to get uneasy about economic conditions. Walter Chrysler afterward recalled, "Early in 1929 it had seemed to me that I could feel the winds of disaster blowing." Alfred Sloan remembered that "on October 4, 1929, shortly before the stock market crash, I addressed a general letter to the [GM] organization noting the end of expansion and promulgating a new policy of economy for the corporation.... As it turned out, I was not, of course, pessimistic enough; indeed, it would soon be a question whether we were able to cope with the unbelievable course of events." Yet Charles Nash, in an address to the National Automobile Dealers Association (NADA), had said as early as 1925: "I read something the other day in an ad where a fellow was boohooing [sic] the idea of the saturation point. I am going to say to you men tonight, regardless of the fact that I will be contradicted in the press and by a lot of shining lights, that the saturation point was reached two years ago; not now but two years ago." Nash thought that the industry had reached "the point of the survival of the fittest" and added that "production must be limited to fit the demand." [8]

Beginning in the 1920–1921 recession, numerous articles in the automobile trade journals dealt with the possibility of market saturation, but unlike Nash they generally failed to face the problem squarely. The tendency instead was to state with bravado rationalizations intended to maintain business confidence. A 1925 editorial in *Motor Age*, for example, claimed: "The retail organization in the automotive industry knows that saturation in automotive ownership does not exist today.... The dealer who is convinced that the saturation point is reached in his market is ready to turn some profitable business over to his competitors." As late as January 1930, *Motor* was contending that people "will continue to buy automobiles. They have been doing it for a quarter century with no letdowns of consequence. They won't walk. They don't like old cars—and they aren't broke. Business executives may be a bit pessimistic because *they* 'lost in the market.' It would do most of them good if they would take a day off and talk to the great common people. They would learn that the stock market is *not* America and that the 'home town folks' are ready to make 1930 a good year." [9]

Mounting evidence ran counter to such optimism. NADA studies showed that replacement demand accounted for over 70 percent of new-car sales as early as 1924—three years before NACC statistics revealed the same shift. In 1926 a field survey conducted by James B. Dalton, the industrial editor of *Motor*, revealed that "not more than 30 percent of all dealers are making money; 30 percent are making a bare living, and the rest are losing money. Dealer mortality has been so heavy that some companies have found it necessary to ship on consignment.... Repossessions by finance companies have further complicated the used car situation and depressed the market."[10]

In July 1929 Dalton reported, "Thumbs down is the attitude of bankers on loans for the wholesale buying of new automobiles to all save the most soundly financed dealers.... With the Federal Reserve constantly stressing the dangers of the credit situation, and with the entire nation jumpy because of its frequent warnings, the automotive industry—more completely dependent than any other upon the use of credit for the merchandising of its products—is feeling a real pinch." The bankers felt that "persons of moderate means who trade in their cars every year or two and are perpetually paying installments on an automobile are carrying things a bit too far." On the eve of the October stock market crash, Dalton wrote, "How long this uninterrupted progress can continue without a major reverse is the question which is perplexing economists and business strategists.... The march forward will be checked by a shortage of credit if by nothing else." He continued, "Business is weaker than it was in 1920. Excessive productive capacity and the bitter competition which has resulted have brought profit margins very low whereas the reverse was true at the close of the war. Production costs and selling prices are so delicately balanced that even a moderate recession in demand would convert a profit into a loss."[11]

"There is precisely one thing wrong with the automobile industry today," Clarence E. Eldridge, sales manager of the REO Motor Car Company, told the Minnesota Automobile Dealers Association as the stock market crashed. "That one thing is that there has been built up by this greatest of all industries a capacity for building, and a capacity for selling, approximately twice as many automobiles as the market, either present or potential, can absorb." Eldridge excoriated the industry for not recognizing earlier the limits to the new car market and for innovations that were intended to stave off market saturation. "The exploitation of high-cost markets, both foreign and domestic; the imposition upon the dealers of arbitrarily determined quotas, together with a reduction of territory, for the purpose of compelling dealers to sell more cars; the exhaustion of the possibilities, so far as creating additional buyers, of installment selling; and finally the utterly short-sighted policy of accelerating the obsolescence of comparatively new cars, for the purpose of temporarily stimulating sales of new cars—all of the methods, sound or

Autocampers near Yellowstone National Park in 1923. The spread of automobile ownership and the building of improved roads after passage of the Federal Highway Act of 1921 put an automobile trip to a remote national park within the reach of middle-class vacationers in the 1920s. This inaugurated a golden age of national park development and stimulated the growth of many tourist-related industries. (Courtesy Library of Congress)

Opposite, top: 1921 converted Model T camper. Early campers had to be self-sufficient. A premium was placed on collapsible equipment that could provide the essential comforts of home in the outdoors. Some ingenious autocampers even designed and built their own portable homes away from home. (Courtesy Henry Ford Museum and Greenfield Village)

Opposite, bottom: American Tourist Camp, North Carolina, 1930. In the 1920s municipally run camps offering free tent space, showers, and cooking facilities to attract the auto-tourist trade proliferated from coast to coast. Private entrepreneurs entered the business after the municipal camps began imposing small fees to discourage undesirable itinerants. "Tearooms" and filling stations often were adjuncts to the camps. (Courtesy Library of Congress)

Entrance to Grandview Cabins, Holyoke, Massachusetts, and interior of tourist cabin, Sea-View Motor Court, Arcata, California, ca. 1941. The more enterprising owners of tourist camps moved in the 1930s toward providing cabins that combined privacy and economy with indoor plumbing, and the AAA began to rate these tourist facilities for its members. The Great Depression witnessed a marked shift in tourist patronage away from downtown hotels in favor of such tourist camps, which by the outbreak of World War II were being upgraded to offer even more than the comforts of home. Because they appealed to local unmarrieds as well as to traveling families, FBI chief J. Edgar Hoover characterized them as "camouflaged brothels." (Courtesy Library of Congress and John Baeder)

Carpenter's drive-in restaurant, Hollywood, California, 1932. Thousands of drive-in fast-food stands were built at the edges of towns in the 1920s and 1930s; at the height of their popularity in the mid-1960s there were some 35,000 in the United States. The drive-in became the forerunner of the contemporary fast-food, limited-menu family restaurant when in 1948 the McDonald brothers dismissed the carhops from their San Bernardino, California, drive-in, reduced their menu to a minimum, and began to develop assembly-line techniques for the preparation of food. (Courtesy Huntington Library)

Opposite, top: 1923 Dodge Custom coupe, the first car with an all-steel, closed body. The closed car permitted all-weather, year-round automobile use. The all-steel body obviated virtually all of the need for handcrafting in body work and permitted automatic welding to replace hand bolting, thus leading to lower labor costs. Sheet steel made bodies stronger and more durable, as well as permitting more latitude in styling. (Courtesy Chrysler Historical Collection)

Opposite, bottom: 1923 Chevrolet with copper-cooled engine. Chevrolet's 1919–1923 experiment with an air-cooled engine was conceived as the key to bringing out a lightweight, inexpensive car to complete with the Model T. The intention was to produce an air-cooled engine with a higher compression ratio, and thus greater fuel economy and power for a given displacement. Heat was dissipated by a front-mounted fan pushing air through copper fins brazed to the engine. Lack of communication and cooperation between design and production engineers and numerous component failures killed off the copper-cooled Chevrolet after only 100 retail sales. The result was that under Alfred Sloan's leadership GM both improved interrelationships ·vithin the firm and adopted a marketing strategy that discouraged technological innovation and eschewed technological leadership. (Courtesy General Motors)

Walter P. Chrysler with 1924 Chrysler Six, the first car to bear his name and the first moderate-priced car with a high-compression (4.5:1) engine. The stylish Chrysler Six also featured four-wheel hydraulic brakes and low-pressure "balloon" tires. The car's low-slung lines compared with other contemporary models were necessitated by its 70-mph cruising speed. (Courtesy Chrysler Historical Collection)

1927 La Salle Model 303. In 1927 General Motors formed a new styling section in its Fisher Body Division headed by Hollywood custom automobile stylist Harley J. Earl. This made the styling of automobiles an institutionalized activity carried out by professional designers, rather than a haphazard activity of engineers or salesmen as the need for a new model arose. Instead of the then conventional wooden models and hammered metal parts, Earl used modeling clay in developing his designs, which permitted him to conceptualize more fluid, rounded shapes. The La Salle, introduced in March 1927, was both Earl's first design for GM and the first successful mass-produced stylist's car. (Courtesy General Motors)

1929 Chevrolet AC Sports Coupe. By the mid–1920s a mechanically superior, annually restyled Chevrolet could be bought for only a few hundred dollars more than an obsolete Model T, and Chevrolet came to outsell Ford in the low-priced field. William S. Knudsen, as president of Chevrolet, accommodated the annual model change to mass production by reverting from special to general machine tools and by decentralizing and jobbing out components manufacture. The 1929 Chevrolet featured a six-cylinder engine and was advertised as "A Six for the Price of a Four." Called the "cast-iron wonder," the six-cylinder 1929 Chevrolet engine remained the basic Chevrolet power plant until 1953. (Courtesy General Motors)

Model A cars being assembled at the River Rouge plant in 1931. The switchover from Model T to Model A production at River Rouge involved closing down the Ford assembly lines for six months and cost some $250 million. Such disruption of production and inordinate cost were irreconcilable with bringing out the essentially new model every three years that Sloanist marketing strategy envisioned. Consequently, the more flexible production techniques innovated at Chevrolet were adapted to Model A production at the Rouge. Assembly machinery also was refined. For example, Model T bodies had been slid from a gravity drop onto chassis driven under them. Here, in contrast, a power crane brings Model A bodies from an upper level and sets them in place on chassis moving along a conveyor line. (Courtesy Ford Motor Company)

Opposite, top: Henry Ford with V-8 engine. The most significant manufacturing innovation of the 1930–1950 period was casting the entire engine block of the 1932 Ford V-8 engine as a single unit. This greatly reduced manufacturing costs, making an eight-cylinder engine practical for low-priced cars. (Courtesy Henry Ford Museum and Greenfield Village)

Opposite, bottom: 1932 Ford V-8 convertible coupe. Introduced in fourteen body styles on March 31, 1932, the $450–$650, 65-horsepower Ford V-8 featured streamlined styling, double drop-frame construction, safety plate glass in all windows, and synchromesh transmission. It has been called "the handsomest of all the company's creations." (Courtesy Ford Motor Company)

Manufacture of one-piece, all-steel "turret tops." The Fisher Body Division of General Motors developed and introduced the turret top on 1935 GM models. This was made possible by technological advances in steel milling that increased the width of steel strips from the conventional 72 inches to 110 inches. The turret top both represented a great safety advance and permitted more economical stamping processes in automobile manufacturing. (Courtesy General Motors)

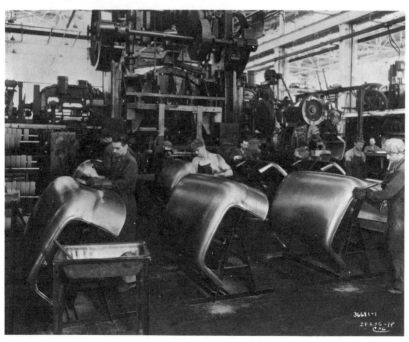

1936 Lincoln Zephyr, one of the more distinctive aerodynamic automotive designs of the prewar period. Under Edsel Ford's leadership as president of the Lincoln Motor Company and the Ford Motor Company after 1922, the Lincoln was progressively restyled to improve its appearance. (Courtesy Henry Ford Museum and Greenfield Village)

1934 Chrysler Airflow. The most advanced aerodynamic styling in a 1930s production car was achieved in this eight-cylinder vehicle. Its full aerodynamic shape developed 40 percent less drag than competing models; and it featured welded unitized construction, all seating within the wheelbase, and an integral trunk. The five-passenger sedan sold for a moderate $1,345. A superior automobile in all respects, the Airflow was far too revolutionary for consumers. Fewer than 11,000 units were sold before it was withdrawn from production in 1937. As a result of the Airflow's failure in the market, Chrysler became the most conservative of the Big Three in styling policy for several decades. (Courtesy Chrysler Historical Collection)

1938 Cadillac 60 Special. In contrast with that of the Chrysler Airflow, the styling of this model so appealed to consumers that they were willing to take smaller trade-in allowances when purchasing it. The elimination of running boards for the first time in the 60 Special enabled the "standard-size" American car to hold six passengers, because the basic body could now be widened to the full tread of the wheels. A sedan styled like a convertible, the 60 Special was a forerunner of the retrogressive, unsafe "hardtop" convertible introduced in the 1949 Buick, Cadillac, and Oldsmobile models. (Courtesy General Motors)

Opposite, top and bottom: 1940 Oldsmobile Series 90 sedan, and a line drawing of the Oldsmobile Hydra-matic transmission. The automatic transmission was the last major innovation in automotive technology. The first fully automatic transmission was the 1940 Oldsmobile's Hydra-matic Drive, which used a fluid coupling and a four-speed planetary gearbox. The contemporary fluid torque-converter automatic transmission was first used on 1937 GM buses and made its appearance in passenger cars in the 1948 Buick Dynaflow transmission. By the 1974 model year some 90 percent of American-made full-size cars were equipped with automatic transmissions. (Courtesy General Motors)

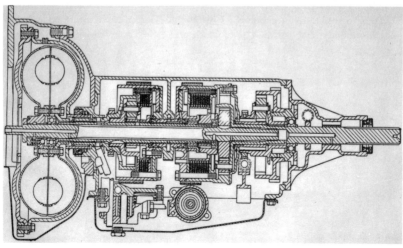

Some of the 854,000 heavy trucks that GM produced for the armed forces during World War II. GM asked for only half of its normal peacetime profit on war orders, and with a 50-percent expansion of its productive capacity stood second only to Du Pont in expansion for the war effort. In addition to turning out several million motor vehicles of various types, before the war ended the American automobile industry had produced for the military some seventy-five essential items, including 27,000 completed aircraft, 450,000 aircraft and 170,000 marine engines, and 5,947,000 guns. (Courtesy General Motors)

Jeeps coming off a Ford assembly line. Developed first by Bantam, then by Willys-Overland in response to a U.S. Army–sponsored competition, the rugged, go-anywhere jeep became "the backbone of all Allied military transport." During the war some 660,000 four-wheel-drive jeeps were produced by Willys-Overland and by Ford. After the war, surplus military jeeps inaugurated a market for off-road recreational vehicles that persists into the present. (Courtesy Henry Ford Museum and Greenfield Village)

unsound, which might sell new cars were put into effect." Stripping away still another myth of the automobile market, Eldridge pointed out that "the basic problem is not one of how to sell used cars or to handle the used car problem, but how more intelligently to adjust production to the absorptive capacity of the market. And that responsibility, I say quite frankly, rests in one place and one place only—with the automobile manufacturers. It is they who by their insatiable ambition, their blind worship at the shrine of the goddess 'quantity production,' have created this situation—this situation which, unless speedily corrected, seems to me to threaten the very existence of the entire merchandising structure of the automobile industry." [12]

Technological Stagnation

The gravity of the situation was compounded by the onset of technological stagnation in the automobile industry. By the late 1920s no manufacturing innovation was in sight of comparable importance to the continuing-strip mill for rolling sheet steel or the continuous-process technique for manufacturing plate glass, much less anything that could have the impact on investment in new plant and equipment that the moving assembly line had had a decade earlier. Moreover, no product innovation in sight could approach in economic importance the stimulus provided by the shift to the closed car in the twenties. Increasingly into the 1930s new investment in the automobile and ancillary industries was being stimulated more by the demands of planned obsolescence and the dictates of style than by basic innovations in automotive and manufacturing technologies. As *Business Week* reported in its issue of November 10, 1934, the result was that "with no overwhelming need for wholesale modernization, the industry would like to roll along for a while without any capital outlay. The cars themselves are good, already have everything a purchaser should want in the way of personal transportation."

With the exception of the automatic transmission, the major mechanical innovations that distinguish cars of the post–World War II period from the 1908 Model T had been incorporated into production cars by the late 1920s. The self-starter was developed by Charles F. Kettering under the supervision of Henry M. Leland in 1911. It gained rapid acceptance after its introduction in the 1912 Cadillac, which also featured a generator-battery lighting and ignition system. The self-starter was an adaptation of the electric cash register motor that Kettering earlier had developed at National Cash Register. As it happened, this electric device sealed the doom of the electric car, by obviating the onerous and dangerous task, especially for women, of using a hand crank to start an internal-combustion engine.

Following the general adoption of the self-starter, the single most significant automotive innovation was the closed steel body. This change alone outmoded the styling of the Model T, onto whose open-car design the closed body was ungracefully grafted. Closed cars used much more plate glass than open cars and required different materials for upholstery. The cost of plate glass was significantly reduced, and its quality improved, by a continuous-process technique introduced and perfected by Clarence W. Avery at Ford between 1919 and 1921. Hudson's innovation of simpler, standardized parts and subassemblies for car bodies resulted in its introduction of the first inexpensive closed car in 1921.

The all-steel body, notes William J. Abernathy, "promised strength with less weight, greater styling possibilities, and mass production economies." These promises were realized as production techniques were improved. Abernathy describes a number of significant developments: "Because of the greater temperature tolerance of steel, paint could be 'baked' on, thereby permitting a faster finishing process. . . . Box annealing, normalizing, and loose rolling processes developed by the steel industry improved the quality of sheet steel. Automatic welding machines, improvements in sound deadening materials, and the monopiece body, all developed by the Budd Manufacturing Company, led to quieter and stronger steel bodies." The spread of automatic welding in body assembly was linked closely to the adoption of the closed steel body. Introduced at Budd in 1925, automatic welding came into extensive use in 1928 at the Ford River Rouge plant in Model A production. Automatic welding reduced assembly costs while increasing the quality of the product. "It produced strong and neat joints with greater speed and uniformity than previous assembly methods. The assembly consumed less material, and the resulting body was lighter." [13]

Edward G. Budd innovated an all-steel body that was introduced in the 1912 Oakland and Hupmobile models and in the 1914 Dodge. Then Dodge in 1923 introduced the first closed sheet-steel body, with wood and waterproof fabric used only on its roof. The closed sheet-steel body was adapted to the Model T in 1925. Cadillac, Chrysler, and Packard also had adopted the closed sheet-steel body by 1928, although as late as 1934 most GM cars still used wood framing with sheet metal on all exterior surfaces except the roof. Steel roofs did not appear on cars until the 1935 model year, when GM introduced its one-piece steel "turret top" and Studebaker came out with an all-steel roof made by Budd.

Only 10.3 percent of cars built in the United States had been closed in 1919, versus 82.2 percent closed in 1927. The shift to the closed car brought not only a greatly increased demand for steel and plate glass and new production techniques, but an entirely new level and type of demand for automotive products and services. Combined with better roads, the closed car encouraged all-the-year-round use of the automobile. The Hoover Committee on Recent Economic Changes pointed out in 1929 that "the effect of this more constant use was to increase the demand for gasoline, lubricants, and tires, and to provide an almost new market for alcohol, glycerine, and other non-freezing preparations, and, not least, to increase the demand for labor for repair and maintenance service." [14]

Kettering and Thomas Midgeley, Jr., of the General Motors Research Corporation, discovered in the early 1920s that the addition of tetraethyl lead to gasoline greatly reduced engine knock. Then in 1926 Graham Edgar of the Ethyl Gasoline Corporation, formed by General Motors and Standard Oil of Indiana to market the product, conceived a scale to rate the octane (antiknock quality) of fuel. Ethyl gasoline and better crankshaft balancing to reduce vibrations were the most important of the breakthroughs that led to the introduction of the first high-compression (4.5:1) engine in a moderate-priced car, the stylish 1924 Chrysler Six.

The Chrysler Six also featured four-wheel hydraulic brakes, developed in 1918 by Malcolm Lougheed (Lockheed) and introduced on the 1920 Duesenberg, the first American car to use a straight-eight engine. Four-wheel mechanical brakes began to be widely adopted as standard equipment in 1923–1924, as were low-pressure "balloon" tires, which had thinner walls and halved tire pressures from about 60 psi to 30 psi. Low-pressure tires in turn led to the introduction of more sensitive steering mechanisms on the 1925 models. As early as 1915, quick demountable rims had replaced clincher types, making tires far easier to change.

The modern V-8 engine, which has remained the basic power plant for large cars, was introduced in a production car by De Dion–Bouton in 1909 and first used in an American-made production car in the 1915 Cadillac. Safety plate glass in all windows and synchromesh transmission, which obviated learning the fine art of double-declutching to avoid clashing the gears, were features of the 1928 Cadillac.

In contrast with the Model T, which came only in black after 1913 because only black enamel would dry fast enough for the Ford production schedule, mass-produced cars of all hues of the rainbow became possible when Duco lacquer made its debut on sheet steel in the "True Blue" of the 1924 Oakland.

Compared with the incorporation of these 1912–1929 innovations in production cars, the mechanical improvements of the 1930–1950 period were far less basic. Probably the most significant manufacturing innovation was casting the entire engine block of the 1932 Ford V-8 as a single unit. This greatly reduced manufacturing costs, making an eight-cylinder engine practical for low-priced cars. The only 1930s innovation in power plant of comparable significance was the production in the late 1930s of the first diesel-powered passenger cars by Mercedes-Benz.

While the styling of cars underwent revolutionary change in the 1930s, under the hood they remained essentially the same. A prime example is that the six-cylinder Chevrolet engine introduced in 1929, called the "cast iron wonder," with minor improvements remained the basic Chevrolet power plant until 1953. However, as evidenced in the 1949 Ford B-A, the first new Ford design since the V-8, by 1950 the average horsepower of American cars had increased to 100 bhp, versus the 20 bhp common in the 1920s.

The mechanical innovations of the 1930s were almost all concerned with riding comfort, handling, and ease of operation. Improved suspension systems were the most important. Mercedes-Benz introduced the first modern independent front suspension in its 1931 six-cylinder model. By the next model year, thirty-one European makes were using some form of independent front suspension, some having fully independent suspension of all four wheels. During the 1930s Ferdinand Porsche also perfected torsion-bar suspension, in which laminated strips of steel twist as they absorb shock, thus increasing resistance in proportion to the strength of the shock. The 1938 Volkswagen prototype employed both torsion-bar and fully independent suspension of all four wheels. In the United States, General Motors began developing independent front suspension in late 1930. It was featured in the 1934 GM models. Ford became the last American automobile manufacturer to adopt independent front suspension in 1949. Packard in 1955 became the first American production car to use torsion-bar independent front suspension.

Automatic controls were developed. Several 1933 cars featured a starter activated by the accelerator instead of by a separate starter pedal. The introduction of the mechanical fuel pump by GM's AC Spark Plug Division in 1926 made possible the use of the down-draft carburetor, which increased the power of the engine by increasing the flow of the fuel-air mixture. However, the distribution of fuel became uneven when the car was on a grade, and this problem motivated the development of the automatic choke. The first was developed by the Pierce Governor Company in 1928. An automatic choke with thermostatic and vacuum controls developed in 1931 by Stromberg was introduced in the 1932 Oldsmobile, and by the 1934 model year the automatic choke had become common. Ford continued to use a manual choke until 1953.

"Freewheeling," which enjoyed a brief vogue after it was innovated at Studebaker in 1930, put the transmission into neutral when the throttle was released. This saved fuel but was dangerous because the braking power of the engine was lost. Freewheeling was displaced by automatic overdrive, introduced in the 1934 Chrysler and DeSoto Airflow models.

By 1934 automatic declutching devices were available on several models, and in 1935 Hudson and Terraplane introduced a new "electric hand" fingertip-control gearshift mounted on the steering column. Fluid coupling and the torque converter, the innovations that were combined eventually into the modern automatic transmission, had been invented for use in marine engines in Germany in the early 1900s. The first fully automatic transmission was the 1940 Oldsmobile's "Hydra-matic Drive," which used a fluid coupling and a four-speed planetary gearbox. Chrysler developed its own automatic transmission in the "Fluid Drive" featured in the 1941 Chrysler, Dodge, and DeSoto models. The fluid torque-converter automatic transmission of the present day was first used in 1937 GM buses and made its appearance in passenger cars in the 1948 Buick "Dynaflow" transmission.

Thus, the era of epochal innovation in automotive technology had ended by the onset of the Great Depression. "None of these changes [of the 1930s] represented any drastic technological innovations; most were ideas that had been thought of and experimented with earlier, but had not in their initial stages proved commercially practical," Rae asserts. "What was happening to the passenger automobile was a constant process of refinement and improvement." [15]

Notably too, the lead in automotive technology by the 1930s was reverting to Europe, as evidenced by the introduction of diesel-powered passenger cars by Mercedes-Benz and the innovation of vastly improved suspension systems at Mercedes-Benz and by Porsche. The most technologically advanced production car of the 1930s undoubtedly was the 1934 Citroën Traction Avant, which featured an all-steel body, unitized construction, streamlined styling, an overhead-valve engine, independent front and torsion-bar suspension, and front-wheel drive. Yet in the throes of the worldwide depression, production of the Traction Avant led to bankruptcy for André Citroën.

The End of Expansion

Far more than automobile manufacturing was affected by the combination of market saturation and technological stagnation in the automobile industry, for the continuation of Coolidge prosperity was tied in most ways to the expansion of automobility. The stabilization of demand for motorcars consequently had catastrophic reverberations. The ending of huge governmental expenditures for new construction of streets and highways seemed imminent by 1929. New residential construction, another mainstay of the boom dependent on increasing motorization, began declining sharply in early 1928. So did the manufacture of tires. The prospects were particularly glum for the petroleum industry, which by 1927 faced a drop in the price of crude oil below the cost of production and heavy losses in refining activities connected with meeting the needs of the motorcar.

In 1923–1924 skyrocketing prices for gasoline had presaged a fuel shortage that touched off investigations of the oil industry by both Progressive Senator Robert M. LaFollette of Wisconsin and the Federal Trade Commission, as well as several muckraking articles by Ida M. Tarbell, the well-known critic of the Standard Oil Company. By the end of 1926, however, huge new oil fields developed in Oklahoma and Texas had led to overproduction, which promised to be lasting because, as Alfred D. Chandler explains, "the market was no longer expanding as it had before 1925. Not only did the vast flow of crude threaten decreasing prices but also a temporary increase in costs ... [because] the new crude, heavy in sulphur, demanded changes in the refining equipment which processed it." As a consequence, Standard Oil of New Jersey's 1927 profit "was the lowest since 1912. Earnings fell from $117.7 million in 1926 to $40.4 million in 1927. Not only did the refining activities show heavy losses, but domestic production showed a small net loss." [16]

Additionally, the automobile boom of the 1920s was either illusory or deleterious for several segments of the economy. The depressed condition of agriculture and the demise of the family farm in that decade were in large part the result of motorization. The larger trading areas brought about by automobility unsettled retail and wholesale trade to the particular detriment of many small-town and downtown retail businesses. The profits of the railroads on short-haul passenger traffic and of the street railways and interurbans dwindled as riders switched to motorcars. Municipal governments lost their tax bases as middle-class automobile commuters moved to the suburbs.

Nor did the boom mean prosperity even for most of the automobile industry. As we have seen, by the mid-1920s most automobile dealers were breaking even or losing money. In the 1920s the franchised dealership system became universal, wiping out the wholesalers who had served as middlemen between the automobile manufacturers and the dealers in the early days of the industry. With the closure of entry into automobile manufacturing in the 1920s and the solidification of the industry into an oligopoly of three giant corporations, most small automobile producers, and with them most parts and accessories manufacturers, faced ruin. "Unhappily, there is more of tragedy, courage and dogged determination than of romance in the events which are now unfolding," wrote James Dalton in the October 1924 issue of *Motor*. "Old and honored names are being erased from the roster and it seems inevitable that more of them must go, either by voluntary liquidation while there is still something to save, or by failure.... The industry is slowly but steadily contracting, *not in the volume of its products but in the number of companies making them*." Dalton predicted: "The effects promise to be far reaching not only for accessories manufacturers but for jobbers and dealers. No vivid imagination is required to visualize the result. It will mean a radical readjustment in methods of distributing a large volume of merchandise which has been highly profitable in the past ... it is practically certain that at least 90 percent of the business will always be in the hands of a comparatively few powerful manufacturers." [17]

The makers of luxury cars and the coachbuilding firms that built custom bodies for production luxury car chassis would be particularly notable casualties. Richard Burns Carson points out that the popular prestige attached in the prosperous twenties to ownership of a unique Duesenberg, Franklin, Lincoln, Marmon, Packard, Peerless, or Pierce-Arrow turned to aspersion with hard times: affluent owners were stoned while driving past breadlines. Moreover, the exorbitant cost of these and lesser luxury cars such as the Chrysler Imperial and the Cadillac V-16 became increasingly unjustifiable even to the wealthy as technological differences were erased vis-à-vis much more moderately priced production cars during the 1930s. Luxury car sales peaked at about 150,000 units (or 5 percent of total American demand) in 1928 and 1929, then declined sharply to less than 20,000 units in 1933. They further evaporated to a mere 10,000 units in 1937, while the rest of the automobile market experienced a general recovery. Duesenberg, Franklin, Marmon, Peerless, and Pierce-Arrow failed as firms; Cadillac V-16, Chrysler Imperial, and Lincoln sales shrank to next to nothing; Packard, the most prestigious luxury marque of the 1920s, was forced to develop an integrated line of cheaper models to survive. Carson sees 1933 as marking the end of the true luxury car market in the United States and of the custom coachbuilding firms. [18]

There was indeed some justice in the outcome that the main benefits of the automobile boom accrued to a relatively small number of capitalists, for the boom was mainly due to vast capital expenditures to reshape the American economy and society to fit the motor vehicle—something largely accomplished by the late 1920s. During the decade the production of capital goods and nonresidential construction rose much more rapidly than the production of commodities designed for direct consumption, including residential construction. This huge expansion in capital investment undoubtedly encouraged an unrealistic emphasis upon the priority of savings for investment. And it encouraged this at the expense of demands for better income distribution and for significant increases in personal disposable income.

The paradox confronting Americans by the late 1920s was that, although the automobile boom was the product of capital investment, automobility had caused a concomitant shift to a new consumer-goods-oriented economy and society. The diffusion of mass-production techniques, innovated in the automobile industry, tremendously increased the output of all commodities. Even more important, as a governmental fact-finding committee was to point out in 1933, "the great expansion in the automobile and electrical industries had far reaching effects in diverting the consumers' purchasing power from old to new products and placing in the hands of consumers stocks of durable products which have a slow rate of obsolescence and which, consequently, need to be replaced only after a lapse of considerable time." (The average life of a passenger car, for example, was seven years.) During the twenties the production of such durable consumer goods increased 72 percent, compared with an increase of less than 15 percent in the production of more staple, perishable commodities.[19]

As we have seen, it was time sales of automobiles that set the precedent for a great expansion of consumer installment credit during the twenties. As the market for automobiles approached saturation after 1925, and as defaults on auto loans rose, the finance companies began to fear that they had overextended credit for automobile purchases. So they tightened credit terms. To diversify their risks, they also encouraged installment purchases of many other types of merchandise. However, consumer installment credit could not be expanded indefinitely to sustain purchases of durable consumer goods.

Personal disposable income did not increase sufficiently and income distribution was inadequate during the 1920s to support the phenomenal increase in the production of durable consumer goods with low replacement demand. The decade was a time of relatively full employment, and the real wages of workers employed in manufacturing rose about 17 percent between 1919 and 1929. Per capita disposable income, however, rose only about 9 percent during that period, and the rise was fairly well concentrated in the upper-middle- and upper-income brackets. The top 5 percent in income received approximately one third of all personal income in 1929. Contrary to the optimistic predictions of Henry Ford and other apostles of industrial efficiency, and despite an almost 50-percent gain in manufacturing output, the number of workers employed in manufacturing remained constant—the big gain in new employment being in relatively poorly paying service trades. The collapse of the trade union movement after the 1920–1921 recession was one important reason why workers did not share adequately in the gains of the automobile boom. Wages and prices remained relatively stable from 1922 to 1929, freezing the level of demand for an ever increasing amount of consumer goods. During the 1920s corporate profits and dividends rose between eight and nine times faster than real wages. Net corporate profits soared from $3.9 billion in 1922 to $7.2 billion in 1929, and bank deposits, almost wholly from the upper and upper-middle classes, increased from $41.4 billion to $57.9 billion.

These excessive savings lacked productive outlets for investment, so they became the main source of the runaway bull market of the late 1920s. Once markets for durable consumer goods had begun to be saturated, there was no incentive to invest money in plant expansion and new equipment. The money ended up instead in diversified stock portfolios, where it accumulated paper profits. Lacking borrowers, the banks put their money in the same place. It was this large volume of capital that could not find a productive use that skyrocketed stock prices from reasonable bets on the future into fantastic gambles on the hereafter.

Inadequate governmental supervision of trading on the stock exchanges, inadequate application of monetary controls to curb speculation, weak banking and corporate structures, and international monetary problems were additional flaws, in an economy riddled with weaknesses, that contributed to bringing about the stock market crash and an ensuing decade of hard times.

The more fundamental weaknesses of Coolidge prosperity, however, were tied in one way or another to the impact of the automobile and the automobile industry. Because the populace as a whole lacked the purchasing power necessary to sustain the automobile boom, by the late 1920s the mass-production techniques innovated in the automobile industry had led to overproduction, which could not be absorbed through advertising, salesmanship, or the extension of consumer installment credit. And once market saturation and technological stagnation in the automobile industry became apparent, there was no incentive for capitalists to invest still more capital in the future of automobility.

The Sage of Dearborn Responds to Hard Times

Henry Ford was one of the few industrial capitalists sufficiently committed to the capitalist system to make a voluntary effort to maintain the economy as it slid into depression following the stock market crash of October 1929. Hoping to stimulate consumption by increasing purchasing power, Ford lowered prices on the Model A in November and raised the minimum daily wage of his workers to $7 in December. Early in 1930 he announced a $25-million program of branch factory construction.

Ford quickly reneged once the severity of the depression had become apparent. He also reduced the profit margins of his dealers on the sale of new cars to the lowest in the industry. And by 1932 the minimum daily wage at Ford had been reduced to $6 for skilled workers, $5 for semi-skilled workers, and $4 for laborers. Even these rates were illusory, because they did not account for the downgrading of many jobs to lower pay scales and an increase in jobbing out components manufacture to outside companies that paid still lower wages than Ford. The number of Ford employees declined sharply from 170,502 in 1929 to 46,282 by 1932, as total employment in Detroit's automobile factories dwindled to less than 40 percent of its 1923–1925 average. Ford had been an opponent of unemployment insurance for workers. Now, in the trough of the Depression, he claimed that only lazy workers could not find jobs. Because Ford, with the help of Bennett's Service Department, managed to resist unionization longer than General Motors or Chrysler, Ford wages for 1937–1941 fell a few cents below the average for all industry in the United States and well below the average for the automobile industry.

In the black ghetto of Inkster, Michigan, adjacent to lily-white Dearborn, a bastion of the Ku Klux Klan, Ford set up a gigantic plantation for his black workers. He paid them only $1 a day in cash of their $4 wage, the remaining $3 in food and clothing from a public commissary. Seeds to plant in garden patches and communal sewing machines were also furnished to Ford's Inkster blacks.

Yet, outside his company, organized labor, the automobile industry, and the Detroit metropolitan area, the myths that had built up around the figure of Henry Ford refused to die. A survey conducted by *Fortune* magazine in 1937 for the National Association of Manufacturers found that 47.2 percent of the respondents still approved of the policies of the Ford Motor Company, versus an insignificant 3.1-percent approval for General Motors and 1.2-percent approval for Chrysler.

Even to grass-roots Americans who had deified Ford for a generation, however, his rhetoric increasingly seemed irrelevant nonsense as the Great Depression wore on. The letters to the Sage of Dearborn dwindled and became bitter and resentful. "Instead of writing to Ford," reports Reynold Wik, "farmers in increasing numbers addressed their remarks to officials in the nation's capital where the power to effect reform resided. The letters found in the [Franklin Delano Roosevelt] library at Hyde Park, New

York, and in the National Archives in Washington, D.C., suggest that farmers believed that relief could be found in federal legislation rather than in the good intentions of business leaders." [20]

Laissez-Faire Expires: Ford and the 1933 Banking Collapse

The Guardian Detroit Bank was formed in 1927 by Edsel Ford and Ernest Kanzler, his brother-in-law and up to 1926 a Ford executive. Within a year the bank had become the nucleus of the Detroit Union Guardian Trust Company, a holding company owning the stock of twenty-five Michigan banks. Kanzler was chairman of the board, and Edsel Ford was the largest stockholder of the Union Guardian Trust Company. Union Guardian financed the Ford Motor Company's Universal Credit Corporation, which in turn financed time sales of the Model A. To counterbalance this powerful Ford-dominated banking group, forty other Michigan banks financed largely by General Motors and Chrysler money merged in January 1930 into the Detroit Bankers Company. The two banking groups together held 57.5 percent of all loans and investments in Michigan and controlled 87 percent of the banking in Detroit. [21]

By the October 1929 crash, the Union Guardian Group held a large portfolio of stocks and had invested heavily in real estate. Within a year the group's stock plummeted from a 1929 high of $350 to $75. To maintain the price of the holding company's shares, so that investments would not have to be liquidated at depressed prices, 110 Union Guardian directors each agreed to purchase at least 60,000 shares and hold them for a year. A committee of five trustees was formed to oversee this stock pool; it included Kanzler and Roy D. Chapin, founder of the Hudson Motor Car Company and secretary of commerce in the Hoover administration.

The price of Union Guardian stock was supported by borrowing at heavy interest rates and cannibalizing the accounts of savers and investors. In violation of both state and federal banking laws, by 1932 the Union Guardian group held 149,574 of its own shares as security for loans. By 1932, too, the parent Guardian National Bank of Detroit had loaned its own officers and directors nearly $3.5 million, an amount equivalent to 34 percent of its capital. The First National Bank of Detroit outdid even this by lending its directors and officers over $33.2 million, a sum greater than its total capital.

The Union Guardian group maintained public confidence in its solvency by shifting money from bank to bank as financial statements came due and by issuing false reports to its stockholders. In 1931, for example, a $3,887,052 net earning before charge-offs was reported to the stockholders, while the official report filed with the Michigan Securities Commission declared a loss of $288,930. The 1933 annual report to Union Guardian stockholders declared a net income for 1932 of $1,316,952; Kanzler later corrected the figure to a "profit in the red" of $1,789,069.

Far from being unique, the malfeasance and deceit of the Union Guardian group typified the pattern of corruption in the American banking system revealed in 1933 in mounds of testimony before the Senate Banking and Currency Committee. Part of the unfolding national scandal was evidence of favoritism in the award of Reconstruction Finance Corporation (RFC) loans, ostensibly intended by the Hoover administration as a means of shoring up weak banks. At a time when total RFC deposits were only $95 million, a $90-million loan was extended to the Central Republic Bank of Chicago, one of whose founders was Charles Dawes, president of the RFC and former vice-president in the Coolidge administration. Union Guardian, which had Secretary of Commerce Roy D. Chapin as a trustee, was given a $14-million RFC loan in 1932 and by January 1933 was seeking another for $20.5 million, for which it could offer as collateral securities worth only $6 million at face (not market) value. Rumors were that Union Guardian was short $14 million of the amount that its depositors had banked and that the Guardian National Bank remained open only because Detroit's welfare funds were on deposit there.

As it turned out, an RFC loan of $51 million was needed to bail out Union Guardian. But the Union Guardian group could come up with mortgages worth only $35 million at depressed market prices as collateral, whereas federal law required that all RFC loans be secured by full collateral. President Hoover was willing to make the loan in violation of the law, but he was stopped short when Senator James Couzens threatened to denounce the loan on the floor of the United States Senate. So Hoover turned to the expedient of trying to convince Henry Ford to bail out Union Guardian. He dispatched Chapin and Undersecretary of the Treasury Arthur Ballantine to Detroit on Friday, February 10.

The Union Guardian Trust Company was, for all practical purposes, already under a Ford trusteeship. The Fords by now had loaned the bank $15.5 million and in addition had permitted it to use $5 million of the Ford Motor Company's municipal bonds as collateral for other loans. But Henry Ford refused to prop up the bank further if the RFC was not willing to provide a loan. On Monday, February 13, Ford told Chapin and Ballantine that he would not risk $50 million of his money "to keep Jim Couzens from making a speech." He threatened as well to withdraw his $32.5 million in deposits from Union Guardian and his $25 million in deposits from the First National Bank of Detroit. To pleas that this would collapse the entire Michigan banking structure, he replied, "Let the crash come."

On Tuesday, February 14, 1933, at 1:32 A.M., following a marathon session at the Union Guardian Building in Detroit, Governor William Comstock proclaimed a state banking holiday that closed 436 banks and trust companies and froze $1.5 billion in assets in the state of Michigan. The closing of the Michigan banks set off a chain reaction that collapsed the national banking structure. As Robert Conot concludes, "Panic spread across the nation.... By March 4 banks in only a handful of states remained open. The economic system of the country had broken down. Laissez-faire had expired."[22]

The New Deal and the Rise of the UAW

Aware that the recovery of the automobile industry was important to restoring prosperity, President Roosevelt took a personal interest in National Recovery Administration (NRA) code drafted for that industry. "The subjects to which the code committee gave greatest attention were hours, wages, and management-labor relations," writes Sidney Fine in his definitive study. Maximum weekly hours for workers were set at 48, and it was stipulated that working hours averaged on an annual basis should not exceed 35 a week, a substantial reduction from the average weekly hours worked in the automobile industry in the 1920s. But Fine notes that 95 percent of the auto workers were already making more than the 43-cent minimum hourly wage set by the code before it was approved by the president on August 26, 1933. Under Section 7(a) of the National Industrial Recovery Act (NIRA), workers ostensibly were given the right to organize and engage in collective bargaining with management through a representative of their choice. Yet Roosevelt overrode his own Labor Advisory Board and permitted an affirmation of the automobile industry's open-shop policy to stand in the code. The automobile code did not encompass the parts and accessories manufacturers, contained no references to trade practices, and failed to define the relationship between automobile manufacturers and their dealers and suppliers. The president's Consumer Advisory Board "pointed out that the code was of little interest to consumers.... It noted that the highly competitive character of the industry protected the consumer in so far as price was concerned." The National Automobile Chamber of Commerce (NACC) was made the code authority and was entrusted with its administration, while neither organized labor nor the consumer was represented. Henry Ford refused to sign, and the Roosevelt administration did not have sufficient will or the power to make him sign. Thus, the code at best reduced average hours, which the Depression was doing anyway, and maintained workers' wages, which accounted for only 10 percent of the wholesale price of a car. As Fine says, "The automobile manufacturers, in final analysis, had their way." [23]

On May 27, 1935, a unanimous decision of the United States Supreme Court in *Schecter Poultry Corporation v. the United States* declared the National Industrial Recovery Act unconstitutional. Probably the best summary of the pathetic ineffectiveness of the automobile industry code was given by Alfred Reeves, who spoke for the Automobile Manufacturers Association (AMA), the successor to the NACC. "Neither the industry nor its employees," said Reeves, "benefitted from the code while it existed and neither have [sic] suffered any loss from its termination." [24] The code certainly did not create jobs for automobile workers or improve the working conditions of those fortunate enough to remain employed. It did nothing to lower the prices of cars for consumers. It did not even lead to higher profits for the manufacturers. And it did nothing to check the attrition of small automobile producers and parts and accessories manufacturers from the automobile industry, which had accelerated in the 1920s and snowballed in the Depression. The main impact of the NIRA was that it stimulated labor organization and gave an impetus for management to pay more attention to labor relations. Section 7(a) encouraged the American Federation of Labor (AFL) to establish a network of "United Automobile Workers Federal Unions," open to automobile workers whose skills did not fit other AFL unions. The automobile manufacturers, in turn, tried to neutralize Section 7(a) by setting up espionage systems to rout union sympathizers from their plants and by trying to organize company unions.

The National Labor Relations (Wagner-Connery) Act (NLRA) of July 5, 1935, replaced Section 7(a) after the NIRA was declared unconstitutional. This so-called Wagner Act set up a National Labor Relations Board (NLRB), empowered to conduct elections to determine workers' bargaining agents and to restrain employers from "unfair labor practices," including the discharging of workers for union membership and the setting up of employer-dominated company unions. Roosevelt at first opposed the Wagner bill but soon reversed himself to declare it "must" legislation. "The Wagner Act was one of the most drastic legislative innovations of the decade," observes William E. Leuchtenberg. "It threw the weight of government behind the right of labor to bargain collectively, and compelled employers to accede peacefully to the unionization of their plants. It imposed no reciprocal obligations of any kind on unions. No one, then or later, fully understood why Congress passed so radical a law with so little opposition and by such overwhelming margins." Certainly an important reason, as Leuchtenberg concludes, was that "the Wagner Act and the movement for industrial unionism were motivated in part by the desire to contain 'unbalanced and radical' labor groups." [25]

The workers in the pre–New Deal automobile industry, observes Fine, "whether native- or foreign-born, white or black, male or female, ... had at least one characteristic in common. They were, in the vast majority, almost entirely innocent of trade unionism in so far as their personal work experience was concerned." John Rae describes the half-hearted attempts of the AFL to unionize them in the late 1920s and early 1930s as "monumental ineptitude.... The leadership of the AFL was obviously more concerned with protecting the jurisdictional rights of existing craft unions than with developing an organizational structure that would meet the needs of the automobile workers." However, no greater success was achieved by the radical International Workers of the World (IWW). [26]

Labor unrest in the automobile industry spread with massive unemployment and the deterioration of working conditions as the Depression deepened. On March 7, 1932, the minuscule, communist-dominated Auto Workers Union staged a march of the unemployed on the Ford River Rouge plant that ended in a violent encounter with the Dearborn police. In 1933 the parts and accessories manufacturers were plagued by spontaneous, sporadic strikes.

Coincident with passage of the Wagner Act, the AFL issued a charter to the International Union, United Automobile Workers of America (UAW). And within the AFL, in November 1935, a group headed by John L. Lewis, Sidney Hillman, and David Dubinsky set up the Committee for Industrial Organization (CIO), with the intention of abandoning the craft union principle of the AFL and of organizing industrial unions in the mass-production industries that had resisted unionization. The CIO separated from the AFL and became the Congress of Industrial Organizations in August 1936, taking along the UAW, headed by Homer Martin and the aggressive young Reuther brothers, Walter and Victor. At this time only about 15 percent of American automobile workers were organized.

By the end of 1936 the UAW had closed most General Motors plants through the new tactic of the sit-down strike. Workers stopped work but remained in the plants so that strikebreakers could not be brought in.

In these sit-downs, as August Meier and Elliot Rudwick point out in their study of black auto workers and unionization, "blacks mostly left the plants, neither joining nor actively opposing the strikers, and by and large these strikes were won virtually without black support.... Like the black elite in cities across the country, Detroit's Negro leadership overwhelmingly sided with the manufacturers." Black automobile workers distrusted the UAW and remained unconvinced that unionization would bring them any benefits. In January 1937, "realizing that the colored employees could be relied upon," the Ford Service Department "for the first time recruited blacks as armed guards—hand picking large, strong men from various departments in the Rouge plant, and arming them with blackjacks and other similar weapons." Ford was not unique in exploiting blacks in the 1930s labor-management confrontations. Later, during the 1939 lockout and strike at Dodge Main in the Hamtramck section of Detroit, the Chrysler Corporation attempted "to capitalize on racial antagonisms" by encouraging blacks to go back to work, in a strategy "calculated to break the strike by producing interracial violence and the calling out of the National Guard." [27]

The refusal of Governor Frank Murphy to call out the National Guard to evict strikers from GM's Chevrolet and Fisher Body plants in Flint, Michigan, led on February 11, 1937, to the capitulation of GM to the UAW-CIO. Chrysler yielded to the union's sit-down tactics two months later. Alfred Sloan, the GM president, was outraged that President Roosevelt and Secretary of Labor Frances Perkins had joined Governor Murphy in maintaining "a steady pressure upon the corporation, and upon me personally, to negotiate with the strikers who had seized our property, until we finally felt obliged to do so." On April 1, 1937, Sloan wrote to the GM stockholders that the strike had not been "actuated by any fundamental causes that affected, in an important degree, the welfare of the workers" and expressed his opinion that the unionization of GM "means the economic and political slavery of the worker, and an important step toward an economic and political dictatorship." [28]

The GM and Chrysler settlements left Ford the holdout against industry unionization and the main strike target of the UAW-CIO. Because the Roosevelt administration had failed to enforce the law fully, the intransigent Ford Motor Company remained in violation of the National Labor Relations Act, the constitutionality of which had been upheld by the United States Supreme Court. Members of the Ford Service Department brutally beat Walter Reuther and several other UAW-CIO organizers in the notorious "battle of the overpass" at the River Rouge plant on May 26, 1937. Then on April 1, 1941, following the discharge of several union members, a spontaneous walkout of Ford workers closed down the River Rouge plant, initiating a UAW-CIO organizing strike.

Although the vast majority of black workers left the plant in the walkout, it is estimated that between 1,500 and 2,500 blacks, along with about 300 white members of the Ford Service Department, remained in the Rouge as strikebreakers. With the exception of a few dissenters—most notably the Reverend Charles Hill and the Reverend Horace White—Detroit's black clergy supported the company. The Ford management position was publicly endorsed by two black Detroit church groups, the Interdenominational Ministers Alliance and the Baptist Ministers Conference. This time, however, the Detroit Urban League failed to back Ford. Even more important, the Detroit branch of the National Association for the Advancement of Colored People (NAACP) followed the national NAACP policy of cooperation with unions. Members of its youth council distributed some ten thousand handbills in churches urging Ford's black workers, "Do Not Be Used as Strikebreakers," and they drove around the Rouge in a hired sound truck exhorting the workers remaining within the plant to leave. Walter White, the NAACP national secretary, flew to Detroit to help in the evacuation effort, but to little avail. In the NLRB election that followed the strike, the majority of black workers endorsed the company-backed, craft-dominated AFL—an anomaly in that they overwhelmingly held unskilled jobs at Ford.

Even without the support of the blacks, the UAW-CIO won about 70 percent of the votes in the NLRB election held at Ford on May 21, 1941. On June 20 Henry Ford finally signed a contract with the UAW-CIO—agreeing, ironically, to more generous terms than had GM or Chrysler, including the deduction of union dues from workers' paychecks. At first after the NLRB election he had threatened to close his plants rather than sign with the UAW-CIO. His abrupt turnaround in recognizing the union and agreeing to its terms was brought about by Clara Ford, who never before had interfered in company business. She was terrified lest riots and bloodshed result from her husband's intransigence, and threatened to leave him. "She became frantic about it," Ford told Charles Sorensen. "She insisted that I sign what she termed a peace agreement. If I did not she was through." [29]

With the signing of the Ford-UAW contract a new era of labor relations in the automobile industry dawned, as workers turned from dependence on Henry Ford's paternalism and fear of Bennett's Service Department to the union shop steward and the skills of UAW-CIO negotiators.

Sloanism

12

As the era of American social and industrial history dominated by Fordism evaporated with hard times, a new era was being inaugurated at General Motors under the leadership of Alfred P. Sloan, Jr.

Ford had remained stubbornly committed to the Model T as a single, static model in a dynamically changing technological milieu. Except for minor face-liftings and the incorporation of such basic improvements as the self-starter and the closed steel body, the Model T remained essentially unchanged long after it was technologically obsolete. Even David Hounshell, who documents "significant changes" in the supposedly changeless Model T, concludes that "by the standards of the mid-1920s, the Model T was outmoded. The ignition, carburetion, transmission, brake, and suspension systems, as well as the styling and appointments, made the Model T appear antique." [1]

The Model T was intended as a farmer's car for a nation of farmers. Its popularity was bound to wane as the United States urbanized and as rural America got out of the mud after passage of the 1916 Federal Aid Road Act and the 1921 Federal Highway Act. Better roads rendered needless the once functional high clearance and hard springing of the rugged but rough-riding "Tin Lizzie." Model T owners tended to trade up to larger, faster, smoother riding, and more stylish cars; and the demand for low-cost, basic transportation that Model T had met tended increasingly to be filled from the backlog of used cars piling up on dealers' lots as the market became saturated. By the mid-1920s, a secondhand car of a more expensive make in good condition could be bought for the same price as a new Model T. In addition, the onset of market saturation for new cars forced general price reductions after 1925 that, for example, pegged only

$200 higher than an obsolete Model T an annually restyled, larger, and far better equipped Chevrolet, which could be bought on the installment plan.

Ford closed his mind to the advice of his executives, the pleas of his dealers, and mounting complaints about the Model T from his customers. He denounced the new emphasis on style and comfort as extravagant and wasteful, and tried to meet the competition by drastically reducing prices to a low of $290 for the coupe and making "everybody dig for profits." The speedup of the assembly line enforced by the Service Department drove workers "to the highest point of efficiency." Ford dealers, too, were forced "to the highest point of efficiency." As Model T production was cut from 1.8 million units in 1923 to 1.3 million units in 1926, the number of Ford dealerships was increased from about 8,500 to 9,800, in the hope that heightened competition among them would stimulate more aggressive salesmanship. Seven out of ten Ford dealers were losing money by 1926; and as some went bankrupt and others switched to General Motors, about a third of the Ford dealerships turned over that year.

Even Henry Ford was forced at last to recognize that the Model T era had ended. Production of the car was halted on May 27, 1927, and the Ford plants were shut down while its successor, the Model A, was hastily designed. A mild recession in 1927 was attributed in part to hundreds of thousands of automobile owners deferring their purchase of a new car until Ford came out with his new model. Some 400,000 orders were received before the Model A had even been seen by the public. At a retooling cost of $18 million, for what was probably up to that time the most extensive changeover of an industrial plant in American history, the assembly lines at River Rouge began to turn out limited numbers of the Model A in November 1927.

The initial response to the four-cylinder, 40-horsepower Model A was enthusiastic. Unlike the revolutionary Model T, however, the Model A was a very conventional car for its time. In 1929 Ford briefly regained the industry lead in sales that had been lost to Chevrolet in both 1927 and 1928. Ford production surpassed 1.5 million units in 1929 and 1.15 million units in 1930, compared with Chevrolet's 950,000 and 683,000 units for those years.

Nevertheless, the decline of the Ford Motor Company vis-à-vis GM and Chrysler continued into the 1930s, despite the fact that the 65-horsepower V-8, introduced in fourteen body styles on March 31, 1932, was a truly advanced automobile in all respects, selling at an exceptionally low price. "I have driven Fords exclusively when I could get away with one," bank robber Clyde Champion Barrow informed Henry Ford in a letter dated April 10, 1933. "For sustained speed and freedom from trouble the Ford has got ever [sic] other car skinned and even if my business hasn't been strictly legal it don't hurt enything [*sic*] to tell you what a fine car you got in the V-8." [2] Only a few years earlier Henry Ford had dismissed six-cylinder cars with the quip, "I have no use for an engine with more cylinders than a cow has teats." His radical move from the four-cylinder Model A to the V-8 was calculated to outdo Chevrolet, which had gone to six cylinders in 1929. The seventy-year-old Ford personally supervised the designing of the V-8 and the conversion of the River Rouge plant for its production. V-8 production was introduced gradually and necessitated less extensive and less costly changes than had the 1927 changeover to Model A production. The $450 to $650 V-8 featured streamlined styling, double drop-frame construction, safety plate glass in all windows, and syn-chromesh transmission. It was, in the words of Allan Nevins and Frank Hill, "very much the handsomest of all the company's creations." [3]

Neither the Model A nor the Ford V-8 could regenerate the Ford Motor Company. Between 1931 and 1970 Chevrolet outsold Ford in every year except 1935 and 1945, and the latter year was an exception only because Ford was the first automobile manufacturer to get back back into civilian production following World War II. Plymouth also cut into Ford sales in the low-priced field after it was introduced in 1929. And Ford's cars in the luxury and moderate-priced brackets—the Lincoln, acquired from the Lelands in 1921, and the Mercury, introduced in 1939 to compete with Pontiac and Dodge—failed to become popular. Only in the sale of light trucks did the Ford Motor Company enjoy a slight lead over its competitors. In the oligopoly that had come to dominate the American automobile industry, by 1936 Ford had dropped to third place in sales of passenger cars, with 22 percent of the U.S. market versus 43 percent for General Motors and 25 percent for Chrysler.

As automobile sales and registrations declined in general, Ford pro-duction collapsed from over 1.5 million units in 1929 to a low of only 232,000 units in 1932, before bouncing back to 600,000 units in 1941, the last full year of civilian automobile production before American entry into World War II. During 1931–1933 the Ford Motor Company lost $120 million after taxes. Profits of $17.9 million in 1936 and $6.7 million in 1937, during a brief revival of the economy, went far, however, toward cancel-ing out an estimated total loss of $26 million over the preceding decade.

Sloan's GM: Multidivisional Structure, Product Policy, and Financial Controls

In sharp contrast with the Ford Motor Company and almost all other automobile manufacturers, General Motors weathered well both the onset of market saturation in the 1920s and the evaporation of the market for new cars during the Depression. GM income after taxes rose from slightly over $72 million (10.32 percent of sales) in 1923. when Alfred Sloan became president, to over $248.48 million (18.94 percent of sales) in 1928. Better forecasting techniques at GM permitted Sloan to predict the onset of the Depression and to pull in the giant corporation's horns. Net income after taxes dropped to only $169,979 (0.04 percent of sales) in the trough of the Depression in 1932 before recovering to $238.482 million (16.57 percent of sales) in 1937. The GM payroll was cut about two thirds during the Depression, while stockholders continued to earn annual dividends ranging from 21 to 75 cents a share on common stock, versus annual common stock dividends ranging from 11 cents in 1923 to 63 cents in 1928. Because investment needs were slight, GM paid record dividends in 1936 and 1937, while working capital increased by more than a third over its 1929 level. Sloan later reported that "in no year did the corporation fail to earn a profit." [4]

Sloan was the automobile industry's first "gray man." First, last, and always an organization man, he abhorred the autocratic rule of colorful "personal" entrepreneurs such as Henry Ford and Billy Durant. Under his leadership General Motors became the archetype of the depersonalized, decentralized corporation run by an anonymous technostructure.

In the "multidivisional structure" that Sloan introduced at GM, strategic decisions affecting the setting of corporate goals and the long-term allocation of resources were centralized in executive and finance committees, while tactical decisions on the day-to-day utilization of these resources were decentralized in the firm's various operating divisions. At du Pont this had resolved problems stemming from a lack of overall cooperation and coordination among operating divisions making very different products. At GM the structure had the opposite function of decentralizing operating decisions down to an appropriate level in a formerly too-centralized firm in which the divisions made essentially the same product. For still different reasons, the multidivisional structure was adopted as well in the 1920s at Standard Oil of New Jersey and at Sears, Roebuck. It was at GM under Sloan, however, that the financial controls and coordination of operations that the structure engendered underwent the most refinement and formalization and were most publicized. [5] To a large extent this was the outcome of GM's ill-fated attempt to introduce an air-cooled engine designed by Charles F. Kettering.

Chevrolet's 1919–1923 experiment with Kettering's invention marked the last attempt by an American automobile manufacturer to pioneer to the stage of production a truly radical engine design. Kettering's "copper-cooled" engine was for a short time seen by GM as the key to bringing out a lightweight, inexpensive car to compete with the Model T. Air cooling offered several theoretical advantages over water cooling, including better fuel economy from an engine that weighed less per horsepower, savings from the elimination of a radiator and other cooling accessories, and an end to engines' freezing in winter and overheating in summer. In practice, however, the air-cooled engines of the day overheated badly, resulting in a loss of power and burned valves. Kettering sought to utilize the superior thermal properties of copper to eliminate this problem and to produce an air-cooled engine with a higher compression ratio, thus affording greater fuel economy and power for a given displacement. Heat was to be dissipated by a front-mounted fan, driven at faster than engine speed, pushing air through copper fins that had been brazed to the engine in a specially designed oven. The project had the enthusiastic personal support of Pierre S. du Pont, the GM president until 1923.

The copper-cooled engine was doomed by a lack of coordination and cooperation on the project among GM units. Production problems were the inevitable result of a lack of communication between Kettering's Dayton, Ohio, Delco laboratory, where the engine was designed, and the factories at Flint and Pontiac, Michigan, where the car that the engine powered was to be produced. Design problems arose also, because it had not been foreseen that numerous other components would have to be redesigned to accommodate to the light weight of the new engine. The copper-cooled Chevrolet was introduced at the 1923 New York automobile show, but only 759 were ever produced, and 239 of these were scrapped in production. Only 100 of the remainder were ever sold to retail customers. "After initial sales," relates Stuart W. Leslie, "complaints came in concerning excess noise, clutch problems, wear on cylinders, carburetor malfunctions, axle breakdowns, and fanbelt trouble." Reduced to a research project in 1923, the copper-cooled-engine program was terminated in 1925. General Motors would not produce another air-cooled car until the 1960–1969 Corvair. "The significant influence of the copper-cooled engine was in what it taught us about the value of organized cooperation and coordination in engineering and other matters," recalled Sloan in 1964. "It showed the need to make an effective distinction between divisional and corporate functions in engineering, and also between advanced product engineering and long-range research." [6]

After the copper-cooled-engine debacle, GM not only paid far more attention to such interrelationships within the firm, but under Sloan's leadership adopted a market strategy that discouraged technological innovation and eschewed technological leadership. Sloan took the position that "the primary object of the corporation . . . was to make money, not just to make motor cars.... The policy ... was valid if our cars were at least equal in design to the best of our competitors in a grade, so that it was not necessary to lead in design or to run the risk of untried experiments." [7] He considered even the safety plate-glass windows of the 1928 Cadillac an unjustified cost.

Control in the corporation under Sloan passed from engineers like Kettering to cost-cutting accountants. Donaldson Brown, the GM vice-president for finance, worked out with Albert Bradley a system of financial controls. They set a 20-percent return on investment as the corporation's expectation. And GM became insulated from the adverse effects of short-term fluctuations in the market for cars by basing unit cost estimates (hence car prices) on a conservative assessment of how many cars GM could expect to sell over a period of years at given prices and average utilization of plant capacity. When demand exceeded these expectations, GM would gain windfall profits, because unit prices had been set on the basis of a lower and consequently costlier level of production. This was called "standard volume pricing." The system of controls called for only a conservative amount out of actual profits to be reinvested in expansion of the business, including research and development. It was thus a strategy geared not for producing a technologically superior product at a lower price, but for guaranteeing the safety of invested capital and ensuring high rates of return in a market assumed to be both saturated and technologically mature.

What Sloan chose to call "constant upgrading of product" is more accurately described as planned obsolescence through cosmetic changes. In diametric opposition to the Ford Model T product philosophy of a single, static model at an ever decreasing unit price, GM attempted to produce "a car for every purse and purpose." Sloanism called for blanketing the market with a car at the top of every price range and encouraging the consumer to trade up from Chevrolet to Cadillac via Pontiac, Oldsmobile, or Buick. Sloanism also called for stimulating sagging sales in a replacement market by inducing the consumer, long before his present car's useful life was over, to trade it in for a newer and higher-priced one. Consumer dissatisfaction with today's car was engendered by the innovation of the annual model change, which called for major styling revisions every three years, functional or not, with minor annual faceliftings in between. The three-year styling cycle was geared to die life, so that retooling costs would not be excessive. The trick here was to maintain an overall GM product identity while differentiating GM car lines from one another and the GM car models in a given line from year to year. GM initiated bringing out annual models in 1923. But the concept evolved gradually and was not fully formalized and regularized until the 1930s.

Sloan intended that this product philosophy would result in GM's gaining each year a larger share of the consumer's dollar.

Styling Comes of Age

The new emphasis on styling engendered by Sloanism was not in itself dysfunctional, especially not in the automotive designs of the 1930s. Styling would only become dysfunctional with the excesses of the 1950s. Indeed, lower-slung, wider, aerodynamically designed cars became essential for safety and performance as cars with more powerful engines cruised at higher speeds on better roads. GM cars of the mid-1920s were 70 to 75 inches in height and 65 to 71 inches wide, compared with heights of 51 to 57 inches and overall width of about 80 inches in the mid-1960s. Sloan explained, "The new closed car [of the 1920s] was a high, ungainly contraption, with narrow doors and a belt line (that is, the line between the windows and the lower part of the body) high above the already high hoods.... [A]s cars were driven more rapidly by more efficient motors, it became dangerous to have vehicles with their center of gravity so far above the ground." [8]

As early as 1921 the GM product policy had stressed "the very great importance of style in selling," and in a letter dated July 8, 1926, to Harry H. Bassett, the general manager of Buick, Sloan expressed his "general views about the need [for GM] to develop a styling program." Sloan was particularly impressed with the low-slung lines of the 1924 Chrysler Six, necessitated by the car's 70-mph cruising speed. He had purchased small wire wheels to get his own Cadillac nearer to the ground. His views about the importance of styling were shared by Lawrence P. Fisher, the general manager of Cadillac, who had been impressed by the special bodies turned out for the cars of Hollywood movie stars in the Los Angeles custom body shop of Don Lee. In early 1926 Fisher hired Harley J. Earl, Lee's chief designer, under special contract as a consultant to Cadillac. Prior to that, in September 1925, Fisher Body (annexed as a division of GM in 1918) had acquired the old-line Fleetwood custom coachbuilding firm of Reading, Pennsylvania, and moved its operations to Detroit to do custom bodies for Cadillac chassis and aid in designing production-car bodies. Then on June 23, 1927, Sloan proposed to the GM executive committee a plan for a new Art and Color Section of fifty persons, to be headed by Earl and funded by the Fisher Body Division. Renamed the Styling Section in the 1930s, its purpose was "to direct general production body design and to conduct research and development programs in special car designs."

Earl's Styling Section gave GM a "long lead" in making the styling of automobiles an institutionalized activity carried out by professional designers, rather than a haphazard activity of engineers or salemen as the need for a new model arose. After World War II both Ford and Chrysler emulated GM in forming styling departments, which were staffed largely by personnel trained under Earl at GM. Earl, who ended his career as a GM vice-president, summed up his design approach in 1954: "My primary purpose for twenty-eight years has been to lengthen and lower the American automobile, at times in reality and always at least in appearance. Why? Because my sense of proportion tells me that oblongs are more attractive than squares." [9]

Earl used modeling clay in developing his designs instead of the then conventional wooden models and hammered metal parts. This permitted him to conceptualize more fluid, rounded shapes. He also departed from common practice by "designing the complete automobile, shaping the body, hood, fenders, headlights, and running boards and blending them into a good-looking whole. This, too, was a novel technique." The 1927 La Salle, Earl's first design for GM, was also, in Sloan's words, "the first stylist's car to achieve success in mass production." Sloan still waxed enthusiastic over the La Salle in 1964. "The effectiveness of the new design can be seen by comparing it with the 1926 Buick," he observed. "The La Salle looked longer and lower; the 'Flying Wing' fenders were drawn deeper than their predecessors; side windows had been reproportioned; the belt line had a new type of moulding; sharp corners had been rounded off, and other design details were added giving it the unified appearance that we were looking for." [10]

The most important innovation in lowering the lines of 1930s cars was "drop-frame" construction. It was used not only in Earl's GM designs but also in the 1932 Ford V-8, various Chrysler cars, and other competitive makes. In drop-frame construction the frame dipped, bringing the passenger compartment down from its high perch upon the axles to its now familiar position between the front and rear axles. This lowered the height and center of gravity of the car, eliminated the need for running boards to help passengers step up into the car, and moved the motor forward over the front axle.

Aerodynamic styling, or streamlining, was another functional styling innovation widely adopted in the 1930s. It reduced drag coefficient, resulting in better fuel economy and performance. Though it only now began to be employed extensively, streamlining had a long history in automotive design. The first streamlined automobile was Camille Jenatzy's 1899 La Jamais Content, an electric car with a sheet-steel body that set a land speed record of 65.9 mph. After that numerous designers used elements of streamlining to reduce air resistance. Streamlining was particularly evident in the Benz Tropfenwagen, a teardrop-shaped racer of the early 1920s, and it reached a zenith in the 1931 Wikov Streamline Saloon, of Czech design. Ferdinand Porsche used aerodynamically styled bodies designed by Reutter of Stuttgart and Drauz of Heilbronn in several Volks-auto prototypes that he developed for Zundapp in 1932 and for NSU in 1933. These bodies bear an unmistakable resemblance to the "beetle" body of the Volkswagen prototypes that Porsche developed for Hitler between 1933 and 1939. That the Volkswagen combined a 60-mph cruising speed with 35-mpg fuel economy was in large part due to its advanced aero-dynamic styling.

Richard Burns Carson argues that the enthusiasm for streamlining among automotive designers in the 1930s emanated from a "new con-sciousness of aviation that permeated all mechanized transportation after Lindbergh's [epic 1927 trans-Atlantic] flight." Even more important, Car-son makes some critical distinctions among three different forms of streamlining—a term that he generally defines as the "unification of formerly uncoordinated elements." First, he distinguishes between "visual streamlining," which "integrates the car's visible features into ever larger, more flowing gestalt wholes," and "aerodynamic streamlining," which "organizes the invisible air currents passing around the car's outer features into larger, smoother, and less turbulent ones. There is a divergence be-tween these two approaches, between appearing streamlined and being aerodynamically streamlined. For the designer, visual streamlining is usu-ally an intuitive process and certainly always an artistic one. By contrast, aerodynamic streamlining seeks reduced air drag and wind noise and increased stability at speed as its goals and uses scientific tools in achieving them." Only in the most advanced automotive designs of the mid-1930s did true aerodynamic streamlining become evident. A third type, "struc-tural streamlining," operated independently of the first two, "concerning itself with hidden structure rather than with outer contours. This 'struc-tural streamlining' transformed distinct component frameworks into sup-porting aspects of a larger framework, thereby eliminating duplication of structural rigidity throughout the car. The end result of structural stream-lining was the unitary welded body that merged chassis and body strength into one." [11]

The first integration of all three types of streamlining in an automo-tive design was achieved in the revolutionary 1934 Chrysler and DeSoto Airflow models. Carson calls the Airflow "Art Moderne's furthest exten-sion of influence in American auto building" but asserts that it was also "the first American production car whose shape was fashioned accord-ing to scientific rather than aesthetic standards." He goes on to observe that "the Airflow's heterodox [welded unitary] construction required a technology that was, at that time, beyond the custom coachbuilders, eliminating the possibility of custom-bodied Airflow cars." Carl Breer, Chrysler's executive engineer, and his staff developed the Airflow body style by testing models in wind tunnels to achieve reduced air resistance and noise. The car's more rigid welded body structure was designed by Dr. Alexander Klemin, chief engineer at the Guggenheim Foundation for Aeronautics. Consequently, it was a "totally engineered car designed from the inside out." At the Chicago Century of Progress fair, an Airflow sedan was displayed next to the new Union Pacific M-1000 Streamliner to suggest similarity in design concepts.[12]

Powered by an eight-cylinder, 4.4-liter engine, the Airflow in motion developed 40 percent less drag than competing models. The five-passenger Chrysler sedan sold for a moderate $1,345. It was one of the first cars to feature welded unitized construction, in which the body and chassis frame are built as an integral structure, rather than the body being a separately built structure bolted onto the chassis frame in assembly. Unitized construction permits greater rigidity for a given weight and a roomier passenger compartment for a given width of body. The full aerodynamic shape of the Airflow combined a deco grille, headlights mounted flush in the front fenders, a split slant windshield, seating entirely within the wheelbase, and an integral trunk. Although the Airflow was a superior automobile in all respects, it was far too revolutionary for consumers. Fewer than 54,000 units were sold before it was withdrawn from production in 1937. Chrysler hurriedly brought out conservatively designed Airstream models in 1935 and after its Airflow experience remained the most conservative of the Big Three in styling policy for several decades.

Unlike his father, Edsel Ford was very style conscious. As president of the Lincoln Motor Company, in 1925 Edsel introduced the "catalogue custom body." By ordering custom bodies in small lots of three to ten, Edsel was able to offer them as options in the Lincoln catalogue at prices significantly lower than one-of-a-kind bodies cost; yet because there was small chance that the owners of the same custom body would ever cross paths, the bodies could be considered individualized. Edsel also pioneered in formalizing the relationship between stylists and automobile manufacturers by bringing Raymond H. Dietrich to Detroit in 1925 from his New York City coachbuilding firm, Le Baron. A new independent firm, Dietrich, Inc., did catalogue custom body work and acted as a consultant on the styling of Lincoln production cars.

Le Baron had been formed in 1920 by Dietrich and Thomas L. Hibbard. Both had begun their careers as draftsmen at the New York City carriage-building firm of Brewster and Company, which began building custom automobile bodies in 1910. "As draftsmen," Carson explains, "their talents were totally subservient to those of the master woodworkers and metal shapers, just as they would have been at . . . any other coach-building house of the time . . . making full-scale drawings of component body parts to aid in the construction of templates." But at Le Baron, Dietrich and Hibbard turned the tables to establish the primacy of the designer, to innovate the "free form designing idea" of conceptualizing the design of the car as a whole, and to develop "a larger new theme of 'automotive architecture,' which amounted to applying the architect's traditional role to the field of luxury auto building. . . . [T]he customer didn't buy an automobile body from Dietrich and Hibbard; what he bought were the complete plans with which an automobile body could be built." [13]

Dietrich's move to Detroit at Edsel Ford's behest presaged the moves there of other designers from the east and west coasts, with the result that by 1929 Detroit was the center for building custom-designed automotive bodies as well as production cars. With the failure of the coachbuilders in the early years of the Depression, the custom designers found employment in the newly created styling departments of Detroit's automobile manu-facturers. Dietrich, for example, was hired by Walter Chrysler as a special consultant on body design in 1932.

Under Edsel Ford's leadership, after 1922 the Lincoln was progres-sively restyled to improve its appearance. And it was Edsel's prodding that caused the Model A to be designed to resemble the much higher priced contemporary Lincoln in its overall styling. With annual modifications in the appearance of the low-slung, streamlined V-8 during the 1930s, the Ford Motor Company in effect followed GM in instituting the annual model change. One of the classic and more distinctive aerodynamically and structurally streamlined automotive designs of the prewar period was the twelve-cylinder 1936 Lincoln Zephyr, designed by John Tjaarda and Eugene T. "Bob" Gregorie. Like the Airflow, the Zephyr featured unitary construction.

The Lincoln Zephyr, the Airflow, and the 1936–1937 front-wheel-drive, unitary-built, coffin-hooded Cord 810–812, designed by Gordon Buehrig, demonstrate that neither the most revolutionary nor necessarily the most aesthetically pleasing aerodynamically and structurally stream-lined cars of the 1930s were designed by Earl's GM Styling Section. Nevertheless, it was at GM that a program of streamlining to eliminate projections and to make cars appear lower and longer first became institu-tionalized. This overall effect was evident in the extended rear deck and integral trunk, which hid the spare tire, innovated in the 1932 Cadillac and then incorporated into the design of the low-priced 1933 Chevrolet. On the so-called A-bodies of the 1933 Chevrolet, the radiator was hidden behind a grille, the gas tank was covered by a "beaver tail," and fender skirts (innovated on the 1932 Graham-Paige) were added. The one-piece steel "turret top" introduced on 1935 GM cars was a styling innovation that both made cars safer and permitted more economical stamping processes in automobile manufacturing. It became possible as a design concept with the perfection of the high-speed strip mill, which produced sheet steel in eighty-inch widths. The elimination of running boards for the first time in a production car in the 1938 Cadillac 60 Special enabled the "standard-size" American car to hold six passengers, because the basic body could now be widened to the full tread of the wheels. A sedan styled like a convertible, the 60 Special was a forerunner of the retrogressive, unsafe "hardtop convertible" introduced in the 1949 Buick, Cadillac, and Oldsmobile models. The styling of the 60 Special so appealed to consumers that they were willing to take smaller trade-in allowances when purchasing it. This demonstrated to Sloan "the dollars and cents value of styling."

What was good for General Motors in this instance, however, was not necessarily good for most automobile manufacturers. The effects of the annual model change and increased emphasis on styling were greatest on stamping processes, where the greatest economies of scale accrue to large-volume producers in automobile manufacturing. So Sloanism combined with the contraction of the automobile market to drive the last nails into the coffins of most of the remaining independents. Many honored marques disappeared. Only a handful would survive into the post–World War II era to compete with the Big Three at the fringes of the market. Furthermore, some stylistic changes put various accessory manufacturers out of business. Sloan recalled, for example, that the integral trunk "was another case where styling changes made some people unhappy, for these developments meant an apparent loss of accessory business in trunk racks, tire covers, and the like, at a time when accessories were very profitable items. But such is the price of progress."[14]

Flexible Mass Production

The annual model change and diversity of product were incompatible with Fordist production methods. At the Ford Highland Park plant, "every machine tool and fixture was fitted for the production of a single product whose every part had been standardized to the minutest detail."[15] Even small changes in the design of the Model T bottlenecked its production. The switchover to Model A production was chaotic. Machine tools highly specialized for Model T production could not be converted to

Model A production, with the result that more than half of the 32,000 machine tools used to produce the Model T had to be redesigned and rebuilt and half of the remaining ones had to be scrapped. That the plant layout optimal for Model T production was not well suited to production of the Model A is evidenced by the change to a final assembly line at the Rouge that was only half as long as the Model T final assembly line at Highland Park.

The switch from Model T production at Highland Park to Model A production at the Rouge involved closing down the Ford assembly lines from late May to November 1927. For some time after that the expansion of Model A production was hampered by the Ford practice of extremely close spacing of machine tools, which exacerbated problems of rearranging plant layout. Hounshell estimates the total cost of the changeover to the Model A, "including experimental and design work, tooling and loss of profits," at about $250 million. Such a disruption of production and the consequent inordinate expense were irreconcilable with bringing out the essentially new model every three years that Sloanist marketing strategy envisioned. It is no wonder that at the Rouge, as a consequence of this costly initial lesson, "Sorensen aimed for greater flexibility in assembly rather than cost advantages through a single-purpose [machine tool] approach." There was an almost complete turnover of supervisory personnel at the Rouge as production-head Sorensen tried, in his own words, "to get rid of all the Model T sons-of-bitches ... get away from the Model T methods of doing things." [16]

Sorensen adapted to the Model A production techniques that had been developed at Chevrolet by William Knudsen, who had set up the Ford branch assembly plants. He had been hired by Sloan on February 1, 1922, a few months after he had resigned from the Ford Motor Company over being constantly overridden by Sorensen and Henry Ford. Knudsen's first assignment at GM was to work out a long-range production plan for Chevrolet. He went on to become president and general manager of Chevrolet in 1924 and, when Sloan moved up to chairman of the board, president of General Motors in 1937. More than any other single factor, it was competition from Chevrolet in the low-priced field that caused the great decline in Ford's share of the market for new cars after 1925.

GM production was far more decentralized and far less vertically integrated than Ford production. Sloan had reasoned that GM would have to make the same profit on capital invested in plant and equipment for the manufacture of its various components as outside suppliers charging reasonable prices for those components. So GM depended more on outside suppliers. This alone gave GM far more flexibility than Ford. Additionally, Knudsen decentralized Chevrolet components manufacture among specialized plants at Toledo, Ohio, and at Flint, Detroit, and Bay City, Michigan, and bought still other components from other GM divisions and from outside suppliers. Assembly, too, was decentralized. "At four assembly plants (Tarrytown, New York, Flint, Michigan, St. Louis, Missouri, and Oakland, California) ... subassemblies and thousands of parts purchased from vendors were brought together to make the Chevrolet.... Knudsen [also] had convinced GM executives that a Fisher body plant should be attached to each assembly plant so that body production could be coordinated precisely with the daily output of each assembly plant." The major innovation at Chevrolet, however, according to Hounshell, was that Knudsen replaced single-purpose machine tools with standard general-purpose machine tools. "For this reason, Chevrolet could accommodate change far more easily than could the Ford Motor Company."[17]

Hounshell dates "flexible" as opposed to "rigid" mass production from these developments at Chevrolet. Perhaps so. Yet it can also be argued that true flexible mass production came not so much with the annual model change as with individualization of product within model runs. And this in turn resulted not from a reversion to general-purpose machine tools but from the advent of the automated automobile factory equipped with automatic transfer machines, other highly specialized automatic machinery, and the computer-controlled assembly line. The automated automobile factory did not become a reality until the 1950s.

Flexible mass production, explains Gerald Bloomfield, "allows a wider range of options of body style, colors, trim, power train, but within permissible standardized limits. The products of this type of mass production have a greater appearance of diversity. Flexible mass production involved a high degree of planning, and became more capital intensive than the earlier stages of rigid mass production." The resulting individualization of product is summed up by Brock Yates: "A Yale physicist whimsically calculated that a 1965 Chevrolet, offered in 46 models, 32 different engines, 20 transmissions, 30 colors, and 400 options, could be purchased in almost as many permutations as there are atoms in the universe." With the automated, computer-controlled assembly line, it became not merely theoretically possible but indeed likely that no two cars from the same model run would be precisely identical.[18]

Automatic production began with the introduction of the transfer machine, described by James R. Bright as "a number of machining stations mounted upon a base (or bases so closely integrated that the effect is the same), and having a work-feeding device integral with the machine and common to all stations." Bright believes that the first transfer machine in automobile manufacturing was used by Morris Motors in England about 1924 and that in the American automobile industry Graham-Paige installed the first true transfer machine in 1929 and the first transfer machine system, using automatic jigs and fixtures in 1931. During the 1930s the use of transfer machines became commonplace in automobile manufacturing, then spread to the production of other items. Transfer machines proved "extremely important in cutting labor cost, increasing quality through uniformity and reduced tolerances, and in reducing manufacturing cycle time." [19]

Because transfer machines alone do only a part of the total operations required in assembly, a system of transfer machines would not in itself constitute automation. Robert Bendiner defines automation as "the controlled operation of an entire factory or process in which the machines as linked units automatically perform their manipulations in specified sequences, with electronic judgment substituted for the perception of the machinist or foreman." For that to occur, automatic controls had to be added to systems of transfer machines. Control was at first (1954–1957) by coded punched or magnetic tape, but increasingly thereafter by the computer. [20]

Under the leadership of Delmar S. Harder—rightly known as "the father of automation"—the Ford Motor Company in 1947 became the first corporation in the world to establish an Automation Department. In 1949 Ford began work on the first factories built to make any notable use of automation—its Buffalo stamping plant and its Cleveland engine plant. In 1955 Peter Drucker hailed the application of automation to automobile manufacturing as "a major economic and technological change, a change as great as Henry Ford ushered in with the first mass production plant fifty years ago." [21]

Until the very recent development of the microprocessor, which permits machine tools to be programmed for a large number of tasks, automation was compatible with individualization of product and the annual model change only in the manufacture of those components which remained basically unchanged from car to car and from model year to model year, such as engines and transmissions. Consequently, automation was first and most fully applied to the production of large runs of standardized mechanical components. Heavy investment in specialized machinery in turn militated against technological innovation in mechanical components, so cars had to remain much the same under the hood. The MIT Report points out that "by contrast, large amounts of semiskilled labor were used in the body plant and the final assembly line to accommodate the year-to-year changes in the product.... In the body plant the producer faced a choice between inflexible automation, with very high production volumes and long unchanged product runs to justify its cost, and flexible manual systems with higher labor content." Because high-volume production of a single static model was essential to realizing economies from replacing workers with automated machinery, the full automation of body welding and final assembly was first instituted in stages between 1953 and 1966 at Volkswagen's Wolfsburg plant in the production of the Beetle, one of the most standardized cars of all time. "This meant low labor content, and it was suited to the labor shortage in postwar Germany," the MIT Report observes. "The alternative system, as developed by most of the other world producers, involved greater use of semiskilled labor for practically all operations and was suited to frequent model changes and simultaneous production of many body styles and accessory combinations."[22]

Sloanism thus had the effect of intensifying the amount and pace of dehumanizing work in automobile manufacturing at the same time that automation theoretically promised to shift it to the machine. This is what Emma Rothschild meant by her 1973 claim that "certain advances in automated production cannot be used (are not 'suitable' for) auto manufacturing" because of "a contradiction between auto marketing and productive improvement."[23] In the mid-1970s about 75 percent of the jobs in automobile manufacturing remained semiskilled or unskilled, versus only about 10 percent for the rest of American industry.

Even where automation displaced human operators, there was degradation of labor to lower skill levels and intensification of the production process. The General Motors Lordstown, Ohio, plant was the most costly and technologically advanced factory in modern automotive history when it opened in June 1970 to produce the subcompact Vega, a design that was expected to remain fixed for several years to enable economies of scale to be realized. The major feature of the plant was twenty-six Unimate robots (programmable, multipurpose automatic machines), capable of welding Vega bodies more precisely and uniformly than could humans. Some 95 percent of body welding was automated, compared with 20 to 40 percent at older automobile factories. Unskilled workers were still needed, however, to feed the robots materials. Maximum possible automation controlled by computers was combined with rigid Taylorization of the work force, permitting Lordstown to run the fastest assembly lines in the world. Each hour, 104 cars were turned out, versus the then usual 55 to 60 per hour. Despite (or because of) extensive automation, Lordstown became a hotbed of labor discontent. A series of labor disturbances, during which over 5,000 grievances were filed against management, culminated in March 1972 with a spontaneous vote by 97 percent of the plant's 8,000 workers to strike in protest against the tempo and discipline of work at Lordstown.

The Bean Counters Take Command

Sloan moved up from the GM presidency to replace Lammot du Pont as chairman of the board on May 3, 1937, with the position redefined at his behest as "chief executive officer." With or without that title, and despite his disdain for "personal" business leadership, gigantic General Motors was largely Sloan's creature from his assumption of its presidency on May 10, 1923, until he retired as GM chairman in favor of Albert Bradley on April 2, 1956. Sloan wielded his immense power with the backing of GM's largest stockholders—particularly the du Ponts. By the time Sloan retired, the du Pont interests owned 23 percent of the GM common stock, collected about 25 percent of the GM dividends, and had five seats on the board of directors. By then, too, GM was purchasing annually more than $26 million worth of du Pont products. These facts are strikingly incongruent with the image of GM as a firm guided by the "objective" decisions of professional management separated from ownership projected in Sloan's 1964 *My Years with General Motors.*

An era ended at GM on June 3, 1957, as hard on the heels of Sloan's 1956 retirement came the decision of the United States Supreme Court that the du Pont controlling interest of GM violated the 1914 Clayton Antitrust Act. The key piece of evidence for the government's case was John J. Raskob's December 19, 1917, report urging the E. I. du Pont de Nemours finance committee to invest $25 million in GM, which "will undoubtedly secure for us the entire Fabrikoid, Pyralin [celluloid], paint and varnish business of those companies, which is a substantial factor." The court ordered that du Pont divest itself of its controlling interest in GM and that no individual sit on the boards of both corporations. "The sundering of the two corporations left General Motors entirely in the hands of professional managers, men whose stock holdings were comparatively smaller," Ed Cray points out. "Executives and board members ... no longer could muster a controlling interest in the company's stock to enforce their decisions. Ironically, the shift in leadership, which might have induced corporate 'democracy,' with the individual shareholders' votes more crucial, had virtually the opposite effect.... Even without the great block of shares voted by du Pont representatives, the new elite routinely would pile up massive majorities on the few proposals upon which the stockholders at large were permitted to vote." [24]

A significant difference between GM and Ford, especially after the 1957 du Pont stock divestiture, was that Ford was a family-controlled firm. The Ford Foundation was established in 1936 as a legal device to maintain family control of the Ford Motor Company while avoiding

Roosevelt's "soak-the-rich" taxes. The Ford Foundation was given a 95-percent equity in the Ford Motor Company in nonvoting common stock. A 5-percent equity of all voting common stock was retained by the Ford family. Had the Ford Foundation not been conceived, Henry Ford's heirs would have paid federal inheritance taxes estimated at $321 million and would have lost control of the company in selling the stock necessary to raise the money. Ironically, however, by the end of 1955 the Ford Foundation had disposed of some $875 million of the Ford fortune and announced plans to diversify its investments. This involved selling nearly 7 million shares of Ford common that were reclassified as voting shares. The result was that almost three-fifths of the Ford voting common stock ended up in the hands of key Ford executives and the general public. Still, that left over two fifths of the stock in the hands of the Ford family.

After a generation of gross mismanagement, Ford was losing about $10 million a month when Henry Ford II took over on September 21, 1945. The Service Department had made fear and demoralization a way of life at Ford. Few executives worth their salt were left. The company lacked both a program of research and development and college-trained engineers. Accounting was so primitive that at least one department estimated its operating costs by weighing the invoices. There was no coordination between purchasing, production, and marketing. For years the financial statements had been closely guarded secrets even within the firm, because of fear that they might damage prestige or prompt an investiagation.

Henry Ford II began the turnaround by hiring at the war's end a team of eight former Air Force officers from the Office of Statistical Control who had been trained at the Harvard Business School. First called the Quiz Kids because of the many probing questions they asked about Ford operations, they soon came to be known as the Whiz Kids for their analyses of Ford's problems. Six of the eight ultimately became Ford vice-presidents, and two—Robert S. McNamara and Arjay Miller—presidents of the Ford Motor Company. Also in 1946 Ford hired as executive vice-president the accountant Ernest R. Breech, president of Bendix Aviation and former general assistant treasurer at GM. Breech recruited an executive team from GM and reconstructed at Ford the GM committee structure and system of financial controls.

The revitalized Ford Motor Company surpassed Chrysler to regain second place in the industry. Ford sales doubled from 549,077 in 1948 to almost 1.2 million in 1950 with the introduction of the 1949 Model B-A, the first new postwar Ford car. The Model B-A's "envelope body," a styling feature previously incorporated in the postwar Kaiser-Frazer cars, eliminated both conventional fenders and running boards. Its incorporation in the Model B-A set a styling trend still in evidence. The Model B-A also featured independent, coil-spring front suspension, called Hydra Coil, which softened the ride. In Leon Mandel's opinion, "it was this change that put the company in contemporary engineering competition with Chevrolet and Plymouth. But its use by all three led the American car down the road to handling complacency. . . . The B-A's ride . . . [was] the clear beginning of the marshmallow feel that would characterize Detroit's products for the next three decades." The sign identifying the Model B-A in the Henry Ford Museum says, "It was visible evidence of the successful revitalization of the Ford Motor Company."[25]

Chrysler alone among Detroit's Big Three failed to institutionalize Sloanism. After the death of Walter Chrysler in 1940, leadership in the firm passed to K. T. Keller, an engineer, then in 1956 to Lester Lum Colbert, a lawyer. Chrysler's deserved prewar reputation for technological innovation and engineering excellence was preserved into the postwar period. Experiments with the gas turbine engine began shortly after the end of World War II. And Chrysler led among American automobile manufacturers in the introduction of disc brakes (1949), the hemispheric combustion chamber (1951), power steering (1951), hydraulic shock absorbers (1952), improved torsion-bar suspension (1957), and the alternator (1960). Yates calls the 1956 Chrysler Torqueflite automatic transmission "the finest automatic ever built."[26] Chrysler also led the industry in 1962 in offering extended warranties. Paradoxically, its products gained a reputation for poor quality control. And throughout the postwar period Chrysler turned out what were overall the most conservatively styled cars in the industry.

Chrysler came to be headed in the 1960s and 1970s by the accountants Lynn Townsend and John J. Riccardo. No one held more than a one-percent equity in Chrysler, and GM management practices were well known and had been popularized in Sloan's 1964 autobiography. Nevertheless, Chrysler failed to emulate GM by instituting even a rudimentary committee structure, clear lines of authority, or a system of financial controls. Lido A. "Lee" Iacocca took over as Chrysler president in November 1978, a few weeks after being fired as Ford president by Henry Ford II. He replaced Riccardo as chief executive officer in September 1979. Iacocca was horrified to learn that Townsend and Riccardo "hadn't brought in any serious financial analysts" and that "nobody in the whole place seemed to fully understand what was going on when it came to financial planning and projecting." No one was responsible for cost control. Overproduction for dumping to dealers at regular sales was a company policy. Manufacturing was not geared to marketing. Design was not geared to manufacturing. A self-perpetuating managerial bureaucracy had left Chrysler fat with highly paid unnecessary executives. Iacocca was dumbfounded that "after thirty years of postwar, scientific management ... in 1978 a huge company could still be run like a small grocery store." The problem was compounded because "for years, Chrysler had been run by men who really didn't like the car business.... [E]ngineering, which had always been Chrysler's ace in the hole, became a low priority under Lynn Townsend. When profits started to fall it was engineering and product development that paid the price."[27] As a consequence, by 1978 the Chrysler Corporation was in debt to some four hundred banks and on the verge of bankruptcy.

The mismanagement at Chrysler was unique, especially the failure to institute financial controls. The other problems described by Iacocca, however, had come by the 1970s to be shared by Ford and GM. Like Townsend, Robert McNamara, who became Ford president in 1960, was a "bean counter," not an engineer. So too was Arjay Miller. John Bugas was a former FBI man who had headed first industrial relations, then overseas operations for Ford before becoming president. Although he received an M.A. in mechanical engineering from Princeton, except for a nine-month stint as an engineering trainee, Iacocca's background at Ford was entirely in sales. Among the postwar Ford presidents up to Iacocca's tenure, only Semon E. "Bunkie" Knudsen, the son of William Knudsen, lured away from GM to become Ford president briefly in 1968–1969, was a trained engineer, with a degree from MIT. Iacocca also points out particularly forcefully that both the Ford committee system and the board of directors were overwhelmed by the personal power wielded by Henry Ford II, with the aid of his brother, William Clay Ford.

So long as Sloan was chief executive officer, some semblance of decentralized decision making remained a reality at General Motors. And during the presidency of Charles E. Wilson, the production people in the GM operating divisions in Detroit actually gained in representation on the board of directors. But the GM decentralized structure and committee system of decision making began to deteriorate during the 1953–1958 presidency of former bookkeeper Harlow H. Curtice. "In operational matters, Curtice was Billy Durant reborn—given to quick decisions, disposing of problems with lavish hand and absolute authority," writes Cray. "Like Durant, he toured factories and instantly dispensed millions of dollars for expansion without so much as a by-your-leave to the finance committee. The committee system of which Alfred Sloan and Pierre du Pont were so proud gradually slipped into disuse; Curtice was frank to assert, 'The best committee is the committee of one.'" Under Curtice and his immediate successors in the GM presidency, the accountants John F. Gordon (1958–1965) and James M. Roche (1965–1967), GM led the American automobile industry in emphasizing nonfunctional styling over engineering, to produce at higher unit profits bigger and bigger cars loaded with more and more accessories. The "automobile men" began to return to power at GM in 1967, when Roche was replaced by Chevrolet general manager Edward N. Cole, an engineer trained at the General Motors Technical Institute. Cole was succeeded in 1974 by Elliott "Pete" Estes, an engineer with long experience at Oldsmobile and Pontiac.

The trend toward control of General Motors by cost-cutting accountants inaugurated by Sloan in the 1920s was exacerbated during the chairmanship of his successor, the accountant Albert Bradley (1956–1958). And during the 1958–1967 tenure of Frederic G. Donner as chairman of the board, the famed GM decentralized structure became largely mythical as power within GM came to be centralized in the corporation's New York City financial headquarters. Under Donner's leadership the "bean counters" took command of giant GM. His successors as chairman all had financial, as opposed to engineering or sales, backgrounds. James M. Roche (1967–1971) moved up to the job from the GM presidency. He was followed by Richard C. Gerstenberg (1971–1974), who had described himself to Senator Abraham Ribicoff's U.S. Senate Government Operations Committee in 1968 as "old Gerstenberg the bookkeeper." Cray characterizes Gerstenberg as "the paradigm of General Motors executives; he was cautious, colorless, virtually unknown beyond the confines of the industry, and a diplomat who brokered adroit compromises between factions on the fourteenth floor.... Within the company he became known as an expert on pricing, budgets, and cost-control—the very heart of the corporation's new emphasis on profits." Thomas A. Murphy, the GM chairman from 1974 to 1980, had spent his entire career in finance after joining GM in 1938 upon his graduation from the University of Illinois. Cray concludes, "The appointments of Gerstenberg and Murphy underscored the shift from a production and merchandising company to a financial and marketing firm." [28]

As Yates says, "Detroit and its dealers were playing a dangerous game of immediate gratification—and eventual self-destruction." He points out that the "numbers-oriented executives" who "came to dominate industry thinking on all levels ... were obsessed by the financial structure of the car business and viewed the product mainly as an abstraction out of which profit or loss could be generated." [29] Consequently, high short-term profits were generated at the expense of manufacturing quality and technological development, to the detriment of the long-range well-being of the American automobile industry. As sales were lost, first to European, then even more dramatically to Japanese competitors in the post–World War II period, American dominance in automobile manufacturing ended. The U.S. share of the world market for motor vehicles plunged from 76.2 percent in 1950 to only 19.3 percent in 1982, as Japan in 1980 overtook the United States to become the leading producer of motor vehicles in the world.

American Challenge, European Response

13

The idea that Sloanism, like Fordism, would become dysfunctional when carried to its illogical conclusion was inconceivable in the pre–World War II era of American dominance in world automobile manufacturing. In 1928 North American manufacturers produced some 84 percent of world motor vehicle exports and had captured some 35 percent of the world automobile market outside the United States. About 10 percent of American automobile production was being exported. Additionally, both Ford and GM had become multinational enterprises. By 1928 Ford was assembling cars in twenty-one countries, GM in sixteen. James Foreman-Peck observes, "By 1928 American multinational production abroad exceeded the total output of both the French and German motor industries. A survey of the mid-1930s concluded that there were very few major markets of the world in which assembly plants had not been established by Ford or General Motors." [1]

The establishment of Ford and GM factories in Europe was particularly notable, for it marked recognition of a newly developing mass market there for cars. While the North American market stagnated during the Great Depression, there was a gradual but steady increase in middle-class motoring in Europe, where economic recovery occurred earlier than in the United States. British registrations increased from 1.4 million in 1929 to 2.59 million in 1938; French registrations increased from 1.3 million in 1929 to 2.27 million in 1938. In Hitler's Germany registrations jumped phenomenally, from only 654,400 when he assumed power in 1932 to 1.67 million in 1938.

With the expansion overseas of Ford and GM, and the emergence of a European-owned industry producing for a mass market, the relative position of the Canadian industry deteriorated. From its inception the

Canadian industry had been essentially the export branch of the American industry. As overseas markets came more to rely on local production, from 1930 to 1939 Canada produced only 1.34 million units, falling to fifth place in world production after the United Kingdom with 3.56 million, France with 1.94 million, and Germany with 1.82 million.

The Multinationalization of Ford and GM

Ford overseas expansion began in 1911 with the formation of the Ford Motor Company, Ltd.—a wholly owned subsidiary of Ford-U.S., capitalized initially at only £1,000 and financed entirely out of profits earned in the United Kingdom. Although Percival Perry ostensibly was in charge of Ford-England, its operations were closely supervised from Dearborn. Product was identical, to the point that the Model T steering wheel remained on the left side of the car in defiance of the British custom of driving on the left-hand side of the road. At first Model Ts were assembled at the Trafford Park plant on the edge of Manchester from cars shipped "completely knocked down" (ckd) from Dearborn. But the proportion of local content was gradually increased to 92 percent by mid-1924 as a policy was implemented of buying Birtish-made components whenever they were of comparable quality and cheaper than components shipped from the United States.

American work rules and methods, however, were uncompromisingly adopted. In 1923 even the customary British Christmas raffle and the foremen's social club were abolished by mandate from Dearborn. The imposition in 1919 of the American exclusive franchise system on the Ford U.K. dealer organization was considered "particularly outrageous." Volume in the British market was simply too small to justify a dealer's handling only one make of car, even if that make was the Model T. So Ford lost or canceled out scores of dealers while he reaped a whirlwind of ill-will in the British automobile trade press. Although he remained the leading U.K. auto producer from 1911 through 1923, Henry Ford was, according to Kenneth Richardson, "very unpopular at the time, and these arbitrary actions, for so they were made to appear, seemed to confirm the view that he was both ruthless and anti-British." [2]

The policies initiated at Trafford Park characterized Ford's overseas operations throughout the Model T era. Wholly owned subsidiaries financed out of local profits produced an identical product. Barrages of directives from Dearborn were filed at branch agencies and plants across the globe in thick loose-leaf operations manuals called Ford Bibles. This rigid imposition of Ford-U.S. policies where local conditions made them inappropriate resulted in significant Ford losses of market shares world-wide after 1925 both to GM and to European producers.

GM followed the opposite strategy of overseas expansion through acquiring interests in strong foreign firms that produced cars designed for local markets. Negotiations to acquire Citroën in 1919 and Austin in 1924–1925 were dropped when it became apparent that both firms had physical plants in poor condition and weak management. Instead GM bought Vauxhall Motors in 1925 and Adam Opel AG in 1929.

At the time of purchase, Vauxhall made a relatively high-priced car and had an annual volume of only about 1,500 units. It did not begin to make money for GM until 1933, when it introduced the Light Six, a small car designed for European conditions. Opel was by far the more important GM wedge in the European market. Its purchase made GM the largest automobile manufacturer in Germany. Opel accounted for 26 percent of the German market and 44 percent of the sales of German-made cars. After 1933 Opel and Vauxhall sales combined exceeded GM's American exports.

The other significant GM acquisition was Holden's Motor Body Builders of Australia, from whom GM had purchased bodies since 1923. In 1931 GM purchased Holden's and merged it with General Motors of Australia, formed in 1926. This solidified the great gains over Ford that GM had made during the 1920s through its Holden's association in the developing Australian market.

The multinationalization of Ford and GM was necessitated by the emergence in the interwar period of strong tariff barriers against further U.S. penetration of European automobile markets. A dramatic reversal of the pre–World War I world tariff structure on automobiles had occurred. The 1913 U.S. tariff of 45 percent on passenger cars valued over $2,000 and 30 percent on cars valued under that was reduced in 1922 to 25 percent or a duty equal to that imposed by the exporting country, but not to exceed 50 percent. In 1930 the U.S. tariff on automobiles was further reduced to 10 percent. In contrast, the U.K. moved away from a policy of free trade in 1915 to the 33⅓-percent McKenna duties, which were retained into the post–World War II period, except for a brief removal in 1924–1925. On the Continent automobile tariffs soared: in France from 9–14 percent in 1913 to a minimum of 45 percent and as high as 180 percent with reciprocity by 1924; in Germany from a mere 3 percent in 1913 to 13 percent by 1924, 25 percent by 1932, and 40 percent by 1937; in Italy from only 4–6 percent in 1913 to an exorbitant 101–111 percent by 1937. Manufacture abroad with a high proportion of local content to avoid these prohibitive tariffs thus became essential if Ford and GM were to retain niches in the most important developing overseas markets for cars.

Adapting to the European Market

"Both indigenous manufacturers and American multinationals, if they wanted to increase their European market shares, had ... to adapt American technological experience." writes Foreman-Peck. "The Americans eventually had to develop a different product for sale in the European market, and both groups had to adapt American process technology to the smaller production runs." Underlying realities were lower per capita European incomes, far higher raw material costs and gasoline prices than in the United States, and discriminatory horsepower taxes. Foreman-Peck estimates, for example, that in 1927 significantly higher French coal prices made sheet metal for body work 134 percent more expensive in France than in the United States, and that steel prices for Ford-England were 50 to 70 percent higher than those for Ford-U.S. "A Dodge analysis of 1927 concluded that the four-cylinder Dodge met few if any of the European requirements," he further observes. "In Germany the cost of fuel was 28–30 cents a gallon, equal to the hourly wage of the highest paid worker, yet the Dodge could only achieve 12–14 miles per gallon. Taxation [based on horsepower formulas] on the 'Four' was $161 per year in Germany, $116.50 in England, and $89 in France." [3]

European horsepower taxes were intended to discriminate against American cars, whether produced in the United States or locally. The horsepower ratings were based on formulas, not brake mean horsepower (bhp) at a given number of revolutions per minute (rpm), and the formulas were discriminatory against the American large-bore, short-stroke engine. The 1906 Royal Automobile Club (RAC) formula used in the U.K., for example, was $ND^2/2.5$, where N is the number of cylinders and D the cylinder diameter. Because length of stroke was not incorporated, the RAC formula was not a measure of cylinder capacity/engine displacement. By this formula the 20-horsepower Model T was rated as a 23-horsepower car, and the purchaser of a Model T in 1923 paid £23 (about $73) more in taxes than the purchaser of an Austin Seven.

Although horsepower taxes based on the RAC formula helped U.K. manufacturers in the home market, the resulting British high-performance, small-bore, long-stroke engine with high piston speeds, and the small cars it powered, were ill suited for export to Commonwealth and other countries where driving conditions approximated those in the United States. "British roads were slow and congested," notes Peter J. S.

Dunnett. "Cars suitable for these conditions were ones which would trundle along easily in top gear at twenty miles per hour with sufficient engine torque to accelerate to forty or fifty miles an hour when the opportunity to pass slow traffic arose. Demand for such high-revving, low-geared cars was, quite simply, incompatible with much overseas demand. . . . British cars tended to emphasize maneuverability, light steering and good engine torque and to de-emphasize high-speed cruising ability."[4]

Conversely, American-type cars were not well suited to European driving conditions. The Model T and other low-priced American-type cars faced even stiffer competition in the interwar period from more fuel-efficient European light cars. The first European car to compete directly with the Model T was the four-cylinder, 8.5-horsepower (by RAC formula) Morris Oxford, assembled from jobbed-out components and introduced in 1913 at the moderate price of £175. The first popularly priced, mass-produced European car was the 1919 four-cylinder, 10-horsepower, four-door Citroën Type A Torpedo. The Type A sold for only 7,500 francs, about a quarter of what a comparable pre–World War I car had cost. By the end of 1920 Citroën had sold nearly 23,000 Type A's, inducing Mathis, Peugeot, and Renault to bring out competitive economy models by 1922.

The best and most successful of the 1920s European light cars was the 1922 Austin Seven, a 7-horsepower car by RAC formula that actually developed 13 horsepower. The Seven's high horsepower-to-weight ratio made it a spectacular performer in hill-climbing contests and in racing competitions. It won the Shelsey Walsh Hill Climb in 1922. Then in 1923 it won the Brooklands Small Car Handicap and went on to take first place in the 750-cc class of the Italian Grand Prix at Monza, becoming the first British car to win a race on the Continent since 1914. In 1924 the Seven established some twenty-two International Class H records. The production car gave a fuel economy of 50 mpg and had a top speed of 52 mph. It sold in 1922 for only £225, in 1924 for a mere £125.

The Seven was rivaled after 1929 by the Morris Minor. The redesigned 1931 two-seat, side-valve Minor became the first British car to sell for as low as £100; and with sales of over 200,000 units within four years, it became the largest-selling pre–World War II British car as well. A special model fitted with a supercharger did over 100 mph at Brooklands; then, under RAC supervision, without the supercharger, the car was driven 107.4 miles at 15 mph on a single gallon of benzole. Advertising coupled the 100-mph speed and 100-mpg fuel economy with the £100 price. Morris Garages, organized as a separate company from Morris Motors, from 1924 also pioneered in the development of the classic light sports car with its MG models.

To meet the new competition, Ford Motor Company policies underwent drastic revision. In August 1928 Sir Percival Perry, fired during the 1919 Ford purge of executives, was rehired, and by November Ford's European operations had been completely reorganized. A new English corporation was created; called Ford Motor Company, Ltd., it acquired all of the assets of the Ford Motor Company (England), Ltd., Henry Ford and Son, Ltd., of Ireland, and the shares of the nine Ford operations on the Continent. Ford-U.S. would continue to hold 60 percent of the new company's stock and thus continue to exercise control. The other 40 percent would be sold in small lots to the British public. The new Ford-England in turn would control 60 percent of the shares of the Continental subsidiaries, with 40 percent being offered to the public in each country. The authorized capitalization of Ford-England was increased from £200,000 to £7 million, and it was made the center of Ford's European operations. To avoid the problem of double taxation by the host countries on the Continent and England, a holding company was formed in 1930—first headquartered in Lichtenstein, then in Luxembourg—that acquired Ford-England's stock in six of the Continental subsidiaries.

The goal here was to encourage the idea in the host countries that Ford was not a foreign corporation. This idea was reinforced by the appointment of directors for the various European subsidiaries who were distinguished citizens of the host countries. Consequently, by 1933 only two of Ford's European and North African branches had American managers. Mira Wilkins and Frank Hill report that by 1936 Ford-England had come to be considered a British company and that "its executives took counsel with Dearborn specialists on production and purchasing, but they rarely requested or received advice as to sales, finance, or labor relations. In these areas they were on their own." [5]

On May 6, 1929, construction was begun on a new plant at Dagenham, near London. With an annual capacity of 120,000 units, the Dagenham plant was planned as Ford's European manufacturing center and as the largest automobile factory outside the United States. In 1930 a small-bore Model A was introduced, but sales proved disappointing. So in the spring of 1932 Ford introduced its first car designed specifically for the European market—the Model Y. Eight-horsepower by RAC formula, the Model Y actually developed 22.5 horsepower. It was manufactured exclusively in Britain. A 10-horsepower (by RAC formula) Model C was added in 1934. "These two vehicles—the Popular and the De Luxe as they came to be called—transformed the British company from a deficit to a profitable enterprise," relate Wilkins and Hill. "With them, Ford in England was again in a position to challenge the leaders of the British automotive industry, the Morris and the Austin." [6] The four-seat Popular undersold the two-seat Austin by £2 10s. and the two-seat Morris by £18. In 1935 Dagenham began producing as well the American-type V-8. By 1937, with 22.3 percent of the British market, Ford ranked third after Morris and Austin.

On the Continent Ford did not do nearly as well. Ford-SAF (Société Anonyme Français) never challenged Citroën, Renault, and Peugeot. After 1935, in addition to the V-8 with a French-designed body, Ford-SAF produced a smaller V-8. Both were named Alsace. A 1934 manufacturing arrangement with Mathis to produce a light four-cylinder car did not work out, and plans for Ford to produce it alone were shattered by Hitler's invasion of Poland on September 1, 1939, just as the machinery for its production was being assembled for shipment from Dearborn.

With a four-cylinder car called the Eifel, made entirely of German content, and the V-8, Ford-AG (the German branch) in 1936 captured 8 percent of the German market for fifth place in passenger car production. In truck production, however, Ford-AG ranked second, producing the four-cylinder Model BB and the eight-cylinder Model 51. The outbreak of the war squelched plans to bring out the Taunus, an attractively styled car that used an Eifel motor on a longer wheelbase.

In Fascist Italy no Ford assembly plant could be built without government permission, and Mussolini's policy was to foster the development of a 100-percent Italian-owned automobile industry. Consequently, with Il Duce's support Fiat monopolized the Italian market while Ford's share was infinitesimal.

Automobile production in the rest of 1930s Europe combined was insignificant, ranging from only 31,326 units in 1931 to 236,727 in 1938.

Adopting Fordist Methods

Fordist production methods were, appropriately, first introduced in Europe by Ford-England at its Trafford Park plant. Some 1,500 workers there assembled 12,500 cars in 1914—a phenomenal productivity rate by European standards. In 1915 Trafford Park began to employ, on a much smaller scale, the special-purpose machine tools, moving assembly lines, and other techniques developed at Highland Park.

European automobile factories remained heavily dependent on American-made machine tools. "Citroën in 1925 used 3,100 machine tools at the main 50-acre works at Javel, selected from the best in the United States," Foreman-Peck points out. "Opel's plant was reported by a visiting delegation from Dodge in 1927 to look almost entirely American. At his Coventry engine factory Morris used a large number of American specialized machines in the same year, and the British industry imported large quantities of American stamping and pressing machinery and lathes." So too were American-made machine tools predominant at Fiat and in the emerging Russian motor vehicle industry. Yet Foreman-Peck concludes significantly that "the use of such advanced machinery did not necessarily guarantee high productivity.... [O]utput per worker was less [in the U.S.S.R.] than in Britain, where in turn American management was sometimes disturbed at the poor productivity." [7]

Europeans were slow to adapt Fordist methods to the production of small, fuel-efficient cars. Primitive attempts at continuous-flow assembly were made in 1913 at both the Fiat works at Turin, Italy, and the Sunbeam factory at Wolverhampton, England, where chassis were moved mechanically from one group of specialized workers to another during assembly. However, progressing beyond this was militated against by Sunbeam's annual sales of less than 2,000 units and by Fiat's wide range of products, variety of automobile models, and failure to standardize. Fordist production methods were not inplemented fully at Fiat until 1936, when it opened its huge new plant at Mirafiori to produce the tiny 13-horsepower, 9,750-lire (£711) Topolino (little mouse). The Mirafiori factory boosted Fiat production some 50 percent in one year, giving the firm 84.9 percent of the total 1937 Italian production of 77,700 units. Citroën in 1919 became the first French manufacturer to adopt the moving assembly line; Renault waited until 1922 to install one.

Ford-England's British competitors lagged still farther behind. Austin began to move toward continuous-flow production after Herbert Austin visited American automobile factories in 1922 to learn firsthand about "the means by which U.S. manufacturers were able to deliver a car from their works for about the same price that our company had to pay for materials and accessories for building a similar-sized car." Yet, as Roy Church reports, "not until the beginning of 1928 had output expanded sufficiently to justify the wholesale mechanization of chassis erection, though in ... 1924–1927 moving lines, electric hand operated [sic] hoists, pulleys, and conveyors had been installed." Following the installation of the moving assembly line at Austin's Longbridge plant, it was quickly adopted by Singer, Standard, and Hillman. Nevertheless, labor productivity in British plants remained significantly lower than in American factories. Notably, in response to the introduction of continuous-flow techniques and the consequent reclassification of job skills, the Longbridge workers walked out on March 25, 1929, in "the most serious strike ever" in Austin's history. [8]

As early as 1914, William Morris too had visited the United States, in an unsuccessful effort to place orders for components for his Cowley. He returned to England with drawings for an American engine that cost £25, as against the £50 he was paying for a similar engine supplied by the British firm of White and Poppe. He again visited the United States in 1925 and returned home this time to form the Pressed Steel Company of Great Britain in association with the Budd Manufacturing Company of Philadelphia, the pioneer in the development of the all-steel body. Budd dies and designs were used to manufacture all-steel bodies for the 1927 and 1928 Morris Oxford.

Although Morris was the largest British producer, he did not install a moving final assembly line until 1934, apparently because demand for cars seemed too low in the U.K. to justify the investment. Continuous-flow production was introduced in 1934 at the new Morris Cowley factory, giving it the capacity to produce 100,000 units a year—greater than the total 1933 German production of 95,700 units and better than half of the total 1933 French production of 189,000 units.

Although theoretically the Morris Cowley plant could produce 20,000 fewer cars a year than the Ford Dagenham plant, in fact it produced far more. Actual production at Dagenham ranged from a mere 24,152 units in 1931 to a high of 94,165 in 1937, then declined to 65,387 in 1939. In contrast, the Morris Cowley plant truned out 96,512 units in 1935; and although precise statistics are not available, production at Cowley is estimated at 90,000 units or more annually for the rest of the 1930s. Moreover, production at Cowley was even more integrated and mechanized than at Dagenham. A car was turned out every two minutes, and Morris claimed to have surpassed mass production with "progressive production." R. J. Overy makes the well-documented claim that after 1934 Morris "controlled the largest and most technically advanced factory of its kind not only in Britain but in Europe as a whole. . . . The main assembly shop at Cowley was the largest and most progressive in Europe, despite Ford's massive investment of 1932/1933 at Dagenham"[9] Still, Morris's total production of 58,248 units in 1934 and 96,512 units in 1935 was dwarfed by Ford's recorded 1934 factory sales of 757,931 units for the United States and 872,849 worldwide.

Underlying problems were the failure of European automobile manufacturers to standardize and the craft tradition entrenched in European automobile factories. The British industry provides striking examples. In the first place, it was fragmented among too many small producers producing too many models. A plan put forward in May 1924 by Herbert Austin to merge his company with Morris Motors and Wolseley Motors was quickly and firmly rejected by William Morris, although the proposed merger of these leading firms had the potential to rationalize and consequently to improve greatly the competitive position of the British industry. Morris sold two basic body types with a dozen body styles in 1927, nine basic body types with twenty-six body styles in 1933. Daimler, the leading British producer of luxury cars, in 1927 offered twenty-three models, exclusive of body styles, with a choice of five different engines and twelve wheelbase lengths. As late as 1934, Austin offered fifty-two models and Hillman thirty-four.

British manufacturers of motors and chassis for higher-priced cars still expected in the late 1920s that the purchaser would order a custom-made body from a specialized body maker. "Their workshops were virtually divided into a number of independent republics of craftsmen, each specializing in a particular production process," writes Richardson. "Blacksmiths, coachbuilders, painters and trimmers, they usually belonged to one of those small unions such as the United Kingdom Coachmakers, which amalgamated into the National Union of Vehicle Builders in 1918.... Most of them had been apprenticed and knew their own jobs to perfection, loving the feel of good wood and the gloss upon finished panels." Twenty-one coats of primer, paint, and varnish—each taking twenty-four hours to dry naturally—were applied by brush, for example, at the Grosvenor Carriage Company, which made bodies for Vauxhall in the early 1920s; when flow painting and drying chambers were belatedly introduced, the time of the painting operations was cut to only two hours.[10]

Production methods were not nearly so antiquated in the Austin and Morris plants. There too, however, in contrast with Ford-England, a strong class tradition separating manual from white-collar work militated against management's intervening to rationalize production on the shop floor. Too many skilled workers with too many prerogatives were divided into too many job-skill classifications. The workers were organized into too many small craft unions, each of which had to be negotiated with separately, and none of which could discipline even its own members. Remuneration was based on an antiquated, individualistic piecework system that was antithetical to the coordination of production and to quality control. Church provides a particularly striking example of this retrogressive pattern of labor relations at Longbridge: "The men demonstrated a preference for independent action, and in 1924 the skilled body makers successfully resisted the introduction of semi-skilled workers to cope with tasks customarily regarded by the men as skilled. They struck in direct contravention of the trade union agreement, and achieved a settlement through direct negotiation with the Austin managers.... The dispute lasted for only two days and was resolved before the union officials had time to become involved."[11]

This concession to wildcat worker demands occurred in a factory where few of the workers were unionized, a factory whose owner, Herbert Austin, was as hard-nosed and outspoken an opponent of labor organization and worker democracy as Henry Ford. As late as 1939 the automobile industry was "the most weakly organized section of British trade unionism. It has been estimated that at the outbreak of the war 'seldom more than a fifth and often only a fiftieth of mass production operatives [in U.K. automobile plants] were union members.'" Not until 1944—three years after the unionization of Ford's American plants—did the workers at Dagenham gain Ford's recognition of their right to join a union, and it took a sit-down strike that disrupted essential war production to extract that recognition. As opposed to the exclusive representation of Ford-U.S. workers by the UAW-CIO, negotiations had to be conducted with twenty trade unions by Ford-England. However, in contrast with the negotiating patterns that had become customary in the U.K. automobile industry, "the Ford Motor Company would recognize unions, but it would deal only with the national officers of those unions. It wanted no bargaining on the shop floor. Like Ford in America it wanted to preserve its right to manage, to control the work rate." [12]

There was, then, something illusory about the large-scale conversions of British and other European automobile plants to American-made specialized machinery and continuous-flow production that took place between the world wars. In industrial organization, in product rationalization, and in labor-management relations, a chasm as wide and deep as the Atlantic still separated the European and American automobile industries.

Remaking Germany: The Volkswagen

During his 1923–1924 imprisonment in Landsberg for riotous behavior, Adolf Hitler read Henry Ford's autobiography, *My Life and Work*, and wrote *Mein Kampf*. Although the Führer never learned to drive, he was a lover of cars, especially fast Mercedes sedans. Jacob Werlin, the salesman who sold him his first Mercedes in 1923, became Hitler's chief adviser on automotive affairs. Werlin was made a member of the Mercedes-Benz board of directors when Hitler became chancellor of Germany, and pouring money into building up the Mercedes racing team became one of Hitler's pet projects. He undoubtedly was unaware that his favorite car had been named for the granddaughter of a Hungarian rabbi.

Hitler's first major public speech after becoming chancellor was given on February 11, 1933, at the Berlin Motor Show. In that speech he announced plans to abolish the registration tax on purchases of new automobiles and motorcycles, to make driving licenses easier to obtain and traffic laws less stringent, to build a network of superhighways across Germany, and to develop a small car for the masses. He declared, "A nation is no longer judged by the length of its railways but by the length of its highways." The theme of remaking Germany into a mass automobile culture was reiterated in Hitler's speeches at subsequent annual Berlin Motor Shows through 1939.

R. J. Overy argues that until 1935 mass motorization was more important than rearmament to Germany's recovery from the Great Depression. "The military expansion before 1935," he writes, "did not involve large increases in personnel, and was largely carried out in secret. The motor sector on the other hand had the advantage that it could rapidly absorb a large number of unemployed with the maximum of publicity. Thus the strength and rapidity of the recovery can be explained with reference to cars and roads rather than tanks and aircraft." [13]

There were six million unemployed in Germany when the Nazis came to power. Hitler estimated in 1935 that his motorization program had produced one million jobs. By 1938 it was providing one and a half million jobs, one out of every twelve, and the structure of the German economy had been altered by the key role that motorization had come to play in only five years. By 1939 some 17,000 kilometers of road had been improved, 3,000 kilometers of new road had been completed, and over 3,000 bridges built. Production of motor vehicles increased from only 52,088 units in 1932 to 342,169 units in 1938, the last peacetime year. Between 1925 and 1930 only 89,000 commercial vehicles had been produced, versus 265,000 between 1933 and 1938. Tractors in use increased from 25,000 in 1929 to 82,000 in 1939. "The transport load as a whole was shifted onto the motor vehicle for private travel while the number of passengers on public transport increased as bus services spread over the German countryside," Overy observes. *Motorisierung Politik* tremedously increased the demand for concrete, steel, machinery and tools, electrical equipment, textiles, tires, and petroleum products. It also encouraged the rise of many small retail businesses, particularly garages and repair shops. All in all, rapid motorization in 1933–1938 under the Nazis wrought a revolution in the German economy and society, and its importance as a "'leading sector' ... would have increased had the Nazi motor plans not been interrupted by the war." [14]

German leadership in automotive technology became increasingly evident in the 1930s. The *Reichsautobahnen* feverishly built to link Germany from border to border were the first integrated network of express highways in the world and became a model for all future highway construction. Germany led in the development of diesel-powered trucks and passenger cars. And German reentry into grand prix competition under heavy government subsidy led to impressive victories by Mercedes Silver Arrows and Porsche-designed Auto Union P-Wagens.

Legally a citizen of Czechoslovakia, Austrian-born Ferdinand Porsche was made a naturalized German by his fellow Austrian Hitler, who considered the Czechs to be subhuman. Porsche received honorary doctorates from the technical universities of Vienna and Stuttgart for his contributions to automotive technology. He shared his Führer's great admiration for Henry Ford and the desire to build a cheap small car for the German masses.

While managing director of Austro-Daimler, shortly after World War I Porsche became interested in building a *Volksauto*—a generic term for any "people's car." His vision was not shared by the Austro-Daimler board of directors. He did, however, build a tiny racing car, the Sacha, for the movie mogul Count Sacha Kolowat that was capable of 106 mph and that won both first and second prizes at the 1922 Targa Florio race in Sicily. Shortly afterward Porsche became technical director of German Daimler, which in 1926 merged with the Benz firm to form Mercedes-Benz. There he was chiefly responsible for designing a number of the great supercharged Mercedes racing cars of the 1920s. Fired in the course of depression-induced cutbacks, he returned to Vienna as technical director of the Steyr Works, which had shifted from arms to automobile production after World War I. Then in January 1931 Porsche established his own independent design and engineering consulting firm in Stuttgart, Germany, where Mercedes-Benz was located.

Porsche designed the P-Wagen racing car for Auto Union, formed in 1932 from Audi, DKW, Horsch, and Wanderer. Grand prix racing cars were limited to a weight of less than 1,653.8 pounds (750 kg). Yet although the ultra-lightweight P-Wagen weighed less than the later VW Beetle, it was powered by a 295-horsepower, V-16, rear-mounted engine. The P-Wagen won three grand prix events in 1934 and set a new flying-mile record of 199 mph in 1935. Robin Fry notes that it "looked more like an aircraft fuselage on wheels than a racing car. . . . In its later development Porsche's wonder car, driven by Bernd Rosemeyer, notched up a formidable number of victories, with speeds of up to 250 mph (402 kph), equal to racing cars even today, bringing much prestige to German motor racing." [15]

The rear-mounted engine and aerodynamic streamlining were design features of the P-Wagen that Porsche wanted to adapt to his Volksauto. And in 1932 he patented torsion-bar suspension, another radical feature intended for his people's car. Porsche developed Volksauto prototypes for

Zundapp in 1932 and for NSU in 1933 that bear striking resemblances to his later VW Beetle.

During a series of meetings with Porsche on the P-Wagen, Hitler discussed his ideas for a people's car, which he referred to as a *Volkswagen*. Porsche responded on January 17, 1934, with an outline of the basic requirements for such a vehicle. The idea of building a cheap, scaled-down bantam was never entertained by Porsche or Hitler. The Volkswagen was to be a closed-body car capable of carrying four persons, with a cruising speed of 60 mph (100 kph) and fuel consumption of 33 mpg (6 liters per 100 km). It was to have an air-cooled engine, in order to eliminate frozen radiators and starting difficulties in winter. It was to be durable and cheap to maintain and repair. It was to be safe and comfortable, and to have a high resale value. Porsche believed that "in the case of the future people's car, there must be no question of a compromise solution. In fact a new basic design solution must be sought which will enable the price to remain acceptable for a wide section of the population and will also be in step with technical progress for many years to come." Porsche thought that such a car could be built to sell for 1,500 reichsmarks (RMK) (about $600). Hitler demanded that its price be below 1,000 RMK. In his speech at the 1934 Berlin Motor Show, the Führer explained, "As long as the car is a vehicle for the rich, it is with bitter feelings on my part that millions of good, hard-working, and industrious people will be excluded from the use of a motor vehicle, which would be particularly beneficial to the less well off, and which would not only prove useful to their way of life, but would also enhance their Sundays and holidays, giving them a great deal of future happiness." [16]

Porsche signed a contract with the Nazi government on June 22, 1934, to build three prototypes of his people's car, for which he was allocated a small budget of 200,000 RMK. Production of its components was to be undertaken by the members of the RDA (Reichsverband der Deutschen Automobilindustrie, or Society of German Automobile Manufacturers), who were forbidden to develop their own Volksautos and therefore resented the unfair competition from the government-subsidized Volkswagen project. Consequently, they gave Porsche only minimal cooperation. The contract stipulated that the purchase price of the car was to be 900 RMK on an output of 50,000 vehicles, about half the price of the cheapest German car on the market. Interest in the car's military potential was evidenced by the stipulation that the Volkswagen be capable of carrying three soldiers plus a machine gun and ammunition. The prototypes were handed over to the RDA for testing on October 12, 1936. Only minor defects were found.

In late May 1937 the Gesellschaft zur Vorbereitung des Volkswagens (the Volkswagen Development Company) was formed, with a capitalization of 480,000 RMK. The capital was supplied by the state-controlled DAF (Deutsch Arbeitsfront, or German Labor Front). The company became Volkswagenwerk GmbH (the acronym GmbH is the equivalent of "Ltd.") in 1938, and its capitalization was increased to 150 million RMK in 1939.

In August 1938 Robert Ley, head of the DAF, announced that the Volkswagen project would be sponsored by the KdF (Kraft durch Freude, or Strength Through Joy). This was the DAF branch charged with organizing recreation and travel for workers. A plan was announced by which a worker could purchase a Volkswagen on a 5-mark-weekly layaway plan for 990 RMK ($396), including insurance, garage, and maintenance costs. However, the actual cost under the plan came to 1190 RMK, and the KdF contract did not in fact obligate the state even to deliver a car once the final payment had been made. Walter Henry Nelson reports that under the KdF plan 336,668 Germans furnished 280 million RMK ($67 million) in capital to build cars that they never received. Hitler officially named the car that would become the Volkswagen the KdF-Wagen; in May 1938 he had dedicated a new plant and surrounding city, near Fallersleben in Lower Saxony, constructed for production of the KdF-Wagen. Plans to begin production with 150,000 units in 1940, to be boosted to an annual 1.5 million units within a decade, were canceled with the invasion of Poland and the outbreak of World War II. Yet layaway payments continued to be collected by the KdF until the war's end in 1945.

The KdF-Wagen purchase plan has been called "the world's biggest installment swindle." During the war the KdF-Wagen plant at Fallersleben, built from KdF "savings," used slave labor to turn out war materials for the Nazis. After the war the remaining funds accumulated in the KdF layaway accounts were confiscated by the Soviet occupation forces. In 1954 the West German supreme court absolved Volkswagenwerk from all responsibility for the KdF contracts. Nevertheless, litigation from disgruntled savers continued. In 1961 a settlement was reached whereby savers who had completed their payments would receive either 600 greatly devalued deutsche marks (DMK) in credit toward a new VW or 100 DMK in cash. About 87,000 claims were settled on these terms by mid-1964, half of the claimants choosing to purchase the car.[17]

Porsche's final KdF prototype, the VW38, was a 1,600-pound, 94.6-inch-wheelbase car with a central-tube frame. It was powered by a flat four-cylinder, 25-horsepower, large-bore/short-stroke, air-cooled, rear-mounted engine, and it featured both fully independent and torsion-bar suspension. Its aerodynamic styling gave it a drag coefficient of only .49. Forty-four VW38 cars were rigorously tested on back roads by SS men sworn to secrecy before it was introduced.

Hitler designated Porsche *Reichs Autokonstrukteur* (State Auto Designer); and in 1938, Nelson records, "Nazi Germany honored its leading designer ... with its own equivalent of the Nobel Prize.... Other 1938 winners were Ernst Heinkel, for his bombers; Willy Messerschmidt, for his fighters; and Dr. Fritz Todt for his Autobahnen. Dr. Goebbels announced the prizes and Adolf Hitler delivered an anti-Semitic harangue."[18]

The extent to which the KdF-Wagen was intended to be a military vehicle rather than a universal car for the German masses remains moot. Hitler undoubtedly was serious about developing a mass automobile culture in Germany, and the KdF-Wagen undoubtedly was conceived by both Hitler and Porsche primarily as a people's car. As noted, however, the earliest specifications mandated that the car be suitable for military use. Jerry Sloniger argues that "a military version ... had really been a prime concern since the first and would be the only one after May 1938. After a showing to German generals all facilities were devoted to it as of June 1940." He further observes that the KdF-Wagen plant at Fallersleben was built with no wood floors, "in anticipation of incendiary attacks. Porsche soon asked if it was a car factory or a war plant. Hitler replied, 'A VW factory and nothing else.' But his aides stipulated no flat or angled windows which might reflect moonlight at hostile airplanes. Officially, German industry had gone on a 'wartime footing' four years before the German army marched into Poland."[19]

During the war a number of versons of the KdF-Wagen were used by the German military as general-purpose vehicles. The most important were the Kommandereur (command car), the Kübelwagen (literally, "bucket car"—the counterpart to the American jeep), and the amphibious Schwimmwagen. Unlike the heavy German trucks, these light, air-cooled military KdF-Wagen models were particularly well suited to desert warfare. Field Marshal Erwin Rommel wrote to Porsche: "Your jeep, which I used in North Africa, saved my life. It didn't pack up when crossing a minefield, when the heavy Horsch trucks traveling behind with the supplies were blown sky high."[20] Yet here too German inferiority in mass production was evident. Only 50,435 Kübelwagens were turned out during the war, versus Allied war production of some 660,000 jeeps.

The chief legacy of the Nazi motorization program, the Volkswagen was also the mainstay of German economic recovery in the post–World War II period. Hitler's car remade Germany into one of the world's foremost automobile cultures. Predicated on the product philosophy of the Model T, the VW Beetle would surpass the Model T to become the best-selling car of all time and to set a new standard of excellence in performance and durability for a low-priced, family car. It would also change significantly the competitive structure of the worldwide automobile industry.

Freedom's Arsenal

14

Ferdinand Porsche visited the United States to study American mass-production techniques in both 1936 and 1937. His entourage on the second trip included Bodo Laffrentz, chief aide to DAF head Robert Ley, and Jacob Werlin, the Führer's adviser on automotive affairs. Porsche met with Henry Ford and discussed the KdF-Wagen. Ford declined an invitation to visit Germany. The envoys mounted a campaign to recruit American-trained German nationals working in the United States and American citizens of German descent to return to Germany to work in the KdF-Wagen plant. The campaign was carried out through 1938 by German consuls in American cities. About twenty technicians were signed up.

When war was declared between Germany and the United States, Porsche wondered how Germany could possibly expect to win, given the great American superiority in mass production that he had witnessed. As late as the outbreak of World War II, the German automobile industry was hopelessly fragmented among some seventeen small firms. Although Hitler's panzer divisions wrote a new chapter in the history of mechanized warfare, the German automobile industry—including the American-owned subsidiaries Opel AG and Ford-Werke AG—produced only 32,994 commercial motor vehicles and a total of only 289,271 motor vehicles of all types during the first six months of 1939. The totalitarian Nazi regime never succeeded in rationalizing the German automobile industry. Even military truck production was not fully standardized until the last year of the war. The superiority of Ford trucks produced in Canada and at Dagenham early became evident to the Germans. On December 15, 1941, for example, Rommel wrote an order to his Afrika Korps commanders: "For desert reconnaissance only captured English trucks are to be employed, since German trucks stick in the sand too often." Thus Germany was ill prepared to fight the global automotive war that it had initiated.

The Nazis Take Over at Ford-Werke and Opel

On November 28, 1938, Field Marshal Hermann Goering announced that the German army needed 100,000 trucks and could no longer depend upon the voluntary efforts of the German automobile industry to supply them. "It will now be necessary for me to interfere," he said. He had Ford and Opel trucks especially in mind. Ford-AG "was now cooperating closely with Hitler's regime," Mira Wilkins and Frank Hill relate, "and, as the summer [of 1939] drew to a close, would become serviceable to him in time of war. As a symbol of its wholly German identity, the company changed its name in July 1939 from the Ford Motor Company AG to Ford-Werke AG." A new truck assembly plant near Berlin turned out "troop-transport-type" vehicles for the Wehrmacht. And the Ford Cologne plant counted on Nazi government contracts for a quarter of its German domestic sales. Wilkins and Hill go on to observe that the Nazis "made them pay dearly for it. They forced the company to manufacture in Germany of German materials practically all the cars it sold there, they compelled no small degree of standardization, set up an export policy that required galling accommodations from both Dagenham and Dearborn, blocked remittances of profits earned in Germany, and imposed truck developments that served their military purposes." With the rapid Nazi conquest of Europe, Hitler came to control the Ford operations in eight countries on the Continent by late 1940. Following the German declaration of war against the United States on December 11, 1941, Hitler seized these Ford European plants as "enemy property." Without the knowledge of Ford-U.S., the German management of Ford-Werke AG for some time before this had been "secretly engaged in the production of war materials." [1]

General Motors has gone on record that after the German invasion of Poland all American personnel resigned from Opel, ending GM control over the day-to-day operations of the firm, and that even nominal GM representation on the Opel board of directors ended with the German declaration of war against the United States. GM claims that "as early as October 1939, the German government had prohibited the transmittal of financial or operational reports from Opel to General Motors" and that "a meticulous search has disclosed no communications whatsoever between Opel and General Motors Corp. after September 2, 1941." A German board of managers appointed by the Nazi government ran Opel after September 3, 1939. A German custodian was formally appointed in 1942 to oversee Opel by the Reich Commissioner for Treatment of Enemy Property. Only under these conditions did Opel become integrated into the Axis war effort as an important supplier of trucks, half-tracks, and aircraft engines.[2]

Neither GM nor Ford, however, has contested that its German subsidiaries played key roles in the Axis war effort or that it legally continued to own those subsidiaries. It has been estimated that the GM Ruesselsheim factory assembled about 50 percent of all the propulsion systems for JU-88 medium-range bombers produced between 1939 and 1945 and that the Ruesselsheim plant helped develop the propulsion system for the ME-262, "the world's first operational jet fighter." It has also been estimated that "GM and Ford German subsidiaries built nearly 90 percent of the armoured 'mule' 3-ton half-tracks and more than 70 percent of the Reich's medium and heavy-duty trucks. These vehicles, according to American intelligence reports, served as 'the backbone of the German army transportation system.'" Thus, unintentionally through their Nazi-controlled subsidiaries, "GM and Ford became principal suppliers for the forces of fascism as well as the forces of democracy."

The situation grew even more ludicrous with the cessation of hostilities. The Soviet occupation forces dismantled the GM Opel plant at Brandenburg and moved all of its machinery and equipment to the Caucasus to satisfy Soviet claims for reparations against Germany, while GM and Ford demanded and received from the United States government reparations for damage inflicted on their Axis properties by Allied bombing. "By 1967 GM had collected more than $33 million in reparations and federal tax benefits for damages to its warplane and motor vehicle properties in formerly Axis territories.... Ford received a little less than $1 million, primarily as a result of damages sustained by its military truck complex at Cologne."

The Failure of Nationalization in Japan

In Japan, recognition of the usefulness of the motor vehicle came in 1923, when the Kanto earthquake destroyed the railway line between Tokyo and Yokohama. Following this disaster, a thousand Model T truck chassis were ordered by the government for the Tokyo transportation system. The Ford Motor Company of Japan was incorporated in Yokohama in 1925, to assemble trucks and cars in Japan from components shipped from Detroit. General Motors Japan of Osaka began to assemble Chevrolet trucks and cars from American-made components in 1926. A 50-percent ad valorum duty was evaded by assembling in Japan, but the tariff on components still was 30 percent.

Ford and General Motors shared about 90 percent of the Japanese market up to the enactment in 1936 of the Motor Vehicle Business Act (or Law Regarding Automobile Manufacturing Enterprise), after which their combined share dropped to about 75 percent. That act reflected the ongoing effort of the military after the September 1931 Manchurian Incident to establish a Japanese-controlled motor vehicle industry. It mandated that all motor vehicle manufacturers producing more than 3,000 units annually be licensed by the government; that half of the capital, management, and stockholders of the licensed manufacturers be Japanese; and that the licensed manufacturers agree to supervision by the Japanese government, especially regarding military orders and objectives. The tariff on imported motor vehicles was raised to 70 percent. Despite these oppressive conditions, both Ford and GM sought and obtained licenses. Ford sought to meet the Japanese ownership mandate by raising new capital for expansion from its Japanese dealers; GM sought mergers with Nissan and Toyota. Both efforts were to no avail. Operating under ever tighter restrictions and production quotas, Ford and GM together ultimately produced an estimated 250,000 total units before the military-controlled government forced them to close their Japanese plants in 1939. An estimated 51 to 60 percent of their Japanese output had been trucks. And these trucks formed the backbone of the Japanese army transportation system in the China campaign.

The Japanese army had exhibited an interest in adopting motor vehicles as early as 1907. And beginning with the Military Motor Vehicle Subsidy Act of 1918, the Japanese government offered subsidies to Japanese-owned automobile manufacturers to produce motor vehicles suitable for military use. Yet few were produced before 1936, because the well-established *zaibatsu* (family-owned business groups), to whom the military were hostile, remained reluctant to risk capital to compete with Ford and GM. Consequently, the military established alliances with newer business groups—principally Toyota and Nissan in the case of motor vehicles.

Kiichiro Toyoda's Toyoda Automatic Loom Works formed a Motor Vehicle Division in 1933, which became the Toyota Motor Company, an independent company, in 1937. The Tobuta Casting Company and Nippon Industries in 1933 formed the Motor Vehicle Manufacturing Company to manufacture a small passenger car with a 750-cc engine called the Datsun. The firm changed its name to the Nissan Motor Company in 1934. Toyota and Nissan became the first Japanese-owned motor vehicle manufacturers licensed under the 1936 act. Trucks accounted for

79.6 percent of Toyota's 1936 production of 1,142 units, 91.1 percent of its 1939 production of 11,931 units. The Datsun passenger car had accounted for 69 percent of Nissan's total 1935 production of 3,800 units. But production of the Datsun was suspended by governmental order in 1938, and truck production came to account for 92.3 percent of the 17,781 units produced by Nissan in 1939. Together, Toyota and Nissan accounted for 89.5 percent of motor vehicle production by Japanese-owned firms in 1939. This declined to 73.1 percent in 1941, when total Japanese motor vehicle production peaked at only 46,468 units.

After the Pearl Harbor attack, with the shift of Japanese military effort from the mainland of China to the islands of the South Pacific, Japanese motor vehicle production, under the control of the army, steadily declined, to a mere 6,754 units in 1945. C. S. Chang observes that, unlike the situation in Germany, this almost total collapse of the Japanese industry "was not a direct result of bombing by the U.S. Air Force. The industry was never a prime target of air attack." Rather, the collapse primarily resulted from a shift in the allocation of scarce raw materials from motor vehicle to aircraft production. "When the main battlefield was China, motor vehicles played a very important role," Chang writes. "However, when the battlefield shifted to the Pacific after World War II began, priority was given to the production of airplanes for the control of scattered areas there." Unlike the United States, Japan had an inadequate supply of steel to produce both trucks and planes. Chang concludes, "Lack of truck transportation—due to decreased production of trucks—undoubtedly contributed to the failure of the Japanese army to solve its logistics problems during the war. It brought, for example, a production decline in many fields of war materials. . . . Raw materials could not reach manufacturers, and the railway system had been damaged by bombing." [3]

Mobilization for the Allies

The Axis powers all made the fatal error of counting on quick victories after bold surprise attacks and lightning-paced offensives. They did not anticipate the drawn-out war of logistics that developed. Japan was even more ill-prepared to fight it than Germany. Italy was ill-prepared even for its mechanized assault on spear-throwing Ethiopians. After the *New York Times* reported in October 1935 that Ford-U.S. had recently sent some 2,200 trucks to Italian Africa, Henry Ford canceled shipment of 800 more that the Italians had paid for in advance, bogging down the drive to Addis Ababa. "Had Ford known about and acted to forbid the orders from the start," note Wilkins and Hill, "and had the League [of Nations] dealt as effectively with [the supply of] other commodities, Mussolini's venture into Ethiopia would have been deep in trouble."[4]

The Axis powers stood no chance of winning a war of logistics in which the motor vehicle and mass production played the key roles. Total combined German, Italian, and Japanese motor vehicle production in 1938, the last peacetime year of full production, was only 436,918 units, versus 444,877 units for the United Kingdom alone and an additional 166,088 units for Canada. Thus, even without conversion of the massive U.S. industry to the Allied war effort, the British Commonwealth nations had a decided edge, especially since the Axis motor vehicle industries were operating at full strength while the U.K. and Canadian industries, like the U.S. industry, had excess plant capacity.

Despite proclamations of neutrality from Dearborn, Ford's British Commonwealth plants were quickly converted to war production during the fall of 1939. The Dagenham plant was camouflaged to protect it from enemy bombers, as production shifted to Fordson tractors, ambulances, trucks up to five-ton capacity, and auxiliary V-8 engines for a variety of military uses. Later the production of Bren carriers and tank trucks was also undertaken there. A new Ford "shadow factory" (secondary production site) was constructed near Manchester to build Rolls-Royce Merlin aircraft engines.

Ford-Canada joined with the Canadian Department of Defense in late 1939 to develop a series of motor vehicles for the military, including four-wheel-drive vehicles, and from the beginning of the war supplied trucks to the Canadian and British forces. Wallace R. Campbell, the head of Ford-Canada, claimed that after the fall of France and the almost complete destruction of British equipment at Dunkirk, Canada became "the most important source of mechanical transportation to the empire." Wilkins and Hill relate that when Hitler sent Rommel to Africa in 1941, "Canadian-built trucks and carriers, along with British-built Ford units, were the mainstay of the African army defending Egypt."[5]

In the United States, meanwhile, President Roosevelt had appointed William S. Knudsen, president of General Motors, to the chairmanship of the National Advisory Defense Committee (NADC). Knudsen left GM to assume his new duties at no salary on May 28, 1940; he resigned as GM president and member of its board of directors to avoid any suspicion of conflict of interest. In late November, at a secret meeting in New York with over one hundred auto industry executives, he called on American automobile manufacturers to give their full cooperation to U.S. defense plans.

Henry Ford had developed the hallucination that Roosevelt was a warmonger controlled by General Motors and the du Ponts and that

United States involvement in World War II was part of a conspiracy to get control of his company. He already had reneged on an early June 1940 agreement with Knudsen to undertake the manufacture of Rolls-Royce airplane engines for the British, and was consequently under attack by the press, especially in the U.K. His son Edsel and deputy Charles Sorensen, however, managed to obtain his reluctant consent to participate in an aircraft-engine program for the U.S. Air Force. His failure to comply voluntarily in this, they knew, would invite the governmental takeover that his paranoia led him to fear.[6]

On November 1, 1940, the Ford Motor Company signed a contract to make Pratt and Whitney airplane engines for the U.S. Air Force, while Packard undertook production of the Rolls-Royce engines for the Royal Air Force. In February 1941 the government approved Ford plans for a vast bomber plant at Willow Run, near Ypsilanti, Michigan. Snags in getting "Will-It-Run" into production delayed acceptance of the first B-24 bombers completely assembled by Ford until September 1942. By then the Ford Motor Company, along with the rest of the American automobile industry, had completely converted to war production and was playing an indispensable role in the war effort. Henry Ford feared that the military personnel at Willow Run were spies sent by Roosevelt to assassinate him and took to carrying an automatic pistol under the cowl of his car.

Following Edsel's untimely death on May 26, 1943, Henry Ford again became president of the Ford Motor Company. Aware of Ford's mental incompetence, Roosevelt toyed with the idea of removing him and having the government operate the company for the duration of the war. It took threats by Edsel's widow and Clara Ford that they would sell their shares of Ford stock out of the family to induce Henry Ford finally to step down in favor of his grandson Henry Ford II, a few weeks after the Japanese surrender in September 1945.

Knudsen was made codirector—with Sidney Hillman, president of the Amalgamated Clothing Workers—of the Office of Production Management (OPM) in January 1941, to coordinate defense production, purchasing, and priorities in consultation with Secretary of War Henry L. Stimson and Secretary of the Navy Frank Knox. The OPM was under the Supply, Priority, and Allocations Board (SPAB), chaired by Vice-President Henry Wallace. When the SPAB was abolished in early 1942, its functions were taken over by the War Production Board (WPB), chaired by Donald M. Nelson. Knudsen was "demoted" to lieutenant general and director of war production in the War Department. He resigned from the army in June 1945, to return to GM as a member of its board of directors.

Charles Erwin ("Engine Charlie") Wilson had replaced Knudsen as president of General Motors on January 6, 1941. Unlike Ford, GM had maintained contact with the War and Navy departments since 1933 regarding its production allotments and the types of contracts on which it would bid in the event of war. By American entry into the war GM already had undertaken over $1.2 billion in defense contracts for the Allies. "In the five years of war production, General Motors ... turned out $12.3 billion worth of military supplies, only one-third of it comparable in form to its civilian production," reports Ed Cray. "The conversion from peacetime to wartime production, beginning with the prewar planning of 1940, had been a gigantic task made the harder by the company's agreement to take on government contracts for only the largest, most difficult projects." Its first contract went to Chevrolet in April 1940 to produce 75-millimeter high-explosive shells. GM assigned government contracts top priority even before American entry into the war. And the corporation made a critical policy decision that it would ask for only a 10-percent pretax profit—half its average peacetime gain. "If the corporation ever had a supreme moment," Cray concludes, "a period of unqualified contribution to the commonweal, it was during the war years of 1940 through 1945. General Motors was second only to E. I. du Pont de Nemours in expansion for the war effort, spending $911 million for new factories and tools, $809 million of that from the public treasury." Still, during the war GM made after-tax profits of over $673 million and increased its productive capacity 50 percent. "A tendency to unguarded loquacity later made Wilson a controversial secretary of defense in the Eisenhower administration, but he was one of the great presidents of General Motors," John Rae notes. "At the end of 1943 he was able to report that every defense contract given to General Motors was in production, on schedule, and yielding more output than the government had considered possible." [7]

The output of the American automobile industry doubled even as the war brought great curtailment in civilian automobile use. The manufacture of motor vehicles for the civilian market ceased on February 22, 1942, despite the reluctance of automobile manufacturers faced with an expanding market for the first time since the 1920s. Tires and gasoline were severely rationed for the duration of the war, and a 35-mph national speed limit was imposed. Motor vehicle miles of travel decreased from 334 billion in 1941 to 213 billion in 1944; highway expenditures fell from their 1938 high of $2,675,000 to a 1944 low of $1,349,000; and receipts from special motor vehicle use taxes dropped from $2,041,000 in 1941 to $1,613,000 in 1944. Cars that had been nursed through the Depression long after they were ready to be junked were patched up further to survive through the war. Consequently, the wholesale value of replacement parts for the domestic market, $718 million in 1941, rose to a new high of $778 million in 1944 after a $472-million low in 1942. Factory sales of passenger cars dropped to a mere 139 units in 1943 and 610 units in 1944, while truck and bus sales declined from slightly over 1.06 million units in 1941 to 699,689 units in 1943 and 737,524 units in 1944.

The Automobile Manufacturers Association sponsored the formation of the Automotive Council for War Production (ACWP) shortly after the Japanese attack on Pearl Harbor. Twelve divisions of the ACWP coordinated the conversion of the industry's resources to the war effort. Alvan Macauley, president of both the AMA and the Packard Motor Car Company, became chairman of the ACWP. Its chief executive officer was George K. Romney, then managing director of the AMA.

Chrysler became the leading producer of tanks. Willys-Overland and Ford were the leading producers of some 2.5 million military trucks, most four-wheel-drive, and 660,000 four-wheel-drive jeeps. Raymond Flower and Michael Wynn Jones call the jeep—the name is an elision of GPV, for "General Purpose Vehicle"—the "crowning success of the war." Developed first by Bantam and then by Willys-Overland in response to a U.S. Army–sponsored competition, the jeep "became the backbone of all Allied military transport.... This plucky little machine seemed willing to go anywhere, do anything, and came to be regarded with great affection by the troops." [8] After the war, surplus military jeeps inaugurated a market for off-road recreational vehicles that persists into the present.

In addition to turning out several million motor vehicles of various types, before the war ended the American automobile industry had produced for the military 4,131,000 engines, including 450,000 aircraft and 170,000 marine engines; 5,947,000 guns; and 27,000 completed aircraft. Altogether, American automobile manufacturers made some seventy-five essential military items during World War II, most of them unrelated to the motor vehicle. These military materials had a total value of $29 billion and constituted one fifth of the nation's entire war production. American superiority in mass-production techniques—techniques developed in the automobile industry—was indeed the main reason for the Allied victory.

The Insolent Chariots

15

Despite the postwar seller's market for cars, not one new firm was able to get off the ground. Closure of entry into the American automobile industry was now complete. Twenty-two million dollars proved insufficient for flamboyant promoter Preston Tucker to get into production his radically designed rear-engined Tucker Torpedo at a cheaply leased Dodge aircraft plant. The Kaiser-Frazer Corporation failed despite the assets of the Graham-Paige Motor Car Company, the resources of shipbuilding and steel magnate Henry J. Kaiser, stock issues totaling $54 million, a $44-million loan from the Reconstruction Finance Corporation, and $30 million in bank loans. Formed shortly before the end of the war in 1945, Kaiser-Frazer produced some 745,928 units before folding in 1955, but in its best years, 1947 and 1948, was able to capture only 5 percent of the U.S. market as the leading independent. Its assembly operations at the converted Willow Run aircraft plant acquired from Ford were inefficient, and it had paid premium prices for its raw materials. But the main reason for failure was insufficient capital. Henry Kaiser estimated later that the company's initial stock offering should have been for three times the amount. John Rae reports that "the most reliable estimates for what would have been required to make a start in the 1950s run from a quarter of a billion to over a billion dollars, exclusive of the dealer organization, and the lower figure was considered very risky."[1]

The Mature American Industry

The American automobile industry further solidified into a joint-profit-maximizing oligopoly dominated by General Motors. The pattern that would characterize automobile manufacturing in the United States into the 1970s with only minor variations was well established by 1955, a banner year in sales. The United States produced about two thirds of the entire world output of motor vehicles, with 94 percent of the huge American domestic market held by Detroit's Big Three. GM had 50 percent, Ford 27 percent, and Chrysler 17 percent. The remaining 6 percent was shared by American Motors, Studebaker-Packard, and all imports, each accounting for a minuscule 2 percent. Additionally, the Big Three received nominal competition in heavy-duty truck production from a few surviving independents. The White Motor Company, which had made only heavy-duty trucks since 1908, absorbed Autocar in 1953, REO in 1957, and Diamond T in 1958 to become the largest independent heavy-duty truck producer. The other survivors with small shares of the heavy truck market were International Harvester, Mack, and Flxible.

A 1982 National Research Council study reports that from the end of World War II until very recently, "competition in any given segment of the U.S. automobile market occurred largely on the basis of economies of scale, styling, and sales and service networks. As befits a maturing industry, innovation became increasingly incremental in nature and, in marketing terms, invisible." The study notes, "It may seem odd to think of manufacturing as anything other than a competitive weapon.... Yet the history of the automobile market in the United States suggests that by the late 1950s manufacturing had become a competitively neutral factor.... [N]one of the major producers sought to achieve a competitive advantage through superior manufacturing performance." [2]

In the first scholarly analysis of the economics of the postwar American automobile industry, Lawrence J. White pointed out that during the 1946–1967 period the industry averaged an 11.51-percent rate of return on total assets and a 16.67-percent rate of return on net worth, compared with average profits for all American manufacturing corporations of 6.64 and 9.02 percent, respectively, on these criteria. While we lack such systematically analyzed data for European automobile manufacturers for the same period, an educated guess is that profits of only about 5 percent on total assets were the normal expectation. [3]

White cited Gordon R. Conrad and Irving H. Plotkin, who had tried to estimate the relationship between rates of return and risk, using a sample of 783 companies grouped into 59 industries. [4] The sample included Detroit's Big Three plus the leading independents, Studebaker-Packard and American Motors. Using the extremely weak criterion that 8.6 percent was the return on a riskless investment in an industry in which some monopoly profits were earned, the researchers found that the five automobile companies had an average rate of return of 17.99 percent and an average variance of 58.13 percent for the 1950–1965 period. When the variance is accounted for in the equation, the expected average rate of return, adjusted for risk for the automobile industry, is 13.4 percent, showing that the actual rates of return included excess profits over and above a generous risk premium. Of the 59 industries examined by Conrad and Plotkin, only the cosmetic industry, notorious for overpricing its products, showed a greater margin between the actual rate of return and the risk-adjusted rate of return. Normal profits, White pointed out, would have meant 3.5-percent lower wholesale prices on new cars.

These high average profits for the American automobile industry as a whole reflected in large part the performance of General Motors, the industry leader, which averaged 14.67 percent on total assets and 20.67 percent on net worth in the 1946–1967 period. Excluding GM, average profits for the American automobile industry on these criteria respectively were 7.76 and 11.41 percent. At the fringe of the market American Motors made average profits of only about 5 percent, and Studebaker-Packard was losing so much money that it folded as an active automobile manufacturer in 1963.

The main reason for GM's far more consistent large profits was Sloanism—GM's marketing strategy of "a car for every purse and purpose," leadership in styling, and the corporate structure and financial controls that vastly increased GM's internal efficiency and insulated the firm against the short-range vicissitudes of the market. Other reasons were GM's sheer size and high degree of vertical integration, which permitted it to define competitive conditions on terms favorable to itself. George Schwartz, assistant director of the UAW research department, pointed out in 1972 the ironic result: "In the auto industry, the lowest risk producer earns the highest return and the highest risk producer the lowest." [5]

"A Civilized Relationship": The Big Three and the UAW

Industry price leader General Motors avoided antitrust prosecution by pricing cars at levels that ensured huge profits for itself while permitting Ford and Chrysler to survive. In this GM was aided by the pattern of bargaining with the UAW that emerged in the immediate postwar period. In 1945 the UAW adopted the "one at a time" strategy of selecting only one of the Big Three as a strike target in negotiations, and contracts were extended to five years in 1950 and to three-year periods after 1955. A 1955 pact among the automobile manufacturers bound all of them to "pattern bargaining": all would agree to essentially the same terms that the union negotiated with the one selected as a strike target. "Whether it be styling, engineering, distribution or pricing, the auto industry always seems to end up playing follow the leader," reported *Time* in early 1973. "If giant General Motors announces higher prices on new-model cars, for example, Ford and Chrysler customarily follow suit—even though they may have earlier announced lower prices for their new cars. During triennial rounds of labor negotiations, identical company wage offers usually appear on the three separate bargaining tables within minutes of one another." [6]

As early as 1946, GM president Charles Wilson told reporters, "We have the union relations I designed, and they are right for our industry and our union. . . . We lose fewer days to strikes than any other major company in this country or in any other unionized country." The violent labor-management confrontations of the late 1930s simmered down after the war to what UAW president Leonard Woodcock in 1970 called "a civilized relationship." After a bitter 113-day strike against GM in the winter of 1945–1946, the UAW until 1970 chose as its strike target every three years one of GM's much weaker competitors. The union could gain from them much more generous settlements, to which GM was bound as well. When at long last the UAW leadership again selected GM as its strike target in 1970, to preserve credibility with its rank and file, the result was one of the costliest strikes in American history. Lasting 67 days, it cost GM $1 billion in profits, the workers $765 million in wages, the federal government $1 billion in taxes—plus $30 million in state welfare benefits and some $375 million in retail sales in Michigan alone.

Pattern bargaining was a major factor in the decline of the marginal independents, who had higher break-even points than the Big Three, and in the consolidation of GM's power. The union's concentration on increased wages and costly fringe benefits actually left GM's huge profit margins untouched. Lee Iacocca explains: "Because the strikes were so devastating, the leaders of the industry would do almost anything to avoid one. In those days we could afford to be generous. Because we had a lock on the market, we could continually spend more money on labor and simply pass the additional costs along to the consumer in the form of price increases." [7]

The automobile industry bought industrial peace at a high price. Settlement of the 1970 GM strike reaffirmed earlier settlements tying wages to the Bureau of Labor Statistics cost-of-living index (COLA) and providing for early retirement ("30 and out"). Contract negotiations in 1948 had resulted in the adoption of a proposal by GM president Charles Wilson tying wages to the cost-of-living index plus an "improvement factor" for increased productivity. Walter Reuther had foolishly bargained this away in 1967 to get still higher wages for some skilled and production workers. The 1970 negotiations reinstituted COLA. As early as 1949 an agreement with Ford had guaranteed a minimum retirement income for workers with thirty years of service. The 1970 GM agreement provided for retirement at a minimum of $500 a month for workers 56 years of age or older with thirty years of service, with reduced benefits after Social Security payments began at age 62. A 1955 agreement with Ford provided for supplemental unemployment benefits in the event of layoffs. Medical benefits were generous in the extreme. By the early 1980s, for example, Blue Cross/Blue Shield had become Chrysler's largest supplier, at a cost of $600 for every car that rolled off its assembly lines.

These concessions were a major source of the postwar American inflationary spiral that persisted into the 1980s, as well as a major reason why the American automobile industry became less and less able to compete with European and Japanese producers.

The Dinosaur in the Driveway

By the late 1950s the American automobile industry and its product were coming under increasing criticism. John Keats caught the new mood well in his witty diatribe against the postwar American car culture, *The Insolent Chariots*, which he "thoughtfully dedicated to the Automobile Manufacturers Association." Said Keats, "The American's marriage to the American automobile is now at an end, and it is only a matter of minutes to the final pistol shot, although who pulls the trigger has yet to be determined." A *New York Times* reviewer summed up that Keats's book portrayed contemporary American cars as "overblown, overpriced monstrosities built by oafs for thieves to sell to mental defectives." [8]

The complaints of the 1950s against the automobile culture were overwhelmingly consumer-oriented and directed against the Big Three. George K. Romney, while managing director of the Automobile Manufacturers Association (AMA), "felt the industry made a mistake in not preventing dealers from overcharging and forcing motorists to buy unwanted accessories during the postwar car shortage." [9] And when the seller's market for new cars changed to a buyer's market with the end of the Korean War in 1953, the sharpened competitive conditions resulted in dealers generally engaging in sales practices that not only were highly unethical but often skirted illegality.

The sales "blitz" was introduced in 1953, and high-pressure tactics came to include grillings by teams of salesmen in special rooms equipped with bugging devices. Customers were subjected to the "plain pack" (inflated charges for dealer preparation of the car); the "top pack" (an inflated trade-in allowance added to the price of the new car); the "finance pack" (exorbitant rates of interest on installment sales, usually involving a kickback to the dealer from the finance agency); the "switch" (luring a customer into a salesroom with an advertised bargain, then getting him to accept a worse deal on another car); the "bush" (hiking an initially quoted price during the course of the sale by upping the figures on a conditional sales contract signed by the customer); and the "highball" (reneging on an initially high trade-in offer after the customer committed himself to buying a new car). The customer might be induced to sign a conditional sales contract offering him a fantastic deal by a personable "liner," who feigned sales inexperience; he would then be turned over to a tough-talking "turnover" man, who bullied him into accepting far worse terms, and a "stick man," who cheated him on the financing. Salesmen often kept the customer from leaving the salesroom by "unhorsing" him—taking his trade-in out of sight to be "appraised," then refusing to bring back the car and/or return its keys. Few customers walked out of a salesroom without feeling that they had been victimized, and many people still shop for a new car with trepidation.

Senator Mike Monroney spoke for most buyers when he said that the retail selling of automobiles by the mid-1950s had come to exhibit "the morality of an Oriental bazaar." Monroney sponsored the Automotive Information Disclosure Act of 1958, which requires that every new motor vehicle being offered for sale bear a sticker (still known as the "Monroney sticker") stating the suggested retail price, specifying which items are standard equipment, and listing individually with suggested retail prices all optional equipment on the vehicle.

Despite disclaimers from Detroit, the evidence is unequivocal that the scandalous treatment of customers by dealers emanated from long-standing policies of the automobile manufacturers. The manufacturers forced their franchised dealers to accept too many cars and to maintain large stocks of unwanted parts and accessories. Allocations of popular models were tied to the acceptance of quotas of slow-selling cars. With the annual model change and the proliferation of models, components were arbitrarily changed in minor ways, forcing dealers to buy expensive new repair tools and needlessly to increase inventories of parts and accessories. Cars came off the assembly line with too many minor flaws that the dealer had to remedy at his expense for the customer. Dealers were forced to contribute to national advertising funds that did little to promote local sales. Books had to be kept in ways that exaggerated the dealers' profits, thereby increasing their taxes. High-volume "stimulator" dealerships were franchised in territories where competition already was ruinous. Phantom freight rates from Detroit were charged on cars assembled at much closer branch assembly plants. Franchises were arbitrarily canceled without adequate compensation for the dealers' investment.

These dealers' complaints were investigated as early as 1938 by the Federal Trade Commission. But nothing was done to correct them until, at the request of the National Automobile Dealers Association (NADA), automobile marketing practices were investigated in 1955–1956 by a subcommittee of the United States Senate Committee on Interstate and Foreign Commerce. With passage of the so-called Automobile Dealers' Day in Court Act of 1956 (Public Law 1026), the worst abuses were corrected, and there was a general easing up of sales pressures on dealers. However, Detroit continued to define dealer-manufacturer relations in ways that encouraged the exploitation of customers so that dealers could maintain average profits about equal to those for all retail businesses.

As for the product itself, consumer dissatisfaction with it mounted during the 1950s. As early as 1938, the automotive engineer Delmar G. Roos, who contributed to the development of the jeep, had stated a commonsense sine qua non of rational automobile design: "The object of an automobile is to transport a given number of people with reasonable comfort, with the least consumption of gasoline, oil, and rubber, and for the slightest operating cost and prime price." An AMA analysis of extensive statistics on automobile use compiled by the Public Roads Administration revealed that 85 percent of all automobile trips in the United States were thirteen miles or less and were for essential purposes. Clearly, it was foolish to use, in the words of the AMA's own Christy Borth, "two tons of automobile to transport a 105-pound blond." A survey undertaken by the Federation of Women's Clubs agreed with this criticism, and the mayors of both New York City and Los Angeles took public stands for smaller cars to reduce smog, traffic congestion, and parking problems. In an article that attracted wide attention, S. I. Hayakawa, the prominent semanticist, who was later to become a U.S. senator, wrote that "except for some interesting experiments at the fringes of the market by American Motors and Studebaker, the dominating forces in the industry—General Motors, Ford, and Chrysler—are still carrying on (in 1958) their assault on consumer intelligence. The Big Three are producing no cars that are not expensive, hideous and (except for a few sizes) costly to operate and powered far beyond any ordinary needs." Bishop G. Bromley Oxam, head of the Methodist Church in the United States, asked, "Who are the madmen who build cars so long they cannot be parked and are hard to turn at corners, vehicles with hideous tail fins, full of gadgets and covered with chrome, so low that an average human being has to crawl in the doors and so powerful that no man dare use the horsepower available?" [10]

During the 1950s American Motors president George Romney was a lone voice in the industry campaigning against what he called the "dinosaur in the driveway." Romney testified in 1958 before the Subcommittee on Antitrust and Monopoly, chaired by Senator Estes Kefauver, that competition in the American automobile industry had not been sufficient "to compel the Big Three to keep their products as modern in this country as the products the two biggest ones [GM and Ford] are building in Europe and in Australia and places like that." [11]

As early as 1926, Charles Nash had become interested in small cars and had wrongly projected a shift to cars under 110 inches in wheelbase because of their superior handling. Nash engineers were the only ones in the American industry to respond to a 1949 American Automobile Association (AAA) protest against nonfunctional styling and excessive size and horsepower. The AAA called for more economical cars. In 1950 Nash introduced its 100-inch-wheelbase, 2,576-pound, six-cylinder Rambler at $1,800. This was the first of the modern generation of compacts. In 1954 Nash added its 85-inch-wheelbase, four-cylinder, subcompact Metropolitan, made in England with specifications identical to those of the MG Midget series. The 1954 "standard-sized" six-passenger, four-door Nash had comparable interior room to that of competitive Big Three models, yet with a 108-inch wheelbase was a foot and a half shorter. The Nash cars after the 1941 "600" featured unitary body and chassis construction, which gave them a greater rigidity-to-weight ratio and hence made them safer than competing Big Three models. The Nash Airflyte series, introduced in the 1949 model year, looked like inverted bathtubs but were among the first commercially successful aerodynamically styled cars, with significantly lower drag coefficients than competing models.

Romney became chief executive officer of American Motors, newly formed from Nash and Hudson, in 1954. Under his leadership AMC became the only American automobile manufacturer to emphasize the small car. The Nash name was abandoned and after 1958 all American Motors cars were known as Ramblers. The 100-inch-wheelbase Rambler American became "the only success story of the American automobile industry in 1958, a year which saw more cars imported than exported for the first time in the century." In this year of business recession, a consumer reaction against ever larger cars was becoming evident. The Eisenhower administration coined the slogan, "You auto buy now," making buying a new car a patriotic duty, as factory sales of American-made cars declined from 7.2 million units in 1957 to 5.1 million units in 1958. Prematurely, as it turned out, Romney wired President Eisenhower, "Consumers are rebelling against the size, the large horsepower and the excessive styling changes made each year by many auto manufacturers." [12]

Detroit's reluctance to enter the small-car market can be explained by a truism in automobile manufacturing—large cars are far more profitable to build than small ones. Fixed investments in plant and machinery, advertising expenses, and labor costs were about the same for a subcompact and a "standard-size" car, and raw material costs did not vary more than perhaps $500. Yet the standard-size car could be sold for as much as several thousand dollars more than the subcompact. Iacocca, for example, pegs the 1984 profit per unit for the Cadillac Seville at $5,500, versus the usual profit of only about $700 per unit on subcompacts.[13] Similarly, dealers' profit margins averaged 25 percent of the wholesale price for standard-size cars, 21 percent for compacts and intermediates, and only 17 percent for subcompacts. In addition to the consideration that the production of small cars shifted sales away from the far more profitable large cars, the buyers of economy cars were less likely to order them loaded with luxury extras, which typically were marked up much higher than was the basic car, earning profits of 50 to 100 percent in some instances.

Led by the low-priced makes—Chevrolet, Ford, and Plymouth—a significant shift toward larger automobiles was inaugurated in the mid-1950s. "Between 1949 and 1959," notes White, "low, medium and high price makes grew in all relevant dimensions. After 1959 the high and medium price makes tended to remain about the same size or shrink slightly, while the low price makes continued to grow." In 1959 the full-size Ford V-8 had a 118-inch wheelbase, was 208 inches long and 76.8 inches wide, and weighed 3,485 pounds, as compared with the Cadillac V-8 dimensions of a 130-inch wheelbase, 225-inch length, 80.2-inch width, and 4,770 pounds. By 1968 the Cadillac V-8 had been reduced in weight to 4,640 pounds, with other dimensions reduced only fractions of an inch, while the Ford V-8 had grown to a 119-inch wheelbase, 213.3-inch length, 78-inch width, and 3,596-pound weight. The result of the trend toward making the smaller models progressively larger was that by 1968 "intermediate-sized cars, represented by the Ford Fairlane and the Oldsmobile F-85, [were] larger than was the full-sized Ford [Model B-A] of 1949."[14]

The major new engine development of the immediate postwar period was the so-called Kettering engine, announced in a 1947 technical paper. This V-8, overhead-valve engine operating at a 7.5 : 1 compression ratio with high-octane gas gave the 1949 Cadillac 160 horsepower on 331 cubic inches of displacement. "It is difficult to determine what was so revolutionary about the engine," White points out. "The V-8 designs had been around for over thirty years; the standard Ford [B-A] had a V-8 engine. Overhead valves (or valve in head) had also been around [since 1904]; the Buick straight-eight had them at the time of Kettering's paper. Everyone knew the effects of high octane gas in permitting high compression (more efficient) engines. But somehow the combination of these elements excited the industry."

The historical importance of the Kettering engine is that it engendered the post–World War II horsepower race. In contrast with the 100-horsepower 1949 Ford Model B-A, White notes, in 1967 "the low-priced three offered V-8s in the 200 horsepower range on their full-sized cars, sixes in the 150 horsepower range, with optional engines offering up to 400 horsepower. The minimum compression ratio in the industry was 8.25:1, with most standard engines falling in the 8.50:1 range; compression ratios as high as 11.01:1 were offered." Along with larger, more powerful engines, automatic transmissions, power steering, power brakes, and air conditioning came to be considered essential equipment, with about 90 percent of the full-size cars having these "options" by the 1974 model year.

The industry indulged in an orgy of nonfunctional styling that subordinated engineering to questionable aesthetic values. "The Cadillac styling team, headed by Harley J. Earl and his protégé, William L. Mitchell, had become fascinated with the rakish, organic lines of the twin engine, twin fuselage, Lockheed P-38 fighter plane, the most dramatic looking combat aircraft of World War II," writes Brock Yates. "They set out to create a new generation of automobiles featuring such aerodynamically inspired fillips as pointed noses, long sweeping pontoon fenders, curved windshields, and a generally elongated length that was inspired by airborne, not land-based transportation." The nonfunctional tail fins introduced on the 1949 Cadillac grew in proportion to set a styling trend to be emulated eventually even by stodgy Chrysler "with what became known as the 'Forward Look.' By 1958 the Chrysler, Dodge, and even the lowly Plymouth, had fins so outlandish that they appeared to have been stolen from the drawing boards of Boeing Aircraft." The 1954 Cadillac featured a "wraparound" windshield that distorted the driver's side vision and teatlike propeller spinner guards on its front bumper that became known as "Dagmars" after a big-busted television star. The "hardtop convertible" was innovated at Kaiser-Frazer and quickly emulated in post-war GM models; its nonconvertible but convertible-looking roof was a safety hazard in that it offered no protection in a rollover. The 1949 Buick featured a grille that Europeans called the "dollar grin" and nonfunctional "mouseholes" or "ventiports" along the sides of its hood, three on the lower-priced and four on the expensive models. Excessive front and rear overhang made cars corner worse and become more difficult to park. Indicating a dramatic reversal of roles, in a 1953 styling paper for the Society of Automotive Engineers (SAE) "Buick engineers . . . boasted how they had developed a special vertically mounted valve layout for their new 322 cubic inch V-8s specifically to conform to the restricted engine bay space allotted to them by the stylists." Yates concludes, "With Mitchell and Earl in control at GM, [Virgil] Exner at Chrysler, and the equally flashy George Walker at Ford, the industry was on the road to styling Babylon at the expense of engineering. . . . A part of the car that was not garishly painted was coated either in white vinyl or chrome." [15]

It would be hard to say which of the many models produced by Detroit was the most bizarre. The 1947 Studebaker Champion, designed by Raymond Loewy, was probably the most radical in its styling and came to be called the "coming or going" Studebaker because it looked much the same from the front and the back. For sheer garishness and grossness, Leon Mandel picks the 1958 Buick and Oldsmobile models. "When reckoning time comes at the end of the era of the automobile, anthropologists specializing in sheetmetal will look upon these two cars as prime examples of the age of excess," he writes. "Huge, vulgar, dripping with pot metal, and barely able to stagger down the highway, they were everything car people hated about the American automobile." [16]

Operating costs skyrocketed, because heavier, more powerful cars with more convenience options guzzled gas and oil and were harder on tires that were generally undersized for the weight of the car to enhance a stylish low profile. Even a large Cadillac got 20 miles to a gallon of gasoline in 1949, but by 1973 American-made passenger cars averaged only 13.5 miles per gallon. The accelerated subordination of utility to style made cars increasingly prone to extensive damage from even minor accidents, so repair bills and insurance premiums soared. Further, motorists paid out countless billions in motor vehicle use taxes to revamp our streets and highways to accommodate ever wider, longer, heavier, and faster motorcars. The average wholesale price of a car increased from $1,270 in 1950 to $1,822 by 1960, twice the rise of all wholesale costs during the decade, as transportation costs rose from 9.5 percent to 11.5 percent of personal disposable income in the United States. All costs considered, the Department of Transportation estimated in 1974 that the average owner would pay out $15,893 to drive his standard-size car 100,000 miles over a ten-year period.

From Sleek Horse to Fat Pig: The Strange Legacy of the Compacts

Increasingly successful penetration of the U.S. market (to 8.1 percent in 1958) by European imports, especially the VW Beetle, and the popularity in the 1958 recession of the compact Rambler and the Studebaker Lark brought about the introduction of the Big Three's first generation of compact and intermediate models, starting in 1960. Among the compacts, the Ford Falcon, Dodge Dart, and Plymouth Valiant were scaled-down conventional cars. The Chevrolet Corvair, on the other hand, was a more radical design powered by an air-cooled, flat-six, aluminum, rear-mounted engine.

The light weight of the Corvair engine, the absence of a drive shaft, and air cooling were definite pluses in a small, fuel-efficient car. However, the Corvair's rear end tended to lift up and its tires to tuck under on high-speed turns in stiff crosswinds, causing an "airout" from the tubeless tires that could send the car out of control. Moreover, like all rear-engined cars, including the VW, the Corvair had a natural tendency to oversteer in the hands of the average driver. Cost cutting on the Corvair went to such an extreme that a $15 stabilizing bar that would have corrected the over-steering problem was omitted, except in the optional sports package of the sporty Monza Coupe version. The son of the general manager of Cadillac was killed in a Corvair that oversteered, and the son of a GM executive vice-president suffered irreparable brain damage in another Corvair accident. Semon E. "Bunkie" Knudsen, general manager of Chevrolet and a GM vice-president, whose niece was brutally injured in a Corvair, ap-proached the GM executive committee and threatened to resign unless he was given permission to redesign the car's suspension, which he did for the 1964 model. John Z. DeLorean, chief engineer at Pontiac, was "absolutely convinced ... that the car was unsafe," so he kept it out of the Pontiac lineup. Then a completely new suspension system, designed by Frank Winchell, was incorporated in the facelifted 1965 Corvair, making it, in DeLorean's words, "one of the safest cars on the road." By then, however, the Corvair had become the focus of Ralph Nader's crusading book *Unsafe at Any Speed.* Sales faltered badly, and the car was withdrawn from production in 1969.[17]

Other GM divisions introduced compacts with conventional water-cooled, front-mounted engines. Buick and Oldsmobile jointly developed the Buick Special/Oldsmobile F-85, which was modified by DeLorean to become the Pontiac Tempest. DeLorean later recalled that the Tempest "rattled so loudly that it sounded like it was carrying half a ton of rocks." He failed to recall that *Road Test* magazine called the Tempest "probably the worst riding, worst all-around handling car available to the American public."[18]

This first generation of American compacts left a strange legacy in the high-performance cars developed in the mid-1960s to appeal to the youth market. Year by year, the compacts grew bigger and were loaded with more accessories. Illegal drag racing by youths on Detroit's Wood-ward Avenue inspired DeLorean to fill a niche in the market by stuffing an enormous 389-cubic-inch V-8 engine into a stripped-down Tempest—the "worst all-around handling car available"—and adding stiffer suspension and heavy-duty brakes. Stealing a designation from Ferrari, DeLorean named the car the GTO. "It was the start of a series of Muscle cars including Ford's Torino Cobra, Mercury's Cougar Eliminator, and Plymouth's Road Runner," Mandel relates. "Europeans could have their real Ferrari GTOs. The American young for $3,200 could get a car that would go almost as fast in a straight line, and survive to take its driver to work at the car wash the next morning. In a land where straight lines stretched from one coast to the other, who needed an alpine racer?" The 1968 Plymouth Road Runner, in Mandel's words, was "the ultimate street ripper of them all.... Like the Pontiac GTO, it began life as a weak kneed Intermediate, but with the addition of the famous Chrysler 426-cubic-inch 'Hemi' (for hemispherical combustion chamber) engine, it became the darling of the street racers." [19]

Lee Iacocca, then general manager of the Ford Division, had an even "better idea." The Ford Motor Company had been sobered by the colossal failure of the 1958–1960 Edsel, a gadget-bedecked road cruiser with a distinctive horse-collar grille designed on the basis of 1954–1955 market surveys. The Edsel was introduced during the 1958 recession, just as a shift in consumer preference toward smaller cars became evident. Aware of a growing market for sportier "personal cars" among young buyers and as second cars, Iacocca used numerous components from the compact Falcon in the design of the first "pony car," the 1965 Mustang, which could be bought with a 260-cubic-inch (later 289-cubic-inch) V-8 optional engine and a four-speed transmission with shift on the floor. "It was the first of the [Ford] long-term plans to put something together for the kids," Iacocca explains. "The [Falcon] components were in the system; all we had to do was put a youth wrapper around it—and this was done for less than $50 million." Mandel calls the Mustang "the most sensational introduction of modern times. Ford sold half a million Mustangs in eighteen months; Lee Iacocca made the cover of *Time* magazine, a legend at barely forty." The base price of the car was only $2,368, but buyers were ordering an average of $1,000 worth of options. [20]

From 550,000 units in 1966, Mustang sales plummeted to only 150,000 units in 1970. "Within a few years of its introduction, the Mustang was no longer a sleek horse. It was more like a fat pig," Iacocca laments. "By 1971, the Mustang had grown eight inches longer, six inches wider, and almost six hundred pounds heavier than the original 1965 model.... [O]ur customers had abandoned us because we had abandoned their car." [21]

"Unsafe at Any Speed": Technological Obsolescence in Detroit

Cars had become less safe. Although Nader's focus on the Corvair was unfortunate, his main contentions were sound. He pointed out forcefully the subordination of safety to styling in automotive design and the dangers of the "secondary collision" to passengers after an accident had occurred. The most complete study of automotive safety versus styling has been done by Joel W. Eastman.[22] He notes, among other things, that in order to make cars nonfunctionally longer, bodies were built with unsafe excessive front and rear overhang from the chassis; several other major styling innovations, particularly the hardtop and the wraparound windshield, were safety hazards. Additionally, the emphasis on comfort over safety meant poorly designed seats, springing that was too soft, and an overall loss of road feel. Until changes were mandated by federal law for the 1968 model year, cars were also poorly designed to protect occupants from injuries in secondary collisions: doors tended to fly open, dashboards had too many needless protrusions, steering columns did not collapse, and cars lacked as standard equipment seat belts to restrain occupants from being thrown through windshields. To its great credit, as early as 1954 the Ford Motor Company introduced a "safety package" consisting of safety door latches, a collapsible steering column, a padded dashboard, and optional seat belts, only to discover that safety did not sell to style-conscious consumers.

Despite a 1955 pact among the automobile manufacturers that forbade them to support formal racing or to advertise horsepower ratings, automobile advertisements continued to stress performance and to portray cars as outlets for antisocial instincts. The agreement not to support racing was widely violated as well, with the Ford Motor Company alone spending an estimated $20 million to $30 million a year on racing activity in the mid-1960s. An industry-sponsored Vehicle Equipment Safety Compact authorized by Congress in 1958 had passed only one safety standard (on tires) by 1965 and had no full-time staff members until 1966.

In 1965 the Senate Government Operations Committee's Subcommittee on Executive Reorganization began investigating automotive safety under the leadership of its chairman, Senator Abraham Ribicoff. Testimony revealed that GM had spent only $1.25 million on safety research in 1965 (GM later claimed it had spent $193 million) while making $1.7 billion in profits. And although the industry continued to deemphasize the role of the car in accidents, it was brought out by Ribicoff that since 1960 over 8 million cars (about one out of every five manufactured) had been recalled for defects, many of them safety related. Indeed, manufacturing quality had deteriorated to the point that by the mid-1960s American-made cars were being delivered to retail buyers with an average of twenty-four defects per unit. Nader, a consultant to the Ribicoff committee, estimated that styling changes accounted for $700 of a car's retail price and suggested that most of this money be diverted to making cars safer.

"Oversized, overpowered, with soggy suspension, vague steering, weak brakes and low-grade tires, the average Detroit automobile of the day was a true ocean liner of the road," writes Yates. "It was smooth and relatively stable when proceeding in a straight line, but it became a slave to inertia when asked to stop or change directions. Ironically almost all these safety hazards were ignored in the Ribicoff hearings." He makes the important point that too much emphasis was put on the poor crashworthiness of American cars in accidents, almost none on the "awful handling and braking" that helped cause accidents.

Yates cites the two-and-a-half-ton 1967 Cadillac Eldorado, with a premium basic price of $6,277, as "a typical General Motors car of the period: powerful, gadget-laden, with a feather-pillow ride. It plowed through tight corners in ungainly fashion, got only ten miles to the gallon, and would run 109 mph in a short burst like an ill-trained athlete." The car's standard hydraulic drum brakes were dangerously inadequate. "To make a panic stop in an Eldorado from 80 mph took well over a football field of distance, nearly a hundred feet more than could be considered acceptable. Exactly 386 feet were required to rein in the car from that speed, which in pre–55 mph days was a common highway velocity, especially on the open roads of the West." Like other American-made cars of the day, the Eldorado had a suspension system that was too soft for the car to handle well on curves and on rough roads, and it came equipped with outdated, inferior bias-ply tires. Yates errs, however, in calling the 1967 Eldorado typical. With a 120-inch wheelbase, it was shorter and lower than other Cadillacs. It was the first car in the world to combine front-wheel drive with variable-ratio steering and automatic level control. And it was the only Cadillac model on which front disc brakes were offered as an option. The Eldorado was in fact one of the more advanced Detroit production cars of its day.[23]

In contrast with the Eldorado, a contemporary Mercedes-Benz 250 sedan cost about $2,000 less, weighed about a thousand pounds less, was 20 inches shorter, and gave about twice the gas mileage. It featured fuel injection, four-wheel disc brakes, fully independent suspension, steel-belted radial tires, and unitary body construction. Fuel injection, introduced on the 1954 Mercedes-Benz 300SL sports car, produces a more even distribution of the fuel, reducing exhaust emissions and increasing fuel efficiency without sacrificing performance. Disc brakes are lighter and mechanically simpler, and have less tendency to "fade" (lose braking power under hard braking) or to slip or grip when wet than drum brakes. Fully independent suspension gives better control of the car and a better ride on rough roads. Steel-belted radial tires are more durable and give far better traction, especially on wet surfaces, than bias-ply tires. Unitary body construction gives greater rigidity for the weight of the car, increasing its safety. The Mercedes-Benz passenger compartment was built rigid to prevent collapse in a rollover and was protected by a front end designed to crush to absorb energy in a collision. The Mercedes-Benz thus was cheaper to buy and operate, easier to handle and park, safer to drive, and more crashworthy than the Cadillac. In addition to being a generation ahead of the Cadillac technologically, the Mercedes-Benz was of vastly superior manufacturing quality, and its classic styling was intended to remain appealing for decades rather than for a few years. The comparison made ludicrous to a rational observer that the word "Cadillac" was still synonymous in the American mind with "excellence."

Yates criticizes the American automobile industry for lagging far behind foreign competitors in the 1950–1980 period in developing and adopting state-of-the-art innovations that improved fuel economy, performance, handling, and safety. The European technological lead, opened in the 1930s, widened after World War II, as American "stylists and engineers were becoming little more than gadget builders, slaving compulsively over such problems as the creation of opera lights or automatic headlight dimmers while the essentials of the automobile—the brakes, suspension, steering—were left virtually unimproved."[24]

The superiority of steel-belted radial tires, introduced by Michelin in 1946, was immediately recognized in Europe, but radials were not generally adopted in the United States until the late 1970s. American cars still in the main had rigid rear axles. Disc brakes were introduced in 1949 on the Chrysler Crown Imperial but then phased out. After being used in the late 1950s on the Triumph T-3, the Citroën, and the Jaguar, and in 1960 on the English Ford, disc brakes were rapidly adopted as standard equipment on European cars in the early 1960s, a decade before front disc brakes combined with less efficient drum rear-wheel brakes came to be standard on American cars. Although the availability of fuel injection as an option had increased, the American industry continued to lag in fuel injection technology. With the exception of Chrysler's continuing experiments with the gas turbine engine, the major innovations in power plants were pioneered abroad—the turbo-diesel at Mercedes-Benz, the Wankel rotary piston at Toyo Kogyo, and the CVCC stratified-charge engine at Honda.

"Sometime in the late 1960s . . . a nagging suspicion about the philosophy of General Motors and the automobile business began to overtake me," recalled ex–GM executive John DeLorean in 1979. He was concerned "that there hadn't been an important product innovation in the industry since the automatic transmission and power steering in 1949 [*sic*]. . . . In place of product innovation, the [American] automobile industry went on a two-decade marketing binge which generally offered up the same old product under the guise of something new and useful. But year in and year out we were urging Americans to sell their cars and buy new ones because the styling had changed. There really was no reason for them to change from one model to the next, except for the new wrinkles in the sheet metal." [25]

Complacency carried a high cost, not only in a dwindling share of the world market for new cars but also in the increasing penetration of the North American market by imports, beginning with the VW Beetle in the 1950s. The United States shifted as early as 1967 from being a net exporter to a net importer of automotive products.

Up from the Ashes

16

Unconcerned over their loss of technological leadership, American automobile manufacturers remained convinced well into the 1960s of their invulnerability to foreign competitors in the world as well as the U.S. market. In a classic reaffirmation of the American auto maker's longstanding advocacy of free trade, Henry Ford II on April 5, 1961, gave a speech in which he argued that the automobile industry, and industry in general, would stagnate without the fullest, freest international competition. He advocated "a strong and growing flow of trade, of capital, of technology throughout the free world." [1]

Tariff barriers on automobiles have tumbled from 1950 to the present. In 1950 tariffs on passenger cars ranged from 10 percent in the United States to 40 percent in Japan, with rates of 33⅓ percent in the U.K. and 35 percent in France, Germany, and Italy. A 1964 pact provided for free trade between the U.S. and Canada in motor vehicles and automotive equipment. The establishment of the European Economic Community (EEC) eliminated tariff barriers between the major auto-producing countries of Western Europe, except Sweden, after 1968 (1978 in the case of the U.K.) and imposed a common external tariff of 17.6 percent. By 1973 tariffs on passenger cars had dropped to 3 percent in the U.S., 6.4 percent in Japan, and 10.9 percent in the EEC countries; and by 1983 they had fallen slightly further to 2.8 percent in the U.S., 0 in Japan, and 10.5 percent in the EEC countries. However, substantial barriers to truly free trade in motor vehicles continue to exist in the form of differential local methods for taxing motor vehicles, local equipment requirements, and import quotas. The existing import quotas in the main have been imposed to prevent the further penetration of markets in the European auto-producing countries by the Japanese.

Big Three Expansion Abroad

In the decades following World War II, both Ford and GM greatly expanded their worldwide, and especially their European, operations. GM's overseas policy remained the acquisition abroad of wholly owned subsidiaries. Ford reverted to this policy in the immediate postwar period, buying out the shareholders in its European affiliates. By 1961 Ford-U.S. owned 100 percent of Ford-England and 99 or 100 percent of its other overseas subsidiaries. An International Division of the Ford Motor Company was formed in 1946 to coordinate Ford operations worldwide. Then in 1967 Ford of Europe, Incorporated, was formed, with headquarters in Brentwood, England, to integrate European development, production, and marketing. GM operations worldwide were coordinated through its Overseas Policy Group, and GM did not integrate its European operations at Opel in Germany and Vauxhall in the U.K. until 1979.

The Ford Motor Company remains the foremost multinational automobile producer in the world. Some 38 percent of total Ford sales in 1979 came from production facilities outside North America, with 25 percent coming from production in EEC countries. In comparison, only 19 percent of GM's production in 1979 came from its plants outside North America, with 12 percent coming from EEC countries. Within the European automobile industry, Ford and GM respectively held fifth and sixth place in 1979 among the ten companies with annual production of more than 100,000 units. And Ford's European operations were its most profitable. While Ford posted losses of EUA (European Unit of Account) 145 million and EUA 1.548 billion on its 1979 and 1980 U.S. operations, Ford-Europe reported profits of EUA 889 million and EUA 248 million. GM's European operations have been far less profitable. While GM sales worldwide exceeded Ford sales by 52 percent in 1979, they amounted to only 76 percent of Ford sales in the EEC countries. Like most other European automobile manufacturers, and in marked contrast to their American operations, Ford-Europe and GM-Europe both concentrated in the postwar decades on producing small, fuel-efficient cars.

Chrysler made a belated, ill-starred attempt to develop as a multinational company by mounting in the late 1950s and the 1960s an ambitious overseas expansion program. It began by importing Simca cars from France in 1957 and purchasing a controlling interest in Simca in 1958. By 1973 Chrysler owned 100 percent of Simca, Barrieros in Spain, and Rootes Motors, producer of the Hillman and the Humber, in the U.K. This gave Chrysler 7.3 percent of Western European output. Subsidiaries were established in Australia and Japan. Assembly facilities were acquired in Argentina, Colombia, and Venezuela.

Simca and Rootes were both in financial trouble and in poor competitive positions in their respective national industries. The major problem was that both were too small vis-à-vis their competitors and could not achieve sufficient economies of scale. That was why they could be bought cheap. So Chrysler made the classic blunder of adding their weaknesses to its own. Chrysler-U.K. was losing so much money by 1975 that the parent company, in deep financial trouble itself, threatened to begin liquidation unless the British government agreed to a bailout. This first Chrysler bailout remains largely unknown in the United States. To save an estimated 25,000 jobs at Chrysler-U.K. and 25,000 more in related U.K. industries, the British government shared Chrysler losses of £72.5 million and provided or guaranteed the firm an additional £90 million in loans, on condition that Chrysler-U.K. be more closely integrated with Chrysler-France.

Despite the British bailout, and the claim of Chrysler-U.K. in 1976 that its financial position was viable, Chrysler-U.S. announced in August 1978 the sale of its European subsidiaries to Peugeot-Citroën (PSA), as part of a general retrenchment program. Peugeot-Citroën took over some £400 million of accumulated debt and paid Chrysler £230 million and 15.5 percent of Peugeot-Citroën stock. Chrysler-U.K. became Talbot, Limited. Chrysler sold its Latin American facilities the following year. Then in 1980 the Chrysler subsidiaries in Australia and Japan were sold to Mitsubishi for 15 percent of Mitsubishi stock and retention of a 35-percent interest in the Australian subsidiary. Thus ended Chrysler's brief history as a multinational. At present Chrysler has operations only in North America.

Ford and GM continue to be the only automobile manufacturers with operations on all continents. In contrast, the Japanese industry has been the least multinational in its operations and remains committed to carrying out all except token manufacturing in the home country. Consolidation of the automobile industry at the international level through mergers, the establishment of overseas subsidiaries, joint manufacturing ventures, and outsourcing of components has progressed so far that the term "multinational" no longer seems an adequate description of organizational reality. As John Rae remarks, "In recent years there have been marked indications that the automobile industry has been moving beyond the conventional multinational form into something that is as yet vaguely defined but can best be described as supranational." [2]

The Postwar Western European Industry

The increased activity of U.S.-based multinationals in Europe was over-shadowed by the resurgence of the European automobile industry. German output increased from 306,064 units in 1950 to over 2.055 million units in 1960, as GM-owned Opel fell from first to third place in the German industry. During the same decade French output increased from 357,552 units to some 1.37 million units, Italian output from 127,847 units to 644,633 units. Although the British industry more than doubled its output from 783,672 units in 1950 to 1.81 million units in 1960, its relative position was declining. Germany surpassed the U.K. to become the second-largest automobile producer in the world in 1956. By 1970 the Japanese as well as the French had surpassed the British in output. By 1980 so had the Italians and the U.S.S.R.

The postwar European automobile industry has remained heavily an export industry, with the pattern of export trade being mainly within Europe. Considered as percentages of domestic production, from 1960 to 1982 for Germany, France, the U.K., and Italy, passenger car exports ranged from 33.2 percent in Italy to 47.6 percent in Germany in 1960, from 33.7 percent in Italy to 58.3 percent in Germany in 1982. Commercial vehicle exports ranged from 12.3 percent of domestic production in Italy to 49.3 percent in Germany in 1960, from 33.8 percent in the U.K. to 67.6 percent in Germany in 1982. These figures contrast sharply with exports accounting for a mere 2.2 percent in 1960 and 7 percent in 1982 of U.S. passenger car production, and only 18 percent in 1960 and 6.7 percent in 1982 of commercial vehicle production. The exports of EEC auto-producing countries have been increasingly destined for other EEC countries as the Japanese have penetrated the American and other external markets. By 1980 Japanese penetration left only France and Germany among the EEC countries with a favorable balance of automotive trade.

The Western European automobile industry was already a highly concentrated one in 1960: 98 percent of French production was accounted for by Renault, Citroën, Peugeot, and Simca; 96 percent of British production by the British Motor Company (BMC), Ford-England, Standard, Rootes, and Vauxhall; 87 percent of German production by Volkswagen, Opel, Mercedes-Benz, and Ford-Werke; and 85 percent of Italian production by Fiat and Alfa-Romeo. By 1979 the automobile industry in the EEC countries could be described as a "normal oligopoly." Peugeot-Citroën (PSA), the largest firm in 1979, accounted for 19 percent of the total EEC output of passenger cars. The four largest firms—PSA, Volkswagen, Renault, and Fiat—accounted for 61 percent. The ten firms with annual production of more than 100,000 units—the aforementioned plus Ford-Europe, GM-Europe, British Leyland (BL), Mercedes-Benz, BMW (Bayerische Motoren Werke), and Alfa-Romeo—accounted for 99 percent of the total output, the remaining one percent of the market being shared by fourteen small independent producers.

Outside the EEC in Western Europe, Volvo and Saab-Scania in Sweden are the only important independent producers and together account for only about one percent of world production. Spain accounts for a little more than 3 percent. Through the Instituto Nacional de Industria (INI) the Spanish government holds a majority interest in the Sociedad de Automoviles de Turismo (SEAT), the largest producer, and controls two small commercial vehicle producers, ENASA and AISA. Ford has established a major subsidiary in Spain. GM has only a minuscule operation. The lion's share of Spanish production is accounted for by subsidiaries of EEC producers—primarily Fiat (which has invested in SEAT), Fasa-Renault, Talbot-Spain, and Citroën-Spain. Like GM, Mercedes-Benz and British Leyland have only token Spanish operations.

The Western European automobile producers are far less multinational enterprises than are Ford and GM. Among the Western European producers only Volkswagen, Fiat, and Volvo produce a significant proportion of their total output outside the parent country. The proportions for 1982 were Volkswagen and Fiat 28 percent and Volvo 30 percent. The bulk of manufacturing outside the parent country by EEC producers is accounted for by operations in Brazil, Spain, Mexico, and Argentina. With the exception that state-owned Renault had a controlling interest in American Motors until bought out by Chrysler in 1987, Volkswagen is the only European producer to manufacture cars in the United States.

The high degree of nationalization, on the one hand, and of family control, on the other, are striking features of the Western European industry. Renault, British Leyland, and Alfa-Romeo are entirely state-owned enterprises. Volkswagen is owned 20 percent by the federal government of West Germany and 20 percent by the state of Lower Saxony. The Peugeot family owns 49.5 percent of PSA stock. The Agnelli family holds a controlling interest of 29 percent of Fiat stock.

European governments also commonly intervene in the market to restructure competitive conditions when this appears to be in their national self-interest. In addition to nationalizing Renault after World War II, for example, the French government in 1974 bailed out Michelin's automobile holdings (Citroën, Panhard et Levassor, and Berliet), then in 1976 played a leading role in the acquisition of Berliet by Renault and the takeover of Citroën by Peugeot. The Japanese penetration of European markets has been thwarted by import quotas of 2,300 Japanese cars annually in Italy, 3 percent of new registrations in France, and 11 percent of new registrations in Great Britain. Furthermore, primarily because of great discrepancies in the rates of the value-added-tax and the imposition of special national surcharges, the EEC is still a far cry from being a "common market." These trade barriers meant that in 1980 the pretax sticker prices of Common Market cars varied up to 80 percent among EEC countries. Thus, neither in its pattern of ownership nor in its practice in the market does the Western European automobile industry conform to American conceptions of how free enterprise should operate in a free market.

The MIT Report points out that whereas the North American industry by the early 1950s concentrated on producing in the largest possible volume a standardized product, the all-purpose road cruiser, "the Europeans fashioned domestically produced products for very different national market conditions, which were due to the wide variations in consumer incomes, vehicle taxes, and geography among the European countries.... In addition, the numerous European manufacturers were pursuing many different technical solutions to the differing design requirements." Consequently, technological innovation flourished in the European automobile industry while it stagnated in the American industry. The Europeans offered a wide variety of engines, including diesels; rear-mounted/rear-wheel-drive and front-mounted/front-wheel-drive, cars; and numerous suspension systems and body types. "Once the tariff walls in Europe began to come down in the late 1950s and early 1960s" the MIT Report continues, "the diversity of the European automobile industry became its greatest strength. When each manufacturer could sell its specialized products in all the markets of Europe, adequate scale to capture full production economies was suddenly available.... Real prices to consumers fell, demand surged upward, and the European industry advanced to the forefront of world motor vehicle manufacturing." [3]

Thus, the Europeans led technologically in all segments of the world automobile market, as exemplified by the Mercedes-Benz and the Jaguar at one extreme and the Volkswagen at the other. Nevertheless, as Jean-Jacques Chanaron points out, it was the small, fuel-efficient European "people's cars" that became "the spearhead of the expansion strategies and the primary reason for the growth and leadership of some of the major European manufacturers. These included Volkswagen (Beetle), Renault (4CV), Citroën (2CV), Fiat (500 and 600), and the British Motor Corporation (Mini)." [4]

With the diffusion of such "people's cars," automobile cultures rapidly developed in the advanced capitalist nations of Western Europe and in Japan. The proportion of world registrations accounted for by the United

States declined dramatically from 76 percent of the total passenger cars and 51 percent of the trucks and buses in 1950 to only 38 percent of each by 1980, and continues to decline. In 1980 the United States continued to lead in the ratio of motor vehicles to population, with one motor vehicle for every 1.4 persons, followed closely, as in 1927, by Canada (1:1.8), New Zealand (1:1.8), and Australia (1:1.9). But the gap between these early leaders in the development of automobile cultures and the advanced capitalist nations of Europe and Japan had almost closed. Among the Western European capitalist nations the ratios were 1:2.4 in France, the Federal Republic of Germany, and Switzerland; 1:2.7 in Sweden; 1:2.8 in Belgium; 1:2.9 in Italy and Norway; 1:3 in Austria and the Netherlands; 1:3.1 in Denmark; 1:3.2 in the United Kingdom; 1:3.4 in Finland; and 1:4.1 in Ireland and Spain. Greece and Portugal were anomalies, with ratios of 1:7.3 and 1:8.2. Although the Japanese automobile culture began to develop only in the early 1960s, by 1980 Japan had a ratio of one motor vehicle for every three persons.

Will There Always Be an England?

The United Kingdom appeared to have the best chance to develop a European automobile culture at the end of the war. At the beginning of postwar expansion the British industry ranked second after the American in world motor vehicle production. Britain's market position declined progressively, however, in the 1960s and deteriorated rapidly after 1975. By 1982 the U.K. had dropped to seventh place in world motor vehicle production, behind Italy, the U.S.S.R., France, West Germany, the United States, and Japan. In commercial vehicle production the U.K. ranked sixth, after the U.S.S.R.; in passenger car production, eighth, after Spain, as well as the U.S.S.R. and Italy. State-controlled Lada in the U.S.S.R. alone produced some 800,000 passenger cars in 1982, versus 405,000 produced by nationalized British Leyland. Return on capital from 1967 to 1971 for the British automobile industry was only 3.5 percent, compared with 12.4 percent for the West German industry.

The British industry's historic problems of poor labor productivity and insufficient rationalization were exacerbated after the war by excessive, unwise, vacillating government regulation. With Continental automobile plants in ashes and the U.S. industry unable to fill domestic— much less world—demand, the Labour government attempted to use England's automobile industry as a "leading sector" in an export drive intended to reduce balance-of-payments difficulties and to relieve pressure on the pound. The Society of Motor Manufacturers and Traders (SMMT)

1949 Ford Model B-A. The revitalization of the Ford Motor Company under Henry Ford II was evidenced by the 100-horsepower 1949 Model B-A, the first new postwar Ford car. Ford surpassed Chrysler to regain second place in the industry as sales doubled with introduction of the Model B-A. Its "envelope body" eliminated conventional fenders as well as running boards to set a styling trend still in evidence. Its independent, coil-spring Hydra Coil front suspension initiated the marshmallow ride and poor handling that characterized American-made cars until the 1980s. (Courtesy Henry Ford Museum and Greenfield Village)

1949 Nash Custom Line Ambassador Series 60. Nash cars after 1941 featured unitary body and chassis construction, which gave them a greater rigidity-to-weight ratio and hence made them safer than competing Big Three models. The 1949 Airflyte series, the first totally redesigned postwar Nash car line, looked like inverted bathtubs but had significantly lower drag coefficients, and thus better fuel economy, than the Big Three models. The Custom Line Ambassador shown here had a 121-inch wheelbase and a six-cylinder, 112-horsepower engine. Despite the functional utility of Nash cars, sales declined as the postwar seller's market evaporated. In 1954 Nash merged with Hudson to form American Motors, the only American manufacturer to emphasize the small car in the 1950s. (Courtesy American Motors)

1949 Cadillac Fleetwood 60 Special. The 1949 Cadillac introduced the first postwar GM styling changes and featured nonfunctional tail fins inspired by the Lockheed P-38 fighter plane. This 133-inch-wheelbase Fleetwood 60 Special additionally featured larger doors, hydraulic window lifts, and nonfunctional chrome slashes on its rear roof pillar. It was powered by the so-called Kettering engine, the major new postwar engine development, announced in a 1947 technical paper. This V-8, overhead-valve engine operating at a 7:51 compression ratio with high-octane gas gave the 1949 Cadillac 160 horsepower on 331 cubic inches of displacement. Nothing about the engine was revolutionary. Its historic importance is that it engendered a postwar horsepower race that lasted into the mid-1970s. (Courtesy General Motors)

Great Smokies family snapshot, 1951. With general prosperity and rising working-class incomes and leisure, tourism became central to the American economy in the post–World War II period. (Courtesy Smithsonian Institution and National Archives)

The first Holiday Inn Hotel Courts, Memphis, Tennessee, 1952. Struck by the lack of comfortable, low-priced accommodations on a 1951 family vacation trip, Kemmons Wilson joined forces with prefabricated-home builder Wallace E. Johnson to pioneer the motel chain. They franchised their Holiday Inn trade name, logo, national advertising, and national referral system to local investors who agreed to erect and maintain motels according to Holiday Inn standards of design and service. Hotel corporations owning their own properties followed them into the motel business in the mid-1950s. (Courtesy Holiday Inns, Inc.)

Howard Johnson's restaurant and adjacent Skyline Motor Court, Waynesboro, Virginia, 1951. In the 1930s Howard Johnson perfected the concept of the family roadside restaurant chain. His easily identifiable restaurants offered both full-meal service and fast-food counters with standardized menus and attractive atmospheres. Following the lead of Holiday Inns, in 1953 Johnson began franchising the motels that had sprung up adjacent to his restaurants to capitalize on the visual association and proximity. After passage of the 1956 Interstate Highway Act, the logos of national motel-restaurant chains became a familiar greeting to tourists at freeway interchanges across the United States. (Courtesy National Archives)

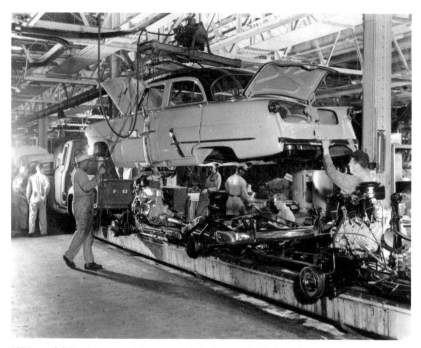

1953-model Ford cars and pickup trucks being assembled on the same line at the Ford River Rouge plant. While cars became increasingly complex and varied within model runs as Fordism was intensified by Sloanism, assembly-line technology remained essentially unchanged at the River Rouge from production of the Model A. Because specialized automatic machinery could only be used profitably for the manufacture of mechanical components that remained relatively unchanged, the need for large amounts of dehumanizing semiskilled labor had grown and the pace of work in the body plant and in final assembly had intensified since the early 1930s. (Courtesy Ford Motor Company)

Opposite, bottom: 1958 Edsel Pacer convertible. After nine years of planning and one of the biggest promotion campaigns in history, the Ford Motor Company introduced the Edsel as "entirely new to the industry" on September 4, 1957. The announced first-year sales goal of 200,000 units evaporated as consumer tastes shifted to smaller cars in the 1958 recession, and only 63,000 Edsels were sold in the 1958 model year. The chrome- and gadget-bedecked Edsel featured a distinctive horse-collar grille and a push-button automatic transmission control centered in the steering wheel hub. The car was withdrawn from production in 1960, and the name Edsel became a synonym for "loser." The model shown was a double loser, for the popularity of convertibles waned as air conditioning came to be considered essential equipment on standard-size cars in the 1960s. (Courtesy Ford Motor Company)

1957 Chrysler New Yorker. After decades of stodgy styling, Chrysler attempted to beat GM at its own game with the "Forward Look" of the 1957 Chrysler models. This 4,330-pound, 126-inch-wheelbase New Yorker had the largest engine available in a 1957 production car: with a 9.25:1 compression ratio, the New Yorker Series V-8 overhead-valve engine developed 325 horsepower at 4,600 rpm on 392 cubic inches of displacement. Safety hazards of the New Yorker's styling included the pillarless hardtop, the wraparound windshield, and excessive rear overhang resulting from exaggerated nonfunctional tail fins. The car's only advanced technical feature was torsion-bar suspension, which had been introduced in 1938 in Ferdinand Porsche's Volkswagen prototype. (Courtesy Chrysler Historical Collection)

1949 Volkswagen Export Model. The 1938 Volkswagen prototype was a four-cylinder, 25-horsepower, closed-body car capable of carrying four persons in comfort at a cruising speed of 60 mph and fuel consumption of 33 mpg. Several military versions saw service during World War II, and civilian production began at the war's end. With the introduction of the improved Export Model in 1949, Beetles began to be exported to the United Kingdom, British Commonwealth countries, and the United States. Although the basic Beetle design was retained, some 2,000 mechanical and stylistic improvements had been incorporated by the mid-1960s, and horsepower was progressively raised to as high as 60 bhp in the 1971 Super Beetle. On February 17, 1972, the Beetle surpassed the Model T to become the best-selling car of all time. (Courtesy Volkswagen of America, Inc.)

Opposite, bottom: 1965 Ford Mustang hardtop. Capitalizing on the youth market for small, sporty cars that had been made evident by the popularity of the Corvair Monza Club Coupe, in April 1964 Ford introduced the first "pony car," the 1965 Mustang. The 108-inch-wheelbase Mustang used the Falcon chassis and many Falcon components. Its base price was only $2,368, but buyers ordered the car loaded with an average $1,000 worth of options. Engines up to a 289-cubic-inch, 271-horsepower V-8 were available. During its first year on the market the Mustang set a new world sales record of over 418,000 units. But Mustang sales plummeted to only 150,000 units in 1970 as, according to Lee Iacocca, the car grew in all relevant dimensions to resemble a fat pig more than a sleek horse. (Courtesy Ford Motor Company)

Top: 1964 Chevrolet Corvair Monza Club Coupe. Increasing penetration of the American market by the Volkswagen and other small imports led the Big Three to introduce the first generation of "compact cars" in the 1960 model year. The Ford Falcon and the Plymouth Valiant were scaled-down versions of conventional American standard-size cars, but the 108-inch-wheelbase Chevrolet Corvair featured fully independent suspension and a novel rear-mounted, aluminum, air-cooled, horizontally opposed six-cylinder engine. The omission of a $15 stabilizing bar to cut costs resulted in the Corvair's tendency to oversteer, and the 1960–1963 Corvair consequently became a focus of Ralph Nader's safety crusade. Although the problem was corrected in the 1964 model year and eliminated in the redesigned 1965 Corvair, the car's reputation was by then irreparably damaged. The sporty Monza Club Coupe, with bucket seats, four-speed manual transmission, and floor-mounted stick shift, was the best-selling Corvair model. (Courtesy General Motors)

Opposite, top: 1964 Pontiac GTO. The first generation of American compacts left a strange legacy in the high-performance "muscle cars" developed in the mid-1960s to appeal to the youth market. Illegal drag racing by youths on Detroit's Woodward Avenue inspired John DeLorean at Pontiac to fill a niche in the market by stuffing an enormous 389-cubic-inch, 325-horsepower V-8 engine into a stripped-down Tempest compact, characterized by *Road Test* magazine as the "worst all-around handling car available to the American public." Stealing a designation from Ferrari, DeLorean named the car the GTO. The Ford Torino Cobra, the Mercury Eliminator, and the Plymouth Road Runner soon followed. (Courtesy General Motors)

Opposite, bottom: 1967 Cadillac Fleetwood Eldorado. Shorter and lower than other Cadillac models, the 120-inch-wheelbase, 340-horsepower 1967 Fleetwood Eldorado was the first car in the world to combine front-wheel drive, variable-ratio steering, and automatic level control as standard equipment. This advanced technology incongruously was matched with a soggy suspension system, outdated bias-ply tires, and inadequate hydraulic drum brakes on all four wheels. The Eldorado was the only 1967 Cadillac model to offer front disc brakes as an option. For a premium base price of $6,277, the Eldorado had a top speed of 109 mph; but at the 70- to 80-mph cruising speeds then prevailing, it got only 10 mpg and took more than the length of a football field to come to a stop. Nevertheless, the Eldorado was one of the most popular personal luxury cars of its day. (Courtesy General Motors)

1967 Mercedes-Benz 250SE Sedan. Postwar German leadership in automotive technology was evidenced not only by Volkswagen at the bottom of the market but by Mercedes-Benz at the top. This sedan featured fuel injection, four-wheel disc brakes, fully independent suspension, steel-belted radial tires, and unitary body construction. Its passenger compartment was built rigidly to prevent collapse in a rollover and was protected by a front end designed to crush to absorb energy in a collision. It was about a thousand pounds lighter and 20 inches shorter than a contemporary Cadillac, and gave about twice the gas mileage. In addition to being a generation ahead of American production cars technologically, the Mercedes-Benz was vastly superior in manufacturing quality, and its classic styling was intended to remain appealing for decades rather than for just a few years. (Courtesy Mercedes-Benz of North America)

1981 Ford Escort three-door hatchback. At a development cost of $3 billion that involved worldwide design and engineering expertise, in 1980 Ford introduced the high-technology Escort. Its components are outsourced from seventeen countries, and it is assembled in five. Since 1981 the Escort has been the best-selling car in the world, and its design features have become standard for small cars. The 94-inch-wheelbase, 2,080-pound Escort utilizes unitized construction. Until mid-1985 its standard power plant was a 1.6-liter, four-cylinder, transverse-mounted engine with front-wheel drive through a transaxle. Standard equipment included rack-and-pinion steering, self-adjusting front disc brakes, and four-wheel independent suspension with MacPherson struts on the front wheels. The 1981–1985 Escort with 1.6-liter engine had an EPA fuel economy rating of 27/44 mpg, unsurpassed by any car in its class. (Courtesy Ford Motor Company)

Robots with Consight computer vision system sorting and transferring rear-end differential housings at GM St. Catherines, Ontario, foundry. Until very recently, robots could be programmed to perform only a few repetitive operations and were primarily used in welding, which they do more precisely than can human operators. The microprocessor and new computer vision systems now give robots the ability to handle complex materials, select and distribute parts, and discriminate in the performance of tasks in much the same way as can a human being. This has revolutionary implications for automobile manufacturing: it permits economies of scale to be realized on much smaller model runs, lowers labor costs, and improves manufacturing quality. By the year 2000 flexible robotics is expected to eliminate 37 percent of the jobs in automobile production. (Courtesy General Motors)

Opposite, top: Ford engineer using a computer to design a component. Traditional engineering know-how and cut-and-try methods are being abandoned in favor of computer-aided engineering (CAE) and computer-aided design (CAD) to complement computer-aided manufacturing (CAM). Here a Ford engineer designs a component on a computer programmed for the stresses to which the component will be subjected. Weak points show in color, and the computer aids in redesign. The boundaries between CAE, CAD, and CAM are disappearing to create computer-integrated manufacturing (CIM). (Courtesy Ford Motor Company)

Opposite, bottom: Prototype of GM Saturn. In 1985 GM formed the Saturn Corporation to build a small car in the United States that will be cost-competitive with imports. The prototype front-wheel-drive Saturn is smaller and 600 pounds lighter than current GM subcompacts. Initial production is expected to be 250,000 units a year, turned out by 3,000 workers on a two-shift operation, an unprecedented labor productivity rate of 83 cars annually per worker. A tradition-shattering contract with the UAW provides that Saturn workers will be paid annual salaries rather than hourly wages and that 80 percent of them will be guaranteed lifelong employment. (Courtesy General Motors)

Interchange of U.S. Highway 101 and State Route 92, San Mateo, California. The American highway network is the most costly public-works construction effort in human history and the most important visible symbol of the transformation of the American landscape by automobility. (Courtesy California Department of Transportation)

was informed at its 1946 dinner by the president of the Board of Trade, Harold Wilson, of a new policy requiring that the motor industry export 50 percent of production; this was later raised to all output not essential for home demand. Compliance was enforced by a government threat to cut off supplies of essential raw materials from newly nationalized industries—especially steel, which was in short supply. Then, after the outbreak of the Korean War in 1950 and to meet NATO commitments, a higher priority in steel allocation was given to rearmament—including new military vehicles—than to automotive exports. In general, actual exports fell short of the annually set targets. Tying steel allocations to export quotas was continued by the Conservatives until in 1952 the steel shortage was declared over and export quotas were abandoned.

The historic problem of the British motor industry was that too many producers made too many models at too high a cost. To compound the priority given to rearmament in steel allocation, quotas were allocated to automobile manufacturers without regard to their efficiency. This kept the marginal producers in business while artificially constraining the output of the more efficient firms. For the latter this meant excess plant capacity and smaller than justified model runs, which in turn raised unit costs and discouraged plant modernization.

British cars were ill designed for American and Commonwealth driving conditions, so they tended to give poor service and prove unreliable abroad. Because so many British models were competing in world markets, there was not sufficient sales penetration by any given model to warrant the establishment of an adequate parts and service network. Parts manufacture was further discouraged because parts did not count in the manufacturers' export quotas. Inferior dealerships resulted from the haste with which dealers were recruited to boost export sales. "Inevitably the reputation of British cars declined," writes Peter Dunnett, "and the long-run demand for the British products decreased." [5]

The British bid for the export trade evaporated when the postwar seller's market ended with the termination of the Korean War in 1953. By then the French, German, and Italian automobile industries, with Marshall Plan aid to build modern factories, and new fuel-efficient models, were outproducing and underselling the British in world markets. To encourage the production of larger-engine cars more suitable for the export market, in 1947 taxation based on the RAC horsepower rating was abandoned in favor first of a tax on engine capacity, then of a flat-rate license duty of £10 per annum. The result was that British cars came to fall between two stools: in the U.S. market they were priced too high to lure enough buyers away from large American-made cars; in Europe they were too expensive to buy and operate relative to the small, efficient new Fiats, Renaults, and Volkswagen Beetles.

The British industry shifted its emphasis to the home market, only to discover that "excess demand" there was far smaller than had been anticipated. Home demand continued to be kept low by government policies. The purchase tax on new cars in 1947 was an exorbitant 33⅓ percent on cars selling for less than £1,000 and 66⅔ percent on the few cars selling for more than that. In 1950 the purchase tax was 50 percent on all cars. From then to 1979 it varied from a high of 60 percent in 1955 to a low of 17 percent value-added tax (VAT) in 1973—even the latter rate being prohibitive by American standards. The terms of installment sales for new cars varied from a high of 50 percent down and 24 months to pay in February 1956 to a low of 20 percent down and 36 months in January 1961.

The private passenger car was still considered a luxury by the British government. But as the railways declined, recognition came that road transport was becoming dominant and that roads would have to be improved. Road expenditures tripled during the 1960s, and express highway mileage increased from 75 miles to 750 miles. Still, in 1970 Great Britain, with 63.8 motor vehicles per mile, had the most congested roads in the world.

Neither the government nor management has yet been able to overcome the antiquated craft union structure and premodern attitudes of workers that prevail in British automobile plants. In contrast with the American pattern of triennial negotiations with the UAW-CIO, British automobile manufacturers must negotiate with twenty-two craft unions. Power in these unions is widely diffused down to the level of the shop stewards, and union officials lack the ability to maintain discipline among or to represent their workers. Work stoppages called by shop stewards for minor grievances are commonplace. In 1977, for example, British Leyland had over 700 work stoppages, including a toolmaker's strike over pay differentials that idled 20,000 workers for a month and cost the failing firm £150 million. The large number of work stoppages crippled productivity and raised costs. The British trade unions opposed the introduction of new technology that eliminated jobs while raising worker productivity. As a consequence, in 1974 the value added to manufacture per employee was only £2,129 at British Leyland, £2,560 at Vauxhall. £2,765 at Chrysler-U.K., and £3,901 at Ford-England, in contrast with £4,767 at Volkswagen, £4,883 at Ford-Werke, £7,966 at Ford-U.S., and £8,600 at GM-U.S. Compounding these already severe labor problems, in the late 1950s the British government adopted a regional policy that provided incentives to the automobile industry to locate new plants in areas of high unemployment. The industry consequently created tens of thousands of jobs in Scotland and Wales, at the great cost of increasing inefficiency by moving away from suppliers of raw materials and parts, who remained located in the Midlands.

Long-overdue rationalization began with the 1952 merger of Morris (which included MG, Wolseley, and Riley) and Austin, the two largest firms, to form the British Motor Company (BMC). The government approved the merger as being in the public interest. It was expected to lower production costs through achieving economies of scale and to strengthen the British-owned sector of the U.K. motor industry in relation to Ford-England and Vauxhall.

The results of the Austin-Morris merger were disappointing. BMC did introduce models featuring unitary body construction and pioneered in bringing out a small front-wheel-drive car in the BMC Mini. But the central problems of standardization and integration never were resolved. "At the time of the merger, BMC produced thirteen different engines and twenty-three different body styles," Dunnett observes. "To be effective in exploiting potential economies of scale the new company required a considerable reorganization: a reorganization that was never truly effected.... BMC continued to try to meet every segment of the market with a wide range of models. Consequently, the overall effect of [the government] competitions policy [which encouraged merger] on conduct during this period was fairly limited."[6] Indeed, the effect seems to have been negative. Despite merger, the share of the British market commanded jointly by Austin and Morris declined from 40.1 percent in 1947 to 36.5 percent by 1960, while Ford-England's share increased from 15.4 percent to 30 percent. In 1960 the combined share of the British market held by Ford-England, GM's Vauxhall, and Chrysler-U.K., all wholly American-owned subsidiaries, was 51.3 percent.

There were still too many producers for the size of the market. Rationalization proceeded further. British Motor Holdings (BMH) was formed in 1965 by the addition to BMC of Jaguar, which had acquired BSA (formerly Daimler) in 1960. Then in 1968, with a loan of £25 million from the Industrial Reorganization Corporation, the British-owned sector of the U.K. automobile industry was further consolidated by the merger of BMH and the Leyland Motor Corporation, a truck and bus manufacturer that had acquired Standard Triumph International in 1961 and Rover in 1965. The merged firm was called British Leyland Motor Corporation (BLMC).

"BLMC was doomed for trouble since it consisted of an accumulation of many outdated plants, too broad a product line and a poorly coordinated marketing network," sums up a recent report to the Commissioners of the European Communities. "Although BLMC was the fifth largest automobile producer in the world at that time, it was not an economically viable operation: it produced twice as many models as did GM but produced only one-fifth of its output.... Productivity was abysmally low.... Chronic labor problems added fuel to the dismal performance." A government-commissioned document, the Ryder Report, estimated in 1975 that it would cost £1.3 billion to save BLMC. The National Enterprise Board (NEB) provided £350 million for reorganization and improvement under the Ryder plan from 1975 to 1977; and the NEB and the Ministry of Industry provided £450 million more for further reorganization and improvement from 1978 to 1980. The name of the firm was changed to British Leyland (BL) in 1975, and the NEB acquired 99.1 percent of its stock.

In 1979 BL still produced 14 models, versus 5 each for Ford-Europe and Volkswagen, and its labor productivity was 3.9 motor vehicles produced per employee, versus 11.1 per employee for Ford-Europe and 10.6 per employee for Volkswagen. From 1970 to 1979 BL's share of the British market declined from 38.4 percent to 19.7 percent, 9 points behind Ford-England, while imports increased their share of the British market from 14.3 percent to 56.3 percent. The report to the Commissioners of the European Communities concludes, "To all practical purposes, BL is no longer a major producer, and there are only slight chances for revival." [7]

From 1970 to 1982 British motor vehicle production continued to decline, from 2,098,000 units to 1,156,000 units. Of the four major producers—BL, Ford-England, Talbot, and Vauxhall—Ford-England has been the only one to make money. Pretax profits from 1975 to 1979, for example, averaged 9.5 percent for Ford, a marginal 1 percent for Vauxhall, and losses of −1.6 percent for BL and −3.2 percent for Chrysler/Talbot. For 1975–1979 Ford-England made profits of £1.007 billion, while BL lost £258 million. Despite massive government intervention to save the British segment, by the late 1970s "the structure of the U.K. motor industry was characterized ... by one inefficient British company, BL, three multinational companies, all of which have become increasingly integrated with their European operations, and an ever increasing number of import offerings." [8] It is probable that the British motor industry, except as a components supplier, will not survive into the twenty-first century.

Superbug

At the end of World War II, the only advanced capitalist country with less promise of becoming a leading motor vehicle producer than war-devastated Germany was Japan. And no car was deemed by the automotive experts of the day to be less suitable for export to world markets than Ferdinand Porsche's ugly duckling.

By 11 p.m. on April 10, 1945, a decision had been reached not to defend Hitler's "Strength-Through-Joy Car" factory and workers' city against the approaching American army. Two thirds of the plant had been destroyed by Allied bombing, although the two giant turbine generators that supplied the electricity and heat for the plant and town had somehow survived. After their SS guards fled and the rabble of "home guards" disbanded, the Polish, Russian, French, Belgian, and Dutch slave laborers turned to destroying what remained of the factory they had kept in production and to looting the homes of its executives. *Time* reported that "every telephone had been torn from the walls, every typewriter had been sledgehammered to junk, every file and record had been scattered and burned." [9] They tore through the contents of a freight train at the local railroad station and got roaring drunk on liberated schnapps. Joined in the pillage by local Germans, they threatened to burn down the town. The chief engineer of the plant was unsuccessful in a late-night attempt to persuade the American forces at nearby Fallersleben to protect the town by immediately occupying it. On the morning of April 11, however, the Catholic chaplain of the German army's punitive battalion attached to the plant and the French priest who had ministered to the slave laborers convinced a young American lieutenant that protection was needed for the U.S.-born children of the German-American engineers that Porsche had recruited. Later that day American tanks rolled into the town. Order was quickly restored.

The Americans were replaced during the summer of 1945 by a unit of the Royal Electrical and Mechanical Engineers. A repair shop for British army vehicles was set up in the plant, which was scheduled for dismantling. Major Ivan Hirst was placed in charge. The British renamed the town Wolfsburg, after the ancient castle and surrounding estate that "Strength-Through-Joy Car City" had displaced. The few German workers who remained in the plant cleaned up debris and began to bring back and put into working order machinery that had been dispersed before the surrender. The one surviving press was used to complete two demonstration cars, and the workers began to turn out hand-tooled Kübelwagens and Schwimmwagens for the British occupation forces. The British troops had become familiar with the military versions of the VW in Africa and thought highly of them. Wolfsburg was jammed with displaced persons. The Russian zone lay five miles to the east. Raw materials to build cars and food for the workers were both in short supply. Completed cars were bartered for both. The work force increased from 450 in April to 6,033 by the end of 1945 and to 7,951 by August 1946. The ten-thousandth Volkswagen, which the car was now called, rolled off the assembly line in October 1946.

One of the first production VWs was sent back to England by the military with the suggestion that the Wolfsburg plant be taken over as part of the British war reparations. The military found the car rugged, and a team from the British Society of Motor Manufacturers and Traders at the war's end had reported favorably on the car to British Military Intelligence. Nevertheless, the automotive experts back home were not impressed in 1946. A commission headed by automotive manufacturer Sir William [later Lord] Rootes examined Volkswagenwerk. The Rootes Commission predicted that it would collapse within two years and that even if the Germans did get the car into production, "it would mean no undue economic competition on the world market against British products." "The vehicle does meet the fundamental technical requirements of a motorcar," the commission reported; but "as regards performance and design it is quite unattractive to the average motorcar buyer. It is too ugly and too noisy.... [A] type of car like this will remain popular for two or three years, if that. To build the car commercially would be a completely uneconomic enterprise." [10]

The Ford Motor Company was then offered Volkswagenwerk—free of charge. Sir Patrick Hennessy, the head of Ford's European operations, opposed the acquisition, because he feared making the Ford German subsidiaries too strong relative to Ford-England. At a conference held in Cologne, Germany, in March 1948 for discussion of the proposition, Henry Ford II reportedly asked the opinion of Ford president Ernest R. Breech, who responded, "Mr. Ford, I don't think what we are being offered here is worth a damn!" [11]

Two months before the Ford rejection, the British Military Government had appointed Heinz Nordoff general manager of Volkswagenwerk. Nordoff had graduated in 1927 with a degree in mechanical engineering from the Berlin-Charlottenburg Technische Hochschule. He began his automotive career writing service manuals for Opel. Within a year he was put in charge of customer service at Opel, then sent to Detroit to learn GM marketing and production techniques. In 1936 he became a member of the Opel board of directors. In 1942 he became head of the Opel truck factory near Brandenburg, which was producing 4,000 units a month for the Nazi war effort. After the war, with his plant in the Soviet occupation zone, he settled first in the American zone at Ruesselsheim, then in the British zone at Hamburg, where he took a job managing a small automobile repair shop. His career at Opel was ended, because the U.S. Military Government had decreed that persons who had served in executive capacities for the Nazis could only work as manual laborers in the American zone. The offer to run Volkswagenwerk thus came as a golden opportunity. As a former Opel man, Nordoff had despised the "repulsive Porsche invention," but as an automotive engineer he soon recognized the Beetle as "an extraordinarily amazing automobile with a special personality [and] unlimited possibilities." He dedicated himself to his job at Wolfsburg with a new enthusiasm. In 1950 he stated, "It is my life's aim to make this plant into the greatest car factory in Europe." [12]

Nordoff changed the sign outside the plant from "Wolfsburg Motor Works" to "Volkswagenwerk" on the day he took over. On April 8, 1949, Volkswagen GmbH was formally turned over to the West German authorities by the British Military Government. Until legal ownership could be established, Volkswagen was run under a trusteeship of the federal government of West Germany that delegated control of the Wolfsburg factory to the state of Lower Saxony. The German Labor Front, which had controlled it under the Nazis, had been declared a criminal organization. The federal government and the state of Lower Saxony continued to contest ownership.

Output rose from 312 cars daily in 1950 to over 1,000 by 1955, as the Wolfsburg plant was modernized, and huge new plants were opened at Hanover and Kassel. To complement the Beetle, commercial vehicles, light trucks, and the VW Microbus were introduced in March 1950; and the Karmann Ghia, a VW chassis with a sports car body designed by Ghia of Turin, Italy, was brought out in 1955. On March 9, 1960, Nordoff announced in a speech in Switzerland that up to that date, despite all attempts to raise productivity, Volkswagen never had been able to meet the demand for its cars and trucks. In 1960 VW produced 865,858 motor vehicles, 42 percent of the total German output. The phenomenal postwar German economic recovery was in large part fueled by the Volkswagen success story.

Beetles were brought back from Germany by servicemen completing their tours of duty. An "Export Model" was introduced in 1949, and in the early 1950s cars began to be exported by Wolfsburg to the United Kingdom, British Commonwealth countries, and the United States. The Beetle had to overcome strong anti-German sentiment and aspersions in the press as "Hitler's car." An American cartoon portrayed the Beetle with a machine gun sticking out of its windshield. Some 75 percent of the Beetles arriving in the U.K. were damaged by vandals while awaiting delivery.

Animosity turned to admiration and affection as the rugged, economical little car proved itself in the world's toughest endurance trials. "In the mid-1950s, Australian racing enthusiasts watched in amazement (and amusement) as the Beetle for the first time entered the field against cars twice the power (and twice its price)," relates Walter Henry Nelson. "The trials, often referred to as the world's severest tests of cars and drivers, covered thousands of miles of Australia's unmade roads, led through the torrid north and over the wet tortuous mountain roads of the southern Great Divide." [13] Beetles scored impressively in the 1955 Redex Trial (1st and 2d); the 1956 Mobilgas Trial (1st, 3d, 4th, and 6th); the 1957 Ampol Trial (1st and 2d); and the 1958 Mobilgas Trial (1st, 2d, 4th, 5th, and 6th). In the 10,738-mile 1957 Mobilgas Rally twenty of the fifty-two cars to finish were Beetles, and six of them took first places. Beetles took the first four places in their class in the 1958 Kenya Coronation Safari Rally, the toughest automobile rally in Africa, in which only half of all competitors even finished. Out of thirty-two starters, seven out of the ten cars to finish the 1958 African Endurance Championship were Beetles, which won the first four places. Out of thirty-four starters in the 1959 Congo Marathon, seven out of the ten cars to finish were again Beetles, which won the first three places. A Beetle won the 3,000-mile 1962 East African Safari, in which only forty-seven of the one hundred and four starters finished.

Horsepower was gradually increased, from an initial 25 hp to as high as 60 hp in the 1971 Super Beetle. The 1953 model achieved an average fuel consumption of 37.7 miles per gallon; the 1,584-cc engine of the Super Beetle still averaged 27.4 mpg. The Beetle was built so tight that a window often had to be cracked before the driver could slam its door shut. The sheet of steel protecting the car's undercarriage made it virtually watertight: there are records of Beetles floating for miles after being carried off in floods. Air cooling solved the problems of freezing and hard starting in winter and of overheating in summer. The low-revving, short-stroke engine meant lower piston speeds, which lengthened engine life and permitted (with the 1,300-cc engine) a top cruising speed of up to 75 mph to be maintained for hours. Rear mounting of the engine gave the car improved traction in mud, sand, and snow. It could climb a 43-degree incline in first gear loaded with four passengers and luggage, or accelerate in 23 seconds from 0 to 60 mph in third gear. Four coats of paint were meticulously applied electrostatically and baked on, and no bare metal was left exposed on any part of the car. One out of every ten employees at Wolfsburg was an inspector; and instead of spot checking, every car was inspected on 115 check points plus finish and interior. All this for a fully equipped car with a base price in the late 1950s of about $1,500! The British automobile magazine *Autocar* concluded that "without question, [the VW Beetle] has no superiors in any price bracket on quality, reliability, and after-sales service." [14]

Volkswagen policy was "service before sales." Overseas dealers were carefully selected. Each was required to maintain a complete inventory of over eight thousand parts. A dealer's allotment of cars was increased only as his service potential grew to accommodate all Volkswagens needing service in his sales area. In 1957 Volkswagen already had 350 dealerships to service the 64,803 Beetles and 14,721 other Volkswagen vehicles registered in the United States.

The issue of ownership was settled on May 9, 1960, when Volkswagenwerk was made a public company. The federal government and the state of Lower Saxony each retained 20 percent of the VW stock. The remaining 60 percent was placed on the market by the West German parliament on June 30, 1960, and was soon 84-percent oversubscribed. The terms of the stock sale provided that shares could be bought only by persons of middle income or below. One third of the subscribers received three shares each of the 3.6 million available; two thirds received two shares each. Of 65,000 Volkswagenwerk employees, only 1,000, who failed to qualify because of their high income bracket, failed to buy stock. This gave Volkswagen the highest proportion of employee shareholders of any major corporation in the world.

By 1954 Volkswagenwerk had become the fourth-largest automobile manufacturer in the world, after only Detroit's Big Three. In 1953 Volkswagen do Brazil was formed. It became the largest automobile manufacturer in Latin America and the largest German-owned overseas enterprise. After four years of assembling knocked-down units from Germany, Volkswagen do Brazil began to turn out Beetles with 100 percent local content. Volkswagen de Mexico began assembling Beetles in 1954 with 60 percent local content, increased to 71 percent by 1979, and to 100 percent after that. A joint venture with the VW Australian distributors was launched in 1957 to make Beetles with 100 percent Australian content for the South Pacific market. Volkswagen of Melbourne suspended all except assembly operations in 1967 and was sold to Nissan in 1975. Smaller plants were established in South Africa and in Nicaragua.

To develop the lucrative North American market and supply it with Beetles, Volkswagen of Canada was formed in 1952, and Volkswagen of America in 1955, with headquarters first in New York City, then in Englewood Cliffs, New Jersey, near the Newark port of entry. Volkswagen sales in the United States reached a record 569,292 units in 1968, and by 1970 Americans had bought over 4 million VW Beetles and other models.

Like the rear-engined Corvair, the Beetle became a casualty of Ralph Nader's safety crusade. Even more important, by the early 1970s rising German labor costs, competition from American compacts, devaluation of the dollar, and stiffer import levies left the Beetle overpriced in the American market. By the first quarter of 1974 the port-of-entry price of a Super Beetle without options or accessories had climbed to $2,849, as opposed to a basic price of $2,442 for a Ford Pinto. By then, too, the Beetle was facing stiff competition from Japanese models. Volkswagenwerk was losing $100 on every car shipped to the United States by 1976, and its share of the U.S. market had eroded to 2.5 percent.

To meet these greatly changed competitive conditions, the decision was reached in 1976 to begin manufacturing in the United States, with 75 percent local content, VW's new model, the Rabbit (called the Golf in Europe). The Rabbit, introduced in 1974, was an advanced design that deserves credit as the first "world car"—a car designed for world markets and produced from components sourced worldwide. Volkswagen Manufacturing of America (VMOA) acquired a plant site for assembly from Chrysler at Westmoreland, near New Stanton, Pennsylvania, and a stamping plant to turn out body panels from AMC at South Charleston, West Virginia. By 1980 the German-controlled Westmoreland plant was turning out 1,050 cars a day. VMOA surpassed French-controlled American Motors to become the fourth-ranking "American" producer of motor vehicles.

The German automobile industry was further rationalized as well by the German expansion and diversification of Volkswagenwerk in the late 1960s. Arrangements were worked out with Mercedes-Benz to share research and development costs. A controlling interest in Audi was acquired in 1965 and in NSU in 1969. They were merged to form Audi NSU Auto Union. In 1969, too, Volkswagen combined forces with independent Porsche of Stuttgart as VW-Porsche to produce the popular rear-engine, air-cooled Porsche 914 sports car.

Although the basic Beetle body style and mechanical features remained unchanged, stylistic refinements as well as technological improvements were progressively incorporated. The 1949 Export Model already was a vastly improved car over the VW38 Porsche prototype. By the mid-1960s over two thousand improvements had been incorporated. It is therefore a mistake to think of the Beetle as a static model until it was outmoded, as a brief survey of some of the more important improvements demonstrates.

Stylistically, the 1958 model featured a rear window 95 percent larger, a front windshield 17 percent larger, windshield wipers that swept a 35-percent larger area, and a reshaped engine lid. The front seats were recontoured to be more comfortable in the 1960 model year. Windshield area was increased another 19.5 percent in 1965, and doors and window pillars were made slimmer. In the 1971 Super Beetle a redesigned front hood and a changed suspension system increased the luggage area by

85 percent. A curved windshield to further increase visibility appeared in the 1973 model. Over the life of the Beetle, ventilation, heating, and other features contributing to passenger comfort were vastly improved.

Mechanically, as noted, a progressive increase in horsepower improved performance. Changes in the suspension system improved cornering and handling: an anti-roll bar was added in 1960, the shock absorbers and the spacing between the front torsion bars were improved in 1966, and the 1971 Super Beetle sported MacPherson strut suspension. In the 1961 model, synchromesh was added to the first gear. The following year the steering mechanism was changed from worm and nut to worm and roller, improving both steering and wear. Independent dual braking became available on some 1968 models, front disc brakes on the 1967 1500 Cabriolet and the 1971 Super Beetle. A semiautomatic transmission became available as an option on the 1968 1500 model. Fuel injection became an option on the 1975 Super Beetle. Safety features and pollution control devices were incorporated as mandated by law in the United States.

On February 17, 1972, when Beetle number 15,007,034 rolled off the assembly line, the Beetle surpassed the Model T to become the best-selling car of all time. World production had peaked in 1971 at 1,291,612 units. German production had peaked two years before at 1,076,897 units, then progressively declined to only 33,239 units in 1977 as assembly lines were switched over to newer Volkswagen models. German production was halted on January 19, 1978, and the Beetle was withdrawn from the American market. It is still being manufactured of 100 percent local content in Pueblo, Mexico, where the 20-millionth Beetle rolled off the assembly line on May 15, 1981.

About two thirds of the over 20 million Beetles ever produced remain in use around the globe, making this vehicle, in Jonathan Wood's words, "perhaps the most remarkable as well as the most enduring passenger car the world has ever known." [15]

On November 20, 1987, Volkswagen announced that it was closing its Westmoreland plant and ending production in the United States. Sales of American-produced Volkswagen passenger cars had slipped from 177,118 units in 1980 to only 53,629 for the first ten months of 1987. Japanese competition was blamed for the decline.

Japan as Number One

17

In the mid-1970s Volkswagen was surpassed as the major foreign-car exporter to the United States, first by Toyota, then by Nissan. By 1978 Honda's American sales too exceeded Volkswagen's. Twenty years before, Japan's entire annual production had been fewer than 100,000 passenger cars. As has been noted, in worldwide production Japan passed Germany to rank second in 1967 and passed the United States to take first place in 1980.

"Given its limited resources, Japan has dealt more successfully with more of the basic problems of postindustrial society than any other country," writes Ezra F. Vogel. "It is in this sense ... that the Japanese are number one." He is correct in his contention that this "Japanese success [has] had less to do with traditional character traits than with specific organizational structures, policy programs, and conscious planning." But his 1979 analysis was outdated by the mid-1980s, if only because it was predicated on a weak dollar in relation to the yen. More important, at least for the automobile industry, he is wrong in his unsupportable assertions that "the effort to explain these Japanese successes as a result of cheap labor is out-of-date, for by 1978 with devaluation of the dollar, Japanese wages were slightly higher than those of in the United States" and that "the modernity of technology used in Japanese manufacturing had edged past the United States by 1973." He is also wrong in claiming that decision making in Japanese firms characteristically proceeds from the "bottom up" rather than from the "top down," that there is "much authority concentrated on low levels," and that "the morale of young workers in their thirties tends to be very high." On all of these counts, the evidence is that the opposite is true.[1]

Economic Nationalism and the Rise of
the Japanese Auto Industry

The Japanese automobile industry from its beginnings has been the most protected and nationalistic in the world. In the 1930s the military-controlled government attempted to build an entirely Japanese-owned and Japanese-controlled automobile industry. Following the war the 70-percent tariff on motor vehicles was reduced to 40 percent, as opposed to 35 percent in Western Europe and 10 percent in the United States, then to 30 percent in 1968, as opposed to 17.6 percent in the EEC countries and 5.5 percent in the United States. This very high level of protection insulated the industry from foreign competition into the early 1970s. Additionally, there were nontariff barriers. "Whether officially violating the General Agreement on Tariffs and Trade or not, Japanese bureaucrats use a variety of ways to support Japanese producers," Vogel informs us. "When foreign cars were more competitive, the Japanese required that foreign cars off the assembly line had to be inspected in Japan before they could be sold there ... and Japanese inspectors could find problems as small as location of mirrors or door handles. It thus was difficult for the foreign car maker, subject to such tactics, and sometimes to delays as well, to enter economically into the Japanese market." [2]

The Japanese automobile industry began its postwar resurgence by filling orders for military trucks from the American occupation forces. These orders became substantial during the Korean War. As late as 1965, Japan produced only 696,000 passenger cars to 1,179,000 commercial vehicles. And production up to the early 1970s was largely for the rapidly expanding and highly protected Japanese domestic market.

Rising incomes in the 1960s brought a phenomenon called "my-carism." In 1970 fully 77.2 percent of the 3,179,000 passenger cars and 68.2 percent of the 2,110,000 commercial motor vehicles produced in Japan were for the domestic market. And although the Japanese automobile industry in 1970 was by no means as efficient in production as the American or the German industry, the high tariff barrier kept total imports at only 19,552 motor vehicles.

The year 1970 was the first in which Japanese records showed more passenger cars (8,779,000) registered than trucks (8,282,000), while outdated three-wheel vehicles still accounted for 243,934 registrations. The small three-wheel truck, uniquely suited to use by small businesses on Japan's narrow streets, had been the most popular vehicle in Japan and the mainstay of Japanese motor vehicle production until about 1960.

As the domestic market reached maturity and imminent saturation in the 1970s, the Japanese automobile industry shifted its emphasis dramatically to exports. By 1976 exports accounted for 50.5 percent of Japan's passenger car production and 30.5 percent of its commercial vehicle production.

Government sponsorship of this shift had been presaged as far back as 1949, when the Ministry of Commerce and Industry was reorganized as the Ministry of International Trade and Industry (MITI). MITI targeted specific industries for protection from foreign competition in order to encourage their development as strong international competitors. In 1955 the automobile industry became one of these, and by the early 1970s it was strong enough to compete abroad. The MITI formula for international success was very conventional—a combination of eliminating foreign competition from the domestic market, eliminating competition among Japanese producers so that economies of scale could be gained, and getting more labor productivity at lower wages than did foreign competitors.

The only part of the MITI formula that failed to materialize was the restructuring of the industry into two passenger car producers, Toyota and Nissan, and a third producer of specialty vehicles and buses. Being merged out of existence was recalcitrantly resisted by Mitsubishi, Toyo Kogyo, Honda, and Isuzu, because they were making satisfactory profits on their own. However, in the July 20, 1967, MITI-sponsored "Hakone Declaration," all six major automobile manufacturers agreed to develop on a national basis, as Japanese-owned and Japanese-controlled companies, under national guidance, to meet MITI export policy objectives.

As befitted the new emphasis on international trade, the Japanese tariff on motor vehicles evaporated—from 40 percent on small cars, 35 percent on large cars, and 30 percent on trucks and buses on May 1, 1968, to zero by 1978. Yet this made absolutely no difference in import penetration of the Japanese market. Imports accounted for 1 percent of new Japanese passenger car registrations in 1968 and 1.2 percent in 1982; in between, they ranged from a low of 0.7 percent in 1970 and 1971 to a high of only 1.8 percent in 1978. In 1982 only 36,119 motor vehicles of all types were imported into Japan, and of these only 3,305 were imported from the United States. The reason is an array of nontariff barriers.

One of these barriers is a split-rate commodity tax on imports, amounting to 15 percent on cars with engines having less than 2,000 cc of displacement and 20 percent on cars with a larger engine displacement. This tax is based on the import value cif (cost, insurance, and freight included in price), rather than fob (free on board from point of origin) as in other countries, while Japanese cars are taxed on their ex–factory value. Imports are also discriminated against by the requirement that they be adjusted to comply with an extensive list of unique Japanese safety and environmental standards.

The commodity tax discriminates in two ways. In addition to restricting imports into Japan, it is used to lower the prices of cars exported from Japan to make them more competitive abroad. Unlike most American taxes, which are built into the retail price of a car, the commodity tax is a value-added tax. An amount equivalent to about $800 of the commodity tax is rebated by the government to the Japanese automobile manufacturers on every unit they export. This makes Japanese cars cheaper at the dock in the United States than in Tokyo.

Beyond these protective tariff and taxation policies, as Alexander D. McLeod documents, "government support measures to strengthen the international competitiveness of the industry included low-interest loans from public financial institutions, government subsidies, special depreciation allowances, the exemption of import duties on necessary machinery and equipment, and authorization for essential technology imports."[3] Loans from the Japanese Development Bank between 1951 and 1955 amounted to ¥1.5 billion, about 10 percent of the investment in plant facilities to manufacture passenger cars. Funds allocated by the Development Bank to the automobile industry under the 1956 Law Concerning Provisional Measures for Development of the Machinery Industry averaged 13.6 percent of fixed investment and, during 1957–1959 and 1964–1965, reached as high as 30 percent. Subsidies and commissions amounting to ¥369 million were paid out by the government between 1951 and 1959 to the Automobile Technology Association and similar organizations. Special depreciation allowances on selected essential machinery went into effect for the automobile industry in 1951 and for the automobile parts industry in 1956, reducing the expenditure to purchase ¥64.36 billion of designated machinery to only ¥11.85 billion, or 18.4 percent of its worth. Moreover, essential machinery and tools not manufactured in Japan were exempted from import duties by the 1954 Tariff Law and the 1960 Provisional Tariff Measures Law.

Finally, the Japanese automobile industry has been aided by the Japanese government's policy of keeping the yen undervalued in relation to the dollar. As a result of this policy, Japanese-made products, including automobiles, are cheaper than equivalent American-made products in both the U.S. and world markets.

William Chandler Duncan makes an important distinction between the reorganization of the Japanese automobile industry by MITI and the more familiar ways in which governments protect "infant industries." The difference is that "though a prosperous and competitive industry was of top priority, the reorganization policy came to center on a political objective, i.e., management control. By 1962 the issue among MITI planners was not how to maximize automobile production but rather how to maximize domestically controlled automobile production."[4]

Japanese car manufacture remained a technologically backward industry into the 1950s. Labor productivity was so low that in 1952, for example, a two-door, 27-horsepower Toyopet cost more than a new four-door eight-cylinder Ford, including transportation and import taxes. Acknowledging the technical superiority of foreign makes, the major Japanese companies sought to establish technical tie-ups with foreign producers. In 1952 and 1953 agreements were signed between Nissan and Austin, between Hino and Renault, between Isuzu and Rootes, and between Mitsubishi and Willys-Overland, stipulating the payment of royalties for technical assistance, the rights to Japanese assembly of imported knockdown units and to eventual components manufacture, and sole import rights for imported cars and parts. Direct investment by the foreign companies was negligible and financed from the royalties that they received.

The assembly of imported knockdown units through these technical tie-ups had been encouraged by the Japanese government. But, as Duncan observes, by 1955 MITI was "pushing for a 'nationalization' of the passenger car industry—i.e., domestic production of parts as well as assembled vehicles." As part of a general "buy Japanese" campaign inaugurated by the Hatoyama government in December 1954, an order went out that all motor vehicles purchased for government use must be domestically produced. In March 1955 MITI announced its "New Policy of Nationalizing Foreign Passenger Cars," which restricted the foreign exchange allocated for automobile parts. "By 1958 all foreign passenger car assembly operations had converted to the use of domestically produced parts. The demand of the 1960s was filled almost exclusively by Japanese companies."[5] A MITI quota limited the import of engines to only 1,000 units a year. A MITI regulation announced in June 1967 limited foreign ownership of stock in existing Japanese companies to 7 percent per investor and a total investment of 15 percent before application for approval had to be made to MITI under the Foreign Investment Law. In automobile manufacturing, both joint ventures with foreign firms and 100-percent foreign-owned subsidiaries in Japan were prohibited.

In response to growing protectionist sentiment in the United States, the Japanese made concessions to American negotiators between 1968 and 1973 that liberalized trade in engines and parts and relaxed limitations on foreign investment. By August 1968 the Japanese had agreed to raise progressively the engine import quota to 30,000 in 1969, 50,000 in 1970, and 70,000 in 1971, with full liberalization (the end of quantitative quotas) for engines and automotive parts beginning in October 1971. The tariff on large passenger cars was reduced to the Kennedy Round rate of 17.5 percent, that on small cars to 20 percent; and after 1978, as noted, tariffs were entirely eliminated. Effective October 1971, the Japanese commodity tax on large cars was equalized at 20 percent (down from 40 percent) in exchange for the repeal of a surcharge on Japanese automotive imports into the U.S. levied by the Nixon administration. It was announced in August 1968 that foreign investment proposals for the assembly of automotive parts in Japan would be considered on a case-by-case basis. Effective April 1971, joint ventures between Japanese and foreign automobile producers involving investment in kind were examined for approval on a case-by-case basis, and the restriction on direct investment in new enterprises was liberalized to permit a maximum of 50 percent foreign ownership. Foreign investment in existing automobile enterprises remained for a short time limited to 35 percent by a MITI guideline, which stipulated that the remaining 65 percent of company shares be controlled by so-called stable stockholders. Then in April 1973 the Foreign Investment Council announced abandonment of the 50 percent limitation except for a few industries. This made 100 percent foreign ownership of a Japanese automobile company at long last a legal possibility.

Under the 35 percent MITI guideline, Detroit's Big Three gained a foothold in the Japanese automobile industry, which they have not strengthened significantly under the Foreign Investment Council liberalization. A Chrysler contract to purchase 35 percent of Mitsubishi over a three-year period was approved in June 1971; but a year later the financially shaky Chrysler announced it would limit its investment to 15 percent. Ford's negotiations for 20-percent ownership of Toyo Kogyo reached an impasse in 1972 over the price Toyo Kogyo demanded for its shares and its desire to prevent Ford from increasing its holdings in the future. Ford did, however, enter into joint ventures with both Toyo Kogyo and Nissan to manufacture automatic transmissions in Japan, and it marketed the Toyo Kogyo–built Courier pickup in the United States. The resumption of negotiations led to Ford's acquiring a 25-percent interest in Toyo Kogyo in 1979. In a contract approved in September 1971, General Motors acquired a 34.2-percent interest in Isuzu, which made only commercial vehicles and accounted for only 3 percent of Japanese production. The contract included provisions for cooperation in safety and antipollution research, cooperation in marketing the small Isuzu truck through the GM sales network, and the establishment of a joint venture for manufacturing automatic transmissions. GM agreed to severe limitations on its control, including a stipulation that the Isuzu chairman of the board and president would remain Japanese. Subsequently, GM also entered into an agreement to sell trucks made by Suzuki under the GM nameplate in the United States and acquired a 5.3-percent interest in that firm. Thus, despite liberalization to the point of permitting 100 percent foreign ownership, direct foreign investment in Japanese automobile companies has remained very limited.

"If direct investment in Japan by foreign vehicle manufacturers was very limited up to 1973, so too was Japanese overseas investment in manufacturing and assembly," writes George Maxcy. "Indeed so small was the proportion of overseas production and assets to that of the parent company that, on some definitions of the MNE [multinational enterprise], even the largest Japanese companies would not have been qualified. Moreover, each of the foreign plants manufactured or assembled solely for its local market, so that no Japanese company had the semblance of a multinational network or system." The fifteen overseas assembly plants in which Japanese auto makers had a financial interest were all small joint ventures with local companies. The largest was Nissan's 85-percent-owned Mexican facility, which produced only 25,000 units in 1973. The annual capacity of Toyota's wholly owned Brazilian facility was a mere 1,200 units. Most of the Japanese overseas operations were in Southeast Asia. Maxcy concludes, "Tariffs and local content requirements meant that some investment by the Japanese firms was needed in each case to preserve access to these markets. That approval by the Japanese government for these investments was obtained is another indication that they were 'necessary,' since the policy throughout this period was one of strongly encouraging exports and restricting overseas manufacturing investment." [6]

That policy remains in effect today. Only under the compulsion of local restrictions and penalties that threaten access to markets have the Japanese automobile producers invested in manufacturing operations abroad. The reason is a unique Japanese combination of a protective government, close relationships with financial institutions and ancillary industries, and an exploitation of labor unparalleled in any other advanced industrial country. The consequence of this unique combination is that automobiles can be produced cheaper in Japan than elsewhere in the world.

Japanese Manufacturing Advantages: Myths and Realities

The automobile manufacturing enterprises that got started in Japan in the 1930s entered a business community in which firms were traditionally organized into family-controlled industrial/financial groups called *zaibatsu* (literally, "financial cliques"). An attempt by the American occupation authorities to break up the zaibatsu after the war had only limited success and minimally affected the automobile industry. For example, Toyoda Loom was forced to divest two thirds of its holdings in Toyota Motors, which in turn had to dispose of its stock in some forty affiliates. The Toyoda Loom holdings were retained by Toyota Motors, however; and it remains a moot point whether, as McLeod claims, "the loss of rights over its affiliations inhibited Toyota Motors' ability to integrate production vertically." [7]

The zaibatsu were replaced by looser conglomerates of industrial enterprises called *keiretsu* that are centered around the "city" banks—such as Mitsui, Sumitomo, and Mitsubishi. These banks obtain funds for reloan to industry from the Bank of Japan, the Japan Development Bank, the Japan Industrial Bank, and the Export and Import Bank. The keiretsu operate through a pattern of affiliation and cooperation based on cross-equity holdings. The MIT Report explains that "the group's lead bank will hold 5 percent or less of the equity in each of the other group enterprises and each of the other group enterprises will hold a small share of the equity in each of the other group enterprises, including the bank. The net result is that the group members hold a controlling interest in each others' enterprises. Foreign ownership is effectively blocked.... In addition, to the benefit of each group member, a system of group cross-checks of producer performance has evolved." [8]

As an illustration of the way in which the keiretsu pattern works, the Sumitomo group came to the aid of Toyo Kogyo after sales of its gas-guzzling rotary-engined cars collapsed as a result of the 1973–1974 energy crisis. With annual revenues of about $200 billion, or three times the annual revenues of GM, the Sumitomo group had more than adequate resources to bail out Toyo Kogyo. "However, the group and the lead bank were deeply concerned about the adequacy of TK's management and were determined to completely understand the true condition of the company before proceeding with massive lending. Their solution was to remove the senior management, headed by the grandson of the firm's founder, and its largest private stockholder.... With its own representatives in charge of Toyo Kogyo, the group proceeded with sufficient lending to finance the simultaneous development of three new models and to completely over-haul the production system." The resulting turnaround saw Toyo Kogyo become profitable once again as both labor productivity and market shares in Europe and the United States increased. The MIT Report observes, "The contrasting experiences of Toyo Kogyo (Mazda) and Chrysler during recent periods of financial crisis illustrate the unusual features of this

Japanese system and the competitive advantage it carries over American and much European financial practice."

The high debt/equity ratios of Japanese automobile companies up to the 1970s reflected not financial weakness, as they would in America and Europe, but the confidence of the banking structure. And these high debt/equity ratios were cushioned by commitments of long-term financial support. The confidence of the banks has proved more than justified, and the debt/equity ratios of Japanese automobile manufacturers have declined steadily. Toyota was debt free by 1977, while between 1971 and 1982 Nissan's debt/equity ratio declined from 37.7:1 to 16.1:1, Honda's from 57.8:1 to 25.1:1. During the same period, in contrast, GM's debt/equity ratio increased from 5.1:1 to 19.6:1, Ford's from 12.6:1 to 26.4:1.

Japanese automobile manufacturers enjoy a huge cost advantage over their American and European competitors that is explained by a combination of lower wages, higher labor productivity, and a unique system of material controls and plant maintenance. The MIT Report estimates "that the U.S.-Japan production cost difference on a small car exceeds $1,500 (at 215 yen = $1) and that some recent estimates of the U.S.-Japan cost gap, setting it lower than $1,000 on a typical small car, are impossible to support given the evidence at hand. With regard to the European producers . . . the Japanese have a substantial, although lesser, cost advantage."

On an annual basis the wages paid to Japanese automobile workers seem to compare fairly well with the wages of automobile workers in other countries. But it must be remembered that most Japanese automobile workers still work a six-day week with only two weeks of annual vacation and that much overtime is required. Although from 1975 to 1980 Japan posted the greatest gains in hourly compensation of automobile workers of any automobile-producing country, the average hourly compensation of Japanese automobile workers in 1980 still was about half that paid to American automobile workers, with fringe benefits being about equal.

Japanese labor-management relations go beyond being paternalistic to be premodern. They are less advanced in some important respects than those instituted at the Ford Motor Company in 1914–1915, far less advanced than those common in American and European automobile factories a generation ago. Wages are paid not on the basis of what workers do but on the basis of a combination of individual skill level, seniority, and the company's performance.

Although the claim remains untested in a long-term declining market for motor vehicles, in principle the permanent workers of the major Japanese auto producers enjoy lifelong employment. Even during crises, as at Toyo Kogyo, layoffs have been rare. This is possible only because cyclical fluctuations in demand are accommodated by increases or reductions in both mandatory overtime and the number of "seasonal" or temporary workers, the latter comprising a significant proportion of the work force in Japanese automobile plants. These seasonal workers are generally farmers from the north seeking winter employment. Annual production schedules are adjusted to take advantage of their availability. They reside in regimented company-owned bachelor dormitories, where their private lives come under the close scrutiny of security guards recruited from the National Self-Defense Forces. No women are hired as permanent workers. Also, wages are lower and working conditions worse in the plants of the components suppliers upon whom all of the major automobile assemblers heavily depend.

Japanese assembly lines are undermanned by Western standards. There are fewer workers on the lines; each worker typically performs more tasks; and a worker is expected to learn a greater variety of "production skills" during his term of employment. Given that one routine task is much like another, it is open to question whether this should be characterized as "upgrading skills through lifelong learning" or as a speedup. Most certainly, Japanese semiskilled automobile workers do not develop into craftsmen over the course of their employment—only into semiskilled workers who are adept at a larger number of routine tasks.

More important to labor productivity, however, work rules in American automobile plants limit the tasks that given workers can perform. In contrast with the usual 400 to 500 work rules in American automobile factories, Japanese plants have only 4 or 5. That Japanese workers are not prevented by work rules from performing a wide variety of tasks results in a need for far fewer workers and consequently far greater labor productivity.

About six times the number of industrial robots in relation to units of output were used in Japanese automobile plants in the early 1980s than in American plants. Notably, however, the Japanese count as "robots" many relatively low-level automatic machine tools that are not considered robots in the American auto industry. Visitors have been impressed by the small number of operators in sight monitoring them. While it is probably true that the Japanese have progressed furthest in mechanizing dehumanizing assembly operations, it is also true that the use of robotics until very recently has been fairly well limited to welding operations, which robots perform more precisely than do humans. The workers out of sight have been out of the visitors' minds. Most jobs in automobile manufacturing still exact a high human toll, and the evidence is that Japanese automobile workers are pushed harder than their Western counterparts.

The "quality control circle" meetings praised as an example of Japanese industrial democracy are held on the workers' own time, generally for the purpose of discussing how to implement management directives without increasing labor costs. This means that Japanese automobile workers in fact have no more effective input into the structure of the workplace than do American automobile workers, somewhat less input than German or Swedish automobile workers, and a good deal less input than British automobile workers.

Unionization, in the Western sense, does not exist in Japanese automobile plants. Both blue- and white-collar employees are members of company-dominated "enterprise unions," affiliated into the Federation of Japanese Automobile Workers' Unions, which is in turn affiliated with Domei, the Japanese Confederation of Labor. These automobile workers' unions have not confronted management with workers' demands since the early 1950s, with the result that work stoppages over wages and conditions of employment do not occur to disrupt production.

It is doubtful whether this means that Japanese automobile workers are more contented with their lot than Western automobile workers. McLeod points out, for example, that a "1970 study of alienation among Japanese automobile workers found a high proportion who felt their jobs made them work too fast, were dull and tiresome, and were too simple." [9] It must further be borne in mind that the work force in Japanese automobile plants is very young, averaging in 1980 only 35 years of age at Nissan, 32 at Toyota, and 30 at Honda. It remains to be seen whether the principle of lifelong employment will be compatible with high labor productivity and low wages as the average age of this work force increases.

The best recent estimate of the U.S.-Japanese labor productivity difference shows a Japanese advantage in 1980 of 39 employee hours per vehicle to 74 hours per vehicle in American plants. Other reliable data show the productivity of Japanese automobile producers to be vastly superior to that of European as well as American producers. In 1979 GM-U.S. produced 10.4 motor vehicles per employee and Ford-U.S. 12.8:1; European productivity ranged from 14.9:1 at Ford-Werke and 14.4:1 at Opel to only 3.9:1 at Mercedes-Benz and 3.5:1 at British Leyland, with Volkswagen productivity at 10.6:1 and Renault at 8.3:1. In contrast, Toyota produced 26.9 motor vehicles per employee and Nissan 22.4:1, better than doubling the labor productivity of their Western competitors.

After analyzing all available labor productivity and hourly compensation data, the MIT Report reaches the conclusion that "the [national] difference in total employee cost per vehicle is large. Use of approximate hourly compensation estimates ... indicates a U.S.-Japan employment cost difference per vehicle approaching $2,000 and a German-Japanese difference roughly half as large." Additionally, Japanese capital costs per vehicle are lower. The report explains that this "is not due primarily to capital costs in Japan but to the fact that Japanese producers seem to require much less plant and equipment per unit produced and to have much lower in-process inventories than the American or German producers."[10]

A research panel charged by the National Academy of Engineering and the National Research Council to study the competitive status of the U.S. auto industry reported in 1982, as its "most striking finding" about the U.S.-Japanese performance gap, "the relative unimportance of the factors connected with technology. Neither automation nor product design is accorded a large measure of explanatory power. Despite the publicity devoted to robotics and advanced assembly plants, such as Nissan's Zama facility, U.S. firms appear to have maintained comparable levels of advanced process techniques and equipment." The panel was unanimous in explaining the great Japanese advantages in cost and quality as due to "an amalgam of several management practices and systems related to production planning and control.... [T]he key to Japan's lead ... appears to be the interaction of the material control system, maintenance practices, and employee involvement."[11]

American automobile manufacturers have tended either to absorb their suppliers or to keep them at arm's length and pit them against one another. In contrast, the Japanese develop cooperative relationships with their outside vendors and link them to the final assembly schedule through the *kanban*, or "just-in-time," system of inventory control. Raw materials, parts, and components are delivered in small lots just before they are needed, by independent suppliers located in close geographic proximity to the point of assembly. This largely eliminates the costly keeping of an in-process inventory and waste in handling materials and components. It is a production system that will not work if there are frequent lengthy breakdowns. "Maintenance programs, preventive and scheduled, are therefore pursued vigorously. Plants operate with only two shifts, and equipment is maintained through nonproduction time. The result is a much lower rate of machine failure and breakdown." Notably, the Japanese copied this system from practice at the Ford River Rouge plant in the 1920s.

Far fewer inspectors are employed in Japanese than in Western automobile plants, because the "just-in-time" system does not permit extensive inspection of incoming materials and components. As a result, responsibility for quality control is pushed back to the suppliers. "This same approach —quality control at the source—is used in production on the line, where workers have the authority to stop the operation if they spot defects or other production problems," the National Academy of Engineering–National Research Council panel observes. "Worker-initiated line stops are central to the concept of *jidoka*: making problems visible to everyone's eye and stopping the line if trouble occurs; all thoughts, methods, and tools to avoid stops are jidoka." The MIT Report concludes that the kanban-jidoka system "establishes a new standard of best practice for the world. It supplements the old Ford system in the plant and the Sloan formula for coordinating the production chain as the recipe for competitive success." [12]

Market Success and Token Production in America

Cars built for the Japanese domestic market characteristically have been small and relatively low powered. There are several reasons for this. Japan is entirely dependent on imported petroleum, so cars must be fuel efficient. City streets are very narrow and congested, making large cars difficult to maneuver and park. The relatively poor condition of Japan's highway network militates against sustained high-speed travel.

Japanese penetration of the lucrative American market began in 1958, when 1,479 passenger cars and 40 light trucks were exported to the United States. Gaining a foothold proved difficult. The first Japanese passenger cars imported, the Datsun L210 (advertised as the Datsun 1000) and the Toyota Toyopet, were too underpowered for freeway driving. "The performance of the Datsun is best described as melancholy," *Road and Track* reported in December 1958. "Even though its gearing is well chosen, the engine is just too small to cope with the car's weight." The magazine went on to note, however, that "the car is really quite good, and with a few relatively simple changes it could go over. It is, even in its present form, better than most of the small British cars currently being sold in this country: not so fast, perhaps, but it should be more reliable and it has a nice solid feeling about it."

Up to the late 1960s the Japanese were a negligible factor in the U.S. market. They exported a mere 7,517 motor vehicles to the United States in 1963 and only 82,035 in 1967. The big breakthrough came in 1968, when American imports of Japanese cars more than doubled to 182,547 units.

The first Japanese passenger car adequate for American driving conditions was the 1965 Toyota Corona. Light, four-cylinder Datsun and Toyota trucks rapidly gained a reputation for ruggedness. And in 1969 the Datsun 240-Z sports car, the first of the distinguished Z line, was chosen Sports Car of the Year by *Road Test* magazine. In 1975 both Datsun and Toyota surpassed Volkswagen in U.S. sales to become the leading exporters of motor vehicles to the United States. Total American imports of Japanese motor vehicles reached 1.37 million units in 1976, 2.4 million units in 1980.

By 1980 Japanese cars and light trucks had established a reputation as the best built in the world. Data gathered from its subscribers by *Consumer Reports* in 1979 rated the assembly quality of American-made cars versus imports on a 10-point scale: the imports had advantages of 7.9 to 6.4 for subcompacts, 7.7 to 6.2 for compacts, and 8.1 to 6.6 for midsize cars. Even more impressive, in 1980 *Ward's Auto World* reported the results of a survey in which U.S. automotive engineers were asked, "What country produces the best-quality cars today?" Forty-eight percent of the respondents selected Japan, 27 percent the United States, and 23 percent West Germany. A 1979 German survey of newly registered cars revealed that five of the six models with the lowest frequency of breakdowns were Japanese.

In the years 1974 and 1975, Maxcy notes, Japanese producers accounted for 70 percent of all motor vehicle imports into the United States, "at a cost to the American economy of almost $8 billion, which represented one-third of the U.S. trade deficit with all countries. And it represented the loss of tens of thousands of jobs in the American motor industry. If protection was ruled out then the only solution to the excessive drain of dollars and jobs seemed to be the establishment of Japanese plants in the U.S. producing cars with a high local content." The Big Three and the UAW joined forces to seek protection from Japanese imports unless the Japanese began to manufacture motor vehicles in the United States.[13]

The first Japanese-owned automobile plant in the United States was the motorcycle plant opened in September 1979 at Marysville, Ohio, by Honda America Manufacturing. Production of the midsize Honda Accord began at the Marysville plant in November 1982. Honda adopted a policy of selling only American-built Accords east of the Mississippi River, only imported Accords in the western states, to avoid side-by-side comparisons. In 1984 some 133,000 domestic-built Accords were sold in the United States, versus 123,000 imported ones. The cars are of comparable quality. In 1986 Honda began turning out the subcompact Civic at Marysville as well, and it introduced a second line of Japanese-built cars under the name Acura.

Before entering automobile manufacturing in 1962, Honda had become a distinguished marque in motorcycle design, production, and racing. Perhaps because of its late start in four-wheel automobile production, and consequently its weak position in the Japanese home market compared to Nissan and Toyota, Honda has been the most internationally minded and technologically oriented firm in the Japanese automobile industry.

It also has been the most progressive in its labor policies, having adopted the five-day week at all factories as early as 1972.

The Honda Compound Vortex Controlled Combustion (CVCC) engine, announced in 1971, became the first engine to comply with the 1975 amendments to the U.S. Clean Air Act. The CVCC engine utilizes a small auxiliary combustion chamber with a separate carburetor. The auxiliary chamber is supplied with a very rich (4:1 to 5:1) air-fuel mixture, while the main chamber is supplied with a very lean (18:1 to 20:1) mixture. This results in significant reductions of both nitrogen oxides and carbon monoxide, while improving fuel economy. An improved exhaust manifold system solves the problem of hydrocarbon emissions. The acceleration performance of the CVCC engine has been improved in the CVCC II system, and a catalytic converter has been added to control hydrocarbons. The CVCC engine was incorporated in the design of the Honda Civic, which began to be exported in 1972. The following year Honda signed licensing agreements with Ford, Chrysler, and Isuzu permitting them to use the CVCC technology.

The technological excellence of Honda cars, combined with American production not subject to import barriers, raised Honda's annual U.S. sales to over half a million units. Honda surpassed Nissan in 1984 and Toyota during the first three months of 1985 to become the leading foreign producer in the American market. Honda America also became in 1985 the fourth-largest domestic producer, selling nearly as many units as AMC and Volkswagen of America combined. American buyers have been willing to pay premiums over the suggested retail prices for Accords, Preludes, and Civics, which remain in short supply. With average sales of 100 cars more per year than Toyota dealers, the Honda dealer network in 1985 led the entire automobile industry in sales per outlet in the United States.

Following Honda's lead, in 1980 Nissan Motor Manufacturing, U.S.A., was incorporated in Delaware. In 1983 Nissan began building light trucks at the rate of 10,000 units a month at an 850-acre plant in Smyrna, Tennessee, near Nashville—a plant whose $300-million cost makes it the largest investment to date by a Japanese company in the United States. The decision to begin production at Smyrna with light trucks rather than passenger cars was made because trucks are simpler to build and, lacking annual model changes, have a more stable market. The production of subcompact Sentra passenger cars was added at Smyrna in April 1985. Nissan plans to turn out 100,000 Sentras a year there by 1988.

General Motors and Toyota began in late 1985 to assemble the Nova—a Toyota-designed subcompact similar to the Corolla, with many Japanese components—at a reopened Chevrolet plant in Fremont, California. GM contributed the plant and $20 million, Toyota $250 million, to form New United Motors, Incorporated, with Tatsuro Toyoda, grandson of the Toyota founder, as president. GM and Toyota each own 50 percent of New United Motors, which is the first U.S.-Japanese joint venture in the United States. Job categories, already reduced substantially in GM's other American plants, have been virtually eliminated at Fremont, where Japanese labor-management practices are being instituted. The Fremont plant is expected to produce about 50,000 cars a year. Toyota also has announced plans to build 200,000 cars at its own plant, site still unspecified, in the United States.

Despite having challenged the GM-Toyota joint venture in the federal courts on antitrust grounds, Chrysler in April 1985 announced its own plans for a joint venture with Mitsubishi. The plans call for a $500-million factory, which will have produced 180,000 Mitsubishi-designed cars by late 1988, and for Chrysler's increasing its share of Mitsubishi stock to 24 percent. Chrysler previously had announced limits on its U.S. expansion as a result of the ending on March 31, 1985, of voluntary restrictions on Japanese motor vehicle exports to the United States. That event notwithstanding, explained Mitsubishi president Toyoo Tate to reporters, the decision to manufacture in the United States was based on the belief that "complete freedom of exporting to the American market will not occur in the foreseeable future." On the same assumption, Toyo Kogyo has formed the Mazda Motor Company, which will begin to produce cars at a new factory in Flat Rock, Michigan, in 1988. Initial production of 240,000 units is planned.

Should all of the plans of Japanese manufacturers announced by mid-1985 materialize, the plant capacity for producing Japanese-designed motor vehicles in the United States will reach some 1.36 million units by 1988, about 10 percent of the anticipated American production. It is expected that by then Japanese makes may account for as much as 44 percent of new-car sales in the United States.

The Japanese Challenge and Our Mounting Trade Deficit

Under intense pressure from the Reagan administration, in 1981 the Japanese government established "voluntary" restrictions limiting exports of motor vehicles, first to 1.68 million, then to 1.85 million units a year. The intention was to give U.S. auto manufacturers a respite from Japanese competition while they retooled to produce small, fuel-efficient cars.

Following reports of record profits by the Big Three in 1984, on March 1, 1985, President Reagan announced that he would heed a Cabinet

Council recommendation and not ask the Japanese government to continue the voluntary restraints when the quota program expired on March 31. Urging "free and fair trade" in return, the president hoped to gain other trade concessions in protected Japanese markets for electronic equipment and agricultural products. While making no trade concessions to the United States, the Japanese government announced its intention to increase motor vehicle exports to the United States by 24.3 percent—to 2.3 million units annually. This voluntary 2.3-million annual quota has since been extended to 1987 by the Japanese government, to the consternation of Japanese automobile manufacturers, who wish all restrictions ended.

Ford chairman of the board Donald E. Petersen lamented that the Reagan decision would "create jobs in Japan at the expense of jobs for American workers." "This is a sad day for America—for American workers and American jobs," said Chrysler chairman Lee Iacocca. He later announced plans to curtail U.S. expansion of small-car production and increase Chrysler imports of Mitsubishi Colts from 87,500 annually to 287,500. UAW president Owen Bieber claimed that "no less than our middle-class standard of living is at stake as America's best jobs are allowed to shift overseas.... We have to question the competence of negotiators who are willing to add $5 billion to $7 billion [annually] to an already frightening trade deficit without securing an agreement from Japan to purchase more goods and services in return." In response to news of the Reagan Cabinet Council recommendation to end the quotas, the UAW earlier had claimed that 150,000 jobs in the American automobile industry would be lost, causing "devastation of a number of automobile comunities around the country," and that the transition of the American automobile industry "to efficient production of new kinds of high-quality, fuel-efficient cars" would be aborted.[14]

In opposition to the responses of Ford, Chrysler, and the UAW, General Motors issued a statement that praised President Reagan for acting "responsibly" in recognition that "the time has come to return to free trade." The raising of the Japanese export quotas permitted GM to implement plans to import annually some 300,000 small cars from Isuzu and Suzuki, to be sold as Chevrolet Sprints and Chevrolet Spectrums.

Consumer advocates, too, praised the lifting of the restraints. It was estimated by the Federal Trade Commission that the import restrictions had saved 44,000 jobs, but at the cost of raising the average price of a Japanese-made car sold in the U.S. by $1,300 and the average price of an American-made car by $600.

Despite the restraints, from 1981 to 1985 the Japanese auto makers actually increased their American profits—from $8.2 billion in 1980 to $12.4 billion in 1984 on 150,000 fewer units. The reason was that the Japanese upgraded their model mixes for U.S. export to include more of their larger cars loaded with more luxury extras. Henry V. "Gene" Leonard, Jr., GM's top Japanese representative, explained: "When your unit volume is limited, you'd be a fool not to switch to a richer mix. . . . As long as the export restraints continue, then the Japanese companies will continue to push their larger cars, loaded with the maximum possible number of options in order to maximize their unit revenues." An unidentified Japanese auto executive quipped, "Quotas are the mother of invention." [15]

Despite the restraints, too, in 1984 the United States accumulated a record $36.8-billion trade deficit with Japan and a $123.3-billion trade deficit worldwide. Half of the trade deficit with Japan was accounted for by automobile imports, and the International Trade Commission estimated that without the restraints the deficit would have been $4 billion higher. Consequently, on March 29, 1985, the United States Senate unanimously approved a resolution urging the Reagan administration to take steps within ninety days to curb Japanese auto imports if Japan failed to buy more American products.

The resolution proved of little consequence. On July 30, 1985, Prime Minister Yasuhiro Nakasone announced a three-year "action program" intended to "make the Japanese market the most open in the world" and thereby "totally exterminate opinions that Japan is unfair"; no real trade concessions to the United States were contained in the program, however. The Reagan administration expressed disappointment that the action fell short of what was needed to stave off growing protectionist sentiment in Congress, but no retaliation was undertaken. The United States trade deficit with Japan shot up to a new record of $49.7 billion in 1985 and has continued to widen.

In addition to adapting to changing market conditions, perfecting the kanban-jidoka system, and exploiting their great labor productivity/labor cost advantages, the Japanese have begun to outpace Europe and the United States as well in innovation in automotive technology. The traditional technological dependence of Japanese automobile manufacturers on the U.S. and Europe has now become a myth. As an indication of this, Japan increased its total share of worldwide automobile patenting from only 11.9 percent in 1970–1971 to 34.5 percent in 1980–1981, while Japan's total share of automotive patenting by final assemblers increased from 15.5 percent to an astounding 56.4 percent over the decade. Europe declined over the same period from 56.3 percent to 36.8 percent in total patenting and from 30.6 percent to 19.7 percent in patenting by final assemblers; the U.S. declined from 31.8 percent to 28.7 percent in total patenting and from 53.9 percent to 23.9 percent in patenting by final assemblers.

The huge profits gained from automotive exports to the United States have been used wisely by the Japanese to establish an independent base in automotive technology. Cost advantages in large part attributable to government labor and trade policies thus ultimately translate into a formidable Japanese challenge to the long-standing technological lead of American and European automobile manufacturers. Whether Japan will soon become number one in automotive technology as well as in production remains to be seen.

New Frontiers

18

With the rebuilding of plant facilities following the massive destruction of World War II, American mass-production methods rapidly came to be institutionalized in European automobile factories. As Jean-Pierre Bardou points out, "technical and organizational readjustment in the industry (in the United States from the 1930s onward and in Europe from the end of the war to the 1960s) was paralleled by a profound change in the composition of the labor force, resulting in a massive hiring of rural and immigrant workers, a heterogeneous group without training." By 1970 blacks constituted 44 percent of Detroit's population and accounted for more than 60 percent of the workers on some Detroit assembly lines. White migrants from Appalachia and recent Arab immigrants also were prominent in Detroit's automobile factories. Assembly lines in Western Europe came to be manned by "interior migrants" from economically backward regions—Bretons in France, Calabrians and Sicilians in Italy—and foreign immigrants from less developed countries. "Most of these workers come from the Mediterranean basin as far as the West European auto industry is concerned. The majority of this group found in each country—North Africans in France, West Indians in England, and the like—indicates the relationship between the source of these workers and the former colonial system." [1]

Unlike the native-born skilled workers who had predominated in European automobile factories before the war, unskilled workers from colonial and rural backgrounds tended to form attitudes toward the workplace either of apathy or of revolt. Unlike the newly arrived immigrants and black migrants who had manned Detroit's prewar assembly lines, second-generation Poles and urban blacks, educated into middle-class values and expectations by the public schools and the mass media, reacted identically to the intensification of Fordism by Sloanism.

Labor turnover, absenteeism, and industrial sabotage in European automobile factories reached even higher levels than in American plants. Turnover by 1970 reached 25 percent per year at Ford-U.S., 35 percent at Volvo, and 100 percent in the foundry at Fiat. Daily absenteeism averaged 10 to 15 percent in Detroit's automobile factories and reached 25 percent at the Fiat Mirafiori plant. Wildcat strikes became common. "Unorganized and unsystematic groups committed such acts of sabotage as streaking paint and ripping upholstery.... Such kinds of behavior revealed more of social and working conditions than did the actual strikes," Bardou relates. Worker reaction appeared similar in the emerging Eastern bloc auto industry. "Soviet workers in auto factories ... react the same as their comrades in capitalist countries to the assembly line.... Dissatisfaction appears in such forms as slowdowns, absenteeism, and 'quits.'" [2]

Unions failed to meet the needs of the new auto workers in Western Europe and in the United States, "because racial [and ethnic] issues became intermixed with labor relations." Although 30 percent of the UAW membership was black in 1969, for example, blacks held only 7 of the 100 key UAW posts. The union had lost touch with its rank and file, particularly its minority members. White workers, too, wanted higher wages and objected to the speedup and to more rigid discipline in the workplace. They held the best jobs in automobile plants, however, and their demands differed on a number of issues, such as seniority rights and training programs for skilled apprentices. Bardou cites the "extreme case" of the Dodge Main plant, located in the Polish-American enclave of Hamtramck. Polish-Americans controlled the town's administration and police force as well as the UAW local at Dodge Main. Almost all supervisory and skilled employees, including skilled apprentices, were white at Dodge Main in the early 1970s, and most were of Polish descent. "The union strategy aimed to defend the interests of the Polish-Americans much more vigorously than those of the blacks and Arabs, chronically unemployed and earning the lowest wages. On this point the situation of the mass of semi-skilled workers in Western Europe is not fundamentally different." The failure of the unions to represent the new workers resulted worldwide in spontaneous workers' movements in conflict with the union establishments as well as with management. Bardou argues that "the conflicts in the United States often represent[ed] only a blurred image of what prevail[ed] in Western Europe.... Riots in Detroit ... and the revolts of Turkish workers in Germany, West Indians in England, and North Africans in France represent many different answers to work situations and types of existence that are basically similar."

Wide publicity was given to attempts in the early 1970s by Saab Scania and Volvo to effect a radical restructuring of the workplace. At Saab's new Sojertale plant in 1972, the production line for assembling engines was replaced with "production teams." Groups of three workers were responsible for assembling entire engines, each worker doing the whole series of assembling tasks. The result was that capital costs for plant and equipment and for job training were higher, while the turnover rate remained about the same. It also proved impossible to do away with repetitive line-production jobs for three quarters of the workers at the Sojertale plant, which produced only 110,000 engines a year. To set up a group assembly system to produce, say, a million engines a year would have involved far more formidable problems, because the group assembly system requires more factory space and the installation of additional costly machine tools in every assembly bay.

Volvo began assembling entire automobiles at its small (600 workers, 30,000 unit annual capacity) new Kalmar plant in 1974. Production teams of fifteen to twenty workers assembled complete cars. The teams worked at their own pace and made collective decisions on the rotation of tasks. The Kalmar plant cost 10 percent more than a conventional automobile factory. Notably, too, the Kalmar plant was solely an assembly operation. No stamping or welding—the processes requiring the most intensive use of unskilled and semiskilled labor—was carried out there.

The rate of absenteeism, 30 percent at other Volvo factories, was halved to 15 percent at Kalmar. It was difficult to know what this meant, however: the plant site was in a provincial town on the Baltic with a population of only 53,000 and chronic unemployment. "It is a striking fact that essentially no immigrant workers are employed at the Kalmar factory, though in the other Volvo plants they number 30 percent," Bardou observes. "It is not by accident, therefore, that the most far-reaching and important experiments in job redesign have taken place in Sweden, where the level of worker education and skill is among the highest in the world." [3]

The alienation of workers caused by Sloanist intensification of Fordism led Emma Rothschild to contend in 1973 that "the American automobile business ... faces decline and possible extinction—a decline that can be seen most clearly in the continuing readjustment of modern American and world industries." She made explicit reference to Charles Darwin's theory of natural selection to predict that under "capitalist Darwinism," capital investment in automobile manufacturing and other "low-technology and labor-intensive industries [would] move to ever less developed countries, with low-paid workers." As a corollary, in the advanced industrial countries "low-technology and mass-production industries [would] lose capital to high-technology or research-based industries." She claimed that such readjustments were being "anticipated eagerly by advanced American business opinion, by partisans of financial corporations and of the more dynamic and science-based multinational companies." [4]

Rothschild cited Japan as an illustration of her thesis. The choice was inappropriate: although low labor costs are a primary reason why Japan has become number one in automobile manufacturing, in all other respects Japan fails to fit Rothschild's model. Japan is an advanced industrial country with a highly developed industrial infrastructure, a well-educated work force and large supply of skilled technicians, and a relatively high standard of living—not an underdeveloped country. Japanese penetration of world markets has been evident not only in automobile manufacturing but in such high-technology-based products as cameras, stereos, television sets, and computers. As a result of nationalistic governmental economic policies, the capital that has fueled the Japanese "economic miracle" has almost all been generated internally or from profits, not exported by Western investors as Rothschild's model suggests. Finally, the profits generated by lower labor costs have been reinvested by Japanese auto makers in research and development, leading to Japan's increasing independence in automotive technology from Western Europe and the United States. Thus, the Japanese automobile industry does not fit Rothschild's conception of a labor-intensive, low-technology, mass-production industry.

Contrary to Rothschild's prediction, the locus of automobile production has not shifted to the underdeveloped Third World, nor does it seem possible that it will in the foreseeable future. The reason for her argument's not being borne out is that it proceeds from fundamentally erroneous conceptions about the economics of automobile manufacturing. She also failed to foresee that by the mid-1980s automobile manufacturing would become a high-technology industry.

The Automobile Industry in the Third World

Out of the total world production of slightly under 36.3 million units in 1982, only 2 million units were produced in Third-World countries. Excluding the production of 411,800 units in the advanced capitalist Republic of South Africa, total African production was Morocco's 16,690 units. Excluding Japanese production of some 10.7 million units, total production in other Asian countries was only 315,723 units, with South Korea accounting for 163,484 of these units and India for 152,249. Latin America, including Mexico, produced some 1.69 million units, with

859,295 units accounted for by Brazil, 472,637 units by Mexico, and 132,116 units by Argentina. Third-World production is thus centered in Latin America, Brazil being the leading Third-World producer by a wide margin.

South Korea has been trying to emulate Japan in building up a strong national-based export industry in a protected home market. Ambitious plans that seem incapable of realization with escalating oil prices call for Korean registrations to increase from 634,114 in 1982 to over 3.5 million by 1991. The South Korean automobile industry is fragmented among three small firms, each of which is technologically dependent on ties to companies in the advanced auto-producing nations. The major Korean producer is Hyundai, a public company with 100-percent Korean equity. Hyundai was formed in 1967 with funds borrowed from Barclay's Bank, the French Banque de Suez, and the Japan Export-Import Bank. The design and technology for its car were purchased from Italian, Japanese, and British firms. Its management was recruited at first from the British motor industry but is now entirely Korean. The first Hyundai cars were exported to the United States in 1986.

Despite a wage rate about half that of Japan, the limited Korean home market and the strong nationalistic bias of government policy discourage investment in the Korean automobile industry by the multinationals, while technological dependence militates against the effective competition of the national-based firms in world markets. The total capacity of the Korean automobile industry in 1986 was only about 500,000 units.

Julian Pettifer and Nigel Turner estimate that only about 15 percent of India's 730 million people have ever ridden in a car and that there are 23 million bicycles and 17 million bullock carts on India's roads, versus only 1.96 million motor vehicles (986,470 passenger cars) registered in 1983.[5] India's extreme poverty makes understandable the low priority given by the government to automotive transportation and the emphasis on manufacture of trucks and buses in national planning since independence. Without a substantial domestic market for passenger cars, India cannot generate sufficient volume to be competitive in the export market.

Foreign investment in the Indian motor industry has been prevented by government policy. This in turn has restricted technological development. The two major passenger car producers are Hindustan Motors and Premier Motors. Hindustan produces the 1954 Morris Oxford under license as the Ambassador; Premier produces the late-1950s Fiat 1100 as the Padmini. Volume is too low to be economical, and manufacturing quality is abominable. "The Indian car manufacturers exploit an overprotected market on the basis of a completely oligopolistic position," an angry customer recently complained in *Business India.* "The whole situation is absurd when you know that you are buying a car whose design is 20 or thirty years old; whose fuel consumption is 20 percent higher than that of a small 10 year old European model; which has been built sloppily, and might break down in anything between 3 days and 3 months." [6]

Despite charges of nepotism and the displacement of some 1,500 farmers from their land, the Gandhi government in 1968 approved building the huge Murati (son of the Wind God) industrial complex outside Delhi so that auto enthusiast Sanjay Gandhi, Indira Gandhi's son, could produce a small "people's car." A prototype car was unveiled in 1972, but the Murati factory never got into production. Murati went bankrupt in 1977, and Sanjay Gandhi was killed in an airplane crash in 1980. The Murati assets were nationalized. Then, in an abrupt policy turnaround, the government solicited proposals for a joint venture from foreign auto makers. An agreement has been reached with Suzuki that by 1989 Murati will produce annually, using Japanese machinery, 100,000 units of a Suzuki-designed small car. This is the single bright spot on the Indian motor industry scene.

Automobile industries were established by national decrees in Brazil in 1956, Argentina in 1959, and Mexico in 1962. Latin American motor vehicle production expanded from only 102,200 units in 1957 to a high 2,174,000 units in 1978, declining to 1,687,000 units in 1982. A tendency toward stagnation because of excess plant capacity and high unit costs became evident in Argentina and Brazil as early as the installation of manufacturing capacity in the mid-1960s. And the Latin American motor vehicle industry as a whole can be described as a stagnant industry since 1974 and 1975, when total production leveled off, respectively, at 1,740,000 and 1,741,000 units.

By the mid-1960s it was obvious that production costs in Latin America were not competitive. Jack Baranson estimates that in 1967 the cost of producing a light truck in Argentina was 245 percent of the U.S. cost, in Brazil 180 percent, and, despite very low local-content requirements, in Mexico 158 percent. Kenneth S. Mericle estimates that in 1965 it cost $3,000 in Brazil to manufacture a vehicle that could be produced for $1,660 in Detroit. Rhys Jenkins estimates that in 1965 Argentinian labor productivity was only a quarter of U.S. levels and less than half of Western European levels. He observes that Argentinian labor productivity remained stagnant; consequently, in 1978 Argentinian unit costs remained about double international levels. Despite an increase in output per worker in final assembly from 4.37 vehicles in 1966 to 8.41 vehicles in 1974, Brazilian labor productivity still lagged behind the best U.S.

and Western European levels of 11.6 vehicles per worker at Ford-U.S. and 14 at Opel in 1970.[7]

The minimum efficient scale in automobile production (identical units per plant per year) is, according to George Maxcy, 100,000 units for the production of engine blocks, 500,000 units for engine and transmission machining and assembling, and 250,000 units for final assembly. These minimal economies of scale have never been met in Latin America. Rich Kronish and Kenneth Mericle point out that "national markets were highly fragmented among a plethora of production firms, ranging from eight in Mexico to twenty-three in Argentina.... [T]he only firm in all of Latin America in 1962 to produce more than 50,000 vehicles in any particular market sector (cars, light vehicles, or buses and trucks) was Volkswagen." This was achieved with the highly standardized Beetle. They further observe that "many of the firms offered a large number of models with frequent model change (and limited parts standardization), which fragmented the national market still further. By 1972 the Argentine industry numbered some 120 separate models, while the Brazilian industry counted 131 and the Mexican industry 76. This proliferation of models, coupled with relatively short model lives, effectively limited (and continues to limit) most models to relatively small and costly production runs." The largest model run of any motor vehicle produced in any Latin American country in 1982 was 42,330 units of the Mexican-made Volkswagen Beetle 1600 sedan.[8]

Kronish and Mericle estimate that the total Latin American market for motor vehicles was only 310,000 units in 1957, the first year of Brazilian manufacturing. "With per capita incomes well below those of developed countries (in 1961, $267 in Brazil, $464 in Mexico, and $895 in Argentina) and with some 70 to 80 percent of the population failing to earn even these figures, effective demand for motor vehicles remained largely confined to the upper class and upper middle class throughout Latin America," they write. "No Latin American country in the late 1950s or 1960s, including Argentina, contained a significant mass market for motor vehicles. Despite higher than average income levels and a distribution of income rather less inequitable than the rest of the area, only 3 percent of Argentine families accounted for one-third of all car expenditures in 1963."[9]

The gap between the rich and the poor has widened since then in Brazil. In 1960 the richest 5 percent of Brazilians received 27.3 percent of the total income, while the poorest 80 percent received 45.6 percent; in 1970 the richest 5 percent received 36.3 percent, while the poorest 80 percent received 36.8 percent. An Economist Intelligence Unit report described Brazil in 1975 as "a regime where few people (even if they are lucky enough to work for a multinational firm) earn more than twice the official wage, which is less than enough to keep a wife and two children in food alone." [10]

By 1971 the terminal sector of the Latin American motor vehicle industry was almost completely denationalized. Subsidiaries of foreign multinationals by then accounted for 100 percent of final assembly in Brazil, 97 percent in Argentina, and 84 percent in Mexico. The Latin American motor vehicle industry is thus a prominent example of "dependent industrialization" and/or "economic imperialism."

The evidence is unequivocal that Brazil's flirtation with the multinational automobile industry is ending in economic and social disaster. In sharp contrast with Mexico's abundant petroleum reserves and consequent petroleum self-sufficiency, Brazil is overwhelmingly dependent on imported oil. In 1973 imported oil accounted for 80 percent of total Brazilian consumption, and 60 percent of this imported oil was consumed by motor vehicles. With the OPEC-induced 1973 oil crisis, the cost of Brazil's imported oil soared from $680 million to $2.7 billion in 1974; and the cost of a gallon of regular gasoline rose 242 percent in real terms by 1977. With the increase in world oil prices, Brazil's net foreign debt increased from $6 billion at the end of 1973 to $47 billion at the end of 1980.

To meet this growing trade deficit, the Brazilian government has attempted unsuccessfully to increase motor vehicle exports, while slowing the growth of the domestic automobile market through tightening consumer credit terms and raising gasoline prices. "In effect the state has raised the income level necessary to own and operate an automobile at the same time as the slowdown in general economic activity has reduced the growth rate of per capita income," Kronish and Mericle conclude. "In addition the state has exempted the motor vehicle firms from the price control system and thereby further constrained demand, a measure that also has increased the firms' markups and per unit profits." [11]

Further, the Brazilian government has attempted to replace petroleum as a motor fuel with ethanol (ethyl alcohol) made from sugar cane or manioc (cassava). No filling station in Brazil sells pure gasoline; normal cars run on a gasoline-alcohol mixture; and the automobile industry is mandated to equip a third of all new cars with ethanol-burning engines. At an estimated expenditure of $15 billion, a new optimal-sized ethanol distillation plant with a daily capacity of 120,000 liters was built every four days during 1980–1984. Each ethanol distillery requires 2.6 million tons of sugar cane annually, hence a planted area of 12,500 to 15,000 acres. "More than 6 million acres of the best agricultural land are now devoted to feeding cars; and . . . production has fallen entirely into the hands of the large plantation owners," Pettifer and Turner relate. "In Sao Paulo State, where much of the alcohol is produced, small holders have been forced to leave their land and become casual day laborers. In the Amazon, enormous tracts of forest are being razed to grow cassava.... [R]ivers are being polluted by the 'vinhoto,' a slop which is left after the distillation is complete, and as a consequence some of the rivers in the state of Sao Paulo have become stinking sewers." About 45 percent of a Brazilian worker's wages already is spent on food, and food prices are constantly rising as the diversion of agricultural land to ethanol production necessitates that more and more food be imported by Brazil. Pettifer and Turner note "the final irony; to help the balance of payments, alcohol is produced on land that could be used to grow much needed food, food that consequently has to be purchased abroad, thus damaging balance of payments." They further note that "modern agricultural methods, more often than not, have a negative energy balance: more energy goes into the inputs—tractor fuels and fertilizer, manufacture of agricultural machinery and the whole technical infrastructure—than is captured by photosynthesis in the field. When the aim is to produce not food but energy, it really makes little sense to put more into the process than you get out of it." [12]

Thus, only the large plantation owners growing sugar cane for ethanol production in Sao Paulo State appear to have gained substantially in the long run from Brazil's attempt to develop a denationalized automobile industry. The question whether Brazilian entrepreneurs could have developed the industry to its present level without the involvement of the multinationals is nonsensical. Nowhere in the Third World has this or anything comparable occurred, and everything we know about the mature automobile industry suggests its impossibility. Ironically, developing Brazil's motor vehicle industry has not proved very profitable for the multinational automobile companies and promises to be even less profitable for them in the future.

Latin American countries are risky ones in which to invest, especially in uneconomical industries such as automobile manufacturing. Military coups have occurred with more regularity than democratic elections in these countries. Class antagonism and revolutionary fervor are strong. Automobile workers in Latin America have become increasingly militant. This is particularly true in Argentina. "In the decade up to the [military] coup of March 1976, the Argentine auto workers emerged as a militant social force that challenged government policies in dramatic fashion and consistently opposed the auto companies' efforts to increase productivity. Indeed they developed a level of militant organization and consciousness that blocked the successful implementation of the companies' efforts," write Judith Evans, Paul Hoeffel, and Daniel James. Even after the military government ruthlessly suppressed labor activity and declared strikes illegal, "reports of drastic cuts in production due to slowdowns and sabotage filtered into the press. These job actions seem to have occurred on a broad front." [13] Class conflict in general has been heightened in Brazil as a result of the military government's austerity program to counteract the mounting trade deficit. Auto workers in Brazil have been in the vanguard of demands for union autonomy and general political democracy, and the military government's labor policy was defied in illegal strikes in 1978 and 1979. Although Mexican automobile workers have been the least militant, they too currently are attempting to organize unions independent from the government-affiliated Confederacion de Trabadores de Mexico. This increasing labor militancy contributes to making Latin America a far less attractive place to invest in automobile manufacturing than it seemed a generation ago.

Motor Vehicle Production in the Advanced Socialist Countries

To the extent that automobile production moves out of the advanced capitalist countries, it is far more likely in the foreseeable future to move into the advanced socialist countries than into the Third World.

Outside the U.S.S.R. in the Eastern bloc, rudimentary automobile cultures have developed. Ratios of passenger cars to population in 1982 were 1:6.3 in Czechoslovakia, 1:6.6 in East Germany, 1:8.8 in Yugoslavia, 1:10 in Bulgaria, 1:11 in Hungary, and 1:14 in Poland. The annual production of motor vehicles in Eastern bloc countries other than the U.S.S.R. in the early 1980s was nearly a million units. Technical ties are increasing among Eastern bloc final assemblers, not only with the U.S.S.R. and one another but also with EEC multinationals. With domestic markets initially developed but far from saturated, the Eastern bloc countries plan some expansion of their automobile industries.

More significantly, in the spring of 1965 Soviet premier Alexei Kosygin denounced "the idea . . . foisted upon us that our country needed no large-scale production of passenger cars" as "subjective" and "economically unfounded." [14] The largest industrial investment of the eighth five-year plan (1966–1970) was building the Fiat-designed Volga motor works (VAZ). By 1975 VAZ was turning out over 600,000 passenger cars. Production was raised to 7.8 cars annually per worker at VAZ, which has become a model for the new use of capitalist "material incentives" to raise labor productivity. A new motor city, Tol'yatti, with a 1979 population of 502,000, was built around the Volga plant. VAZ produces the Lada car in cooperation with other Eastern bloc countries, who exchange components for finished vehicles. By the early 1980s VAZ Lada ranked thirteenth among world passenger car manufacturers, with annual production of over 800,000 units. Three other U.S.S.R. final assemblers—Moskovitch, Zaz Zaporojetz, and GAZ Volga—turn out an additional 515,000 units.

During the eighth five-year plan the U.S.S.R. more than doubled expenditures on automating automobile manufacturing with imported Western technology. Twenty-five new component factories were built, and all existing automobile factories were modernized. Of particular note, the Moskovitch car plant in Moscow was renovated and its capacity doubled to 200,000 units with the aid of Renault. With the aid of West Germany, the installation of automated, computer-controlled assembly lines modernized truck plants throughout the U.S.S.R.

Investment in the Soviet motor vehicle industry was upped from 3.5 billion rubles to a massive 5 billion in the ninth five-year plan (1971–1975). Some 3.3 billion rubles were allocated alone to build the gigantic Kama River truck works, and 800 million more for the adjacent new motor city of Naberezhnye Chelny, population 301,000 in 1979. Annual capacity of the Kama River plant is 150,000 heavy three-axled trucks and 250,000 diesel engines. This is production on a phenomenal scale—the total annual U.S. production of similar heavy three-axled trucks does not usually exceed 100,000 units.

"During the first half of the tenth five-year plan (1976–1980)," writes W. H. Parker, "the ministry of the motor industry exceeded its planned targets by 860 million rubles' worth of production. . . . The transformation of a small, backward and parochial industry into a large, modern and highly productive organization had been accomplished." [15]

In 1982 Soviet final assemblers produced 1,307,000 passenger cars, 780,000 trucks, and 85,700 buses. A small export industry is beginning to develop even while the home market remains virtually untapped, with only one motor vehicle for every sixteen persons, one passenger car for every twenty-nine persons. Cars cost three to five times an average worker's annual wage and must be paid for in cash after a wait of a year or more for delivery. Still, a lively black market for used cars persists in the U.S.S.R., and these sell at higher prices than new ones. "Private automobile owners are concentrated primarily among members of the professional and managerial elite resident in urban areas," John M. Kramer reports. "The absence of a well-developed road network and insufficient maintenance facilities in rural areas further contributes to the concentration of most automobiles in Russia's urban centres. Present policy envisages between 150 and 200 cars per 1,000 residents in the largest urban centres by the year 2000, which is roughly the level of car ownership found in Prague, Czechoslovakia, in 1975." [16]

The restriction of automobile ownership to the elite, Kramer points out, carries "political risks ... especially dangerous for a society supposedly dedicated to the gradual elimination of inequalities and the eventual creation of a classless society, since it raises the difficult ideological question of why some in socialist society should have private automobiles while most use public transport." [17] It is uncertain whether such restriction by state policy can long continue in the U.S.S.R.

The Triumph of the Automobile

19

If the industrialized countries of Eastern Europe are now experiencing the automobile revolution largely as a matter of highway transportation by trucks and buses, far less affected by the motor vehicle are the nations of the Third World. At the extreme, the People's Republic of China in 1980 had only one motor vehicle for every 1,135 persons, one passenger car for every 18,673 persons. Fully 88 percent of the world's motor vehicles are owned by the 17 percent of the world's population living in its most affluent countries. "In most of continental Asia today, and in much of Africa and Central and South America, the likelihood of owning a car must seem as remote to the average man as it was beyond the dreams of the farm labourers in nineteenth-century Europe," write Julian Pettifer and Nigel Turner. "Some 7 percent of the world's population own private cars and only a tiny proportion of that minority of mankind lives in the Third World. In most countries car ownerhsip is still what it always has been: the ultimate symbol of wealth and privilege." [1]

Family ownership of cars in Europe ranges from about 55 percent in Great Britain to 75 percent in Sweden, with multiple-car ownership by European families estimated at about 10 percent. Jean-Jacques Chanaron points out that "because the proportion of families owning cars can still increase and because multimotorization is just beginning, European markets are far from zero growth." Nevertheless, he observes, "Two significant factors differentiate Europe [as an automobile market] from the United States. Evident in the major European metropolises is a relative under-motorization, encouraged by the existence of public transit systems and aggravated by a 'de-motorization' movement generated and fed by problems of traffic and parking. In Paris, for example, of 100 families that could own cars, taking account of the proportion of people employed and of age and income levels, only 64 actually do." Only about 50 percent of Japanese families owned cars as of 1980. Yet because of "some particular physical limits" of the Japanese market, Chanaron believes that "a rate of motorization equal to that of Western Europe in 1975 would lead in Japan to a total saturation of its roads, streets, and cities. Unless palliated by a major technical innovation, it would raise the level of pollution and other nuisances to an extent that the public would find unacceptable." [2]

Even in the United States, the most affluent country in the world, automobile ownership did not expand to include the urban working class until the period 1950–1970. Expansion then followed from a new level of general affluence engendered by forced savings during the war years; by the aggressiveness of unions after the war to ensure a more equitable distribution of wealth; by demand for American products to rebuild a devastated Europe; and by continuing huge government expenditures for defense, social programs, and public works. Among the latter, the most important in directly encouraging mass personal automobility was the Interstate Highway Act of 1956.

Motor vehicle registrations in the United States consequently more than doubled, from 49.2 million in 1950 to 108.4 million in 1970—by which date only 17 percent of American households lacked personal automobility, and the market for new cars appeared to be approaching saturation. Growth in new-car sales slackened during the 1970s, especially as the cost of personal automobility increased with escalating fuel prices following the 1973–1974 and 1979 oil shocks. By 1980 some 87.2 percent of American households owned one or more motor vehicles, 51.5 percent owned more than one, and fully 95 percent of domestic sales were for replacement. Automobile ownership in the United States, then, has spread to all except the hard-core poor, people too infirm or too handicapped to drive, and those who prefer alternatives to individualized automotive transportation.

Public Policy and the Decline of Public Transit

By 1956, when the Interstate Highway Act was passed, the railroads' share of common-carrier passenger miles had declined to 34.9 percent, the electric interurbans' share to an infinitesimal 0.3 percent. More important, in the words of George W. Hilton and John S. Due, "all common carriers were being dwarfed by the automobile, which was rapidly approaching a figure of 90 percent of all intercity passenger miles. Examiner Howard Hosmer of the Interstate Commerce Commission, in a widely cited report, suggested that at the average rate of withdrawal of railroad passenger service trains in the postwar era, passenger service other than commutation would be non-existent by 1970." [3]

The triumph of the private passenger car over rail transportation in the United States was meteoric. Passenger miles traveled by automobile were only 25 percent of rail passenger miles in 1922 but were twice as great as rail passenger miles by 1925, four times as great by 1929. Meanwhile, the total volume of travel in the United States expanded over fivefold during the twenties.

Regular intercity motor bus service developed concurrently with intercity travel by private automobile. It was extended and consolidated during the 1920s, Greyhound and National Trailways emerging as the most important highway common carriers. But the bus could not compete with the car any more than could rail transportation, regardless of cost efficiency.

Convincing testimony that cost efficiency was not enough to keep common carriers competitive with the motorcar was provided to the California Railroad Commission in 1936 by officials of both Pacific Greyhound and the Southern Pacific Railroad, which owned a 39-percent interest in Pacific Greyhound as well as a controlling interest in the Pacific Electric interurban railway. W. E. Travis, president of Pacific Greyhound and a member of the board of directors of the Greyhound Corporation, told the commissioners, "Regardless of service or rates, there are certain classes who will not use the bus lines. There is a large group of people who might be called nontravelers who, if they travel at all, do so infrequently, if only a short distance, and then by private car.... The greatest number of travelers at the present time are those who use their private cars." Lee D. Jones, general manager of Pacific Greyhound and a former Southern Pacific executive, amplified the point: "The private automobile is used more for convenience and pleasure by the person driving than because of the cost of operation.... Even with commute rates as low as two thirds of a cent a mile given by railroads in suburban territories, nevertheless there are hundreds of people in these districts driving back and forth to work and disregarding what rates have been placed into effect; the railroads have not been able to draw these people back to the trains." Buses faced the same problem. "You will find on the road between San Francisco and Los Angeles or between Los Angeles and San Diego, hundreds of people traveling in private automobiles daily, even though our round-trip [bus] rates are less than one and one-half cents a mile. The same conditions exist in the moving of labor, such as fruit pickers, lettuce workers, and others, who either use their machines to transport their families or go in together and buy machines to travel from place to place." [4]

One of the big losses in railroad patronage to the motorcar during the

1920s had been the traveling salesman, or "drummer." To attract this category of "commercial traveler" to intercity bus service, in mid-1936 Pacific Greyhound introduced $10 scrip books good for 700 miles of travel over a six-month period. The books obviated having to purchase tickets and made the average rate for highway travel only 1.4 cents per mile. Yet the firms approached by Pacific Greyhound's marketing people showed little interest, and only 180 books were sold over a three-month period. Jones explained: "We are constantly told that no matter if we make our fares one-half cent a mile they would still prefer the use of the private car for their business, explaining that it is not conceivable that any common-carrier service can be made to equal the necessary flexibility for travel by the commercial man. . . . The commercial man is on the road to get business for his firm and to sell its commodities, and the saving in transportation does not justify any slowing down of the speed in the making of sales."

These men claimed, then, that the private passenger car had won out over mass transit not because it was cost-efficient or technologically superior but because travelers preferred the freedom and convenience it gave them. Other evidence, however, suggests that the promotion of highway transportation by special-interest groups and resulting public policy decisions were perhaps more important to the decline of public transit than consumer choice in a free market.

Regulation remained a constraint on profitable operation as the unregulated motor vehicle cut into the business of short-haul passenger traffic. The interrelationship between regulation, competition from the motor vehicle, declining service, and declining ridership was an extremely complex, chicken-and-egg problem. The Hoover committee in 1929 pointed out, for example, that the loss of commuters in suburban traffic to motorcars "brought about curtailment of train service or abandonment of branch lines, when such action is permitted by the regulatory authorities, and the effect of poorer railway service has been to stimulate the transfer of passengers to the highway." [5]

Notably, the Federal Coordinator of Transportation in 1935 traced operating losses in railway passenger service not to the cost efficiency or technological superiority of the motorcar but to poor business practices. He reported, for example, that "railway passenger service operating loss in 1933 was due: to a service lacking in popular appeal; to ineffective sales promotion; and to preventable wastes in baggage service, in handling head end traffic, in duplication of terminal and station operations, in utilization of oversized power and equipment and of excessive and unnecessary number of cars in the trains, in improvident local train service, in competitive duplication of limited trains and sleeping and parlor car accommodations, and in the prodigal operation of dining and buffet services." [6]

The evidence presented by Hilton and Due similarly suggests that the electric interurbans failed for a complex set of socioeconomic, as opposed to technological, reasons. The case of Pacific Electric demonstrates that some of the more important interurbans were conceived as adjuncts to real-estate development schemes rather than as transportation companies expected to make a profit in their own right. They were irrationally overbuilt and were overcapitalized with heavily watered stock. They faced problems in obtaining right-of-way. In contrast with motor vehicles, which ran on roads paid for by the public, electric trains used roadbed, rails, and wires built and maintained as a business expense. Finally, the electric interurbans were overly regulated by government, so that unprofitable operations could not be terminated and fares and rates could not be raised to levels that ensured a reasonable return on invested capital. Given such a formidable set of problems, it is a wonder that the interurbans lasted as long as they did. Most lost money for several years before folding. Pacific Electric, the largest intercity electric traction system in the United States, hung on until 1961, when the last train was discontinued on the Los Angeles–Long Beach line.

"With approval or dismay, scholars of the motor age have described the rise of individual transportation as a result of several factors, most of which were beyond anyone's control," Paul Barrett complains. In a 1975 article on the decline of public transit and the triumph of the automobile in Chicago between the world wars, he demonstrates that "some factors that we might be inclined to take as givens (in particular technical progress and 'middle class aspirations') turn out to be in part the results of public decision making." These decisions were "grounded in the popular conception of transit as a private business and the automobile as a public good." The evidence demonstrates "that distance from central place and the presence of good single family housing are better correlated with declining transit ridership than is the quality of service." His conclusion is that Chicagoans "changed their mode of transportation for reasons which often had little to do with either transportation or technology." The argument is only slightly qualified in his 1983 book. "Certainly a different local transit policy in Chicago would not have prevented the rise of the automobile," he concedes. "It might, however, have provided alternatives for the urban commuter." [7]

This first case study of the triumph of the automobile over electric traction in a major American city is instructive. Eschewing both unregulated free enterprise and municipal ownership, Chicago in 1907 adopted municipal ordinances defining mass transit as a regulated, privately owned business, which was expected to make a profit on operations and pay taxes. Although the 5-cent fare was sacrosanct, the transit companies were guaranteed a 5-percent return on capital investment—a commitment that encouraged overcapitalization through the retention of worthless securities and keeping outdated equipment on the books. The city received 55 percent of the transit companies' net profits, which resulted by 1935 in an additional transportation cost exceeding $188 million to Chicago streetcar riders paying 5-cent fares. This unnecessary expense was greater than the entire inflated value of the Chicago Surface Lines in 1930, and over $155 million of it was diverted to nontransit purposes by Chicago's commercial-political policymakers. The Board of Supervising Engineers empowered to regulate the transit companies proved ineffective, and the system of mixed public and private controls served only to retard the adoption of transit innovations, including even the replacement of streetcars with motor buses. Furthermore, mass-transit planning was effectively divorced from overcall city planning with the implementation after 1909 of Daniel Burnham's Plan of Chicago by the business-dominated Chicago Plan Commission.

As the prospects for direct profits from fares diminished in the 1920s, private investors became reluctant to provide capital for improvements in transit service. As early as 1917, New York, Boston, and Philadelphia were subsidizing mass transit, and these cities have retained viable systems to the present time. But like the overwhelming majority of American cities, Chicago failed to follow their lead. Consequently, the financial community, which passed judgment on the viability of traction securities, came to set the terms for transit policy in Chicago. The hegemony of the bankers was confirmed when the Chicago Surface Lines went into receivership in 1972. A committee of bankers, organized by utility magnate Samuel Insull, worked out an arrangement to refinance the company. Ratified by Chicago's voters in a "traction referendum" of July 1, 1930, this arrangement gave the company a permanent franchise, failed to provide for effective regulation, and belatedly ended the fixed fare and compensation provisions of the 1907 ordinance. Barrett believes that because "municipal ownership in any meaningful sense had been ruled out, the 1930 agreement was probably the best the city could have obtained. It at least freed transit to operate like other businesses—adjusting fares to costs and making, if it could, an attractive return. If mass transit could not become, like the street, a genuine public responsibility, it might at least attract needed investment as a genuine private enterprise."[8] But the change had come at least two decades too late.

In contrast to mass transit, in Chicago and in all American cities the private passenger car was massively subsidized by publicly funded street improvements to accommodate automobile traffic. This accommodation antedated by a generation or more the motorization of the urban working class. So working-class streetcar riders in effect were taxed by city planners and politicians to make possible middle-class automobile use. Unlike public policy toward mass transit, public policy toward the automobile was directed simply at solving practical problems of traffic congestion and public safety. Whereas the regulation of mass transit most often was destructive of its continuance, "traffic regulation [of automobiles], initially negative, soon became positive and accommodative, because it dealt directly with a large and growing group of citizens, and because the mutual adjustment of the city and the automobile presented the city with an urgent problem of pressing concern to important interest groups." [9]

Providing the automobile an infrastructure of vastly improved city streets was not cost-effective in comparison with what it would have cost to provide excellent urban mass transit. In his defense of the unlimited accommodation to the motorcar by city planners, even Mark Foster points out that "Chicago spent the staggering sum of $340 million over a thirty-year period [from 1910 to 1940] on street widening alone, to little avail. That was more than twice the estimated cost of a comprehensive subway system at 1923 prices." The shortsightedness of New Deal "planning" is also painfully evident, for Foster further notes that "the WPA [Works Progress Administration] provided ten times as much assistance to street and highway projects as it did to mass transit." [10]

The most extreme statement of the case that the automobile's ascendancy over mass rail transit in cities was not primarily the result of consumer choice in a competitive market was made in 1974 by Bradford C. Snell, assistant counsel to Senator Philip A. Hart's antitrust subcommittee investigating the restructuring of the automobile and ground transportation industries. Snell alleged that General Motors had played a dominant role in a "conspiracy" that had destroyed a hundred electric surface rail systems in forty-five cities between 1932 and 1956. This was part of a far larger attack on GM, which included allegations that the corporation had collaborated in the Nazi war effort during World War II and that it had pressured the railroads into adopting diesel locomotives that Snell claimed were less efficient than electric-powered ones. GM refuted all of Snell's charges. [11]

In 1925 GM acquired Yellow Coach, the largest manufacturer of both intercity and intracity buses in the United States. By the early 1930s Yellow Coach was also the nation's largest producer of pneumatic-tired trolley coaches—vehicles that ran on the pavement but were powered from overhead electric wires like streetcars. GM also was the largest stockholder in the Greyhound Corporation until 1948 and had formed a holding company called the National Highway Transport Corporation (NHTC) to provide intercity bus service in the Southeast. NHTC became Altantic Greyhound Lines. By mutual agreement Greyhound bought only Yellow Coach buses; and after 1928, Snell contended, GM began a policy of "pressuring" railroads into replacing commuter rail service with jointly owned Greyhound-railroad bus routes. GM maintained an active role in Greyhound management and in 1932 arranged for a million-dollar cash loan to the financially troubled intercity bus company.

GM entered intercity bus operations with the formation in 1932 of United Cities Motor Transit (UCMT). In 1955 GM general counsel Henry Hogan testified before the Senate Judiciary Committee that UCMT had been created after GM "decided that the only way this new market for [city] buses could be created was for it to finance the conversion from streetcars to buses in some small cities." A few small cities in Michigan and Ohio were motorized, and Hogan observed that "in each case [GM] successfully motorized the city, turned the management over to other interests, and liquidated its investment." In 1935 UCMT was dissolved after being censured by the American Transit Association for attempting to motorize Portland's electric transit system.

According to Snell, the turning point in the decline of electric traction in cities came with the motorization of New York City's surface lines by GM and the Omnibus Corporation in 1935. John Ritchie was simultaneously chairman of Yellow Coach and president of Omnibus, which in addition was linked to the GM-controlled Hertz Corporation. The switch from electric streetcars to buses in New York City was largely completed in only eighteen months, but the last streetcar did not disappear until 1957.

In 1936 National City Lines (NCL) was formed by a combination of equipment suppliers headed by GM, Standard Oil of California, and Firestone Tire and Rubber. The purpose of this holding company was to motorize urban transit systems; its operating pattern was the same as that pioneered by UCMT. Streetcar companies were bought up, then resold after being motorized. Snell alleged that the sales contracts prohibited the new owners from purchasing any transit equipment powered by anything other than gasoline. The contracts did not, however, require the purchase of GM buses or other suppliers' products. Yellow Coach abruptly curtailed its production of electric-powered trolley buses in 1938 in favor of new diesel-powered buses. In 1938 Pacific City Lines (PCL) was organized as an NCL affiliate to motorize West Coast streetcar systems, beginning with those in Fresno, San Jose, and Stockton, California. In 1943 American City Lines (ACL), another NCL affiliate, was formed, which in four months began the conversion to buses in nineteen more cities, including the dismantling of Pacific Electric in Southern California. At a cost of $9 million, NCL had motorized the street railway systems of the major cities in sixteen states by 1950. GM terminated its NCL affiliations in 1949.

After they could no longer pay their way, eighteen NCL properties were sold to municipal transit districts at high profits. These included the Los Angeles Transit Lines in 1958 and the Key System, which served the Oakland and East San Francisco Bay area, in 1960. NCL realized $6.5 million from the Los Angeles sale and $5.1 million from the Key System transactions. In these and other cases the municipal transit districts had to subsidize the systems that they had acquired. A particularly sore point was that the Key System tracks on the lower deck of the Bay Bridge had been torn up and the right-of-way paved for highway transportation at the very time when the newly formed Bay Area Rapid Transit District (BART) was seeking a trans-bay route for its trains.

GM responded in detail to Snell's "false and damaging claims." As we have seen in an earlier chapter, the company made a strong rebuttal to the allegation of collaboration with the Axis in World War II. GM similarly presented convincing evidence that Snell's other charges were untrue and that the corporation had not had "a destructive impact on mass transportation in this country." It was pointed out, for instance, that an exhaustive investigation by the U.S. Department of Justice had exonerated GM completely on charges that the corporation had used its power as the nation's largest shipper to pressure railroads into switching over to diesel locomotives. Evidence was also cited that the diesel locomotive was a progressive new product that had revolutionized the railroad industry.

As for electric traction in cities, GM claimed that it had been in decline long before NCL was formed, and that flexible buses were a substantial improvement over less efficient streetcars running on fixed rails. Pacific Electric, for example, had begun to curtail rail passenger service as early as 1917. It "steadily expanded its motor bus operations in the 1920s and 1930s," and "by 1939, the year before it is claimed that GM had any role in acquiring the system, over 35 percent of the total passenger miles were on buses." Rail passenger losses over the system except for 1923 and the war years 1943 and 1944 "were a financial catastrophe."

Documentation was found in "the literature of the time" that demonstrated "why the public favored the bus." Contrary to Snell's contentions, the motor bus "provided greater cost efficiency and operating flexibility." It was estimated that the average motor bus in New York City could operate at about four fifths the cost of a streetcar. In 1936 Mayor Fiorello La Guardia had welcomed "modern buses replacing antiquated trolleys" and "removal of the remaining obsolete traffic-obstructing trolley lines."

Whatever problems the Key System may have had in the 1950s under NCL control were not GM's responsibility, for GM had terminated all of its supply contracts with and investment in NCL in 1949. Furthermore, prior to the acquisition of the Key System by NCL in 1946 a number of contracts for the removal of tracks and the repaving of city streets had been approved by the Oakland City Council, and the decision to remove the tracks from the lower deck of the Bay Bridge was made by the state government, not NCL. "General Motors did not generate the winds of change which doomed the streetcar systems," the corporation claimed in its defense. "It did, however, through its buses, help to alleviate the destruction left in their wake. Times were hard and transportation systems were collapsing [in the 1930s]. GM was able to help with technology, with enterprise and, in some cases, with capital. The buses it sold helped give mass transportation a new lease on life which lasted into the postwar years."

That the demise of electric traction had begun more than a decade before the formation of NCL is incontrovertible. Still, the streetcar remained a more important carrier of passenger than the motor bus until World War II. The trolley coach became a contender only in the vastly reduced public transit market of the mid-1950s. In 1937 some 7.161 billion passengers rode streetcars in the United States, versus 3.489 billion motor bus passengers and a mere 289 million trolley coach passengers. By 1942 streetcar passengers barely exceeded motor bus passengers, 7.290 billion to 7.245 billion, and trolley coach ridership had tripled to 898 million. Motor bus riders exceeded streetcar riders in 1947, 10.2 billion to 8.1 billion, and trolley coach ridership had quadrupled to 1.3 billion. By 1955 all modes of public transit were in decline. Streetcars experienced the sharpest drop in patronage, while trolley coaches were affected the least. In 1955 some 7.250 billion passengers were carried by motor buses, versus only 1.207 billion by streetcars and 1.202 billion by trolley coaches.

Clearly it was not the shifting of passengers from the streetcar to the comparatively cost-efficient motor bus that killed off public transit. Neither was it the failure to shift them to the still more cost-efficient trolley coach. The culprit was the costwise highly inefficient private passenger car, which in the 1950s began making dramatic inroads into ridership on all modes of public transit. From this perspective the conversion of transit systems to motor buses was, as GM claimed, a stopgap measure that permitted them to survive during a period of transition to almost complete auto dependence.

The Highway Lobby

The conversion of urban transit systems to motor buses by GM and other automotive suppliers was not intended as an end in itself, suggests David James St. Clair; rather, it was an entering wedge in a far broader campaign to expand greatly the ownership and use of automobiles in cities. In response to market saturation in the late 1920s, St. Clair claims, "progressive leaders, such as Sloan at GM, engineered a campaign designed to alter the environment in which automobiles were sold. The goal was to reorder society to accommodate increased automobile use and ownership, and therefore increased automobile production. The objective was to create a different social environment in which the automobile would play a larger role." Because farmers were already entirely auto-dependent and a disappearing breed, there was only one place to seek more customers. "In order to augment sales and overcome the saturation of the market, American cities had to be opened up to the automobile, i.e., made compatible with the automobile," St. Clair contends. "This required the construction of an urban freeway network and the suppression of competing modes of transit. The industry was aware of this and actively pursued this policy through its lobbying for urban freeways and through its activities in destroying public transportation." [12]

The automobile industry's great stake in urban freeways was acknowledged in testimony given in 1955 before the House Public Works Committee by James J. Nance, president of both the Automobile Manufacturers Association (AMA) and Studebaker-Packard. Nance was testifying in favor of a complete interstate highway system, including controversial urban freeway portions. He forthrightly acknowledged: "Obviously we have a selfish interest in this program, because our products are no good except on the road. Unless we know that there is going to be an expansion of the roads of this country and an expansion to take care of the saturation which we are rapidly approaching on our present highway system, it is very difficult for us to plan over the next ten years as to what our expansion is going to have to be." [13]

A 1961 study entitled *Future Highways and Urban Growth*, commissioned by the AMA and undertaken by Wilbur Smith and Associates, a New Haven consulting firm, made clear why urban freeways were essential to the expansion of the automobile industry. Seventy-one percent of the American population already lived in major metropolitan areas in 1960, and it was projected that 78 percent would by 1980. Growth in urban areas was strongest in the suburbs, while the percentage of population living in central cities had remained relatively constant. Clearly, it was the urban market that was expanding. And it was in cities that automobile ownership and use were lowest.

"Los Angeles had become the auto industry's prime example of what a city could become," St. Clair observes. "As a result of freeways and the decline of public transit ridership, Los Angeles clearly stood out as an exception to the usual pattern of urban auto ownership." Los Angeles in 1949 had one car for every family, or for every 2.5 people. In contrast, Chicago had one car for every 1.5 families or 5.1 people, New York City one car for every 2.5 families or 8.7 people. St. Clair assumes that "the Los Angeles ratios were indicative of the potential market across the country." He estimates that if the Los Angeles ratios had been approximated in the 95 largest population counties in the United States, 8,198,256 additional vehicles would have been owned on the person-per-car ratio or 5,002,881 additional vehicles on the family-per-car ratio over actual 1949 registrations of 13,161,275 automobiles.[14]

As Nance testified, urban freeways were essential to the realization of these possibilities. Freeways would help disperse the population into outlying areas not served by public transit. "Density and income being equal, fewer cars are owned and used by persons living near the central city than those in outlying areas," Wilbur Smith's study observed. "Quality of public transportation is a factor since areas with efficient and frequent public transit often have lower car ownership and use than areas with poor transit service. High-density areas are often in proximity to employment and commercial outlets, thereby minimizing the need for private transportation." Furthermore, Smith found, "freeway users travel almost three times as far as other urban drivers." He anticipated that "by 1980, up to 16 percent more vehicle miles of travel will result from the use of urban freeways than if there were no freeway systems."[15] This increased use combined with increased ownership would have an exponential impact on replacement demand for cars as well as on sales of gasoline, lubricants, tires, and parts.

Although toll express highways were operating profitably in the urbanized East, James Cope, the vice-president of Chrysler, explained in 1953 testimony to Congress on behalf of the AMA that "no method has ever been devised to adapt the toll principle to urban highway needs."[16] Relatively long driving stretches between toll collections were necessary if roads were truly to be express highways. Keeping toll collection to a minimum in turn required much more limited access than freeways allowed. Consequently, toll roads generated only about 30 percent new traffic, as opposed to 60 percent for the tax-supported "free" express highways that the auto makers lobbied for and obtained in 1956.

As downtown traffic congestion grew into a problem during the

1920s, improving city streets to accommodate increasing automobile traffic had become an important goal of automobile interests. Yet, as Foster points out, "while the automobile industry consciously and aggressively created urban markets, it made no particular effort ... to promote the car as a commuting tool for urban workers." Indeed, it was widely assumed, particularly in electric traction publications, "that the automobile alone could never provide sufficient transportation for all family members in a modern city" and that "most urban trips would continue to involve mass transit." Moreover, the increased use of the motorcar in urban transit was promoted by several special-interest groups other than the automobile manufacturers—chambers of commerce anxious to boost tourism, realtors who "perceived the automobile as creating more investment and sales opportunities," highway engineers, and landscape architects who gained contracts and commissions from better access to public parks. These groups could count on a broad base of popular support. Bond issues to improve city streets were approved by voters with monotonous regularity.[17]

Nevertheless, there was virtually no interest in urban freeways outside Southern California, where construction of them only began in earnest after World War II. The first publicly financed limited-access highway, as well as the first urban freeway, was New York City's Bronx River Parkway, completed in 1923. Following this, city planner Robert Moses began to link parts of the New York City park system together with automobile parkways. As late as 1941, however, as Mark H. Rose reports, highway planning for the postwar years was considered vital by American leaders primarily because "road construction, if done expeditiously and located properly, would open up jobs. Beginning around 1942, a few Americans focused on more grandiose projects."[18]

The Southern California freeway system was first proposed in the 1937 Traffic Survey of the Automobile Club of Southern California and was made possible by state legislation passed in 1939. Of the entire California freeway system, only six miles of the Arroyo Seco Parkway (now the Pasadena Freeway) were finished by the outbreak of World War II, and postwar progress in completing the system was much slower than is now generally recognized. For example, the San Diego Freeway was not extended over the Santa Monica mountains into the San Fernando Valley until 1962, and the western end of the Santa Monica Freeway was not completed until 1964.

The postwar highway lobby formed in the 1930s. In 1937 the AMA organized its safety division into an "independent" Automobile Safety Foundation (ASF), which, as St. Clair reports, "never really supported vehicle safety legislation at either the state or federal level" but "never missed an opportunity to promote highways." From 1939 on, it was "one of the automobile industry's most active lobbying organizations, testifying at Congressional hearings far more often than the AMA."[19]

To prevent the diversion of gasoline taxes to other purposes during the Great Depression, Alfred Sloan conceived the National Highway Users Conference (NHUC) in 1932. He remained its chairman until 1948, when he was succeeded in that role, as later in the position of chairman of General Motors, by Albert Bradley. From 1946 until passage of the 1956 Interstate Highway Act, the NHUC coordinated the lobbying activities of highway transportation interests. It boasted some three thousand member groups but was dominated by GM. In 1951 the NHUC launched Project Adequate Roads to publicize the need for an interstate highway system. The NHUC merged with the ASF in 1969 to form the Highway Users Foundation for Safety and Mobility (HUFSAM).

Additionally, an informal group of highway transportation interests that Helen Leavitt dubs "the Road Gang" began meeting Tuesdays for lunch and holding round-table discussions on postwar highway legislation in 1942. The group had some 240 members, including representatives of the automobile manufacturers and dealers, automobile clubs, oil companies, truckers and the Teamsters Union, highway engineers, and state highway administrators. The Road Gang was secretive about its activities, so little is known about the group.

Even though about 80 percent of war materials in World War II had been moved by rail, the alleged strategic need for an interstate system for national defense became the main argument of the highway lobby. In 1956 the official name of the system became the National System of Interstate and Defense Highways. National defense was the major justification for increasing the federal share of funding from the 60–40 ratio in the 1944 Federal Aid Highway Act to 90–10 in the 1956 Interstate Highway Act and for permitting federal funds from general tax revenues as well as special user taxes to be used for building the system. St. Clair and Leavitt both demonstrate convincingly that, contrary to the contention of the Road Gang, the Interstate System was never essential to national defense.

St. Clair also calls attention to the circular reasoning of the arguments made by the automobile industry that urban freeways were essential to the accommodation of future automobile traffic. His point here is that while the industry's projected increases in urban travel provided its rationale for urging that urban freeways be part of the Interstate System, the projected increases assumed the completion of the urban freeways being argued for. And Leavitt makes a particularly strong case against the claim that the urban freeways were needed to alleviate traffic congestion.

Even the Road Gang was divided over whether urban freeways should be part of the Interstate System. Long-distance truckers were interested only in a system of interconnected, through highways and opposed diversion of funds either to rural secondary routes or to urban freeways. Conversely, the automobile industry considered urban freeways central to the proposed Interstate System. A smaller point of disagreement was the extent to which urban freeways should be conceived in the context of urban planning and urban reform. "Since federal and state road engineers controlled the program, they had few incentives to include urban renewal, social regeneration, and broader transportation objectives in their programming," Rose reports. "Their task, as they saw it, was one of promoting traffic efficiency by constructing roads.... Basically, then, traffic patterns of motorists and truckers and decisions of engineers determined the outlines of Interstate construction." The more significant differences among highway interests were reconciled "after they lost legislation in Congress [in 1955] because of differences over the details of finance. By 1956, the press for more roads and a bill which asked few sacrifices, especially from major truck operators, dissolved these differences." In brief, true to the American pragmatic tradition of pork-barrel politics, everyone got the roads they wanted once the problem of funding had been resolved by providing to pay for the system out of a nondivertible Highway Trust Fund collected from special user taxes. "The 1956 Highway Act, which authorized stepped-up construction of the national expressway system and hearty and regular increases in aid for building urban, primary, and farm-to-market roads, emerged from this social and political milieu," Rose concludes. "It was a highway building program pure and simple, one which federalized state and local road building practices and ideals." What the highway interests "managed to secure, then, was federal funding for localistic and largely impermeable commercial and professional subcultures." [20]

Passage of the 1956 Interstate Highway Act ensured the complete triumph of the automobile over mass-transit alternatives in the United States and killed off, except in a few large cities, the vestiges of balanced public transportation systems that remained in 1950s America. Because they were not conceived as parts of broader metropolitan area plans, the urban freeways constructed as a major part of the Interstate System bisected and destroyed a number of cohesive urban neighborhoods and some city parks, at great social cost and public expense.

The lion's share of funding for the Interstate System came from special use taxes on cars, gasoline, tires, lubricants, and parts paid into the Highway Trust Fund, which could be used only for highway expenditures until August 13, 1973. On that date President Richard M. Nixon signed a compromise $22.9-billion highway aid bill providing for the first diversion of the fund to urban mass transit and extending the timetable for completion of the Interstate System to June 30, 1979. By the time the sacrosanct Highway Trust Fund was broken, 82 percent of the Interstate System was completed, and another 16 percent was under construction. With the nation facing an imminent fuel shortage and a long-term energy crisis, President Nixon called for decreased automobile use and imposed a national 55-mph speed limit over the system's 80-mph express highways.

United States Highway Administration data for 1977 reveal that transportation by private passenger car accounted for some 83 percent of all trips made in the United States, versus only 2 percent by bus and streetcar, 0.3 percent by subway and elevated rail transportation, and 0.5 percent by "other" public transportation, including trains, airplanes, and taxis. For domestic automobiles in 1981, principal use was 44.7 percent to and from work, 31.7 percent local transportation, 15.2 percent pleasure trips, 9.6 percent business use, and 1.7 percent travel to school.

American versus European Highway Policy

Viable cost-efficient rail transportation, including the Paris Métro in France and urban mass transit in Germany, persists in Europe despite relatively high levels of automobile ownership and use. And in Japan, world leadership in automobile production and an automobile culture coexist with excellent mass transit, exemplified by the bullet trains, which are also subsidized. These facts unequivocally demonstrate that mature automobile cultures are compatible with excellent mass-transit systems. Why then did the automobile revolution end up virtually wiping out urban mass transit and rail passenger service in the United States?

A comparative analysis of European and American transportation policies by James A. Dunn, Jr., suggests some answers. He contrasts the European policy paradigm of centralized, authoritative planning with the American paradigm of relying on the invisible hand of the market. Rail transportation in France and urban mass transit in West Germany historically have been viewed not as commodities exchanged for profit in a competitive marketplace but as social services to be provided by government on the basis of rational planning. This has meant that the development of highway transportation in Europe has been coordinated by the state to be complementary to rather than competitive with the railroads and with urban mass transit. Rail and urban mass transit are subsidized from very high gasoline taxes that additionally tend to curb automobile use. And highway systems are not extended or improved beyond points compatible with railroad networks. Europeans have been especially reluctant to build urban freeways.

Dunn's comparison of highway policy in Great Britain and in the United States is particularly instructive. Unlike the purchase of automobiles by individuals, which falls within the American conception of transportation choice being determined in the marketplace, providing the infrastructure of highways and streets essential for automobile use requires centralized planning here as well as in Europe and emanates from political decisions and the political process, not the market. What needs to be accounted for is why, unlike European governments, the federal, state, and local governments in the United States have consistently provided massive funds for building the world's best highway infrastructure, to the virtual exclusion of aid for the rail infrastructure. The answer lies in the historic nondivertibility of highway revenues collected from gasoline and other special user taxes.

Paradoxically, the principle of nondivertibility was innovated not in the United States but in Great Britain, when a bargain was struck between the government and upper-class motorists in debate over the 1909 Development and Road Improvement Funds Bill. The bill provided for a 3-pence-per-gallon tax on imported gasoline and a graduated horsepower tax, to be administered by a central board and spent on roads. Chancellor of the Exchequer Lloyd George explained to Parliament that the motorists were "willing and even anxious to subscribe to such a purpose, so long as a guarantee is given in the method and control of expenditure that the funds so raised will ... be devoted exclusively to the improvement of roads." As Dunn observes, however, "there was a crucial difference between this British style of earmarking and the subsequent American methods. The promise to spend motor vehicle and motor fuel tax revenues only on roads was made in Parliament and was thus on the public record, but it was not written into the law! ... [N]owhere in the law was it stipulated that the Road Board had to spend all the funds it received. Nor did it specifically prohibit the government from withdrawing all or some of the unspent road funds and using them for other purposes." [21]

The gentlemen's agreement between Parliament and British motorists was broken in 1926 by Chancellor of the Exchequer Winston Churchill, who called the idea of a nondivertible road fund "nonsense," "absurd," and "an outrage upon the sovereignty of Parliament and upon common sense." Beginning in 1926, Churchill used the accumulated surplus from the Road Fund to meet general obligations, and he introduced new taxation policies whereby the entire gasoline tax and a third of the horsepower tax on cars were to be paid each year directly into the treasury instead of into the Road Fund. In Dunn's words, "This left the fund with a much narrower revenue base and the precedent that unspent balances could be taken by the treasury at any time."

As a result of these policies, the percent of highway revenues expended on highways in Great Britain declined from a low 60.3 percent in 1950 to only 34 percent in 1970, versus the 100-percent expenditure of nondivertible highway revenues on highways in the United States. Consequently, by 1973, when the Nixon administration ended nondivertibility of the Highway Trust Fund, Great Britain had 70.5 motor vehicles per mile of road and a viable mass-transit system, versus 30.7 motor vehicles per mile of road and public transit in ruins in the United States.

"Most contemporary critics of highway policy have focused their attention on the federal government's Highway Trust Fund," Dunn points out. "But one should remember that the state funds collect and earmark twice as much money as the federal fund. In 1972, for example, the states collected $11.2 billion in highway-user taxes, while the federal government collected slightly less than $5.4 billion." As we have seen, gasoline taxes, collected in all states by 1929, had become the main source of revenue for highway expenditures in the United States. "Coalitions of state automobile clubs, taxpayers' associations, and road user groups, aided by their national affiliates and groups sponsored by the auto industry itself, worked to promote ironclad earmarking," Dunn writes; "their favorite device was to insert an amendment into the state constitution." Minnesota became the first state to adopt an earmarking amendment in 1920, and by 1962 sixteen states had done so. "In states where an amendment was not possible, earmarking schemes based on normal legislation were introduced. In 1974 forty-six of the fifty states had specially earmarked highway trust funds."

Earmarking not only came late—well after a mature automobile culture had developed in the United States—but cannot be considered a manifestation of some unique American affection for the road and the car. Both at the state level beginning in the 1920s and at the federal level after 1934 and especially in the 1950s, the nondivertibility of highway revenues was achieved by the lobbying efforts of special-interest groups of highway users, especially the automobile industry and the automobile clubs, at a time when almost half of American families did not own automobiles and were therefore dependent on some form of public transportation. Thus, the irrational proliferation of the American automobile culture during the period 1956–1973, and the concurrent destruction of alternative transportation systems, cannot be explained away as the choice of consumers expressed in a free market, as the inevitable result of the superiority of the road and the private passenger car over other modes of transit, or as the ultimate consequence of a mystic and mythical American love affair with the automobile.

Decline and Resurgence

20

"When the history of the automobile is written, scholars will necessarily focus careful attention on the crucial period of the late sixties and the early seventies," John Jerome predicted in 1972. "During that period the largest industry the world had ever known ... peaked out. The automobile industry began to die." Jerome considered the railroads to have been "the ultimate example of a throwaway economy." However, he thought that "automobiles have a shorter past and a shorter future. It is unlikely that public control of corporate excess will become powerful enough to kill the automobile so long as there is any profitability to be wrung from it. But as our technology becomes more sophisticated, so does our cost accounting, and new costs—social ones—are being fed into a ledger at a much faster rate than new areas of automotive profitability can be discovered." His conclusion was, "The automobile must go." [1]

Jerome's book was one of the more important in the "death of the automobile" literature that enjoyed a brief vogue in the early 1970s. Other noteworthy titles were Helen Leavitt's 1970 *Superhighway—Super-Hoax*, Kenneth Schneider's 1971 *Autokind vs. Mankind*, Ronald Buel's 1972 *Dead End*, and Emma Rothschild's 1973 *Paradise Lost*. Up to this point, as we have seen, the complaints against the American automobile culture appearing between hard covers had been overwhelmingly consumer-oriented and directed against the automobile industry rather than the road and the car in themselves. John Keats's *The Insolent Chariots*, the most notable and outspoken, was a biting satire on Detroit's styling excesses and shoddy marketing practices. Ralph Nader's 1965 *Unsafe at Any Speed*, the most influential, was a narrowly based attack on the automobile industry that did not question the benefits of mass personal automobility per se. The critics of the early 1970s, in contrast, saw the ending of what Rothschild called "the auto-industrial age," especially in urban transit, as both inevitable and desirable.

The 1973 and 1979 oil shocks capped the critics' concerns about automotive safety, atmospheric pollution, traffic congestion, urban sprawl, and devastation of the natural environment. Oil dependence and escalating fuel prices seemed to represent a far greater threat to the future of mass personal automobility than its alleged social costs. To make matters worse, the automobile industry was widely conceived as stagnant in both its product and production technologies. Making cars more fuel efficient, like making them safer and less polluting a decade earlier, had to be forced on the automobile industry by federal legislation. And in explaining why federal standards could not be met, the auto makers projected an image of defensiveness and helplessness.

Increasing Japanese penetration of our domestic and world markets by the end of the 1970s also called into question the continuing economic viability of our "leading sector" industry. Would the world's foremost automobile culture soon be dependent not only on OPEC for oil but also on the Japanese for motorcars? With the shift overseas of motor vehicle and related industry jobs—17 percent of all American jobs in 1981— where would the economic base be to support our current level of automobile ownership and use?

Resuscitating Mass Transit

By the late 1970s mass transit had been transformed from an essentially private business expected to make a profit into a publicly owned and subsidized social responsibility. Mass transit ridership plummeted from 13.8 million in 1950 to 7.5 million in 1960 and to 5.9 million in 1970. As private transit companies went broke, leaving many small and medium-sized cities with no alternative to the automobile, government became involved. The publicly owned metropolitan transit districts that replaced the private companies integrated mass transit into more comprehensive urban planning and developed a broad base of political support. Indeed, mass transit came to be considered a panacea for urban problems much as the automobile had been considered one at the turn of the century. The new involvement of the federal government was particularly notable.

The first legislation providing for federal aid for urban mass transit was the Housing Act of 1961, which authorized $42.5 million in loans and grants to urban mass-transit companies and commuter railroads. The Urban Mass Transportation Act of 1964 provided $50.7 million for capital grants on a two-thirds federal funding basis for metropolitan areas with comprehensive transit plans. Then in 1968 the Urban Mass Transit Authority (UMTA) was created in the Department of Transportation to oversee experiments to improve urban mass transit in the United States. Funding remained minuscule until the mid-1970s, however. In 1965 only $51 million in federal capital grants was approved for urban mass transit, versus $4.105 billion spent for highway construction; in 1970 only $133 million was approved for mass transit, versus $4.678 billion for highway construction. In contrast, federal capital grants for mass transit totaled $1.430 billion in 1975, while highway construction expenditures increased only slightly to $4.821 billion. In 1974 federal legislation first provided for assistance in offsetting operating deficits. Gordon J. Fielding assesses the magnitude of the change in federal involvement: "Prior to 1961 there had been no federal role in transit assistance, and even as late as 1970, the federal contribution was overwhelmed by state, regional, and local contributions. By 1978, however, the federal government actually funded a greater percentage of the total operating and capital subsidy in the United States than all other government levels combined." [2]

The recognition that there were limits to energy resources, which sank into the minds of policymakers in the 1970s, made rehabilitating mass transit seem critical. By the time of the first diversion of the Highway Trust Fund to urban mass transit in 1973, the American Automobile Association remained the only important holdout against diversion. Even the Motor Vehicle Manufacturers Association had dropped its opposition. Ford and GM both formed mass-transit divisions, and there was speculation for a time that they might diversify into "total transportation" companies by the turn of the century—companies whose main business would be selling modular transportation systems to municipal governments.

In contrast with the narrow concentration of the federal government on highway transportation up to 1973, by the early 1980s there was strong federal and local commitment to building balanced transportation systems. Total federal expenditures on ground transportation from 1980 through 1984 show $14.932 billion spent on urban mass transit and an additional $8.198 billion on railroads (Amtrak), versus $36.541 billion on highway construction.

The most significant diversion of highway revenues to urban mass transit has come as a result of the Surface Transportation Act of 1982, as implemented by the Highway Revenue Act of the same year. President Ronald Reagan's November 1982 message to Congress on the draft bill made clear the administration's intention to treat urban mass transit and highway transportation as interdependent rather than competitive. The main goal of the legislation was to rehabilitate our eroding highway system. Nevertheless, one cent of the five-cent-per-gallon gasoline surtax imposed by the legislation was earmarked for urban mass transit; and the federal government committed itself to paying up to 80 percent of the capital costs for building or refurbishing urban rapid rail systems. The legislation also provided for subsidization of up to 50 percent of their operating deficits, even though the administration in 1981 had announced its intention to end all operating assistance by 1985. Metropolitan governments responded to the federal initiative with ambitious construction programs. As of the end of 1984, sixteen cities planned to extend existing rapid rail systems a total of 167.5 miles at an estimated cost of $12.325 billion, while ten more cities planned to build new rapid rail systems totaling 297.6 miles at an estimated cost of $11.106 billion.

The most impressive rapid rail system under construction is the Metro in Washington, D.C., intended by President Lyndon B. Johnson to be a national showcase and an example for other cities to emulate. Construction money for the Metro was appropriated under special legislation so that the system would not have to compete for funds. Capital costs for the planned 101-mile rail network have mushroomed from an initial estimate of $2.5 billion to a current estimate of $12 billion, and the targeted 1979 completion date will be exceeded by at least fourteen years. The Metro currently carries about 350,000 riders on weekdays, a load 10 percent less than projections, and ran an operating deficit of $190 million in 1984. On the credit side, however, in an article highly critical of urban rapid rail transit, *Business Week* reports that "in some ways Metro really is a model for the country. It is clean, fast, and surprisingly free of crime ... it is even a tourist attraction." [3]

Less spectacular but probably more important is the effort by many metropolitan transit districts to upgrade their bus fleets by buying modern buses and extending service. The number of motor buses in public transit service, excluding sightseeing and school buses, increased from an estimated 49,600 in 1960 to 62,114 in 1982, while the number of electric railway cars decreased slightly from 11,866 to 10,926 over the same period. Miles of bus route doubled from 56,696 in 1960 to 122,169 in 1980. A few cities have even developed plans for special accommodation to buses.

Should these trends continue and existing plans materialize, the balanced transportation systems that critics of the road and the car advocated in the early 1970s will have become a reality in American cities by the turn of the century. At present, however, there is doubt whether this will occur and whether, even if it does, mass transit will meet the high expectations of its proponents. "American transit has reached a crossroads," Fielding observes. "More than a decade of public investment in transit has not changed the propensity of Americans to commute by automobile....

Also, transit's ability to solve energy, environmental and social ills has come under serious question. And there is growing recognition that the fiscal appetite of transit is both voracious and out of control." [4]

So far, improved public transit has proved unable to recapture riders from the private passenger car. Between 1970 and 1982 only slight increases in vehicle miles operated were registered—from 1.409 billion to 1.669 billion for buses and from 448 million to 450 million for electric railways. Over the same period, the number of paying passengers carried by buses also increased slightly, from 4.058 billion to 4.417 billion, but that number declined from 1.746 billion to 1.528 billion for electric railways. During the 1970s there was actually a decline nationwide of 10.6 percent in the use of public transit for metropolitan-area work trips.

Ridership has failed to materialize despite improved service and despite fares that are kept low. Since 1979 operating assistance for transit from federal, state, and local governments has been greater than operating revenues—$4.587 billion versus $3.152 billion in 1982. Since 1978 transit expenses have been greater than all revenues and operating assistance combined—$8.324 billion versus $8.044 billion in 1982. "As a result of the subsidies that they accepted, transit managers lost the incentive to operate their systems efficiently," Fielding reports. "Transit's success was now being measured in terms of fare stabilization, ridership gains, service expansion, and compliance with a host of special requirements governing labor practices, vehicle procurements, and service to the elderly and handicapped. This combination proved financially devastating."

The most significant obstacle to lowering transit operating expenses has been Section 13(c) of the 1964 Urban Mass Transportation Act. This was the price for labor support essential to passage of the legislation. Section 13(c) provided that the terms and conditions of employment of transit workers would not worsen with the transfer of transit systems from private to public ownership. The transit unions have used Section 13(c), in Fielding's words, "to obstruct changes in work rules and capital investments which would have increased labor efficiency." As a consequence, by far the greatest beneficiaries of government subsidization of transit have been the 197,000 transit employees. In 1982 the transit payroll amounted to $3.736 billion—some $648 million more than operating revenues. Clearly, for transit to succeed on a cost-efficiency basis, substantial automation of service combined with massive reduction and rationalization of the work force is essential.

Actually, nowhere in the world does urban rapid rail transit pay its own way except in densely populated Hong Kong, which suffers from perhaps the worst traffic congestion in the world at a ratio of only one motor vehicle for every 27 persons. Outside the United States transit is considered an essential public service and as such is not expected to pay its own way. Accordingly, the most important standard for evaluating transit in Europe is the quality of service, not its cost effectiveness. Although the opposite historically has been true in the United States, by the early 1980s "American transit had been given unrealistic social and political objectives, incompatible with operating and financial efficiency." This leads Fielding to conclude, "it is still not clear whether transit should be evaluated as an essential public service, with due consideration of the inherent costs of government intervention; or as a business, with cost-effectiveness and self-sufficiency the prime objectives. And there is growing concern, given the unique character of the industry, that the latter objective may not be economically feasible." [5]

Regulating the Automobile

As the automobile came to be perceived as a social problem, federal standards were adopted in the United States concerning automotive safety (1966), emission of pollutants (1965 and 1970), and energy consumption (1975). Up to 1975 there were 273 changes in federal standards and regulations pertaining to automobiles and light trucks. Since 1975 a major difficulty for the automobile manufacturers has been achieving the Corporate Average Fuel Economy (CAFE) level of 27.5 miles per gallon mandated by the 1975 Energy Policy and Conservation Act while meeting the stringent antiemission standards of the 1970 Clean Air Act.

Fulfilling federal safety, emissions, and energy requirements has all but ended the annual cosmetic model change, put a new emphasis on functional design, and stimulated innovation in automotive technology. Retail price increases to cover the cost of meeting federal standards since 1968, adjusted to 1983 dollars, amounted to $1,699.20 of the average $10,481 retail price of an American-made passenger car by the 1984 model year—$475.92 for safety equipment and $1,223.28 for emission controls and changes to improve fuel economy.

Safety

As measured by traffic fatality rates per 100 million miles traveled, the United States has the best traffic safety record in the world, and that record has improved progressively over time. In 1981, for example, traffic fatalities per 100 million motor vehicle miles were only 3.1 in the United States, versus 3.4 in Finland, 3.5 in the U.K., 4.3 in Canada and Denmark, 4.7 in Japan, 4.9 in Austria, 5.1 in the Netherlands, 6.1 in Italy, 6.3 in

Germany, 7.1 in France, 7.9 in Belgium, and 11.4 in Spain. In these countries as well as in the United States, traffic fatalities have declined as the driving population has become more experienced, but especially as roads have been improved. The crucial role of limited-access, express highways in reducing traffic deaths is demonstrated by the traffic fatality rate of 1.28 for Interstate highways in the United States in 1982, versus 3.12 for highways not in the Interstate System.

The U.S. rate of traffic fatalities per 100 million miles of motor vehicle travel declined from an average of 18.20 during 1923–1927 to 10.52 during 1943–1947; with further improvement of highways, especially under the Interstate Highway Act of 1956, it fell to only 5.53 in 1966, when safety standards for 1968 model-year cars were mandated by passage of the National Traffic and Motor Vehicle Safety Law. By 1972 the traffic fatality rate had been further reduced to 4.28, even though almost half of the U.S. motor vehicle population antedated the 1968 model year and despite the failure of most drivers to use the seat belts required as equipment by law—a failure to which were attributed 10,000 of that year's 56,278 traffic deaths.

The lowering of speed limits in several states in 1973 as a fuel conservation measure was followed by the imposition of a 55-mph national speed limit on January 1, 1974. In addition to fuel savings, a dramatic drop in the traffic fatality rate to 3.33 in 1974 was attributed to lower highway speeds. Virtual completion of the Interstate System, the 55-mile-per-hour speed limit, and the incorporation of federal safety standards into the motor vehicle population further combined to reduce the traffic fatality rate in 1983 to a low of 2.73 and the total number of traffic deaths to 44,300.

Despite the decline in the traffic death rate, there was good reason for concern about automotive safety in the mid-1960s. In absolute numbers, traffic fatalities had risen sharply from 34,763 in 1950 to 39,628 in 1956, had dipped to 38,070 in 1960, and then had accelerated to 53,041 in 1966 and peaked, as noted, at 56,278 in 1972. How could one explain this rising carnage? Highways were being greatly improved after passage of the Interstate Highway Act of 1956, at the very time that the ratio of traffic fatalities per capita was dramatically increasing. A major reason undoubtedly was the phenomenal increase of inexperienced drivers on American roads, as family ownership of cars grew from 59 percent in 1950 to 83 percent in 1970. But a more compelling explanation at the time was that far more powerful, far less maneuverable cars, designed for looks rather than the protection of occupants in a collision, were traveling at faster speeds on our express highways. The result was that concern over automotive safety shifted its focus from road conditions and driving skills to the designed-in dangers of the car itself.

In 1964 Congress set safety standards for motor vehicles purchased by the General Services Administration (GSA) for the federal government. By late 1965 several government groups and individual officials in addition to Senator Abraham Ribicoff's Subcommittee on Executive Reorganization were concerned with the issue of automotive safety. The most important were the staff of Senator Gaylord Nelson; the Senate Commerce Committee, chaired by Senator Warren Magnuson; and Joseph Califano, a special assistant to President Lyndon Johnson in charge of working up a 1966 legislative program that included a traffic safety bill. That an administration-backed bill would become law was guaranteed by the poor performance of automobile industry executives before congressional committees and by a scandalous case of personal harassment of Ralph Nader by GM, for which GM president James Roche apologized before the Ribicoff Committee and a national television audience. Nader brought a civil suit against GM for invasion of privacy, which the corporation settled out of court for $425,000.

The National Traffic and Motor Vehicle Safety Act of 1966 established an agency under the secretary of commerce whose function was to set safety standards for new cars beginning with the 1968 model year. This agency became the National Highway Traffic Safety Administration (NHTSA) in the Department of Transportation. The seventeen standards issued by the GSA for 1967 model cars purchased by the government were the first ones adopted. These standards included seat belts, padded visors and padded dashboards with recessed control knobs, safety door latches and hinges, impact-absorbing steering columns, dual braking systems, standard bumper heights, and glare-reduction surfaces. Twenty-eight standards had been adopted by the 1969 model year. The act also attempted to goad automobile manufacturers into eliminating defects from their cars by requiring public announcements of recalls. This resulted in the recall of 30.6 million motor vehicles by mid-1972. To induce state governments to institute periodic safety inspections of all motor vehicles registered, in 1973 NHTSA set standards giving states the choice of periodically inspecting brakes, steering, suspension, and tires or losing 10 percent of their federal highway funding. It had been determined that wear of these components caused 6 percent and contributed to an additional 11 percent of all motor vehicle accidents.

The major problem in implementing NHTSA safety standards remains the refusal of Americans to buckle up their seat belts. Despite the well-documented and well-publicized knowledge that they reduce serious and fatal injuries in accidents by about half, seat belts are used by only about 15 percent of Americans, compared with 85 percent of West Germans and 90 percent of Swedes. Laws have been enacted in almost all states and the

District of Columbia requiring the use of child-restraint devices. Until very recently, however, states have been reluctant to require adult seat belt use. In this the United States stands in marked contrast to the rest of the world. Seat belt use is required by law in 33 countries, including all of Western Europe, Canada, Japan, Australia, New Zealand, Israel, South Africa, Brazil, the U.S.S.R., and several other Eastern bloc countries.

Rather than working for federal legislation requiring Americans to buckle up, NHTSA first tried mandating that cars be equipped with ignition interlock systems that prevented them from being started unless seat belts were fastened. The public outcry was so great that the ignition interlock ruling was repealed by Congress in 1976. The market for the ignition interlocks that NHTSA had forced the auto makers to develop collapsed in one year from 11 million units to zero.

As early as 1969, NHTSA had given notice of its intention to require that cars be equipped with "inflatable occupant restraint systems," otherwise known as air bags, which would inflate automatically upon frontal impact to protect the driver and front-seat passenger. A controversy ensued that is still not resolved. In 1984 NHTSA issued a ruling requiring that all new passenger cars sold in the United States be equipped with "passive restraints" by the 1990 model year. Passive restraints may include air bags, seat belt systems automatically activated by entering the vehicle, and/or energy-absorbing interiors and laceration-resistant windshields. They must protect the driver and front-seat passenger in a 30-mph crash into a stationary barrier. Passive restraints are to be phased in with 10 percent of 1987 models, 25 percent of 1988 models, and 40 percent of 1989 models. The kicker in the NHTSA ruling is that the passive restraint requirements will be rescinded if states representing two thirds of the U.S. population enact by April 1, 1989, laws mandating seat belt use that will become effective by September 1, 1989. Such laws had been enacted by a number of states by mid-1985, and NHTSA mounted a seat belt use awareness program.

Air bags give less protection than seat belts, because they only protect in frontal collisions. They are useless in side impacts, rear enders, and rollovers. So seat belts still must be worn for adequate protection. Air bags are expensive. GM estimates that, with no profit to itself, full front-seat air bags would cost $1,100 per unit at production of 250,000 units per year, or $850 at 3 million per year, versus only $45 for front seat belts. GM has led in air bag technology, with dismal results. In 1974 the company invested $80 million in an air bag program to produce 300,000 units offered as options on 1974–1976 Cadillacs, Buicks, and Oldsmobiles. Even though the bags were priced below cost at $300, they ended up costing GM $8,000 each, because only 10,000 were ordered by consumers.

As cars have become safer, concern about automotive safety has reverted to the driver, particularly to the drinking driver. In the mid-1970s it was estimated that alcohol abuse was involved in about half of all our highway fatalities, and the Department of Transportation estimates that in the ensuing decade 250,000 Americans have been killed and 700,000 injured in alcohol-related automobile accidents. Tougher state and local laws and more vigorous law enforcement against drinking and driving have become increasingly evident across the nation. In December 1983 a presidential commission on drunk driving recommended stiffer penalties for drunk drivers, making alchohol consumption in automobiles illegal, and the adoption of a nationwide minimum drinking age of 21 because of the close correlation between the minimum drinking age and the frequency of alcohol-related accidents.

Federal legislation passed in 1987 gave the states the right to increase the speed limit to 65 mph on portions of rural express highways. The impact on traffic safety remains to be seen.

Emissions

Recognition that cars were a major source of air pollution came in the 1950s in smog-ridden Southern California. As with automotive safety, the automobile industry did little toward solving the problem until forced by government. Although a joint committee to study the role of the automobile in causing atmospheric pollution was formed by the Automobile Manufacturers Association in 1953 and a cross-licensing agreement covering pollution control devices was signed in 1954, manufacturers were reluctant to add devices that would raise costs without adding sales appeal. "The compiled correspondence between Kenneth Hahn, Los Angeles County Supervisor, and the auto companies from 1953–1967 on the subject of automotive air pollution seems to be an accurate reflection of the companies' attitudes," notes Lawrence White. "While assuring Hahn of their sincerest interest in the subject, they tended to take refuge behind the AMA committee and behind the issuance of technical papers; more information was needed, they said, more research required. And, besides, better maintenance of vehicles would probably solve most of the problems." [6]

In 1966, of an estimated 146 million tons of pollutants discharged into the atmosphere in the United States, 86 million tons were attributed to motor vehicle traffic. For every 10,000 miles traveled, the average car without pollution controls discharged into the atmosphere 1,700 pounds of carbon monoxide, 520 pounds of hydrocarbons, and 90 pounds of nitrogen oxides. Motor vehicles were the major source of these pollutants and of lead compounds. While both the level of pollutants and the proportion attributable to motor vehicles varied from place to place and over time, from 60 to 80 percent of atmospheric pollution generally was attributed to motor vehicles, with a figure of 97.5 percent reported for Orange County, California, in 1973.

California framed the first legislation to reduce motor vehicle emissions. Positive crankcase ventilation (PCV) systems to reduce hydrocarbon discharge were required on all cars sold in California beginning with the 1963 model year. Exhaust control devices to reduce emissions of carbon monoxide, oxide of nitrogen, and lead compounds became mandatory in California beginning with the 1966 model year. The automobile manufacturers balked at installing nationally the devices required by law in California. But public pressure to do so became irresistible once it was seen from California's experience that the basic technological problems had been solved.

The Motor Vehicle Air Pollution and Control Act of 1965 resulted in national standards comparable to California's for the 1968 model year. These standards allowed an average of no more than 275 parts per million hydrocarbon emissions and 1.5 percent carbon monoxide emissions. By the 1970 model year the standards had been raised to permit no more than 180 parts per million of hydrocarbons and 1.0 percent carbon monoxide emissions. Controls to eliminate pollutants from gasoline evaporation also were required nationwide by 1971.

The passage in 1970 of Senator Edmund Muskie's amendments to the Federal Clean Air Act brought a further reduction of about 90 percent in emissions—in grams per vehicle mile, to 0.41 carbon monoxide and 3.4 hydrocarbons by 1975, and to only 0.40 nitrogen oxide by 1976 (versus actual 1970 emsissions, in grams per vehicle mile, of 46 carbon monoxide, 4.7 hydrocarbons, and 6.0 nitrogen oxide). In 1973 the Environmental Protection Agency (EPA), charged with enforcing the Clean Air Act, bowed to industry pressure—automobile manufacturers insisted that the 1975–1976 standards could not be met—and granted the manufacturers a two-year extension. Industry critics noted that the 1975–1976 standards already had been met by three imports—the rotary-engine Mazda, the CVCC-powered Honda, and the diesel-powered Mercedes-Benz.

Rather than risk large amounts of capital on developing new engine technologies, Detroit pursued the conservative path of proliferating the desmogging devices on already overly complicated conventional engines. By the early 1970s desmogged conventional engines got 10 to 15 percent less gas mileage than earlier uncontrolled engines, were more difficult and expensive to maintain, and had unsafe tendencies to surge from idle, stall, and "diesel" (keep running after the ignition key was turned off). And despite the performance-impairing devices, EPA tests in early 1973 demonstrated that the vast majority of cars built between 1968 and 1971 failed to meet existing antipollution standards.

The main way American auto makers met the 1977 federal emission standards with conventional engines was to install the catalytic converter, to be used with unleaded fuels. Catalytic converters were required on all 1975 model cars sold in California, and in that model year GM installed them on all its cars nationwide, Chrysler on 75 percent of its cars, and Ford on 70 percent of its cars. The catalytic converter had been perfected by GM. It became the only short-run option for meeting government standards, even though the National Academy of Sciences had declared it the least promising way in the long run of controlling exhaust emissions. The catalytic converter is a technology basically intended for large conventional engines. Consequently, foreign cars with smaller engines were able to meet federal emissions standards by alternative engine technologies, and only 9.6 percent of imports were equipped with catalytic converters in the 1977 model year.

Chrysler argued unsuccessfully for meeting the standards through fast-burn/lean-burn technology. Adoption of the catalytic converter further weakened Chrysler's position in the American automobile industry, because as the least backwardly integrated of the Big Three it had to purchase its catalytic converters while GM sold them at a profit. As a result, equipping a conventionally powered car with the total emissions system required by 1977 cost $200 a unit at GM versus over $400 at Chrysler.

Fuel Economy

The 1975 Energy Policy and Conservation Act (EPCA) mandated that American auto makers each achieve the Corporate Average Fuel Economy (CAFE) level of 27.5 miles per gallon by the 1985 model year, to be phased in beginning with 18 mpg in the 1978 model year, while still meeting the stringent antiemission standards of the 1970 Clean Air Act. CAFE is the annual production-weighted average of the overall fuel consumption for a manufacturer's full line of vehicles. In 1974 the fleet average for American-made cars was only 13.2 mpg, versus 22.2 mpg for the import fleet. The EPCA provided a stiff civil penalty of $5 for each tenth of a mile that the fleet average of an automobile manufacturer fell below the CAFE standard in a year, multiplied by its total production for that year. In recognition that conditions might change, Congress gave authority to the secretary of transportation to lower the CAFE standard for 1985 and later model years from 27.5 mpg to 26 mpg. And in 1980 Congress approved a proposal that the automobile manufacturers might accrue credits by exceeding the standard in any year, these credits to be calculated on the same basis as the penalty for not meeting the standard. Accumulated credits could be carried forward for three years, or anticipated credits could be projected for three years to offset a current CAFE deficit.

To encourage further the production of more fuel-efficient cars, the "gas guzzler tax" contained in the 1978 Energy Tax Act provided for graduated taxes on purchases of new cars with combined city/highway fuel economy ratings 5 mpg or more below the CAFE standard. In 1980 these taxes ranged from $200 on cars averaging 14.5–15.0 mpg to $550 on cars averaging 0–12.5 mpg. The 1985 tax range was from $500 on cars averaging 20.5–21.0 mpg to $2,650 on cars averaging 0–12.5 mpg.

Underlying the Energy Policy and Conservation Act and the Energy Tax Act was the grim reality of increasing American oil dependence in an increasingly oil-short world. Domestic oil reserves in mid-1973 were reported to be 52 billion barrels—about a ten-year supply—and the United States was importing about 27 percent of its crude petroleum. Gasoline prices were rising, and an imminent fuel shortage was being predicted months before the Organization of Arab Petroleum Exporting Countries (OAPEC) implemented oil diplomacy following the October 1973 war with Israel. OAPEC announced production cuts of at least 5 percent a month until Israel withdrew from occupied territories and the "legitimate rights" of the Palestinians were restored. The cuts were to be borne by the "enemies" of the Arab cause, which turned out to mean that only the United States and the Netherlands were under a "total embargo" by December. OAPEC also announced that henceforth oil prices would be determined unilaterally by the producing nations rather than through negotiations with the major oil companies.

Posted prices for Persian Gulf oil rose 130 percent over the October price of $5.11 to $11.65 per barrel by January 1974; a year earlier the price had been $2.59 per barrel. Other oil-producing nations naturally followed suit: Nigerian oil jumped from $6.00 to $10.80 per barrel, and new export taxes raised the price of Canadian oil from $6.40 to $10.40 per barrel. In response, the Nixon administration's Cost of Living Council authorized a $1 per barrel increase in "old" domestic crude oil—enough alone to raise the retail price of gasoline 2.3 cents a gallon—and generously pegged at $10 per barrel "new" domestic crude (oil produced in excess of the quantity produced in 1972).

Long lines developed at filling stations because of shortages until the embargo was lifted on March 13, 1974. By then the average retail price of regular gasoline in the United States had climbed to 54 cents a gallon, as opposed to 38 cents a year earlier. In anticipation of rising fuel prices, sales of small cars rose to 39 percent of total U.S. sales and as high as 60 percent in the Los Angeles area during the first four months of 1974. In December 1973 sales of cars with wheelbases under 112 inches surpassed sales of "standard-size" cars for the first time in history; they continued to account for 53 percent of the market during the first quarter of 1974, while inventories of larger models piled up to double the normal 60–65 days in storage lots and dealers' showrooms. First-quarter 1974 sales slipped 27 percent below those in the first quarter of 1973, and first-quarter profits were down 85 percent at GM, 66 percent at Ford, and 98 percent at Chrysler. With 90 percent of its production in small cars, AMC was the only American automobile manufacturer to increase its sales in the first quarter of 1974. Automobile workers were laid off in great numbers, as assembly lines were shifted to the production of smaller models.

GM began significant downsizing of its cars in the 1975 model year. By 1979 gasoline prices in the United States had risen some 80 percent over their 1970 level, putting an end to the era of the all-purpose road cruiser as the predominant type of American car.

The market conditions first made apparent by the 1973–1974 OAPEC embargo became permanent with the "oil shock" following the 1979 Iranian revolution. The establishment in Iran of a Moslem fundamentalist state hostile to the United States meant that Persian Gulf oil no longer could be counted on to fuel the American automobile culture. As a result of the oil shock and further OAPEC price increases, gasoline prices in the United States rose 109 percent between 1978 and 1981, compared with 22 percent in Western Europe and 9 percent in Japan. The cost of gas and oil for an intermediate-size car in the United States, 4.18 cents per mile in 1974, shot up from 4.11 cents in 1979 to 5.86 cents in 1980, then leveled off at 6.74 cents in 1982 and 6.64 cents in 1983.

Oil prices appear to have stabilized in the mid-1980s. World demand has been reduced by conservation measures, vast new reserves have begun to be tapped in Mexico and the North Atlantic, and the successor to OAPEC, the Organization of Petroleum Exporting Countries (OPEC), has lost its ability to enforce prices and production quotas among its member nations. In the spring of 1986 this became evident in significant declines in prices at the pump.

The reversal in oil prices, however, is apt to be as short as it is sweet to motorists. The long-term trend inevitably must be toward significantly higher oil prices. On April 5, 1984, for example, ABC News reported a Royal Dutch Shell prognosis, based on Saudi Arabian reserves, that gasoline prices could be expected to double within a decade from their then current $1.20 average and to increase by as much as sixfold early in the twenty-first century. With no alternative to some form of internal combustion engine in sight as a viable automotive power plant, this necessitates great advances in fuel economy over the 1985 CAFE standards if mass personal automobility is to survive into the next century.

Nadir

Decline in world and domestic demand and an abrupt shift to smaller, more fuel-efficient cars following the 1979 oil shock brought the American automobile industry to its lowest ebb in history. The small-car share of the U.S. market doubled from 27 percent in 1978 to 54.2 percent in 1979, and rose further to 61.5 percent by 1981. The share of the U.S. market held by imports correspondingly increased from 17.7 percent in 1978 to 27.9 percent in 1982, because despite years of warning that the era of the gas guzzler was over, the oil shock caught the Big Three with insufficient small-car production capacity to adjust to the changed demand pattern.

The American automobile industry's historic pattern of primary dependence on internal financing was broken in 1979, when funds from operations fell $4.6 billion below capital needs for new plants and equipment to meet the changed demand pattern. The shortfall reached a record $10.7 billion in 1980, then gradually declined to $1.4 billion in 1983 before a surplus of $3.2 billion was recorded for the first half of 1984. "The long-term debt of the top four U.S. producers rose from $3.3 billion at the end of 1978 to nearly $9.5 billion at the end of 1982, while industry net working capital fell almost 100 percent from $12.3 to $0.4 billion during the same period," observed the 1984 Report of the Secretary of Commerce to Congress on the automobile industry. "By late 1982, aggressive cost-cutting measures had halted the severe financial drain of the previous four years, but industry balance sheets remained extremely weak." [7]

Chrysler was the hardest hit. Only a government guarantee of Chrysler's loans saved the corporation from bankruptcy. In addition to the general problem of adjustment to changed market conditions following the oil shock and to Chrysler's history of mismanagement, federal safety and emissions standards affected Chrysler more severely than larger, more integrated GM and Ford. Indeed, Lee Iacocca rationalized going to the government for aid largely through the argument that "government helped us get into this mess, so government should be willing to help us get out." He explained in 1984, for example, that some $19 billion in research and development costs on automotive safety since 1966 had been spread by GM over 5 million units, by Ford over 2.5 million units, and by Chrysler over only 1 million units a year and that even greater economies of scale had accrued to GM and Ford in the manufacturing of the mandated equipment. He further noted "the sheer volume of staff time and paperwork necessary to report on our EPA regulatory confirmation. In 1978 alone [Chrysler] had to file 228,000 pages to the EPA!"[8] In sharp contrast with the cooperative research among Japanese auto makers to meet federal standards, American automobile manufacturers were forbidden to pool their knowledge by our antiquated antitrust laws.

Meeting Governmental Mandates

Industry critics have viewed the impact of federal standards very differently. "When Detroit claimed that it would be impossible to meet the emission deadlines mandated by the Clean Air Act, Japanese manufacturers produced vehicles that met them and at modest cost," note C. Kenneth Orski, Alan Altshuler, and Daniel Roos. "More recently, while U.S. industry spokesmen publicly doubted ... that 1985 fuel economy standards could be achieved without size and performance sacrifices that the public would find unacceptable, foreign companies led the way in demonstrating that the combination of excellent performance and low fuel consumption was both technically feasible and attractive in the market." They go on to assert that "were it not for government intervention, the [American] automotive sector would be even worse off [vis-à-vis foreign competition].... [P]ractically every recent move by U.S. automakers to adopt advanced features—lightweight metals, high-strength plastics, electronic ignition management devices—can be traced to the influence of government regulations."[9]

Significant technological progress has been made in increasing fuel economy while decreasing emissions and improving performance through electronic engine controls. Chrysler introduced its lean-burn system in 1976. Ford introduced electronic engine controls on its 1978 Pintos and Mercury Bobcats for the California market. GM installed electronic engine controls on 4,000 of its 1978 California cars. By the early 1980s electronic engine controls had come into general use.

By 1983 passenger car emissions of hydrocarbons and carbon monoxide had been reduced 96 percent and nitrogen oxides 76 percent from precontrol levels. Hydrocarbon emissions had been reduced from 10.6 grams per mile to 0.41 grams, carbon monoxide from 84 grams to 3.4 grams, and nitrogen oxides from 4.1 grams to 1.0 grams. As a source of air pollution in the United States, in 1982 motor vehicles accounted for 63 percent of carbon monoxide, 39 percent of nitrogen oxide, 26 percent of volatile organic compounds, 15 percent of suspended particulates, and

2 percent of sulphur oxides. By 1983 some 67 percent of all cars in operation in the United States were equipped with a catalytic converter or equivalent technology as well as fuel evaporation and exhaust and crankcase control devices. Only 5.2 percent of cars on the road remained with no controls.

CAFE standards were met or exceeded by American auto makers through the 1982 model year. American Motors and Chrysler have continued to meet or exceed CAFE standards, as has the import fleet. GM and Ford, however, stopped meeting the standards after 1983, as consumers reverted to buying larger cars with the stabilization of gasoline prices. To avoid stiff penalties, both Ford and GM petitioned the secretary of transportation to lower the CAFE standard to 26 mpg for 1985 and subsequent years. Compared to a 1984 standard of 27 mpg, the actual domestic fleet average was 25.4 mpg and the import fleet average 31.5 mpg. Among domestic producers in 1984 GM averaged 24.7 mpg, Ford 25.8 mpg, Chrysler 27 mpg, and American Motors 35.2 mpg. Perhaps an even better illustration of the progress made is that family-size cars today achieve better fuel economy than compact models did in 1975.

Renaissance

In 1982, at a conference of automotive historians and industry representatives sponsored by the Detroit Historical Society, Ford president (now chairman of the board) Donald Petersen spoke about "new realities," which represented "a major crossroads for our industry. They require that American industry—and its array of new magic machines—become competitive in every respect.... [T]he industry will have to change dramatically to survive. And change it will." To document his point, Petersen reported that "across-the-board retooling under way in our industry is the most massive peacetime private-sector reconversion ever attempted, anywhere. At a cost of more than $80 billion, it involves the retooling and re-equipping, by 1985, of 49 new engine and transmission lines and 89 new or fully re-equipped assembly lines. Few machine tools or parts will remain unchanged in the industry's 260 domestic plants and the plants of more than 5,000 suppliers of automotive parts and materials." Additional substance was given to Petersen's assertions by the fact that in 1982 alone the American automobile industry spent almost $4.5 billion on research and development, more than any other single industry in the United States.[10]

Critics of the early 1970s who had viewed the American automobile industry as technologically stagnant or hopelessly impaled on the horns of a Fordist/Sloanist dilemma were being proved wrong a decade later. More than simply showing survival ability in the face of the Japanese challenge, the American automobile industry by the early 1980s was experiencing an organizational and technological renaissance.

The revitalization of the American automobile industry has been particularly associated in the public mind with the "turnaround" of Chrysler under Iacocca's chairmanship. As we have seen, Chrysler disposed of its overseas operations in 1978–1979. Iacocca also took immediate steps upon becoming chairman in 1979 to modernize the Chrysler management, to improve relationships with dealers, and to upgrade the quality of Chrysler cars. In unprecedented moves, Douglas Fraser, president of the UAW, was given a seat on the Chrysler board of directors, and a joint UAW-Chrysler Management Quality Program was inaugurated.

Then in December 1979 negotiations with the federal government resulted in passage of a controversial loan guarantee act that permitted Chrysler to survive at about half its former size. The act created a loan guarantee board authorized to issue up to $1.5 billion in loan guarantees over the next two years, to be repaid by 1990. These guarantees were fully secured by Chrysler's assets, which were conservatively estimated by the government at $2.5 billion in liquidation value, so no public funds were ever at risk. Other stipulations were that current lenders to Chrysler were required to extend $400 million in new credit and $100 million in concessions on existing loans; foreign lenders were required to extend an additional $150 million in credit; suppliers had to provide Chrysler with $180 million, $100 million of which had to be in stock purchases; the governments of states and municipalities where Chrysler had plants were to provide the corporation with $250 million; Chrysler had to raise $300 million through the sale of assets and issue $50 million of new stock; concessions of $462.2 million were required from UAW employees, and pay cuts or freezes of $125 million from nonunion employees. Before receiving the first $550 million in guaranteed loans in June 1980, Chrysler issued to the loan guarantee board warrants entitling the bearer to purchase at $13 some 14.4 million shares of Chrysler stock, which was then selling at $5.

A far leaner and tougher corporation emerged. In addition to selling off its operations abroad to raise operating revenues, Chrysler sold Chrysler Defense, the nation's only maker of military tanks, to General Dynamics for $348 million. Twenty plants were closed, and the remaining plant facilities modernized. White-collar personnel were trimmed from 40,000 in 1978 to 21,000 in 1983, while salaries were reduced up to 10 percent. Concessions by the UAW averaged $10,000 a worker during the first nineteen months of the loan guarantee, and labor productivity was raised 50 percent. As a result of these cutbacks and increased labor productivity,

Chrysler's fixed costs were cut in constant dollars from $4.7 billion in 1979 to $3.54 billion in 1983, and the firm's break-even point was reduced from 2.4 million units to 1.1 million units. Sales increased with the introduction of the fuel-efficient, front-wheel-drive K-series and the popular Caravan, Voyager, and Dodge Mini Ram minivans. The Aries and Reliant K-cars won *Motor Trend's* Car of the Year award for 1981. Between 1979 and 1983 Chrysler claims a 36-percent improvement in the quality of its cars, on the basis of repairs done under warranty. It also claims the lowest number of recalls of any automobile manufacturer.

Government-guaranteed loans totaling $1.2 billion were fully repaid in 1983, seven years early. With Chrysler stock at $30, the government put up the warrants at auction to the highest bidder. Chrysler bought them back and retired them at a cost of $311 million. Over the three-year period of the loan guarantees, Chrysler also had paid $404 million in interest, plus $33 million in administrative fees to the government and $67 million to lawyers and investment bankers.

Losses of $1.77 billion in 1980 and $475.6 million in 1981 were translated into profits of $170.1 million in 1982, $700.9 million in 1983, and a record $2.38 billion in 1984. Chrysler's debt/equity ratio in 1984 was 19.7 percent, down from 69.8 percent in 1982 and the lowest ratio in seventeen years. Chrysler's share of the North American market reached 11.6 percent in 1984. The corporation's relationships with lending institutions and its labor force were becoming normal for the first time in years.

While the regeneration of Chrysler has received wide publicity, an even more impressive turnaround at Ford has gone largely unnoticed. After net losses of $1.54 billion in 1980, $1.06 billion in 1981, and $657.8 million in 1982, the Ford Motor Company posted record after-tax profits of $1.87 billion in 1983 and $2.91 billion in 1984. In 1984 Ford's share of the U.S. passenger car market reached 19.2 percent, the highest level in five years and a 2-percent increase over 1983, while Ford led in European automobile sales with a record 13 percent of the market. Between 1980 and 1984 Ford closed seven plants, reduced salaried employees by more than 20,000, and reduced hourly employees by 44,000. As a consequence, Ford lowered its break-even point 40 percent, to 2.5 million vehicles, and reduced its operating costs some $12 million a day, or $4.5 billion annually.

The driving force of the Ford turnaround has been Donald Petersen, president of Ford under Philip Caldwell, who replaced Henry Ford II as chairman in 1979. Petersen became chief executive officer with Caldwell's retirement in 1985. Petersen is a product-oriented engineer with a Stanford M.B.A. He attended the Bob Bondurant School of Performance

Driving in Northern California so that he could personally evaluate Ford cars on the test track. Training executives in performance driving has since become Ford policy. Petersen personally supervised the introduction of six new Ford models in twenty months at a development cost of $10 billion. The 1983 Ford Thunderbird/Mercury Cougar and the 1984 Ford Tempo/Mercury Topaz broke sharply with conventional design concepts. Their advanced aerodynamic designs have made Ford the styling pacesetter in the automobile industry. Petersen also put a new emphasis on manufacturing quality at Ford. *Consumer Reports* has rated Ford cars the most improved, and Ford claims an average improvement of over 50 percent in the quality of its cars and light trucks from 1980 to 1985. *Motor Trend* named as its Car of the Year the Ford Taurus sedan for 1986 and the Ford turbocharged Thunderbird coupe for 1987. In 1986 Ford surpassed GM in profits for the first time in 62 years.

Under the chairmanship of Roger B. Smith, a revitalized General Motors has recently undergone the most important organizational change in its history since development in the 1920s of the decentralized multidivisional structure. The corporation has also made a massive commitment of resources to ensure the technological leadership that Sloanism eschewed. That these changes have been instituted under Smith's leadership is especially noteworthy, because his background at GM was in finance.

In early 1984 GM established for its North American operations an organizational structure consisting of two cars groups and the Body and Assembly Group. One car group includes Chevrolet, Pontiac, and GM Canada; the other includes Oldsmobile, Buick, and Cadillac. (Previous to this organizational change, GM consolidated its worldwide truck and bus engineering and assembly operations into the corporate Worldwide Truck and Bus Group.) The Body and Assembly Group—Fisher Body, General Motors Assembly Division, and Guide—has been phased out, and body engineering and assembly responsibilities have been integrated fully into the two car groups. The new structure reverses Frederic Donner's centralization of GM into the the hands of the bean counters. Decentralizing decisions down to the engineers and sales experts in the operating divisions is expected to improve greatly GM's ability to respond to fast-changing markets. It is also expected to lead to a greater diversity in GM's line of passenger cars.

Recently, GM has advanced toward implementing its intention to lead in technological innovation: it has successfully completed a program of strategic diversification to increase its high-technology capabilities. In the summer of 1984 GM purchased, for $2.55 billion, Electronic Data Systems Corporation of Dallas, Texas, a computer-services company. And in June 1985 GM outbid Ford and Boeing Aircraft to acquire Hughes

Aircraft Company, for $2.7 billion in cash and 50 million shares of a new class of common stock. Smith explained that the acquisition of Hughes would help GM to "redefine" the automobile "from a mechanical product with a few electrical subsystems to one with major electromechanical and electronic elements." The *Wall Street Journal* reported that GM expects the Hughes acquisition to result in "a marketing edge over competitors. It sees lasers one day helping guide vehicles under poor visibility conditions; microelectronics and sensors under the hood improving engine performance; cockpit-like computerized dashboards, and space age materials in a range of uses. And on the factory floor, Hughes's advanced computer science especially artificial intelligence capabilities—could offer far more efficient ways to assemble a car."[11]

The World Car, Downsizing, and the New Technology

Beyond significant organizational changes within Detroit's Big Three, the organization of the automobile industry has become increasingly multinational—as evidenced by the location of assembly plants in host countries, joint manufacturing operations, control of domestic auto makers by foreign investors and foreign governments, captive imports, and the outsourcing of components manufacture to the lowest foreign bidder. These trends make it increasingly difficult to speak of an American automobile industry, or to know precisely what one means by an American automobile.

National differences in automobile design reflecting unique domestic market conditions have all but disappeared, and design is now fairly well standardized worldwide. In the early 1980s Detroit turned to the production of "world cars"—cars designed by engineers and assembled from components made in many countries for worldwide markets. The first of these cars were the 1980 Ford Escort/Mercury Lynx and the 1981 GM J-series.

The world-car concept is best exemplified by the Ford Escort/ Mercury Lynx. With minor local variations, the Escort/Lynx is assembled in the United States, the United Kingdom, West Germany, Portugal, and Brazil. Its components are outsourced from seventeen countries. It has been the best-selling car in the world since 1981, and its design characteristics have become standard for state-of-the-art small cars.

The Escort/Lynx is available as a four-passenger two-door hatchback, four-door hatchback, or station wagon. It has a wheelbase of 94.2 inches, height of 53.3 inches, front tread of 54.7 inches, rear tread of 56 inches, and width of 63 inches. The hatchback versions have an overall length of 163.9

inches and a curb weight of 2,080 pounds, the station wagon a length of 165 inches and a curb weight of 2,176 pounds. Until mid-1985 the Escort/Lynx was powered by a 1.6-liter, four-cylinder, transverse-mounted engine with front-wheel drive through a transaxle, a combination that increases fuel economy, improves handling, and adds room to the passenger compartment. A 1.9-liter fast-burn engine that gives better performance at the same fuel economy became standard in the 1985½ models. A 2.0-liter diesel and an electronic fuel-injected conventional engine are offered as options. The Escort/Lynx conventional engine features a compound valve semihead configuration and specially designed pistons to improve combustion. Four- or five-speed manual transaxles are standard, depending on the engine, with an automatic transaxle available as an option. The Escort/Lynx features as standard equipment rack-and-pinion steering, front disc brakes, and four-wheel independent suspension with MacPherson struts on the front wheels. The front disc brakes and front-end alignment are self-adjusting. Unitized body construction results in a more rigid, hence safer, body compartment and reduces rattles.

The trend toward overall downsizing continues. The average weight of American-made passenger cars has been reduced from 3,800 pounds in 1975, when downsizing began, to only 2,700 pounds in 1985. This has been accomplished not only by making cars smaller but also by the greatly increased use of lighter-weight materials—plastics, cast-aluminum engines, and new high-strength steels that permit thinner gauges and as much as 20 percent weight reductions in materials. The development of lighter and stronger materials continues, with ceramics and plastics reinforced with glass or graphite fibers emerging as replacements for steels, and with adhesive bonding replacing welding.[12]

Ford engineers estimate that a reduction in drag coefficient from Cd .40 to Cd .36 in an Escort-size car saves half a mile per gallon of gas in city driving and two miles per gallon on the highway. Ford hopes to achieve an 18-percent improvement in the aerodynamic efficiency of its cars by 1990 compared with 1977, which alone would translate into an average increase in fuel economy of 1.5 mpg. The advanced aerodynamic Ford Probe IV concept car has a rating of only Cd .15, a drag coefficient previously equaled only in land-speed record cars and jet aircraft.

Electronic sensors and controls have become standard equipment, and their further sophistication can be expected. At the present state of the art, it is estimated that it would take a person with a hand calculator about 45 years to perform the calculations that the Ford EEC-IV computer, used to control engines on about two thirds of 1984 Ford cars, performs each minute. The computer-controlled Ford 2.3-liter "high swirl combustion" engine can react to as many as 250,000 commands each second. Other emerging technologies that are radically altering cars under the hood include fast-burn/lean-burn engines, turbocharging/supercharging, the continuously variable (as opposed to step) automatic transmission (CVT), and air suspension systems.

The Electronic Age Dawns: Computer-Integrated Manufacturing and Flexible Robotics

Traditional engineering know-how and cut-and-try methods are being abandoned in favor of computer-aided engineering (CAE) and computer-aided design (CAD) to complement computer-aided manufacturing (CAM). By eliminating much of the need for engineering manpower, CAE and CAD greatly reduce both the cost and the lead time for developing new models. Electronic scanners trace the form of a clay model to gather precise data that is stored in the computer in three-dimensional form. The computer then directs a pen over a drawing board to produce engineering drawings for die making. The computer not only can be used to design parts but also can be programmed to show the effects of the stresses to which the parts will be subjected. Weaknesses in design are shown in colors, and the computer aids in redesign. "The product design, development, and manufacturing process of the future will rely on the integration of a wide range of computer-based application programs," the Ford technical staff predicts. "Properly implemented, the boundaries between CAE, CAD, and CAM will disappear, and the term 'computer-integrated manufacturing' (CIM) can properly be used to refer to this level of development." [13]

Chrysler has installed a unique computer network that uses a central data bank for all design and engineering functions; the car maker has also undertaken a joint venture with Control Data Corporation to develop a new generation of CAD software. Chrysler claims that its 1984 Chrysler Le Baron and Dodge Lancer GTS were the world's first completely computer-designed cars.

In 1983, at a cost of $400 million, Chrysler's Windsor plant in Ontario, Canada, was retooled to produce Caravan, Voyager, and Dodge Mini Ram minivans. This was the first in-line-sequenced automobile plant. Ninety-seven percent of the body welding—there are 3,800 body welds in each minivan—is performed by 112 robots at Windsor. The entire ten-mile assembly line is computerized. Each unit is locked into the assembly process according to a predetermined schedule; it passes through 1,837 assembly stations before emerging as a finished vehicle. Chrysler's Sterling Heights Assembly Plant, opened in 1984 to assemble the Le Baron and the Lancer GTS, is an even more fully integrated in-line-sequenced plant. It is equipped with 57 welding robots, 32 material handling robots, and 162 lasers and cameras that inspect 350 points on the car bodies passing through assembly. Chrysler employs the "just-in-time" inventory system at Windsor and Sterling Heights, necessitating high quality control and precise coordination in manufacturing. A single defect in a part, or a delay in its delivery, can shut down the entire factory. Chrysler expects to install such advanced systems in all of its plants by 1988 and to revamp all of its car lines by 1990.

The most extensive single plant modernization has been GM's construction of Buick City from the sixty-year-old Buick assembly plant at Flint, which had been scheduled to be shut down in 1986. GM planned Buick City, together with the UAW, as "a totally integrated facility" with "total employee involvement." Buick City employs the kanban-jidoka system. Some 90 percent of the parts used are manufactured within a 300-mile radius, and several suppliers are relocating within sight of the complex. The plant's 250 flexible robots perform a variety of assembly operations, including windshield and back glass setting and wheel and tire installation. A guided vehicle system replaces the traditional conveyor in engine and chassis assembly. More modular components, such as fully assembled dashboards, are used. No provision is made for repair or inspection, because none is needed. In cooperation with three Flint educational institutions and the UAW, 630 employees have been given "high-technology training" and the skills to train the other 4,000 to 5,000 employees required to operate the entire assembly complex. The corporation reports, "The realization of the 'Buick City' concept will bring GM closer to the goal of establishing a totally automated and computer-integrated automotive manufacturing facility." [14]

The revolution that has taken place in automobile manufacturing is due primarily to the introduction of the electronic machine tool. Until very recently, robots could be programmed to perform only a few repetitive operations. Now, however, the microprocessor gives robots the ability to handle complex materials, select and distribute parts, and discriminate in the performance of tasks in much the same way as can a human operator. For example, new robot welding systems can perform precise and uniform welds on a variety of models moving through the assembly process in random order, and parts can be moved from machine to machine as required by the model rather than following a fixed itinerary. The MIT Report observes that this new flexible robotics system at Volkswagen "takes the first steps along the path to automated final assembly, with robots installing the engine, brake lines, battery, and wheels. The system is able to produce not only Golfs in several body styles but also Jettas without changing tools or stopping production. In addition, Volkswagen and other producers are experimenting with more flexible tooling and automated material handling in engine and transmission plants to permit, for example, machining of a whole family of engines on the same transfer lines." [15]

Flexible robotics thus has reconciled Fordism and Sloanism, with truly revolutionary implications for automobile manufacturing. It permits economies of scale to be realized on much smaller model runs. This means both that we can expect more diversity of product and that small specialized producers can remain competitive within the automobile industry. Manufacturing techniques are more precise, improving quality. Labor costs are significantly lowered, because flexible robots can perform routine tasks much more cheaply than can human beings. This promises soon to erase the labor cost advantages of Japan and Third-World countries. To program, monitor, and repair robots requires a far more skilled work force than to perform repetitive assembly-line tasks.

Half of all current sales of robots in the United States are to the automobile industry, and the adoption of flexible robotics is proceeding at a rapid pace. In 1987 some 26,000 robots were being used in final assembly plants in the American automobile industry, and about the same number in the auto factories of Western Europe. The Japanese claimed 90,000, but counted as "robots" many fairly low-level automatic machine tools.

It is estimated that the general adoption of electronic machine tools will eliminate 40 to 70 percent of the jobs in automobile production. The MIT Report conservatively projects that total employment in automobile manufacturing in the United States, Japan, and the seven Western European Auto Program Countries will shrink 37 percent, from 3,642,400 workers in 1979 to 2,279,600 by the turn of the century, even as the number of motor vehicles in the world grows from 396.2 million in 1979 to 678.5 million in the year 2000. "Significant gains in productivity are anticipated from this [flexible robotics] system," understates Jean-Pierre Bardou. "But the salient point is that the introduction of electronic machine tools challenges the traditional sequential operation process, whether it is a line formed by human operatives or a line formed by a succession of machines. If the assembly line someday disappears, this will not only mark a page turned in the history of the automobile industry, but also in the history of labor." Stephen Meyer III puts it another way: "Industrial engineers finally may have found their technical solution to the problem of 'the human element in production.' But who, or what, will the labor historian of the future study?" [16]

The most ambitious attempt "to leapfrog the foreign competition" is GM's Project Saturn, launched in 1982 after a study revealed that the

Japanese could build a small car for about $2,000 under GM's cost. The goal of Project Saturn is to build a small car in the United States that is cost-competitive with imports. It has been given the largest commitment of resources of any GM experimental project. In conjunction with Saturn, GM and the UAW announced in late 1983 the formation of a study center to explore alternative ways to make cars in the United States. Saturn is intended "to be an advanced manufacturing process for an automobile employing new tools, new facilities, new management systems, and new forms of employee participation never before realized in General Motors. . . . [I]mprovements that flow from Saturn in product design, manufacturing, and assembly will be applied throughout the corporation." [17]

In early 1985 GM announced the creation of a separate, wholly owned subsidiary to build the Saturn car. The prototype Saturn is smaller and 600 pounds lighter than current GM subcompacts. It is slated to go into production in 1990. Saturn Corporation will operate its own manufacturing and assembly complex and set up its own distribution system, initially of some 100 franchised dealers. Although the Saturn headquarters will be in Detroit, its plant is being built in Spring Hill, Tennessee, 30 miles south of Nashville. Initial production is slated at 250,000 units a year, turned out by 3,000 workers on a two-shift operation, an unprecedented labor productivity rate of 83 cars annually per worker. A tradition-shattering contract with the UAW provides that the Saturn workers will be paid annual salaries rather than hourly wages and that 80 percent of them will be guaranteed lifelong employment.

About 80 percent of the technology that will be employed to produce the Saturn is already in use, the remaining 20 percent being new technology innovated at GM. CAE, CAD, and CAM for Saturn are being developed simultaneously, with CIM as the result. A computer-designed fender, for example, will be stamped out by a computer-designed die. All stamping presses will have quick die-change capability and will use a new die-making material developed by GM. Special attention is being given to increasing the number of parts made from a given amount of raw material and to decreasing the amount of energy used in processing operations. Advances in high-speed machining technology will permit boring, drilling, and milling operations to be performed much faster. The Saturn assembly line will be much shorter than traditional lines, because extensive use will be made of modular assembly of subsystems of the car by teams of workers in an environment designed for optimal workplace ergonomics. Just-in-time inventory control will be used. Sophisticated new data-processing systems will permit the Saturn plant to operate with a minimum of paperwork. GM expects to have 4,000 computer graphics terminals in place by 1990, versus 1,000 in 1981.

After being outbid for Hughes Aircraft by GM, Ford began looking for another major high-technology acquisition to bolster its already strong position as a leader in automotive electronics and satellite communications through Ford Aerospace and Communications Corporation. And Chrysler, in the same month that GM acquired Hughes—June 1985—announced its acquisition of Gulfstream Aerospace for $637 million.

Thus the Automobile Age, three generations of historical development dominated by the impact of the motor vehicle and the automobile industry, melds into the era of space exploration and an emerging Age of Electronics.

Epilogue
The Future of the Automobile

Mass personal automobility appears to have a new lease on life. In contrast with the disappointing past, disillusioning present, and clouded future of mass transit in the United States, the renaissance in automotive technology is making cars safer, less polluting, and more energy efficient with every model year. Predictions of the imminent death of the automobile have given way to a new optimism. The MIT Report comes to the particularly rosy conclusion that "the automobile's future as the prime means of personal transport is quite secure because of the flexibility of the basic concept and robustness of automotive technology.... [T]here is no basis whatever for projecting that in the end auto technologists will fail to cope. Thus, the auto industry can continue to be one of the world's foremost manufacturing activities far into the future, serving the need for personal transportation in developed and developing nations." [1]

Notably, however, the futurists are merely projecting that present trends will persist for another decade and a half to the year 2000. Thus they deal with a sociological rather than a truly historical time span. The long-range future of mass motorization—say, over the next half-century—remains as problematic and clouded as that of mass transit.

There can be no doubt that the automobile will continue into the twenty-first century to be the dominant mode of personal transportation in the advanced capitalist countries and that there will be some growth in automobile ownership and use in both the advanced socialist countries and the Third World. The MIT Report forecasts that by 2000 demand for passenger cars will have increased to 48.8 million units and that 536 million passenger cars will be owned in the world, versus an actual demand of 30.5 million cars and ownership of 396.2 million in 1979. Demand for commercial motor vehicles is expected to increase from 10.8 million units in 1979 to 18 million units in 2000, and commercial motor vehicle owner-ship from 86.4 million units to 142.5 million units. The composite MIT forecast for both passenger cars and commercial motor vehicles is that by 2000 world demand will be 66.75 million units, the world stock of motor vehicles 678.5 million units.

Other forecasts are only slightly more conservative. The Organi-zation for Economic Cooperation and Development (OECD) estimates that by 2000 there will be 529 million passenger cars in the world and that world demand for automobiles will have increased from 35.2 million units in 1985 to 46.6 million units, with demand in the North American market increasing from 12.4 to 13.4 million units and in Western Europe from 11.2 to 13.6 million units. The OECD projects that the North American share of the world market for cars will have declined from 35 percent in 1985 to 29 percent in 2000, and the Western European share from 31 to 29 percent, while the Latin American share will have increased from 7 to 12 percent, the Asian from 18 to 19 percent, the African from 2 to 3 percent, and the Eastern European from 6 to 8 percent.

Of far more significance than these optimistic short-term projections of total world demand and ownership is that replacement demand is expected to climb from 58 percent of total world demand in 1980 to 76 percent by 2000, with replacement demand being as high as 87 percent in both North America and the EEC countries and nowhere in the world lower than the 50 percent estimated for Latin America. The OECD fur-ther foresees that population densities will place ultimate saturation points on automobile densities at 700 cars per thousand persons in the United States, 600 per thousand in France and Germany, and 450–500 per thousand in Italy, Japan, Sweden, and the United Kingdom. Should de-mand in these advanced capitalist countries increase as anticipated, ulti-mate saturation of the world market for cars will be a reality very early in the twenty-first century.

Thus the world market for motorcars is projected to become satu-rated on the criterion of replacement demand in the very near future and on the criterion of ecology in the foreseeable future at levels that would leave the private passenger car "the prime means of personal transport" only in the United States and a few of the world's other affluent nations. Public transit undoubtedly will remain by far the most important means of personal transport in Eastern Europe and at least as vital as the private passenger car in Western Europe and in Japan. Even in most developed nations the automobile is not now the prime means of personal transport; and especially in the socialist countries, but also throughout Western Europe and in Japan, social policy historically has limited automobile ownership and use to levels well below their potentials given a free market. There is every reason to expect that such policy will continue and grow firmer as petroleum resources dwindle in an oil-short world. The Third World will continue to depend overwhelmingly on foot and animal traction for personal transportation, unless an unlikely revolutionary change occurs in the distribution of the world's wealth. Indeed, the idea of mass personal automobility serving the transportation needs of the "developing" nations compounds a myth into an absurdity, for the world currently is divided into two types of nations—the overly developed and the never-to-be developed.

Automobility is incredibly expensive and can be supported at the current American level only in super-affluent America. How long it can be supported even here remains to be seen. The average fixed cost per day of owning a passenger car in 1985 was $6.69, with operating costs at an average of 27.2 cents per mile. The average 1985 expenditure for a new car was $11,629, or 22.7 weeks' income for a family earning the median income of $27,144. The futurists are holding continued American prosperity as a constant in their calculations, even though it is not a variable but an imponderable in an era of mounting gigantic trade deficits and stagnating economic growth.

Despite some impressive recent advances in automotive technology, there is no alternative in sight to the internal-combustion engine burning a petroleum product. Improvements in storage batteries over the years have failed to result in a viable electric car for all-around use, and powering cars by electric fuel cells, much less by nuclear or solar power, is still in the dream stage of development. World petroleum resources not only are dwindling but are largely controlled by the OPEC cartel, which sets far higher crude oil prices than would result from a free market. Further, OPEC nations know the uses of oil as a political weapon and have engaged in oil diplomacy that includes cutting off crude oil supplies to adversaries. No one can estimate how these imponderables will affect automobility over even the immediate future.

On the other hand, it is indisputable that mass transit at present can utilize a wider variety of types of energy than can the motorcar, and the preponderance of evidence is that mass transit is also more energy efficient. Furthermore, although cars have become far safer and less polluting than they were two decades ago, mass transit remains safer and cleaner still, as well as considerably cheaper when all costs are considered.

A major stake that the advanced capitalist countries have had in the continuation of mass personal automobility has been the centrality of automobile manufacturing to their national economies. For example, about one out of every six jobs in the United States in 1982 was in the motor vehicle and related industries. In 1977—the most recent year for which such figures are available—automobile dealers accounted for 28.5 percent of all retail trade in the United States, automotive wholesalers for 11.7 percent of all wholesale trade, and automotive service establishments for 12 percent of all service business.

Should the MIT Report's optimistic prediction materialize—a 62-percent increase in motor vehicle output over 1979 by the year 2000—the world automobile industry undoubtedly will be able to remain prosperous well into the twenty-first century by filling replacement demand alone for some 678.5 million motor vehicles. "This 62-percent increase in total output, when translated into broader economic terms, means that the motor vehicle industry is almost certain to continue as the world's largest manufacturing enterprise," the report concludes. "Therefore the key question about the future of the automobile and its industry . . . is not whether the future holds security and growth for the industry as a whole but rather which producers at which locations in the world will account for the increases in output."

Conventional wisdom has assumed that the twenty final assemblers in the automobile industry in the advanced capitalist countries would be reduced by 2000 to perhaps as few as six truly multinational "mega-producers." The MIT Report identifies "four factors that alter this vision of the future. These are the introduction of microprocessor-controlled flexible production methods, the ready availability of new product technologies, the perfection of a new system of social organization for the production process, and the failure of the world's auto purchasers to demand a single size and type of car." For these reasons it is anticipated that "there are likely to be about as many automakers 20 years from now as today. Departures from the industry will be minimal. . . . The declining minimum efficient scale in manufacturing will give the medium-size and specialist producers a more level field on which to compete. . . . In addition, new forms of cooperation being developed among final assemblers will increase the survivability of specialists and medium-line producers."

This is not to say, however, that the automobile industries of Western Europe and the United States will be able to survive the Japanese challenge. The MIT Report finds "a major competitive imbalance among the developed countries" that strongly favors the Japanese auto makers. "Because the present competitive gap between the best Japanese producers and the weakest Western producers is so great, and because the process of adjustment by its nature will require many years to complete, it is evident that the potential for dramatic shifts in share among national auto industries and for disaster for individual producers will persist for many years. To make matters worse, the adjustment process will proceed in a macroeconomic environment that is likely to be only marginally better than that of the period since 1973." [2]

Despite this major competitive imbalance among the developed countries, none of the MIT Auto Program participants advocated that Western nations take strong measures to protect their automobile industries. Opinion was divided between participants espousing the classic free-trade position—arguing the abstract benefits of competition, the futility of protectionism, and the specter of a global trade war—and proponents of limited government intervention to preserve jobs. In the real world, protectionism historically has been essential to the development of every national automobile industry, and none has been more protected than the Japanese. The Japanese still do not practice free trade. Western European nations in general have erected strong trade barriers against Japanese auto imports. The Japanese have built automobile plants abroad only in response to threats of strong protectionist measures. And without strong protection the jobs of American automobile workers will continue to move overseas at the same time that employment shrinks some 37 percent in the worldwide automobile industry by the year 2000.

Regardless of these short-term possibilities for the future of the automobile and the automobile industry, it is clear that the Automobile Age—half a century of historical development dominated by the motor vehicle—had ended by the early 1970s. The automobile has not been a historically progressive force for change in American civilization since at least the 1960s. Unlimited accommodation to mass personal automobility ended as government came to recognize automotive safety, pollution, and energy consumption as major social problems and consequently to regulate the automobile industry and to invest in mass transit. Although the automobile industry still provided one out of every six jobs in the United States, its hegemony in our society and economy had been progressively eroded over the preceding generation by the expansion of government, which provided one out of every five jobs by 1970. With increased international involvement, the rise of a nuclear warfare state, and the exploration of outer space, new industries associated with aerospace and electronics, together with the federal government, have become more important forces for change than the mature automobile industry. Significantly, the current renaissance in automotive technology is a renaissance almost entirely engendered by electronic and aerospace technology; the major technological forces for change in American lifeways at present are the computer, the robot, the laser beam, and telecommunications. Nowhere else in the world is the automobile apt to have the all-encompassing impact in the future that it has had on American civilization in the past.

The ending of the Automobile Age undoubtedly marks a significant turning point in world as well as American civilization. Whether the age of electronics that is already revolutionizing daily life and the life of nations holds a better or a worse future for mankind remains to be seen. So does it remain to be seen whether the renaissance in automotive technology can make mass personal automobility viable even in the most affluent nations long past the turn of the twenty-first century. To project trends further than that would be to engage in futile speculation, for the history that will be made will be the result not of discoverable inevitabilities but of conscious human choice, effort, and striving.

Notes

1 The Automotive Idea

1. William Plowden, *The Motorcar in Politics, 1896–1970* (London: The Bodley Head, 1971), p. 24.

2. "The Woods Electric Vehicle," *Scientific American* 38 (November 7, 1900): 308.

3. Cleveland Moffett, "Automobiles for the Average Man," *American Monthly Review of Reviews* 21 (June 1900): 706.

4. Lynwood Bryant, "The Development of the Diesel Engine," *Technology and Culture* 17 (July 1976): 439.

5. Hiram Percy Maxim, *Horseless Carriage Days* (New York: Harper and Brothers, 1937; Dover paperback edition, 1962), pp. 3–4.

2 The Emerging Industry

1. James M. Laux, *In First Gear: The French Automobile Industry to 1914* (Montreal: McGill–Queen's University Press, 1976), p. 69. This is the definitive source on the early French automobile industry.

2. S. B. Saul, "The Motor Industry in Britain to 1914," *Business History* 5 (December 1962): 22–38.

3. Saul, "The Motor Industry in Britain," pp. 26–27.

4. Saul, "The Motor Industry in Britain," p. 22.

5. "Salutatory," *Horseless Age* 1 (November 1895): 1.

6. John B. Rae, *American Automobile Manufacturers: The First Forty Years* (Philadelphia: Chilton, 1959), pp. 8, 203.

7. "Manufacture in New England," *Motor Age* 1 (September 12, 1899): 4.

8. Gerald R. Bloomfield, *The World Automotive Industry* (Newton Abbot, London, and North Pomfret, Vt.: David and Charles, 1978), pp. 122–123; Rae, *American*

Automobile Manufacturers, p. 59; George S. May, *A Most Unique Machine: The Michigan Origins of the American Automobile Industry* (Grand Rapids, Mich.: William B. Eerdmans, 1975), p. 343.

3   A Car for the Great Multitude

1. "Fairly Howling," *Motor World* 1 (October 11, 1900): 17; W. W. Townsend, "The Future of the Industry Assessed," *Motor Age* 3 (February 6, 1901): 999; the Anderson letter was printed in full in the *Detroit News*, January 14, 1927.

2. Jean-Pierre Bardou, Jean-Jacques Chanaron, Patrick Fridenson, and James M. Laux, *The Automobile Revolution: The Impact of an Industry*, translated from the original 1977 French edition and edited by James M. Laux. (Chapel Hill: University of North Carolina Press, 1982), p. 22. Hereafter cited as Laux et al., *The Automobile Revolution*.

3. James J. Flink, *America Adopts the Automobile, 1895–1910* (Cambridge, Mass.: MIT Press, 1970); Nicolas Spinga, "L'Introduction de l'automobile dans la société française entre 1900 et 1915," Maîtrise d'Histoire Contemporaine sous la direction de Monseiur Lévy-Leboyer et de Patrick Fridenson, Université de Paris-X-Nanterre, 1972–1973, p. 47. I am indebted to Phylinda Wallace for an excellent translation of Spinga's work.

4. Joseph Interrante, "The Road to Autopia," in David L. Lewis and Lawrence Goldstein, eds., *The Automobile and American Cutlure* (Ann Arbor: University of Michigan Press, 1983), p. 90.

5. Kenneth Richardson, *The British Motor Industry, 1890–1939: A Social and Economic History* (London: Macmillan, 1977; Archon Books edition, 1978), p. 190.

6. "Our Correspondence Column," *Automobile* 2 (August 1900): 137; Motorphobia," *Horseless Age* 12 (September 30, 1903): 348–349.

7. James R. Doolittle, *The Romance of the Automobile Industry* (New York: Klebold Press, 1916), pp. 322–323.

8. George O. Draper, "A View of the Tour from One Participating," *Horseless Age* 16 (July 26, 1905): 153.

9. Chester S. Ricker, "Sixth Annual A.A.A. Reliability Tour," *Horseless Age* 24 (July 14, 1909): 49.

10. Hugh Dolnar, "The Ford 4-Cylinder Runabout," *Cycle and Automobile Trade Journal* 11 (August 1, 1906): 108; *Detroit Journal*, January 5, 1906.

4   Fordism

1. J. A. Kingman, "Automobile Making in America," *American Monthly Review of Reviews* 24 (September 1901): 302.

2. Lawrence H. Seltzer, *A Financial History of the American Automobile Industry* (Boston: Houghton Mifflin, 1928). The Chapin quote was transcribed by Seltzer from notes taken in an interview in Detroit on December 11, 1924.

3. Laux, *In First Gear*, p. 179.

4. Stephen Meyer III, *The Five Dollar Day: Labor Management and Social Control in the*

Ford Motor Company, 1908–1921 (Albany: State University of New York Press, 1981), pp. 2, 46, 50; R. J. Overy, William Morris: Viscount Nuffield (London: Europa Publications, 1976), p. 89; Laux et al., The Automobile Revolution, p. 102.

5. Henry Ford, in collaboration with Samuel Crowther, My Life and Work (Garden City, N.Y.: Doubleday, Page, 1922), p. 59.

6. See "Report of the Committee on the Machinery of the United States of America," presented to the House of Commons in pursuance of their address of July 10, 1855, printed by Harrison and Sons, London; "New York Industrial Exhibition, Special Report of Mr. George Wallis," and "New York Industrial Exhibition, Special Report of Mr. Joseph Whitworth," presented to the House of Commons by command of Her Majesty, in pursuance of their address of February 6, 1854, printed by Harrison and Sons, London. These documents are reprinted with an introduction in Nathan Rosenberg, ed., The American System of Manufactures (Edinburgh and Chicago: Edinburgh University and Aldine Publishing Company, 1969).

7. S. B. Saul, "The American Impact on British Industry," Business History 3 (December 1960): 19–20.

8. Laux, In First Gear, p. 202; Richardson, The British Motor Industry, pp. 103–104.

9. Nathan Rosenberg, "Technological Change in the Machine Tool Industry, 1840–1910," in his Perspectives on Technology (Cambridge: Cambridge University Press, 1976), pp. 9–31.

10. Laux et al., The Automobile Revolution, pp. 57–58, 63.

11. James Foreman-Peck, "The American Challenge of the Twenties: Multinationals and the European Motor Industry," Journal of Economic History 42 (December 1982): 869.

12. Walter P. Chrysler, in collaboration with Boyden Sparkes, Life of an American Workman (New York: Dodd, Mead, 1937), pp. 134–136.

13. Charles E. Sorensen, with Samuel T. Williamson, My Forty Years With Ford (New York: Norton, 1956), pp. 113–114.

14. David A. Hounshell, From the American System to Mass Production: The Development of Manufacturing Technology in the United States 1800–1932 (Baltimore: Johns Hopkins University Press, 1984), p. 9.

15. Sorensen and Williamson, My Forty Years with Ford, p. 116.

16. Robert Conot, American Odyssey (New York: Bantam Books edition, published by agreement with William Morrow, 1975), p. 169.

17. Ford and Crowther, My Life and Work, p. 83.

18. Allan Nevins and Frank E. Hill, Ford: The Times, The Man, The Company (New York: Charles Scribner's Sons, 1954), p. 456.

19. Allan Nevins and Frank E. Hill, Ford: Expansion and Challenge (New York: Charles Scribner's Sons, 1957), pp. 284–285, 287.

20. Laux et al., The Automobile Revolution, p. 95.

21. Reynold M. Wik, Henry Ford and Grass Roots America (Ann Arbor: University of

Michigan Press, 1972), p. 238; Sorensen and Williamson, *My Forty Years with Ford*, p. 124; Nevins and Hill, *Ford: The Times, The Man, The Company*, p. 474.

22. Sorensen and Williamson, *My Forty Years with Ford*, p. 42; John Kenneth Galbraith, *The Liberal Hour* (Boston: Houghton Mifflin, 1960), pp. 155, 164–165.

23. William Greenleaf, *Monopoly on Wheels: Henry Ford and the Selden Patent Suit* (Detroit: Wayne State University Press, 1961), pp. 174–175. This is the definitive source on the Selden patent controversy.

24. "Independent Makers Meet in Detroit," *Automobile* 12 (March 4, 1905): 349; "American Motorcar Manufacturers' Association," *Automobile* 15 (November 29, 1906): 704.

25. Greenleaf, *Monopoly on Wheels*, p. 250.

5   The Rise of the Giants

1. Walter E. Flanders, "Large Capital Now Needed to Embark in Automobile Business," *Detroit Saturday Night*, January 22, 1910.

2. Laux, *In First Gear*, p. 143; Saul, "The Motor Industry in Britain to 1914," p. 37.

3. Nevins and Hill, *Ford: The Times, The Man, The Company*, pp. 403–404.

4. Nevins and Hill, *Ford: Expansion and Challenge*, p. 111.

5. Alfred P. Sloan, Jr., *My Years with General Motors* (Garden City, N.Y.: Doubleday, 1964), p. 4.

6. Bernard Weisberger, *The Dream Maker: William C. Durant, Founder of General Motors* (Boston: Little, Brown, 1979), pp. 98–99. This is the definitive biography of Durant.

7. Weisberger, *The Dream Maker*, p. 110.

8. Quoted in Seltzer, *A Financial History*, p. 157.

9. Benjamin Briscoe, "The Inside Story of General Motors," *Detroit Saturday Night*, January 15, 22, 29, and February 5, 1921.

10. Briscoe, "The Inside Story."

11. Ed Cray, *Chrome Colossus: General Motors and Its Times* (New York: McGraw-Hill, 1980), pp. 66–67. This is the best and most comprehensive history of General Motors.

12. Cray, *Chrome Colossus*, p. 140.

13. Weisberger, *The Dream Maker*, p. 164.

14. Chrysler and Sparkes, *Life of an American Workman*, pp. 148, 161.

15. Howard E. Coffin in *The Society of Automotive Engineers Transactions* (1910): 125–126.

16. "Standardizing the Automobile," *Scientific American* 100 (January 16, 1909): 40.

17. Sorensen and Williamson, *My Forty Years with Ford*, p. 31.

6 War and Peace

1. Harry W. Perry, "Our Industry's Part in the War," *Motor* 31 (January 1919): 52.

2. "The Automobile in War," *Motor Age* 3 (October 11, 1900): 199–200.

3. Quoted in Michael Sedgewick, *Fiat* (New York: Arco Publishing Company, 1974), p. 87.

4. Quoted in Nevins and Hill, *Ford: Expansion and Challenge*, p. 55.

5. Roy Church, *Herbert Austin: The British Motor Car Industry to 1941* (London: Europa Publications, 1979), p. 52.

6. John B. Rae, *The American Automobile Industry* (Boston: Twayne, 1984), p. 61.

7. Ford and Crowther, *My Life and Work*, pp. 91–92.

8. Church, *Herbert Austin*, p. 188.

9. Mira Wilkins and Frank E. Hill, *American Business Abroad: Ford on Six Continents* (Detroit: Wayne State University Press, 1964), pp. 108–109, 157.

10. Sloan, *My Years with General Motors*, p. 60.

11. Sloan, *My Years with General Motors*, p. 26.

12. Alfred P. Sloan, Jr., in collaboration with Boyden Sparkes, *Adventures of a White Collar Man* (New York: Doubleday, Doran, 1941), pp. 104, 107, 112, 120.

13. Sloan, *My Years with General Motors*, p. 38.

14. Quoted in W. A. P. John, "That Man Durant," *Automobile* 39 (January 1923): 71.

7 Modern Times

1. Maurice Hindus, "Ford Conquers Russia," *Outlook* 146 (June 29, 1927): 280–283.

2. Wik, *Henry Ford and Grass-Roots America*, p. 4.

3. Quoted in Wilkins and Hill, *American Business Abroad*, p. 270.

4. David L. Lewis, *The Public Image of Henry Ford* (Detroit: Wayne State University Press, 1976), pp. 138–154.

5. Wik, *Henry Ford and Grass–Roots America*, pp. 125, 212.

6. Ford and Crowther, *My Life and Work* and *Today and Tomorrow* (Garden City, N.Y.: Doubleday, Page, 1926); Ford, *My Philosophy of Industry*, authorized interviews with Fay L. Faurote (New York: Coward-McCann, 1929). The quotes in the next eight paragraphs on Ford's philosophy of industry are taken from these sources, passim. Although the writing was done by Crowther and Faurote, the ideas expressed undoubtedly either were Ford's or were authorized as such by Ford.

7. Harry Braverman, *Labor and Monopoly Capital: The Degradation of Work in the Twentieth Century* (New York: Monthly Review Press, 1974).

8. Horace L. Arnold and Fay L. Faurote, *Ford Methods and the Ford Shops* (New York: Engineering Magazine Co., 1915), pp. 41–42.

9. Ford and Crowther, *My Life and Work*, p. 95.

10. Nevins and Hill, *Ford: The Times, The Man, The Company*, p. 553.

11. Arnold and Faurote, *Ford Methods*, p. 46.

12. Nevins and Hill, *Ford: Expansion and Challenge*, p. 534; Robert S. Lynd and Helen M. Lynd, *Middletown: A Study in Modern American Culture* (New York: Harcourt, Brace, 1929), p. 31.

13. Ford and Crowther, *My Life and Work*, pp. 80, 105, 115.

14. Ford and Crowther, *My Life and Work*, pp. 111–112.

15. Meyer, *The Five Dollar Day*, p. 101.

16. Meyer, *The Five Dollar Day*, p. 111.

17. Samuel S. Marquis, *Henry Ford: An Interpretation* (Boston: Little, Brown, 1923), pp. 34, 149.

18. Ford and Crowther, *My Life and Work*, pp. 129, 146.

19. Nevins and Hill, *Ford: The Times, The Man, The Company*, p. 534.

20. Marquis, *Henry Ford*, p. 155.

21. Meyer, *The Five Dollar Day*, pp. 169, 173.

22. Meyer, *The Five Dollar Day*, pp. 176, 183.

23. Keith Sward, *The Legend of Henry Ford* (New York: Holt, Rinehart, and Winston, 1949), pp. 311–312; Jonathan N. Leonard, *The Tragedy of Henry Ford* (New York: G. P. Putnam's Sons, 1932), pp. 230, 235–236.

24. August Meier and Elliott Rudwick, *Black Detroit and the Rise of the UAW* (New York: Oxford University Press, 1979), pp. 12–13.

25. Zaragosa Vargas, "Mexican Auto Workers at Ford Motor Company, 1918–1933" (unpublished Ph.D. dissertation, University of Michigan, 1984), p. 40.

26. Meier and Rudwick, *Black Detroit*, pp. 8–9. They cite Herbert R. Northrup et al., *Negro Employment in Basic Industry: A Study of Racial Policies in Six Industries* (Philadelphia: University of Pennsylvania Press, 1970), p. 57.

27. Meier and Rudwick, *Black Detroit*, p. 17.

8   Diffusion

1. John Kane Mills, "Speaking of Incomes," *Motor* 35 (February 1921): 21–22, 64; NACC, *Facts and Figures of the Automobile Industry*, 1924 ed., p. 10; James H. Collins, "The Motor Car Has Created the Spirit of Modern America," *Motor* 39 (January 1923): 186.

2. Interrante, "The Road to Autopia," pp. 95, 103.

3. NACC, *Facts and Figures*, 1925 ed., p. 10, and 1927 ed., p. 38; "2,700,000 Families in Two-or-More Car Class," *Motor Age* 51 (April 4, 1927): 30.

4. Interrante, "The Road to Autopia," p. 94.

5. Lynd and Lynd, *Middletown*, pp. 64–65, 254–255, 513–517.

6. Robert S. Lynd and Helen M. Lynd, *Middletown in Transition: A Study in Cultural Conflicts* (New York: Harcourt, Brace, 1937), pp. 26, 245, 266–267.

7. Joel A. Tarr, *Transportation Innovation and Changing Spatial Patterns in Pittsburgh, 1850–1934* (Chicago: Public Works Historical Society, 1978), pp. 32, 36–37.

8. Howard L. Preston, *Automobile Age Atlanta: The Making of a Southern Metropolis, 1900–1935* (Athens, Ga.: University of Georgia Press, 1979), p. 111.

9. Dan Lacy, *The White Use of Blacks in America* (New York: McGraw-Hill, 1972), p. 216; Helen Leavitt, *Superhighway—Super Hoax* (Garden City, N.Y.: Doubleday, 1970).

10. Norman T. Moline, *Mobility and the Small Town, 1900–1930: Transportation Change in Oregon, Illinois* (Chicago: University of Chicago Press; Department of Georgraphy research paper no. 12, 1971), p. 31.

11. "The Motor Car in England," *Scientific American* 72 (December 12, 1896): 423.

12. "The Status of the Horse at the End of the Century," *Harper's Weekly* 43 (November 18, 1899): 1172; "One More Revolution," *Independent* 55 (May 14, 1903): 1163.

13. Quoted in Mitchell Gordon, *Sick Cities: Psychology and Pathology of American Urban Life* (Baltimore: Penguin Books, 1965), p. 13.

14. William F. Dix, "The Automobile as a Vacation Agent," *Independent* 56 (June 2, 1904): 1259–1260.

15. William J. Lampton, "The Meaning of the Automobile," *Outing Magazine* 40 (September 1902): 699.

16. Ashleigh E. Brilliant, "Some Aspects of Mass Motorization in Southern California, 1919–1929," *Southern California Quarterly* 47 (October 1965): 191.

17. Robert M. Fogelson, *The Fragmented Metropolis: Los Angeles, 1850–1930* (Cambridge, Mass.: Harvard University Press, 1967), pp. 144–145.

18. Reyner Banham, *Los Angeles: The Architecture of Four Ecologies* (New York: Harper and Row, 1971), pp. 77–78.

19. Martin Wachs, "Autos, Transit, and the Sprawl of Los Angeles," *American Planning Association Journal* 50 (Summer 1984): 298, 300.

20. Mark S. Foster, "The Model T, the Hard Sell, and Los Angeles's Urban Growth: the Decentralization of Los Angeles During the 1920s," *Pacific Historical Review* 4 (November 1975): 476.

21. Wachs, "Autos, Transit," p. 300; Banham, *Los Angeles*, p. 82; Spencer Crump, *Ride the Big Red Cars: How Trolleys Helped Build Southern California* (Corona del Mar, Ca.: Trans-Anglo Books, 1962), p. 100.

22. C. Warren Thornwaite, *Internal Migration in the United States* (Philadelphia: University of Pennsylvania Press, 1934), p. 18; Wachs, "Autos, Transit," p. 302.

23. Quoted in Foster, "The Model T, the Hard Sell," p. 470.

24. Wachs, "Autos, Transit," pp. 302–303.

25. Foster, "The Model T, the Hard Sell," p. 483.

26. Blaine A. Brownell, "A Symbol of Modernity: Attitudes Toward the Automobile in Southern Cities in the 1920s," *American Quarterly* 24 (March 1972): 24.

27. Blaine A. Brownell, "Automobiles and the City: The Impact of the Motorcar on Southern Urban Areas in the 1920s," paper read at the annual meeting of the Southern Historical Association, Houston, Texas, November 19, 1971, pp. 3–4.

28. Preston, *Automobile Age Atlanta*, pp. xv, xvii, 16.

29. Sam Bass Warner, Jr., *Streetcar Suburbs: The Process of Growth in Boston, 1870–1900*, second edition (Cambridge, Mass.: Harvard University Press, 1962), pp. 22, 64, 157, 165.

30. Preston, *Automobile Age Atlanta*, p. 50.

31. Preston, *Automobile Age Atlanta*, pp. 153–154.

32. Quoted in Preston, *Automobile Age Atlanta*, p.136.

33. Preston, *Automobile Age Atlanta*, pp. 148, 155.

34. *Recent Social Trends in the United States*. Report of the President's Research Committee on Social Trends, 2 vols. (New York: McGraw-Hill, 1933), p. 443.

35. Interrante, "The Road to Autopia," p. 94; Jean Gottman, *Megalopolis: The Urbanized Northeastern Seaboard of the United States* (Cambridge, Mass.: MIT Press, 1961).

36. *Recent Social Trends*, pp. 1357–1358.

37. "The Parking Problem," *Automobile* 35 (December 21, 1916): 1044; Edward Hungerford, "Stop! You Are Congesting the Streets" and "Will Passenger Cars Be Barred from City Streets?" *Motor* 39 (February 1923): 23–24ff. and 39 (March 1923): 34–35ff.

38. Brownell, "Automobiles and the City," pp. 14, 17; Robert A. Walker, *The Planning Function of Local Government: A Report of the Local Planning Committee of the National Resources Board* (Washington, D.C.: National Planning Resources Board, July 28, 1939), p. 131.

39. Lynd and Lynd, *Middletown in Transition*, p. 265; Jane Jacobs, *The Death and Life of Great American Cities* (New York: Random House, 1961).

40. Michael Berger, *The Devil Wagon in God's Country: The Automobile and Social Change in Rural America, 1893–1929* (Hamden, Conn.: Archon Books, 1979), p. 207.

41. *Recent Economic Changes in the United States*. Report of the Committee on Recent Changes of the President's Conference on Unemployment, 2 vols. (New York: McGraw-Hill, 1929), pp. 556, 560.

42. John L. Shover, *First Majority—Last Minority: The Transforming of Rural Life in America* (Dekalb, Ill.: Northern Illinois University Press, 1976), p. 4.

43. Moline, *Mobility and the Small Town*, pp. 122, 138.

44. Quoted in Alfred D. Chandler, Jr., *Strategy and Structure: Chapters in the History of American Industrial Enterprise* (Cambridge, Mass.: MIT Press, 1962), p. 236.

45. *Recent Economic Changes*, p. 342.

46. Joan Halloran, "Effects of Changes in Communication Upon Business Services

of Iowa Agricultural Villages, 1920–1935," *University of Iowa Journal of Business* 18 (November 1937): 10.

47. Shover, *First Majority—Last Minority*, pp. 75–76.

48. Shover, *First Majority—Last Minority*, p. 97.

9 The Family Car

1. Laux et al., *The Automobile Revolution*, p. 205.

2. "The Family Car," *Motor* 35 (February 1921): 19.

3. Lynd and Lynd, *Middletown*, p. 254.

4. Lynd and Lynd, *Middletown*, p. 137.

5. Ashleigh E. Brilliant, "Social Effects of the Automobile in Southern California During the 1920s" (unpublished Ph.D. dissertation, University of California, Berkeley, 1964), pp. 42, 48.

6. Brilliant, "Social Effects of the Automobile," pp. 58, 61.

7. David L. Lewis, "Sex and the Automobile: From Rumble Seats to Rockin' Vans," in Lewis and Goldstein, *The Automobile and American Culture*, pp. 123, 138.

8. Lewis, "Sex and the Automobile," pp. 131–132.

9. Lewis, "Sex and the Automobile," p. 133.

10. Ruth Schwartz Cowan, *More Work for Mother: The Ironies of Household Technology from the Open Hearth to the Microwave* (New York: Basic Books, 1983), p. 85.

11. Chester H. Liebs, *Main Street to Miracle Mile: American Roadside Architecture* (Boston: New York Graphic Society/Little, Brown, 1985), p. 196.

12. Liebs, *Main Street to Miracle Mile*, pp. 213–214.

13. Folke T. Kihlstedt, "The Automobile and the Transformation of the American House, 1910–1935," in Lewis and Goldstein, *The Automobile and American Culture*, pp. 162–163.

14. Kihlstedt, "The Automobile and the Transformation," pp. 162–163.

15. Banham, *Los Angeles*, pp. 213–214.

16. Lynd and Lynd, *Middletown*, pp. 95, 257.

17. Bessie Averne McClenahan, *The Changing Urban Neighborhood: From Neighbor to Night Dweller* (Los Angeles: University of Southern California Press, 1929), pp. 38, 70; Emory S. Bogardus, *The City Boy and His Problems: A Survey of Boy Life in Los Angeles* (Los Angeles: Rotary Club of Los Angeles, 1926), pp. v–vi.

10 On the Road

1. Foster Rhea Dulles, *A History of Recreation: America Learns to Play* (New York: Appleton-Century-Crofts, 1965), p. 319.

2. "The Second Annual Good Roads Convention." *Horseless Age* 24 (September 29, 1909): 335; *The Lincoln Highway* (New York: Dodd, Mead, 1935).

3. Peter J. Hugill, "Good Roads and the Automobile in the United States, 1880–1929," *Geographic Review* 72 (July 1982): 336, 342.

4. John C. Burnham, "The Gasoline Tax and the Automobile Revolution," *Mississippi Valley Historical Review* 48 (December 1961): 445–447.

5. U.S. National Park System, *Public Use of the National Park System* (Washington, D.C.: U.S. Government Printing Office, 1977), p. 1.

6. Alfred Runte, "Pragmatic Alliance: Western Railroads and the National Parks," *National Parks and Conservation Magazine* 48 (April 1974): 14–21.

7. Robert Shankland, *Steve Mather of the National Parks* (New York: Knopf, 1954), pp. 146–147; Abbey is quoted in William C. Everhart, *The National Park Service* (New York: Praeger, 1972), p. 93.

8. Quoted in Shankland, *Steve Mather*, p. 152.

9. John B. Rae, *The Road and the Car in American Life* (Cambridge, Mass.: MIT Press, 1971), pp. 36–39, 42.

10. *Recent Social Trends*, p. 1360.

11. Everhart, *The National Park Service*, p. 35.

12. Lewis Gannett, *Sweet Land* (Garden City, N.Y.: Sun Dial, 1937), pp. 160–161.

13. *Preserving a Heritage: Final Report to the President and Congress of the National Parks Centennial Commission* (Washington, D.C.: U.S. Government Printing Office, 1973), p. 99.

14. John Ise, *Our National Park Policy: A Critical History* (Baltimore: Johns Hopkins University Press, 1961), p. 656.

15. Ise, *Our National Park Policy*, p. 30.

16. Paul Schullery, "A Reasonable Illusion," *Rod and Reel* 5 (November–December 1979): 54.

17. Earl Pomeroy, *In Search of the Golden West* (New York: Knopf, 1954), pp. 113, 130, 149.

18. Lynd and Lynd, *Middletown*, p. 261.

19. Everhart, *The National Park Service*, p. 234; U.S. Congress, Senate, Committee on Energy and Natural Resources, Subcommittee on Parks and Recreation, *Transportation Access to the National Park System, Hearing*, 94th Cong., 1st sess., June 8, 1977 (Washington, D.C.: U.S. Government Printing Office), p. 27.

20. Roger N. Clark, John C. Hendee, and Frederick L. Campbell, "Values, Behavior, and Conflict in Modern Camping Culture," *Journal of Leisure Research* 3 (Summer 1971): 144–145, 156.

21. Schullery, "A Reasonable Illusion," p. 51.

22. U.S. Congress, Senate, Committee on Interior and Insular Affairs, Subcommittee on Parks and Recreation, *National Park Service Concessions Oversight, Hearing*, 94th Cong., 2nd sess., March 10, 1976 (Washington, D.C.: U.S. Government Printing Office, 1976), pp. 246–247.

23. Warren J. Belasco, *Americans on the Road: From Autocamp to Motel, 1910–1945* (Cambridge, Mass.: MIT Press, 1979), pp. 3, 71.

24. Quoted in Belasco, *Americans on the Road*, p. 44.

25. Belasco, *Americans on the Road*, p. 107.

26. Belasco, *Americans on the Road*, p. 139.

27. Belasco, *Americans on the Road*, p. 142.

28. John J. McCarthy and Robert Littell, "Three Hundred Thousand Shacks," *Harper's* 167 (July 1933): 182, 184.

29. Liebs, *Main Street to Miracle Mile*, p. 180; "America Takes to the Motor Court," *Business Week* 15 (June 1940): 21–22.

30. Liebs, *Main Street to Miracle Mile*, p. 184; Seymour Freegood, "The Motel Free-for-All," *Fortune* 59 (June 1959): 119.

31. Kemmons Wilson, *The Holiday Inn Story* (New York: Newcomen Society, 1968), p. 8.

32. Liebs, *Main Street to Miracle Mile*, pp. 201–202.

11 Hard Times

1. Thomas C. Cochran, *The American Business System: A Historical Perspective, 1900–1955* (Cambridge, Mass.: Harvard University Press, 1957), p. 4.

2. Peter Temin, *Did Monetary Forces Cause the Great Depression?* (New York: W. W. Norton, 1976).

3. "Bond Houses Now in Open Enmity," *Motor World* 24 (July 7, 1910): 26; "Nothing to the Mortgage-on-the-Farm-to-Buy-a-Car Scare," *Horseless Age* 26 (September 7, 1910): 324–325.

4. "Get Cash, Pay Cash—Ford," *Automobile* 33 (July 22, 1915): 178; Nevins and Hill, *Ford: Expansion and Challenge*, p. 148.

5. "Studebaker Adopts Credit Plan," *Motor World* 29 (December 7, 1911): 723.

6. Ray W. Sherman, "Take Your Hat Off to the Man Who Buys on Time," *Motor* 44 (October 1925): 27.

7. *Recent Economic Changes*, pp. 416–417.

8. Chrysler and Sparkes, *Life of an American Workman*, p. 197; Sloan, *My Years with General Motors*, pp. 171, 173; Charles W. Nash, "The Automobile Dealer Has Rights," *Motor* 43 (March 1925): 30–31.

9. "What Is Saturation?" *Motor Age* 47 (February 5, 1921): 31; Ray W. Sherman, "1930 Should Be a Good Year," *Motor* 53 (January 1930): 67.

10. "NADA Finds Most Sales of Today Are Replacements," *Motor Age* 48 (August 27, 1925): 34; James B. Dalton, "Only 30 Percent of Dealers Are Making Money," *Motor* 46 (July 1926): 28–29.

11. James B. Dalton, "The Bankers Are Getting a Bit Cool," *Motor* 52 (July 1929): 28–29; and "Credit Warnings Not Mere Bogey," *Motor* 52 (October 1929): 34–35.

12. Clarence E. Eldridge, "One Million Too Many Cars," *Motor* 52 (November 1929): 30–33.

13. William J. Abernathy, *The Productivity Dilemma: Roadblock to Innovation in the Automobile Industry* (Baltimore: Johns Hopkins University Press, 1978), pp. 183, 185.

14. *Recent Economic Changes*, p. 323.

15. John B. Rae, "The Internal Combustion Engine on Wheels," in Melvin Kranzberg and Carroll W. Pursell, Jr., eds., *Technology in Western Civilization*, vol. 2 (London: Oxford University Press, 1967), pp. 127–128.

16. Chandler, *Strategy and Structure*, p. 208.

17. James B. Dalton, "Is the Parts Maker at the End of the Alley?" *Motor* 42 (October 1924): 30–32.

18. Richard Burns Carson, *The Olympian Cars: The Great American Luxury Automobiles of the Twenties and Thirties* (New York: Knopf, 1976), pp. 48–52.

19. *Recent Social Trends*, pp. 232–234.

20. Wik, *Henry Ford and Grass-Roots America*, p. 195.

21. Conot, *American Odyssey*, pp. 384–392, provides the only account of the Ford involvement in the Union Guardian Trust Company and the impact that its failure had in engendering the banking collapse of 1933.

22. Conot, *American Odyssey*, p. 392.

23. Sidney Fine, *The Automobile Under the Blue Eagle* (Ann Arbor: University of Michigan Press, 1963), pp. 51, 69, 74.

24. Quoted in Fine, *The Automobile Under the Blue Eagle*, p. 413.

25. William E. Leuchtenberg, *Franklin D. Roosevelt and the New Deal, 1932–1940* (New York: Harper and Row, 1963), pp. 151, 336.

26. Fine, *The Automobile Under the Blue Eagle*, p. 13; John B. Rae, *The American Automobile: A Brief History* (Chicago: University of Chicago Press, 1965), pp. 128–129.

27. Meier and Rudwick, *Black Detroit*, pp. 35, 37, 39, 67–68.

28. Cray, *Chrome Colossus*, p. 308; *Los Angeles Times*, April 2, 1937.

29. Sorensen and Williamson, *My Forty Years with Ford*, p. 253.

12 Sloanism

1. Hounshell, *From the American System to Mass Production*, p. 276.

2. The letter is reproduced in full in Julian Pettifer and Nigel Turner, *Automania: Man and the Motorcar* (London: Collins, 1984), p. 243.

3. Nevins and Hill, *Ford: Expansion and Challenge*, p. 595.

4. Sloan, *My Years with General Motors*, p. 199.

5. See especially Chandler, *Strategy and Structure*.

6. Stuart W. Leslie, "Charles F. Kettering and the Copper-Cooled Engine," *Technology and Culture* 20 (October 1979): 767; Sloan, *My Years with General Motors*, p. 94.

7. Sloan, *My Years with General Motors*, pp. 64–66.

8. Sloan, *My Years with General Motors*, p. 267. For the most comprehensive history of automobile styling, see Paul C. Wilson, *Chrome Dream: Automobile Styling Since 1893* (Radnor, Pa.: Chilton Book Company, 1976).

9. Quoted in Sloan, *My Years with General Motors*, p. 274.

10. Sloan, *My Years with General Motors*, p. 269.

11. Carson, *The Olympian Cars*, p. 37.

12. Carson, *The Olympian Cars*, pp. 41, 46, 96–98.

13. Carson, *The Olympian Cars*, pp. 54–60.

14. Sloan, *My Years with General Motors*, p. 276.

15. Hounshell, *From the American System to Mass Production*, p. 288.

16. Hounshell, *From the American System to Mass Production*, pp. 263, 289, 298.

17. Hounshell, *From the American System to Mass Production*, pp. 265–266.

18. Bloomfield, *The World Automotive Industry*, p. 42; Brock Yates, *The Decline and Fall of the American Automobile Industry* (New York: Empire Books, 1983), pp. 60–61.

19. James R. Bright, "The Development of Automation," in Kranzberg and Pursell, *Technology in Western Civilization*, vol. 2, pp. 643–644.

20. Robert Bendiner, "The Age of the Thinking Robot and What It Will Mean to Us," *The Reporter* 12 (April 7, 1955): 12.

21. Peter Drucker, "The Promise of Automation," *Harper's* 210 (April 1955): 41.

22. Alan Altshuler et al., *The Future of the Automobile: The Report of MIT's International Automobile Program* (Cambridge, Mass.: MIT Press, 1984), pp. 135–136. Hereafter cited as MIT Report.

23. Emma Rothschild, *Paradise Lost: The Decline of the Auto-Industrial Age* (New York: Knopf, 1973), p. 145.

24. Cray, *Chrome Colossus*, pp. 386–387.

25. Leon Mandel, *American Cars* (New York: Stewart, Tabori and Chang, 1982), p. 264.

26. Yates, *Decline and Fall*, p. 107.

27. Lee Iacocca with William Novak, *Iacocca: An Autobiography* (New York: Bantam Books, 1984), pp. 154–157.

28. Cray, *Chrome Colossus*, pp. 353, 479–480.

29. Yates, *Decline and Fall*, pp. 220–221.

13 American Challenge, European Response

1. Foreman-Peck, "The American Challenge of the Twenties," p. 867.

2. Richardson, *The British Motor Industry*, p. 221.

3. Foreman-Peck, "The American Challenge of the Twenties," pp. 870, 873–874.

4. Peter J. S. Dunnett, *The Decline of the British Motor Industry: The Effects of Government Policy, 1945–1979* (London: Croom Helm, 1980), p. 52.

5. Wilkins and Hill, *American Business Abroad*, p. 291.

6. Wilkins and Hill, *American Business Abroad*, p. 286.

7. Foreman-Peck, "The American Challenge of the Twenties," pp. 870–872.

8. Church, *Herbert Austin*, pp. 70, 99, 150.

9. Overy, *William Morris*, p. 54.

10. Richardson, *The British Motor Industry*, p. 45.

11. Church, *Herbert Austin*, p. 148.

12. Huw Benyon, *Working for Ford* (London: Allen Lane, 1973), p. 45.

13. R. J. Overy, "Cars, Roads, and Economic Recovery in Germany, 1932–1938," *Economic History Review* 28 (August 1975): 477.

14. Overy, "Cars, Roads, and Economic Recovery," pp. 481–482.

15. Robin Fry, *The VW Beetle* (Newton Abbot, London, and North Pomfret, Vt.: David and Charles, 1980), p. 43.

16. Quoted in Fry, *The VW Beetle*, p. 46.

17. Walter Henry Nelson, *Small Wonder: The Amazing Story of the Volkswagen*, revised edition (Boston: Little, Brown, 1967), pp. 58–65, 284–285.

18. Nelson, *Small Wonder*, p. 83.

19. Jerry Sloniger, *The VW Story* (Cambridge: Patrick Stephens, 1980), p. 32.

20. Quoted in Fry, *The VW Beetle*, p. 83.

14 Freedom's Arsenal

1. Wilkins and Hill, *American Business Abroad*, pp. 283–284, 320.

2. Bradford C. Snell, *American Ground Transportation* and *The Truth About "American Ground Transportation"—A Reply by General Motors*. Reproduced as Appendix, part 4A, of U.S. Congress, Senate, Committee on the Judiciary, *The Industrial Reorganization Act: Hearings Before a Subcommittee of the Judiciary on S. 1167*, 93rd Cong., 2nd sess., 1974 (Washington, D.C.: U.S. Government Printing Office, 1974). Among Snell's allegations was that GM and Ford willingly cooperated with the Nazis during World War II. GM responded strongly and convincingly in denying the charges. The quotes in this and the following two paragraphs can be found on pp. 108–109, 143.

3. C. S. Chang, *The Japanese Auto Industry and the U.S. Market* (New York: Praeger, 1981), p. 33.

4. Wilkins and Hill, *American Business Abroad*, p. 260.

5. Wilkins and Hill, *American Business Abroad*, pp. 323–324.

6. See Sorensen and Williamson, *My Forty Years with Ford*, pp. 255–260.

7. Cray, *Chrome Colossus*, pp. 317–318; Rae, *The American Automobile Industry*, p. 91.

8. Raymond Flower and Michael Wynn Jones, *100 Years on the Road: A Social History of the Car* (New York: McGraw-Hill, 1981), pp. 161–162.

15   The Insolent Chariots

1. Rae, *The American Automobile Industry*, p. 101.

2. *The Competitive Status of the U.S. Auto Industry: A Study of the Influences of Technology in Determining International Industrial Competitive Advantage.* Report prepared by the Automobile Panel, Committee on Technology and International Economic and Trade Issues of the Office of the Foreign Secretary, National Academy of Engineering, and the Commission on Engineering and Technical Systems, National Research Council (Washington, D.C.: National Academy Press, 1982), pp. 100, 122. The chairman of the Automobile Panel was William J. Abernathy. This is the definitive statement on the competitive status of the U.S. auto industry in the early 1980s.

3. Lawrence J. White, *The Automobile Industry since 1945* (Cambridge, Mass.: Harvard Universty Press, 1971), p. 248.

4. Gordon R. Conrad and Irving H. Plotkin, "Risk/Return: U.S. Industry Pattern," *Harvard Business Review* 46 (March/April 1968): 90–99.

5. Lowell Dodge, H. L. Duncombe, Jr., and George Schwartz, "*The Automobile Industry since 1945* by Lawrence J. White: A Discussion," *Political Science Quarterly* 87 (September 1972): 437.

6. "Autos: Follow the Leader," *Time* 101 (January 29, 1973): 59.

7. Iacocca and Novak, *Iacocca*, p. 312.

8. John Keats, *The Insolent Chariots* (Philadelphia: Lippincott, 1958), p. 13; *New York Times Book Review*, September 23, 1958.

9. Tom Mahoney, *The Story of George Romney* (New York: Harper, 1960), p. 122.

10. Mahoney, *George Romney*, pp. 196, 203; Cray, *Chrome Colossus*, p. 398. The Hayakawa article originally appeared in *Etc.*, the magazine for the International Society of General Semantics, then was reprinted in *Advertising Age* and in *Madison Avenue* in 1958.

11. Romney's testimony is recorded in U.S. Congress, Senate, *Administered Prices— Automobiles.* Hearings before the Subcommittee on Antitrust and Monopoly, Senate Judiciary Committee, Part 4 (Washington, D.C.: U.S. Government Printing Office, 1958), pp. 2849–2897.

12. Mahoney, *George Romney*, pp. 204–205.

13. Iacocca and Novak, *Iacocca*, pp. 215, 217.

14. The source for the quotations in this and the following two paragraphs is White, *The Automobile Industry*, pp. 216–220.

15. Yates, *Decline and Fall*, pp. 185–189.

16. Mandel, *American Cars*, p. 393.

17. J. Patrick Wright, *On a Clear Day You Can See General Motors: John Z. DeLorean's Look Inside the Automotive Giant* (Grosse Pointe, Mich.: Wright Enterprises, 1979), pp. 55–56; Ralph Nader, *Unsafe at Any Speed: The Designed-In Dangers of the American Automobile* (New York: Grossman, 1965).

18. Wright, *On a Clear Day*, p. 91; Cray, *Chrome Colossus*, p. 585.

19. Mandel, *American Cars*, pp. 305, 319.

20. Mandel, *American Cars*, p. 308.

21. Iacocca and Novak, *Iacocca*, p. 76.

22. Joel W. Eastman, *Styling vs. Safety: The American Automobile Industry and the Development of Automotive Safety, 1900–1966* (Lanham, Md.: University Press of America, 1984).

23. Yates, *Decline and Fall*, pp. 187, 205, 257.

24. Yates, *Decline and Fall*, p. 257.

25. Wright, *On a Clear Day*, p. 4.

16 Up from the Ashes

1. Quoted in Wilkins and Hill, *American Business Abroad*, p. 432.

2. Rae, *The American Automobile Industry*, p. 170.

3. MIT Report, pp. 18–21.

4. Laux et al., *The Automobile Revolution*, p. 173.

5. Dunnett, *Decline of the British Motor Industry*, p. 40.

6. Dunnett, *Decline of the British Motor Industry*, pp. 57–58.

7. Commission of the European Communities, *Concentration, Competition, and Competitiveness in the Automobile Industries and in the Automotive Components Industries of the European Community*. Report prepared by Professor Christian Marfels, Dalhousie University, Halifax, Nova Scotia, Canada (Luxembourg: Office for Official Publications of the European Communities, 1983), pp. 96–97.

8. Dunnett, *Decline of the British Motor Industry*, p. 158.

9. Cited in Nelson, *Small Wonder*, p. 92.

10. Quoted in Nelson, *Small Wonder*, p. 98.

11. Quoted in Nelson, *Small Wonder*, p. 4.

12. Quoted in Nelson, *Small Wonder*, p. 136.

13. Nelson, *Small Wonder*, p. 249.

14. Quoted in Nelson, *Small Wonder*, p. 136.

15. Jonathan Wood, *The VW Beetle: A Collector's Guide* (London: Motor Racing Publications, 1983), dust jacket.

17 Japan as Number One

1. Ezra F. Vogel, *Japan as Number One: Lessons for America* (Cambridge, Mass.: Harvard University Press, 1979), pp. viii–ix, 144–145.

2. Vogel, *Japan as Number One*, p. 241.

3. Alexander D. McLeod, "An Institutional Study of the Japanese Automobile Industry" (unpublished Ph.D. dissertation, University of California, Irvine, 1982), p. 161.

4. William Chandler Duncan, *U.S.-Japan Automobile Diplomacy: A Study in Economic Concentration* (Cambridge, Mass.: Ballinger, 1973), p. 83.

5. Duncan, *U.S.-Japan Automobile Diplomacy*, pp. 72, 75.

6. George Maxcy, *The Multinational Motor Industry* (London: Croom Helm, 1981), pp. 112–113.

7. McLeod, "An Institutional Study," p. 147.

8. The source for the quotations in this and the following three paragraphs is the MIT Report, pp. 149–151, 155.

9. McLeod, "An Institutional Study," pp. 221–222. See also Satoshi Kamata, *Japan in the Passing Lane: An Insider's Account of Life in a Japanese Auto Factory*, translated and edited by Tasuro Akimo, introduction by Ronald Dove (New York: Pantheon, 1982).

10. MIT Report, p. 161.

11. The source for the quotations in this and the following paragraph is *The Competitive Status of the U.S. Auto Industry*, pp. 101, 104.

12. *The Competitive Status of the U.S. Auto Industry*, pp. 104–105; MIT Report, p. 161.

13. Maxcy, *The Multinational Motor Industry*, p. 134.

14. *Los Angeles Times*, February 21, 1985, and March 2, 1985.

15. Lawrence Minard, "Saab, Mercedes, Volvo, BMW, Jaguar, Watch Out!" *Forbes* 134 (September 10, 1984): 42.

18 New Frontiers

1. Laux et al., *The Automobile Revolution*, pp. 247–248.

2. The source for the quotations in this and the following paragraph is Laux et al., *The Automobile Revolution*, pp. 251–263.

3. Laux et al., *The Automobile Revolution*, p. 268.

4. Rothschild, *Paradise Lost*, pp. 191–192.

5. Pettifer and Turner, *Automania*, p. 113.

6. Quoted in Maxcy, *The Multinational Motor Industry*, p. 265.

7. Jack Baranson, *Automotive Industries in Developing Countries* (Washington, D.C.: International Bank for Reconstruction and Development, 1969), p. 40; Rich Kronish and Kenneth S. Mericle, eds., *The Political Economy of the Latin American Motor Vehicle Industry* (Cambridge, Mass.: MIT Press, 1984), p. 54.

8. Maxcy, *The Multinational Motor Industry*, p. 201; Kronish and Mericle, *Political Economy*, pp. 276–277.

9. Kronish and Mericle, *Political Economy*, p. 276.

10. "Brazil Has Second Thoughts about the Multinationals," *Multinational Business* 3 (1975): 20.

11. Kronish and Mericle, *Political Economy*, p. 290.

12. Pettifer and Turner, *Automania*, pp. 117–118.

13. Kronish and Mericle, *Political Economy*, pp. 155–156.

14. Quoted in John M. Kramer, "Soviet Policy Toward the Automobile," *Survey* 22 (Spring 1976): 17.

15. W. H. Parker, "The Soviet Motor Industry," *Soviet Studies* 35 (October 1980): 525.

16. Kramer, "Soviet Policy Toward the Automobile," p. 21.

17. Kramer, "Soviet Policy Toward the Automobile," p. 33.

19   The Triumph of the Automobile

1. Pettifer and Turner, *Automania*, p. 109.

2. Laux et al., *The Automobile Revolution*, pp. 198, 200.

3. George W. Hilton and John S. Due, *The Electric Interurban Railways in America* (Stanford, Cal.: Stanford University Press, 1960), p. 118.

4. The source for the quotations in this and the following paragraph is Gregory Lee Thompson, "The Development of Intrastate Bus Competition and Its Relationship to the Southern Pacific," manuscript chapter of his "The Passenger Train in the Motor Age: The Decline in California, 1910–1941" (unpublished Ph.D. dissertation, University of California, Irvine, 1987). He cites as his source California Railroad Commission, Case Files for Applications, 20170–20173, *Santa Fe Case*, decided 1938. The source is now in the private collection of James Seal, Santa Monica, California.

5. *Recent Economic Changes*, p. 273.

6. *Passenger Traffic Report*. Prepared by the Section of Transportation Service for the Federal Coordinator of Transportation, 1935, p. 8.

7. Paul Barrett, "Public Policy and Private Choice: Mass Transit and the Automobile in Chicago Between the Wars," *Business History Review* 59 (Winter 1975): 474, 497; and *The Automobile and Urban Transit: The Formation of Public Policy in Chicago, 1900–1930* (Philadelphia: Temple University Press, 1983), p. 215.

8. Barrett, *The Automobile and Urban Transit*, pp. 165–166.

9. Barrett, *The Automobile and Urban Transit*, p. 6.

10. Mark S. Foster, *From Streetcar to Superhighway: American City Planners and Urban Transportation, 1900–1940* (Philadelphia: Temple University Press, 1982), pp. 93, 166.

11. Snell, *American Ground Transportation*, and *The Truth About "American Ground Transportation"—A Reply by General Motors*. The quotes in this section are from these sources, passim.

12. David James St. Clair, "Entrepreneurship and the American Automobile Industry" (unpublished Ph.D. dissertation, University of Utah, 1979), pp. 167–168.

13. Quoted in St. Clair, "Entrepreneurship," p. 313.

14. St. Clair, "Entrepreneurship," pp. 176–178.

15. Quoted in St. Clair, "Entrepreneurship," pp. 180, 182.

16. Quoted in St. Clair, "Entrepreneurship," p. 194.

17. Foster, *From Streetcar to Superhighway*, pp. 55, 60–61.

18. Mark H. Rose, *Interstate: Express Highway Politics, 1941–1956* (Lawrence, Kansas: Regents' Press of Kansas, 1979), p. 17.

19. St. Clair, "Entrepreneurship," pp. 205–206.

20. Rose, *Interstate*, pp. 96, 98.

21. The source for the quotations in this and the following paragraphs is James A. Dunn, Jr., *Miles to Go: European and American Transportation Policies* (Cambridge, Mass.: MIT Press, 1981), pp. 100–104, 116–117. Dunn cites Plowden, *The Motorcar in Politics*, as the source of his information on the British Road Fund.

20 Decline and Resurgence

1. John Jerome, *The Death of the Automobile: The Fatal Effect of the Golden Era, 1955–1970* (New York: Norton, 1972), pp. 13–14, 18.

2. Gordon J. Fielding, "Changing Objectives for American Transit: Part 1, 1950–1980," *Transport Review* 3 (1983): 294.

3. "Mass Transit: The Expensive Dream," *Business Week* 2857 (August 27, 1984): 62–69.

4. Fielding, "Changing Objectives," p. 288.

5. Fielding, "Changing Objectives," pp. 288–289, 295, 297.

6. White, *The Automobile Industry since 1945*, p. 231.

7. *The U.S. Automobile Industry, 1983*, Report to the Congress from the Secretary of Commerce, December 1984 (Washington, D.C.: U.S. Government Printing Office, 1985), p. 34.

8. Iacocca and Novak, *Iacocca*, p. 197.

9. C. Kenneth Orski, Alan Altshuler, and Daniel Roos, "The Future of the Automobile," *Transatlantic Perspectives* 2 (March 1980): 4–5, 8.

10. Donald E. Petersen, "The Magic Machine at the Crossroads," address given at the

national conference, "The Automobile and American Culture," sponsored by the Detroit Historical Society, Wayne State University, October 1, 1982.

11. "High Tech Drive: GM May Set New Trend," *Wall Street Journal*, June 6, 1985.

12. See especially Emmett J. Horton and W. Dale Compton, "Technology Trends in Automobiles," *Science* 225 (August 1984): 587–593.

13. Horton and Compton, "Technology Trends," p. 591.

14. "Buick City," *1984 General Motors Public Interest Report*, pp. 11–13.

15. MIT Report, p. 136.

16. Laux et al., *The Automobile Revolution*, p. 271; Meyer, *The Five Dollar Day*, p. 202.

17. "Saturn: A Radical Departure," *1985 General Motors Public Interest Report*, p. 12.

Epilogue   The Future of the Automobile

1. MIT Report, p. 247.

2. MIT Report, pp. 120, 181, 183, 187, 189.

Index

Muncie, Indiana. *See* Middletown
Murati Motors (India), 351
Murphy, Governor Frank, 227
Murphy, Thomas A., 249
"Muscle car," 289, 310–311 (illus.)
Muskie, Senator Edmund, 387
Mussolini, Benito, 113, 257, 273

Nader, Ralph, 288, 290–291, 324, 377, 384
Nakasone, Prime Minister Yasuhiro, 344
Nance, James J., 368–369
Napier, D., and Son, Ltd., 20
Napier, Montague, 22
Nash, Charles W., 46, 66, 68, 87, 192, 284
Nash cars
Airflyte series (1949), 284, 302 (illus.)
Metropolitan (1954), 284
1941 "600," 284
Quad Truck (World War I), 102 (illus.)
Rambler (1950), 284
"young man's model," 161
Nash-Kelvinator, 164
Nash Motor Car Company, 68, 77, 83–84, 284
National Advisory Defense Committee (United States, World War II), 273
National Association for the Advancement of Colored People (NAACP), 228
National Association of Automobile Manufacturers
Atlanta, Ga., show (1909), 145
Cleveland, Ohio, Good Roads Convention (1909), 170
National Automobile Chamber of Commerce (NACC), 55, 71, 77, 130–131, 192, 224–225
National Automobile Dealers Association (NADA), 192, 283
National City Lines (NCL), 365–367
National Cyclists' Union (Great Britain), 4
National Grange, 170
National Highway Traffic Safety Administration (NHTSA), 384–385
National Highway Transport Corporation (NHTC), 365

National Highway Users Conference (NHUC), 371
National Industrial Recovery Act (NIRA), 224–225
National Labor Relations Act, 1935 (NLRA) (also called Wagner-Connery Act), 225–227
National Labor Relations Board (NLRB), 225, 228
National League for Good Roads, 5
National parks (United States), impact of automobile on, 171–182, 194 (illus.)
National Park Service (NPS), 172, 174–175, 177
National Parks Highway Association, 173
National Park System. *See* National parks
National Recovery Administration (NRA), 224
National Socialist Party (Germany). *See* Nazis
National System of Interstate and Defense Highways. *See* Interstate Highway Act
National Traffic and Motor Vehicle Safety Act (1966), 383–384
National Trailways, 360
National Union of Vehicle Builders (Great Britain), 260
Navy Department Advisory Committee (United States, World War I), 77
Nazis (National Socialist Party, Germany), 113, 262, 264, 266, 269–270, 322
Negroes. *See* Blacks
Neighborhood, impact of automobile on, 135, 168
Nelson, Senator Gaylord, 176, 384
Nelson, Walter Henry, 265–266, 323, 425n
Neubauer, Henry and Albert C., Paris firm of, 53
Nevins, Allan, 49–50, 57, 59, 115, 117–118, 123, 190, 231
New Beeston Cycle and Motor Company, 21
New Deal. *See* Roosevelt, President Franklin D.

Smith, Samuel, 35
Smith, Wilbur, and Associates, 368–369
Smith, Willis Warren, 161
Snell, Bradford C., 364–366, 423n
Socialist countries, advanced. *See* Eastern bloc; Union of Soviet Socialist Republics
Socialist Party, 124
Sociedad de Automoviles de Turismo (SEAT) (Spain), 298
Société Civil des Voitures Electriques, Système Kriéger, 8
Society of Automotive Engineers (SAE), 8, 55, 71, 77, 286
Society of Motor Manufacturers and Traders (SMMT) (Great Britain), 300, 321
Sociological Department, Ford, 121–122, 124
Sorensen, Charles E., 47–48, 50–51, 72, 86, 126, 228, 241
South, impact of automobile on the, 145–150
Souther, Henry, 71
Southern California. *See* California; Los Angeles
Southern Pacific Railroad, 140–142, 172, 360
South Korea: automobile industry, 349–350
Spain: automobile industry, 295, 298
Spark, Alex, 125
Spark plug, electric, 11
Speed limit, national 55-mph, 383, 386
Spencer Trask and Company, 189
Spinga, Nicolas, 28
Sprague, Frank, 3
Standardization of parts, intercompany, 71
Standard Motor Company, Ltd., 20, 258, 297
Standard Oil Company, 32, 59
   of California, 365
   of Indiana, 214
   of New Jersey, 217, 232
Standards, United States federal automotive
   effect on automobile industry, 391–392
   emissions, 382, 386–388

fuel economy, 382, 388–389
   met by automobile industry, 392–393
   safety, 382–386
Standard Triumph International, 318
Standard volume pricing, 234
Stanley, Francis E. and Freelan O., 6–7
Stanley Steamer, 7
Star Motor Company, Ltd., 20
Starley, James Kemp, 4
Steam-powered car, 1–2, 6–7, 24
Steel
   High Speed, 46
   vanadium alloy, 37, 46
Steel body, all-, 213, 259
Steinway, William, 15
Stetson, Francis, 63
Stettinius, Edward R., Sr., 106
Steyr Works AG, 263
Stock Exchange, New York, 65, 106, 220
Stock market crash (October 29, 1929), 110, 189, 193, 220–222
Stokes, E. C., 158
Stone, General Roy, 5
Storrow, James J., 65–66, 68, 87
Strauss, Albert, 65
Streamlining. *See* Aerodynamics
Streetcar, electric, 3, 137–138, 141–142, 144, 146–149, 155, 178, 217, 362–367
Streets. *See* Roads
Studebaker, P. H., 23
Studebaker Brothers Manufacturing Company, 64
Studebaker cars, 216, 287
Studebaker Corporation, 64, 83–84, 108, 190, 216
Studebaker-EMF (reorganized as Studebaker Corporation in 1912), 64
Studebaker-Packard Corporation, 278–279, 368
Styling, 235–240, 247, 249, 286–287, 290–293, 396
Styling Section (General Motors), 235–236, 239
Suburbs, development by automobile of, 139–144, 147–151, 155, 188
Sunbeam Motor Car Company, Ltd., 20, 258